BUSINESS ANALYSIS & VALUATION

USING FINANCIAL STATEMENTS

BUSINESS ANALYSIS & VALUATION

USING FINANCIAL STATEMENTS

5e

KRISHNA G. PALEPU, PhD
Ross Graham Walker Professor of Business Administration
Harvard University

PAUL M. HEALY, PhD, ACA
James R. Williston Professor of Business Administration
Harvard University

SOUTH-WESTERN
CENGAGE Learning

Australia • Brazil • Japan • Korea • Mexico • Singapore • Spain • United Kingdom • United States

SOUTH-WESTERN
CENGAGE Learning

Business Analysis & Valuation: Using Financial Statements, 5th edition
Krishna G. Palepu and Paul M. Healy

Senior Vice President, LRS/Acquisitions & Solutions Planning: Jack W. Calhoun

Editor-in-Chief: Rob Dewey

Senior Acquisitions Editor: Matt Filimonov

Senior Developmental Editor: Craig Avery

Editorial Assistant: A. J. Smiley

Senior Market Development Manager: Natalie Livingston

Senior Brand Manager: Kristen Hurd

Marketing Manager: Heather Mooney

Marketing Communications Manager: Sarah Greber

Marketing Coordinator: Eileen Corcoran

Senior Art Director: Stacy Shirley

Production Management, Internal Design, and Composition: PreMediaGlobal

Media Editor: Bryan England

Rights Acquisition Director: Audrey Pettengill

Rights Acquisition Specialist, Text and Image: Audrey Pettengill

Senior Manufacturing Planner: Doug Wilke

Cover Designer: Red Hangar Design

Cover Image(s): ©iStock Photo/franckreporter

For product information and technology assistance, contact us at **Cengage Learning Customer & Sales Support, 1-800-354-9706**

For permission to use material from this text or product, submit all requests online at **www.cengage.com/permissions**. Further permissions questions can be emailed to **permissionrequest@cengage.com**

Library of Congress Control Number: 2012948788

Student Edition ISBN 13: 978-1-111-97230-1

Student Edition ISBN 10: 1-111-97230-3

Student Edition with CD ISBN 13: 978-1-285-42618-1

Student Edition with CD ISBN 10: 1-285-42618-5

South-Western
5191 Natorp Boulevard
Mason, OH 45040
USA

Cengage Learning is a leading provider of customized learning solutions with office locations around the globe, including Singapore, the United Kingdom, Australia, Mexico, Brazil, and Japan. Locate your local office at: **www.cengage.com/global**

Cengage Learning products are represented in Canada by Nelson Education, Ltd.

For your course and learning solutions, visit **www.cengage.com**

Purchase any of our products at your local college store or at our preferred online store **www.cengagebrain.com**.

Printed in the United States of America
1 2 3 4 5 6 7 16 15 14 13 12

F inancial statements are the basis for a wide range of business analysis. Managers use them to monitor and judge their firms' performance relative to competitors, to communicate with external investors, to help judge what financial policies they should pursue, and to evaluate potential new businesses to acquire as part of their investment strategy. Securities analysts use financial statements to rate and value companies they recommend to clients. Bankers use them in deciding whether to extend a loan to a client and to determine the terms of the loan. Investment bankers use them as a basis for valuing and analyzing prospective buyouts, mergers, and acquisitions. And consultants use them as a basis for competitive analysis for their clients.

Not surprisingly, therefore, we find that there is a strong demand among business students for a course that provides a framework for using financial statement data in a variety of business analysis and valuation contexts. The purpose of this book is to provide such a framework for business students and practitioners. The first four editions of this book have succeeded far beyond our expectations in equipping readers with this useful framework, and the book has gained proponents in accounting and finance departments in business schools in the United States and around the world.

CHANGES FROM THE FOURTH EDITION

In response to suggestions and comments from colleagues, students, and reviewers, we have incorporated the following changes in the fifth edition:

- Data, analyses, and issues have been thoroughly updated.
- Where appropriate, lessons have been drawn from current events such as the global financial crisis of 2008 and the ongoing European debt crisis.
- The financial analysis and valuation chapters (Chapters 6–8) have been updated with a focus on firms in the U.S. retail department store sector, primarily TJX and Nordstrom. In addition, we have provided a more cohesive overall discussion of the four key components of effective financial statement analysis that this book examines by introducing these companies in our discussion of strategy analysis in Chapter 2 and staying with them through the accounting, financial, and prospective analyses that follow.
- We have provided a greatly expanded examination of the impact of accounting adjustments (introduced in Chapter 4) on company analysis by analyzing both unadjusted and adjusted financial ratio and cash flow measures for TJX and Nordstrom in Chapter 5, and by then using adjusted numbers for TJX in the prospective analysis of Chapters 6–8.
- The topic of U.S. GAAP/IFRS convergence is introduced and examined, with discussion and examples in comparing companies reporting under U.S. GAAP and IFRS, and a brief discussion on important remaining differences between U.S. GAAP and IFRS.
- An expanded discussion of fair value accounting is included, given its increasing use globally and also its much discussed role in the 2008 financial crisis.
- We have streamlined and greatly enhanced the readability of the discussion on the theory behind valuation techniques in Chapters 7 and 8.
- In our Text and Cases edition, we have included new and updated Harvard Business School cases. In all, we include 27 cases in this edition.

- We are introducing with this edition an online version of the BAV modeling tool, which represents a significant enhancement of the tool over the previous spreadsheet-based version. This comprehensive modeling tool implements the analytical framework and techniques discussed in this book, and allows students to easily import the financial statements of a company into the model from three major data providers—Thomson ONE, Capital IQ, and the Compustat database of the Wharton Research Data Services—as well as to import manually created statements. A user-friendly interface allows the analyst to navigate through the tool with ease. The tool facilitates the following activities: (1) recasting the reported financial statements in a standard format for analysis; (2) performing accounting analysis as discussed in Chapters 3 and 4, making desired accounting adjustments, and producing restated financials; (3) computing ratios and free cash flows as presented in Chapter 5; (4) producing forecasted income, balance sheet, and cash flow statements for as many as 15 years into the future using the approach discussed in Chapter 6; (5) preparing a terminal value forecast using the abnormal earnings, the abnormal returns, and discounted cash flow methods as discussed in Chapters 7 and 8; and (6) valuing a company (either assets or equity) from these forecasts as also discussed in Chapters 7 and 8. We have seen that the BAV modeling tool can make it significantly easier for students to apply the framework and techniques discussed in the book in a real-world context, and we feel that the new online version, with its enhanced data import flexibility and improved overall interface, further enhances the usability and usefulness of this tool.

KEY FEATURES

This book differs from other texts in business and financial analysis in a number of important ways. We introduce and develop a **four-part framework for business analysis and valuation** using financial statement data. We then show how this framework can be applied to a variety of decision contexts.

Framework for Analysis

We begin the book with a discussion of the role of accounting information and intermediaries in the economy, and how financial analysis can create value in well-functioning markets (Chapter 1). We identify four key components, or steps, of effective financial statement analysis:

- Business strategy analysis
- Accounting analysis
- Financial analysis
- Prospective analysis

The first step, **business strategy analysis** (Chapter 2), involves developing an understanding of the business and competitive strategy of the firm being analyzed. Incorporating business strategy into financial statement analysis is one of the distinctive features of this book. Traditionally, this step has been ignored by other financial statement analysis books. However, we believe that it is critical to begin financial statement analysis with a company's strategy because it provides an important foundation for the subsequent analysis. The strategy analysis section discusses contemporary tools for analyzing a company's industry, its competitive position and sustainability within an industry, and the company's corporate strategy.

Accounting analysis (Chapters 3 and 4) involves examining how accounting rules and conventions represent a firm's business economics and strategy in its financial statements, and, if necessary, developing adjusted accounting measures of performance. In the accounting analysis section, we do not emphasize accounting rules. Instead we develop general approaches to analyzing assets, liabilities, entities, revenues, and expenses. We believe that such an approach enables students to effectively evaluate a company's accounting choices and accrual estimates, even if they have only a basic knowledge of accounting rules and standards. The material is also designed to allow students to make accounting adjustments rather than merely identify questionable accounting practices.

Financial analysis (Chapter 5) involves analyzing financial ratio and cash flow measures of the operating, financing, and investing performance of a company relative to either key competitors or historical performance. Our distinctive approach focuses on using financial analysis to evaluate the effectiveness of a company's strategy and to make sound financial forecasts.

Finally, in **prospective analysis** (Chapters 6–8) we show how to develop forecasted financial statements and how to use these to make estimates of a firm's value. Our discussion of valuation includes traditional discounted cash flow models as well as techniques that link value directly to accounting numbers. In discussing accounting-based valuation models, we integrate the latest academic research with traditional approaches such as earnings and book value multiples that are widely used in practice.

Although we cover all four steps of business analysis and valuation in the book, we recognize that the extent of their use depends on the user's decision context. For example, bankers are likely to use business strategy analysis, accounting analysis, financial analysis, and the forecasting portion of prospective analysis. They are less likely to be interested in formally valuing a prospective client.

Application of the Framework to Decision Contexts

The next section of the book shows how our business analysis and valuation framework can be applied to a variety of decision contexts:

- Equity securities analysis (Chapter 9)
- Credit analysis and distress prediction (Chapter 10)
- Merger and acquisition analysis (Chapter 11)
- Communication and governance (Chapter 12)

For each of these topics we present an overview to provide a foundation for the class discussions. Where possible we bring in relevant real-world scenarios and institutional details, and also examine the results of academic research that are useful in applying the analysis concepts developed earlier in the book. For example, the chapter on credit analysis shows how banks and rating agencies use financial statement data to develop analyses for lending decisions and to rate public debt issues. This chapter also presents academic research on how to determine whether a company is financially distressed.

USING THE BOOK

We designed the book so that it is flexible for courses in financial statement analysis for a variety of student audiences—MBA students, master's in accounting students, executive program participants, and undergraduates in accounting or finance. Depending upon the audience, the instructor can vary the manner in which the conceptual materials in the chapters and end-of-chapter questions are used. To get the most out of the book, students should have completed basic courses in financial accounting, finance, and either business strategy or business economics. The text provides a concise overview of some of these topics. But it would probably be difficult for students with no prior knowledge in these fields to use the chapters as stand-alone coverage of them.

If the book is used for students with prior working experience or for executives, the instructor can use almost a pure case approach, adding relevant lecture sections as needed. When teaching students with little work experience, a lecture class can be presented first, followed by an appropriate case or other assignment material. Alternatively, lectures can be used as a follow-up to cases to more clearly lay out the conceptual issues raised in the case discussions. This may be appropriate when the book is used in undergraduate capstone courses. In such a context, cases can be used in course projects that can be assigned to student teams.

ACKNOWLEDGMENTS

The first edition of this book was co-authored with our colleague and friend, Victor Bernard. Vic was the Price Waterhouse Professor of Accounting and Director of the Paton Accounting Center at the University of Michigan. He passed away unexpectedly on November 14, 1995. While we no longer list Vic as a co-author, we wish to acknowledge his enduring contributions to our own views on financial analysis and valuation, and to the ideas reflected in this book.

We also wish to thank Scott Renner for his tireless research assistance in the revision of the text chapters and in refining the online BAV model; Trenholm Ninestein of the HBS Information Technology Group for his help in the development of the online BAV model; Chris Allen and Kathleen Ryan of HBS Knowledge and Library Services for assistance with data on financial ratios for U.S. companies; the Division of Research at the Harvard Business School for assistance in developing materials for this book; and our past and present MBA students for stimulating our thinking and challenging us to continually improve our ideas and presentation.

We especially thank the following colleagues who gave us feedback as we wrote this edition: Patricia Beckenholdt, University of Maryland University College; Timothy P. Dimond, Northern Illinois University; Jocelyn Kauffunger, University of Pittsburgh; Suneel Maheshwari, Marshall University; K. K. Raman, University of North Texas; Lori Smith, University of Southern California; Vic Stanton, University of California, Berkeley; Charles Wasley, University of Rochester.

We are also very grateful to Laurie Palepu and Deborah Marlino for their help and assistance throughout this project. Special gratitude goes to Rob Dewey and Matt Filimonov for their publishing leadership on this edition, to our colleagues, and to Craig Avery and Heather Mooney at Cengage and Kalpana Venkatramani, project manager at PreMediaGlobal, for their developmental, marketing, and production help. We would like to thank our parents and families for their strong support and encouragement throughout this project.

Krishna G. Palepu
Paul M. Healy

Krishna G. Palepu is the Ross Graham Walker Professor of Business Administration and Senior Associate Dean for International Development at the Harvard Business School, Harvard University. He also serves as Senior Adviser to the President for Global Strategy at Harvard University. Prior to assuming his current leadership positions, Professor Palepu held other positions at the School, including Senior Associate Dean, Director of Research, and Unit Chair.

Professor Palepu's current research and teaching activities focus on strategy and governance. In the area of strategy, his recent focus has been on the globalization of emerging markets. He is a co-author of the book on this topic, *Winning in Emerging Markets: A Road Map for Strategy and Execution*. He developed and taught a second year MBA course, "Globalization of Emerging Markets," which focuses on these issues. In addition, Professor Palepu chairs the HBS executive education programs "Global CEOs Program for China" and "Building Businesses in Emerging Markets."

In the area of corporate governance, Professor Palepu's work focuses on board engagement with strategy. Professor Palepu teaches in several HBS executive education programs aimed at members of corporate boards: "How to Make Corporate Boards More Effective," "Audit Committees in the New Era of Governance," "Compensation Committees: New Challenges, New Solutions." Professor Palepu has served on a number of public company and nonprofit Boards. He has also been on the Editorial Boards of leading academic journals, and has served as a consultant to a wide variety of businesses. In addition, he is a researcher at the National Bureau of Economic Research (NBER).

Professor Palepu has a doctorate in management from the Massachusetts Institute of Technology and an honorary doctorate from the Helsinki School of Economics and Business Administration.

Paul M. Healy is the James R. Williston Professor of Business Administration and Senior Associate Dean, Director of Research at the Harvard Business School, Harvard University. Professor Healy joined Harvard Business School as a Professor of Business Administration in 1997. His primary teaching and research interests include corporate governance and accountability, equity research at financial services firms, strategic financial analysis and financial reporting. Professor Healy teaches in several executive education programs and is faculty co-chair of Strategic Financial Analysis for Business Evaluation. Professor Healy received his B.C.A. Honors (1st Class) in Accounting and Finance from Victoria University, New Zealand, in 1977, his M.S. in Economics from the University of Rochester in 1981, his Ph.D. in Business from the University of Rochester in 1983, and is a New Zealand CPA. In New Zealand, Professor Healy worked for Arthur Young and ICI. Prior to joining Harvard, Professor Healy spent fourteen years on the faculty at the M.I.T. Sloan School of Management, where he received awards for teaching excellence in 1991, 1992, and 1997. In 1993–94 he served as Deputy Dean at the Sloan School, and in 1994–95 he was a visiting professor at London Business School and Harvard Business School.

Professor Healy's research includes studies of the performance of financial analysts, corporate governance, the performance of mergers, corporate disclosure, and managers' financial reporting decisions. His work has been published in leading journals in accounting and finance. In 1990, his article "The Effect of Bonus Schemes on Accounting Decisions," published in *Journal of Accounting and Economics*, was awarded the AICPA/AAA Notable Contribution Award. His text *Business Analysis and Valuation* was awarded the AICPA/AAA's Wildman Medal for contributions to the practice in 1997, and the AICPA/AAA Notable Contribution Award in 1998.

Chapter 7 **Prospective Analysis: Valuation Theory and Concepts** *7-1*

PART 3   BUSINESS ANALYSIS AND VALUATION APPLICATIONS

PART

1

FRAMEWORK

Chapter 1

A FRAMEWORK FOR BUSINESS ANALYSIS AND VALUATION USING FINANCIAL STATEMENTS

This chapter outlines a comprehensive framework for financial statement analysis. Because financial statements provide the most widely available data on public corporations' economic activities, investors and other stakeholders rely on financial reports to assess the plans and performance of firms and corporate managers.

A variety of questions can be addressed by business analysis using financial statements, as shown in the following examples:

- A security analyst may be interested in asking: "How well is the firm I am following performing? Did the firm meet my performance expectations? If not, why not? What is the value of the firm's stock given my assessment of the firm's current and future performance?"

- A loan officer may need to ask: "What is the credit risk involved in lending a certain amount of money to this firm? How well is the firm managing its liquidity and solvency? What is the firm's business risk? What is the additional risk created by the firm's financing and dividend policies?"

- A management consultant might ask: "What is the structure of the industry in which the firm is operating? What are the strategies pursued by various players in the industry? How have these factors affected the relative performance of different firms in the industry?"

- A corporate manager may ask: "Is my firm properly valued by investors? Is our investor communication program adequate to facilitate this process?" or "Is this firm a potential takeover target? How much value can be added if we acquire this firm? How can we finance the acquisition?"

- An independent auditor would want to ask: "Are the accounting policies and accrual estimates in this company's financial statements consistent with my understanding of this business and its recent performance? Do these financial reports communicate the current status and significant risks of the business?"

The structure of state economies during the twentieth and early twenty-first centuries has generally fallen into one of two distinct and broad ideologies for channeling savings into business investments—capitalism and central planning. The capitalist market model broadly relies on the market mechanism to govern economic activity, and decisions regarding investments are made privately. Centrally planned economies have used central planning and government agencies to pool national savings and to direct investments in business enterprises. The failure of the central planning model is evident from the fact that at this point most of these economies have partly or entirely abandoned it in favor of the market model. As a result, in almost all countries in the world today, capital markets play an important role in channeling financial resources from savers to business enterprises that need capital.

Financial statement analysis is a valuable activity when managers have in-depth information on a firm's strategies and performance and a variety of institutional factors make it unlikely that they fully disclose this information. In this setting, outside analysts attempt to create "inside information" from analyzing financial statement data, thereby gaining valuable insights about the firm's current performance and future prospects.

To understand the contribution that financial statement analysis can make, it is important to understand the role of financial reporting in the functioning of capital markets and the institutional forces that shape financial statements. Therefore, we first present a brief description of these forces followed by a discussion of the steps that an analyst must perform to extract information from financial statements and provide meaningful forecasts.

THE ROLE OF FINANCIAL REPORTING IN CAPITAL MARKETS

A critical challenge for any economy is the allocation of savings to investment opportunities. Economies that do this well can exploit new business ideas to spur innovation and create jobs and wealth at a rapid pace. In contrast, economies that manage this process poorly tend to dissipate their wealth and fail to support business opportunities.

Figure 1-1 provides a schematic representation of how capital markets typically work in a broad sense. Savings in an economy are widely distributed among households. There are usually many new entrepreneurs and existing companies that would like to attract these savings to fund their business ideas. While both savers and entrepreneurs would like to do business with each other, matching savings to business investment opportunities is complicated for at least three reasons. First, entrepreneurs typically have better information than savers on the value of business investment opportunities. Second, communication by entrepreneurs to investors is not completely credible because investors know entrepreneurs have an incentive to inflate the value of their ideas. Third, savers generally lack the financial sophistication needed to analyze and differentiate among the various business opportunities.

These information and incentive problems lead to what economists call the "lemons" problem, which can potentially break down the functioning of capital markets.[1] It works like this: Consider a situation where half the business ideas are "good" and the other half are "bad." If investors cannot distinguish between the two types of business ideas, entrepreneurs with bad ideas will try to claim that their ideas are as valuable as the good ideas. Realizing this possibility, investors value both good and bad ideas at an average level. Unfortunately, this penalizes good ideas, and entrepreneurs with good ideas find the terms on which they can get financing to be unattractive. As these entrepreneurs leave the capital market, the proportion of bad ideas in the market increases. Over time, bad ideas "crowd out" good ideas, and investors lose confidence in this market.

The emergence of the institutions that make up a fully formed capital market system can prevent such a market breakdown. Financial intermediaries such as venture capital and private equity firms, banks, mutual funds, and insurance companies focus on aggregating funds from individual investors and distributing those funds to businesses seeking sources of capital. Information intermediaries such as auditors and company audit committees serve as credibility enhancers to provide an independent assessment of business claims. Information analyzers and advisors such as financial analysts, credit rating agencies and the financial press are another type of information intermediary that collect and analyze business information used to make business decisions. Transaction facilitators such as stock exchanges and brokerage houses play a crucial role in capital markets by providing a platform that facilitates buying and selling in markets. Finally, regulators

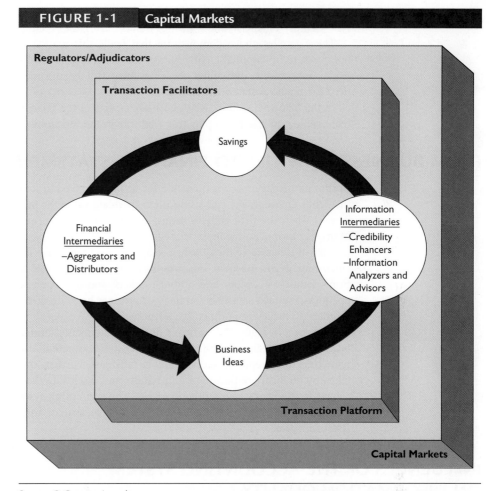

FIGURE 1-1   Capital Markets

Source: © Cengage Learning

such as the Securities and Exchange Commission (SEC) and the Financial Accounting Standards Board (FASB) in the United States create appropriate regulatory policy that establishes the legal framework of the capital market system, while adjudicators such as the court system resolve disputes that arise between participants.[2] In a well-functioning capital market, the market institutions described above add value by both helping investors distinguish good investment opportunities from bad ones and by directing funding to those business ideas deemed most promising.

Financial reporting plays a critical role in the effective functioning of the capital markets. Information intermediaries attempt to add value by either enhancing the credibility of financial reports (as auditors do) or by analyzing the information in financial statements (as analysts and the rating agencies do). Financial intermediaries rely on the information in financial statements to analyze investment opportunities, and they supplement this with information from other sources, including the analysis and perspective of the information intermediaries.

Ideally, the different intermediaries serve as a system of checks and balances to ensure the efficient functioning of the capital markets system. However, this is not always the case, as on occasion they mutually reinforce rather than counterbalance each other. This can arise from imperfections in financial and information intermediaries' incentives, governance issues within the intermediary organizations themselves, and conflicts of interest, as evidenced by the spectacular failures of companies such as Enron and WorldCom in the early part of the new century,[3] and more recently companies such as Lehman Brothers, New Century Financial, and a host of others during the recent global financial crisis.

The examples above demonstrate that while this market mechanism over time has been seen to function efficiently with prices reflecting all available information on a particular investment, individual securities may still be mispriced, thereby justifying the need for financial statement analysis.

In the following section, we discuss key aspects of the financial reporting system design that enable it to effectively play this vital role in the functioning of the capital markets.

FROM BUSINESS ACTIVITIES TO FINANCIAL STATEMENTS

Corporate managers are responsible for acquiring physical and financial resources from the firm's environment and using them to create value for the firm's investors. Value is created when the firm earns a return on its investment in excess of the cost of capital. Managers formulate business strategies to achieve this goal, and they implement them through business activities. A firm's business activities are influenced by its economic environment and its own business strategy. The economic environment includes the firm's industry, its input and output markets, and the regulations under which the firm operates. The firm's business strategy determines how the firm positions itself in its environment to achieve a competitive advantage.

As shown in Figure 1-2, a firm's financial statements summarize the economic consequences of its business activities. The firm's business activities in any time period are too numerous to be reported individually to outsiders. Further, some of the activities undertaken by the firm are proprietary in nature, and disclosing these in detail could be a detriment to the firm's competitive position. The accounting system provides a mechanism through which business activities are selected, measured, and aggregated into financial statement data.

INFLUENCES OF THE ACCOUNTING SYSTEM ON INFORMATION QUALITY

Intermediaries using financial statement data to do business analysis have to be aware that financial reports are influenced both by the firm's business activities and by its accounting system. *A key aspect of financial statement analysis, therefore, involves understanding the influence of the accounting system on the quality of the financial statement data being used in the analysis.* The institutional features of accounting systems discussed below determine the extent of that influence.

Feature 1: Accrual Accounting

One of the fundamental features of corporate financial reports is that they are prepared using accrual rather than cash accounting. Unlike cash accounting, accrual accounting distinguishes between the recording of costs and benefits associated with economic activities and the actual payment and receipt of cash. Net income is the primary periodic performance index under accrual accounting. To compute net income, the effects of economic transactions are recorded on the basis of *expected*, not necessarily *actual*, cash receipts and payments. Expected cash receipts from the delivery of products or services are recognized as revenues, and expected cash outflows associated with these revenues are recognized as expenses.

The need for accrual accounting arises from investors' demand for financial reports on a periodic basis. Because firms undertake economic transactions on a continual

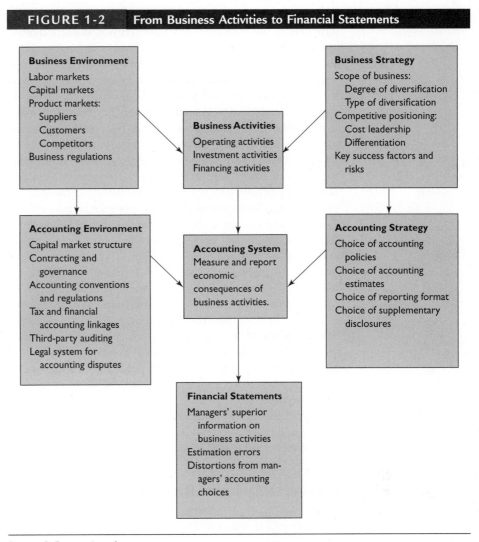

FIGURE 1-2   From Business Activities to Financial Statements

Business Environment
Labor markets
Capital markets
Product markets:
   Suppliers
   Customers
   Competitors
Business regulations

Business Activities
Operating activities
Investment activities
Financing activities

Business Strategy
Scope of business:
   Degree of diversification
   Type of diversification
Competitive positioning:
   Cost leadership
   Differentiation
Key success factors and
   risks

Accounting Environment
Capital market structure
Contracting and
   governance
Accounting conventions
   and regulations
Tax and financial
   accounting linkages
Third-party auditing
Legal system for
   accounting disputes

Accounting System
Measure and report
economic
consequences of
business activities.

Accounting Strategy
Choice of accounting
   policies
Choice of accounting
   estimates
Choice of reporting format
Choice of supplementary
   disclosures

Financial Statements
Managers' superior
   information on
   business activities
Estimation errors
Distortions from man-
   agers' accounting
   choices

Source: © Cengage Learning

basis, the arbitrary closing of accounting books at the end of a reporting period leads to a fundamental measurement problem. Since cash accounting does not report the full economic consequence of the transactions undertaken in a given period, accrual accounting is designed to provide more complete information on a firm's periodic performance.

Feature 2: Accounting Conventions and Standards

The use of accrual accounting lies at the center of many important complexities in corporate financial reporting. Because accrual accounting deals with *expectations* of future cash consequences of current events, it is subjective and relies on a variety of assumptions. Who should be charged with the primary responsibility of making these assumptions? In the current system, a firm's managers are entrusted with the task of making the appropriate estimates and assumptions to prepare the financial statements because they have intimate knowledge of their firm's business.

The accounting discretion granted to managers is potentially valuable because it allows them to reflect inside information in reported financial statements. However, since investors view profits as a measure of managers' performance, managers have incentives to use their accounting discretion to distort reported profits by making biased assumptions. Further, the use of accounting numbers in contracts between the firm and outsiders provides another motivation for management manipulation of accounting numbers. Income management distorts financial accounting data, making them less valuable to external users of financial statements. Therefore, the delegation of financial reporting decisions to corporate managers has both costs and benefits.

A number of accounting conventions have evolved to ensure that managers use their accounting flexibility to summarize their knowledge of the firm's business activities and not disguise reality for self-serving purposes. For example, the measurability and conservatism conventions are accounting responses to concerns about distortions from managers' potentially optimistic bias. Both these conventions attempt to limit managers' optimistic bias by imposing their own pessimistic bias.

Accounting standards, promulgated by the FASB in the United States and similar standard-setting bodies in other countries, also limit potential distortions that managers can introduce into reported numbers. These uniform standards, such as Generally Accepted Accounting Principles (GAAP) in the United States and the International Financial Reporting Standards (IFRS) internationally, attempt to reduce managers' ability to record similar economic transactions in dissimilar ways, either over time or across firms.

Increased uniformity from accounting standards, however, comes at the expense of reduced flexibility for managers to reflect genuine business differences in their firms' financial statements. Rigid accounting standards work best for economic transactions whose accounting treatment is not predicated on managers' proprietary information. However, when there is significant business judgment involved in assessing a transaction's economic consequences, rigid standards that prevent managers from using their superior business knowledge would be counterproductive. Further, if accounting standards are too rigid, they may induce managers to expend economic resources to restructure business transactions to achieve a desired accounting result.

Feature 3: Managers' Reporting Strategy

Because the mechanisms that limit managers' ability to distort accounting data add noise, it is not optimal to use accounting regulation to eliminate managerial flexibility completely. Therefore, real-world accounting systems leave considerable room for managers to influence financial statement data. A firm's reporting strategy, i.e., the manner in which managers use their accounting discretion, has an important influence on the firm's financial statements.

Corporate managers can choose accounting and disclosure policies that make it more or less difficult for external users of financial reports to understand the true economic picture of their businesses. Accounting rules often provide a broad set of alternatives from which managers can choose. Further, managers are entrusted with making a range of estimates in implementing these accounting policies. Accounting regulations usually prescribe *minimum* disclosure requirements, but they do not restrict managers from *voluntarily* providing additional disclosures.

A superior disclosure strategy will enable managers to communicate the underlying business reality to outside investors. One important constraint on a firm's disclosure strategy is the competitive dynamics in product markets. Disclosure of proprietary information about business strategies and their expected economic consequences may hurt the firm's competitive position. Subject to this constraint, managers can use financial statements to provide information useful to investors in assessing their firm's true economic performance.

Managers can also use financial reporting strategies to manipulate investors' perceptions. Using the discretion granted to them, managers can make it difficult for investors to identify poor performance on a timely basis. For example, managers can choose accounting policies and estimates to provide an optimistic assessment of the firm's true performance. They can also make it costly for investors to understand the true performance by controlling the extent of information that is disclosed voluntarily.

The extent to which financial statements reveal the underlying business reality varies across firms and across time for a given firm. This variation in accounting quality provides both an important opportunity and a challenge in doing business analysis. The process through which analysts can separate noise from information in financial statements, and gain valuable business insights from financial statement analysis, is discussed in the following section.

Feature 4: Auditing

Auditing, broadly defined as a verification of the integrity of the reported financial statements by someone other than the preparer, ensures that managers use accounting rules and conventions consistently over time and that their accounting estimates are reasonable. Therefore, auditing improves the quality of accounting data.

Third-party auditing may also reduce the quality of financial reporting because it constrains the kind of accounting rules and conventions that evolve over time. For example, the FASB considers the views of auditors in the standard-setting process. Auditors are likely to argue against accounting standards producing numbers that are difficult to audit, even if the proposed rules produce relevant information for investors.

The legal environment in which accounting disputes between managers, auditors, and investors are adjudicated can also have a significant effect on the quality of reported numbers. The threat of lawsuits and resulting penalties has the beneficial effect of improving the accuracy of disclosure. However, the potential for a significant legal liability might also discourage managers and auditors from supporting accounting proposals requiring risky forecasts, such as forward-looking disclosures.

The governance structure of firms includes an audit committee of the board of directors. The audit committee is expected to be independent of management, and its key roles include overseeing the work of the auditor and ensuring that financial statements are properly prepared. This governance mechanism further serves to enhance the quality and accountability of financial reporting.

LEGISLATION AFFECTING FINANCIAL REPORTING AND AUDITING

In the United States, the Sarbanes-Oxley Act of 2002 made important changes in financial reporting and auditing. The Dodd-Frank Wall Street Reform and Consumer Protection Act of 2010 introduced new regulations for the banking sector, including several new requirements likely to affect financial reporting and auditing.

Sarbanes-Oxley Act

In the aftermath of the collapse of the dot-com bubble and high-profile accounting scandals such as Enron and WorldCom, the U.S. Congress passed the bipartisan Sarbanes-Oxley Act (SOX as it has come to be known) in July 2002. The margin by which the bill was enacted— it passed by a vote of 424 to 3 in the House of Representatives and a vote of 99 to 0 in the Senate—and the far-reaching nature of the reforms reflected the degree to which the public's confidence in the quality of corporate financial reporting had been undermined.

SOX mandated certain fundamental changes to corporate governance as related to financial reporting and altered the relationship between a firm and its auditor. Some of the highlights included:

- Creation of a not-for-profit accounting oversight board, the Public Company Accounting Oversight Board (PCAOB), to ensure standards for auditing and the ethics and independence of public accounting firms;
- Mandating stricter guidelines for the composition and role of the audit committee of the Board of Directors, including director independence and financial expertise;
- Enhancing corporate responsibility for financial reporting by requiring the CEO and CFO to personally certify the appropriateness of periodic reports;
- Requiring management to assess and report on the adequacy of internal controls, which then needs to be certified by the auditor;
- Providing greater whistleblower protection;
- Allowing for the imposition of stiffer penalties, including prison terms and fines, for securities fraud;
- Prohibiting accounting firms from providing certain non-audit services contemporaneously with an audit and mandating audit partner rotation;
- Prescribing conflict of interest rules for equity research analysts; and
- Increasing the funding available to the Securities and Exchange Commission to ensure compliance.

Since the adoption of SOX, similar legislation has been passed in Japan, the EU, Canada, Israel, Australia, and France, among others, indicating general agreement on the importance of tighter reporting standards.

Dodd-Frank Wall Street Reform and Consumer Protection Act of 2010

The Dodd-Frank Act was passed in 2010 in response to the financial crisis on Wall Street. The new legislation mandated important new changes in the governance of banks, including:

- The creation of a new independent consumer protection agency to ensure that consumers receive the information they need to shop for financial products;
- Increased monitoring of banks, including restrictions on proprietary trading;
- New procedures to facilitate the orderly liquidation of failed banks;
- Increased transparency of the trading of financial instruments, which should facilitate fair value accounting for these instruments;
- Increased oversight of ratings agencies;
- Provisions for shareholders to have a non-binding vote on executive compensation; and
- Increased disclosures on the assets underlying complex financial securities.

FROM FINANCIAL STATEMENTS TO BUSINESS ANALYSIS

Because managers' insider knowledge is a source of both value and distortion in accounting data, it is difficult for outside users of financial statements to separate information from distortion and noise. Not being able to undo accounting distortions completely, investors "discount" a firm's reported accounting performance. In doing so, they make a probabilistic assessment of the extent to which a firm's reported numbers reflect its economic performance. As a result, investors frequently have an imprecise assessment of an individual firm's performance. Financial and information intermediaries can add value by improving investors' understanding of a firm's current performance and its future prospects.

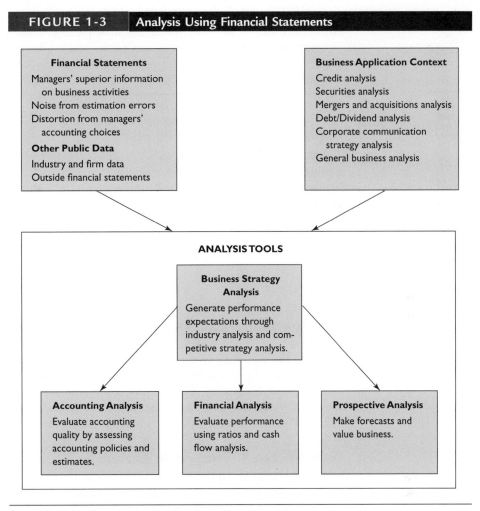

FIGURE 1-3   Analysis Using Financial Statements

Financial Statements

Managers' superior information
  on business activities
Noise from estimation errors
Distortion from managers'
  accounting choices

Other Public Data

Industry and firm data
Outside financial statements

Business Application Context

Credit analysis
Securities analysis
Mergers and acquisitions analysis
Debt/Dividend analysis
Corporate communication
  strategy analysis
General business analysis

ANALYSIS TOOLS

Business Strategy Analysis

Generate performance expectations through industry analysis and competitive strategy analysis.

Accounting Analysis

Evaluate accounting quality by assessing accounting policies and estimates.

Financial Analysis

Evaluate performance using ratios and cash flow analysis.

Prospective Analysis

Make forecasts and value business.

Source: © Cengage Learning

Effective financial statement analysis is valuable because it attempts to get at managers' inside information from public financial statement data. Since intermediaries do not have direct or complete access to this inside information, they rely on their knowledge of the firm's industry and its competitive strategies to interpret financial statements. Successful intermediaries have at least as good an understanding of the industry economics as the firm's managers do, as well as a reasonably good understanding of the firm's competitive strategy. Although outside analysts have an information disadvantage relative to the firm's managers, they are more objective in evaluating the economic consequences of the firm's investment and operating decisions. Figure 1-3 provides a schematic overview of how business intermediaries use financial statements to accomplish four key steps: (1) business strategy analysis, (2) accounting analysis, (3) financial analysis, and (4) prospective analysis.

Analysis Step 1: Business Strategy Analysis

The purpose of business strategy analysis is to identify key profit drivers and business risks, and to assess the company's profit potential at a qualitative level. Business strategy analysis involves analyzing a firm's industry and its strategy to create a sustainable competitive advantage. This qualitative analysis is an essential first step because it enables the analyst to better frame the subsequent accounting and financial analysis. For example, identifying the key success factors and key business risks allows the identification of key accounting policies. Assessment of a firm's competitive strategy facilitates evaluating whether current profitability is sustainable. Finally, business analysis enables the analyst to make sound assumptions in forecasting a firm's future performance.

Analysis Step 2: Accounting Analysis

The purpose of accounting analysis is to evaluate the degree to which a firm's accounting captures its underlying business economics. By identifying places where there is accounting flexibility, and by evaluating the appropriateness of the firm's accounting policies and estimates, analysts can assess the degree of distortion in a firm's reported numbers. Another important step in accounting analysis is to "undo" any distortions by recasting a firm's accounting numbers to create unbiased accounting data. Sound accounting analysis improves the reliability of conclusions from financial analysis, the next step in financial statement analysis.

Analysis Step 3: Financial Analysis

The goal of financial analysis is to use financial data to evaluate the current and past performance of a firm and to assess its sustainability. There are two important skills related to financial analysis. First, the analysis should be systematic and efficient. Second, it should allow the analyst to use financial data to explore business issues. Ratio analysis and cash flow analysis are the two most commonly used financial tools. Ratio analysis focuses on evaluating a firm's product market performance and financial policies, while cash flow analysis focuses on a firm's liquidity and financial flexibility.

Analysis Step 4: Prospective Analysis

Prospective analysis, which focuses on forecasting a firm's future, is the final step in business analysis. Two commonly used techniques in prospective analysis are financial statement forecasting and valuation. Both these tools allow the synthesis of the insights from business analysis, accounting analysis, and financial analysis in order to make predictions about a firm's future.

While the intrinsic value of a firm is a function of its future cash flow performance, it is also possible to assess a firm's value based on the firm's current book value of equity and its future return on equity (ROE) and growth. Strategy analysis, accounting analysis, and financial analysis, the first three steps in the framework discussed above, provide an excellent foundation for estimating a firm's intrinsic value. Strategy analysis, in addition to enabling sound accounting and financial analysis, also helps in assessing potential changes in a firm's competitive advantage and their implications for the firm's future ROE and growth. Accounting analysis provides an unbiased estimate of a firm's current book value and ROE. Financial analysis allows an in-depth understanding of what drives the firm's current ROE.

The predictions from a sound business analysis are useful to a variety of parties and can be applied in various contexts. The exact nature of the analysis will depend on the context. The contexts that we will examine include securities analysis, credit evaluation, mergers and acquisitions, and the assessment of corporate communication strategies. The four analytical steps described above are useful in each of these contexts. Appropriate use of these tools, however, requires a familiarity with the economic theories and institutional factors relevant to the context.

There are several ways in which financial statement analysis can add value, even when capital markets are reasonably efficient. First, there are many applications of financial statement analysis whose focus is outside the capital market context—credit analysis, competitive benchmarking, and analysis of mergers and acquisitions, to name a few. Second, markets become efficient precisely because some market participants rely on analytical tools such as the ones we discuss in this book to analyze information and make investment decisions. This in turn imposes greater discipline on corporate managers to develop an appropriate disclosure and communication strategy.

SUMMARY

Financial statements provide the most widely available data on public corporations' economic activities; investors and other stakeholders rely on them to assess the plans and performance of firms and corporate managers. Accrual accounting data in financial statements are noisy, and unsophisticated investors can assess firms' performance only imprecisely. Financial analysts who understand managers' disclosure strategies have an opportunity to create inside information from public data, and they play a valuable role in enabling outside parties to evaluate a firm's current and prospective performance.

This chapter has outlined the framework for business analysis with financial statements, using four key steps: business strategy analysis, accounting analysis, financial analysis, and prospective analysis. The remaining chapters in this book describe these steps in greater detail and discuss how they can be used in a variety of business contexts.

DISCUSSION QUESTIONS

1. John, who has just completed his first finance course, is unsure whether he should take a course in business analysis and valuation using financial statements since he believes that financial analysis adds little value, given the efficiency of capital markets. Explain to John when financial analysis can add value, even if capital markets are generally seen as being efficient.

2. In 2009, Larry Summers, former Secretary of the Treasury, observed that "in the past 20-year period, we have seen the 1987 stock market crash. We have seen the Savings & Loan debacle and commercial real estate collapse of the late 80's and early 90's. We have seen the Mexican financial crisis, the Asian financial crisis, the Long Term Capital Management liquidity crisis, the bursting of the NASDAQ bubble and the associated Enron threat to corporate governance. And now we've seen this [global economic crisis], which is more serious than any of that. Twenty years, seven major crises. One major crisis every three years." How could this happen given the large number of financial and information intermediaries working in financial markets throughout the world? Can crises be averted by more effective financial analysis?

3. Accounting statements rarely report financial performance without error. List three types of errors that can arise in financial reporting.

4. Joe Smith argues that "learning how to do business analysis and valuation using financial statements is not very useful, unless you are interested in becoming a financial analyst." Comment.

5. Four steps for business analysis are discussed in the chapter (strategy analysis, accounting analysis, financial analysis, and prospective analysis). As a financial analyst, explain why each of these steps is a critical part of your job and how they relate to one another.

NOTES

1. See G. Akerlof, "The Market for 'Lemons': Quality Uncertainty and the Market Mechanism," *Quarterly Journal of Economics* (August 1970): 488–500. Akerlof recognized that the seller of a used car knew more about the car's value than the buyer. This meant that the buyer was likely to end up overpaying, since the seller would accept any offer that exceeded the car's true value and reject any lower offer. Car buyers recognized this problem and would respond by only making low-ball offers for used cars, leading sellers with high-quality cars to exit the market. As a result, only the lowest quality cars (the "lemons") would remain in the market. Akerlof pointed out that qualified independent mechanics could correct this market breakdown by providing buyers with reliable information on a used car's true value.

2. T. Khanna and K. Palepu, *Winning in Emerging Markets: A Road Map for Strategy and Execution* (Boston, MA: Harvard Business Press, 2010), 54–58.

3. See P. Healy and K. Palepu, "How the Quest for Efficiency Corroded the Market," *Harvard Business Review* (July 2003): 76–85.

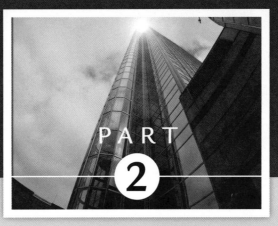

PART 2

BUSINESS ANALYSIS AND VALUATION TOOLS

Chapter 2

STRATEGY ANALYSIS

Strategy analysis is an important starting point for the analysis of financial statements. Strategy analysis allows the analyst to probe the economics of a firm at a qualitative level so that the subsequent accounting and financial analysis is grounded in business reality. Strategy analysis also allows the identification of the firm's profit drivers and key risks. This in turn enables the analyst to assess the sustainability of the firm's current performance and make realistic forecasts of future performance.

A firm's value is determined by its ability to earn a return on its capital in excess of the cost of capital. What determines whether or not a firm is able to accomplish this goal? While a firm's cost of capital is determined by the capital markets, its profit potential is determined by its own strategic choices: (1) the choice of an industry or a set of industries in which the firm operates (industry choice), (2) the manner in which the firm intends to compete with other firms in its chosen industry or industries (competitive positioning), and (3) the way in which the firm expects to create and exploit synergies across the range of businesses in which it operates (corporate strategy). Strategy analysis, therefore, involves industry analysis, competitive strategy analysis, and corporate strategy analysis.[1] In this chapter, we will briefly discuss these three steps and use the U.S. retail department store industry, Nordstrom Inc., and the Tata Group, respectively, to illustrate the application of the steps.

INDUSTRY ANALYSIS

In analyzing a firm's profit potential, an analyst has to first assess the profit potential of each of the industries in which the firm is competing. While specific industry profitability can change over time as the industry evolves, in general the profitability across industries has tended to differ systematically. For example, an analysis of financial results of all U.S.-based companies between 1991 and 2009 shows a ratio of earnings before interest and taxes to the book value of assets of 4.9 percent. However, the average returns varied widely across specific industries: for example, the passenger airline industry group (SIC code 4512), which has struggled with intense competition and low profitability since deregulation in the late 1970s, has seen a 1.8 percent return over the study period. In contrast, the pharmaceutical preparations industry group (SIC code 2834) returned 14.6 percent on average over the period.[2] These are illustrative—there are even more extreme examples. What causes these profitability differences?

There is a vast body of research in industrial organization on the influence of industry structure on profitability.[3] Relying on this research, strategy literature suggests that the

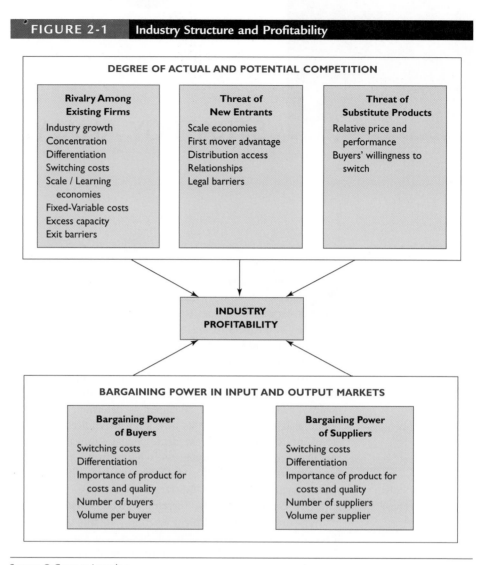

FIGURE 2-1   Industry Structure and Profitability

Source: © Cengage Learning

average profitability of an industry is influenced by the "five forces" shown in Figure 2-1.[4] According to this framework, the intensity of competition determines the potential for creating abnormal profits by the firms in an industry. Whether or not the potential profits are kept by the industry is determined by the relative bargaining power of the firms in the industry and their customers and suppliers. We will discuss each of these industry profit drivers in more detail below.

Degree of Actual and Potential Competition

At the most basic level, the profits in an industry are a function of the maximum price that customers are willing to pay for the industry's product or service. One of the key determinants of the price is the degree to which there is competition among suppliers of the same or similar products. At one extreme, if there is a state of perfect competition in the industry, micro-economic theory predicts that prices will be equal to marginal cost, and there will be few opportunities to earn supernormal profits. At the other extreme, if the industry is dominated by a single firm, there will be potential to earn monopoly profits. In reality, the degree of competition in most industries is somewhere in between perfect competition and monopoly.

There are three potential sources of competition in an industry: (1) rivalry between existing firms, (2) threat of entry of new firms, and (3) threat of substitute products or services. We discuss each of these competitive forces in the following paragraphs.

Competitive Force 1: Rivalry among Existing Firms

In most industries the average level of profitability is primarily influenced by the nature of rivalry among existing firms in the industry. In some industries firms compete aggressively, pushing prices close to (and sometimes below) the marginal cost. In other industries firms do not compete aggressively on price. Instead, they find ways to coordinate their pricing, or compete on non-price dimensions such as innovation or brand image. Several factors determine the intensity of competition among existing players in an industry:

Industry Growth Rate If an industry is growing very rapidly, incumbent firms need not grab market share from each other to grow. In contrast, in stagnant industries the only way existing firms can grow is by taking share away from the other players. In this situation one can expect price wars among firms in the industry.

Concentration and Balance of Competitors The number of firms in an industry and their relative sizes determine the degree of concentration in an industry.[5] The degree of concentration influences the extent to which firms in an industry can coordinate their pricing and other competitive moves. For example, if there is one dominant firm in an industry (such as Microsoft or Intel in the 1990s), it can set and enforce the rules of competition. Similarly, if there are only two or three similarly sized players (such as Coca-Cola and Pepsi in the U.S. soft drink industry), they can implicitly cooperate with each other to avoid destructive price competition. If an industry is fragmented, price competition is likely to be severe, as can be seen in the hotel/motel and construction industries.

Degree of Differentiation and Switching Costs The extent to which firms in an industry can avoid head-on competition depends on the extent to which they can differentiate their products and services. If the products in an industry are very similar, customers are ready to switch from one competitor to another purely on the basis of price. Switching costs also determine customers' propensity to move from one product to another. When switching costs are low, there is a greater incentive for firms in an industry to engage in price competition. The PC industry, where the standardization of the software and microprocessor has led to relatively low switching costs, is extremely price competitive.

Scale/Learning Economies and the Ratio of Fixed to Variable Costs If there is a steep learning curve or there are other types of scale economies in an industry, size becomes an important factor for firms in the industry. In such situations, there are incentives to engage in aggressive competition for market share. Similarly, if the ratio of fixed to variable costs is high, firms have an incentive to reduce prices to utilize installed capacity. The airline industry, where price wars are quite common, is an example of this type of situation.

Excess Capacity and Exit Barriers If capacity in an industry is larger than customer demand, there is a strong incentive for firms to cut prices to fill capacity. The problem of excess capacity is likely to be exacerbated if there are significant barriers for firms to exit the industry. Exit barriers are high when the assets are specialized or if there are regulations which make exit costly. The competitive dynamics of the global automotive industry demonstrates these forces at play.

Competitive Force 2: Threat of New Entrants

The potential for earning abnormal profits will attract new entrants to an industry. The very threat of new firms entering an industry potentially constrains the pricing of existing firms within it. Therefore, the ease with which a new firm can enter an industry is a key determinant of its profitability. Several factors determine the height of barriers to entry in an industry:

Economies of Scale When there are large economies of scale, new entrants face the choice of having either to invest in large capacity which might not be utilized right away, or to enter with less than the optimum capacity. Either way, new entrants will at least initially suffer from a cost disadvantage in competing with existing firms. Economies of scale might arise from large investments in research and development (the pharmaceutical or jet engine industries), in brand advertising (soft drink industry), or in physical plant and equipment (telecommunications industry).

First Mover Advantage Early entrants in an industry may deter future entrants if there are first mover advantages. For example, first movers might be able to set industry standards or enter into exclusive arrangements with suppliers of cheap raw materials. They may also acquire scarce government licenses to operate in regulated industries. Finally, if there are learning economies, early firms will have an absolute cost advantage over new entrants. First mover advantages are also likely to be large when there are significant switching costs for customers once they start using existing products. For example, switching costs faced by the users of Microsoft's Windows operating system make it difficult for software companies to market a new operating system.

Access to Channels of Distribution and Relationships Limited capacity in the existing distribution channels and high costs of developing new channels can act as powerful barriers to entry. For example, a new entrant into the domestic auto industry in the United States is likely to face formidable barriers because of the difficulty of developing a dealer network. Tesla Motors, the California-based electric automobile manufacturer that has gained a lot of positive press for its sporty electric roadster, called out this risk in its 2010 pre-IPO S1 filing with the SEC.[6] In addition, its 2010 strategic partnership with Toyota has been seen by many as a way to leap this barrier by gaining access to Toyota's extensive dealer network. Existing relationships between firms and customers in an industry are another barrier that can make it difficult for new firms to enter an industry. Examples of industries where this is a factor include auditing and investment banking.

Legal Barriers There are many industries in which legal barriers such as patents and copyrights in research-intensive industries limit entry. Similarly, licensing regulations limit entry into taxi services, medical services, broadcasting, and telecommunications industries.

Competitive Force 3: Threat of Substitute Products

The third dimension of competition in an industry is the threat of substitute products or services. Relevant substitutes are not necessarily those that have the same form as the existing products but those that perform the same function. For example, airlines and car rental services might be substitutes for each other when it comes to travel over medium distances. Similarly, plastic bottles and metal cans substitute for each other as packaging in the beverage industry. In some cases, threat of substitution comes not from customers' switching to another product but from utilizing technologies that allow them to do without, or use less of, the existing products. For example, energy-conserving technologies allow customers to reduce their consumption of electricity and fossil fuels.

The threat of substitutes depends on the relative price and performance of the competing products or services and on customers' willingness to substitute. Customers' perception of whether two products are substitutes depends to some extent on whether they perform the same function for a similar price. If two products perform an identical function, then it would be difficult for them to differ from each other in price. However, customers' willingness to switch is often the critical factor in making this competitive dynamic work. For example, even when tap water and bottled water serve the same function, many customers may be unwilling to substitute the former for the latter, enabling bottlers to charge a price premium. Similarly, designer label clothing commands a price premium even if it is not superior in terms of basic functionality because customers place a value on the image or style offered by designer labels.

Bargaining Power in Input and Output Markets

While the degree of competition in an industry determines whether there is *potential* to earn abnormal profits, the *actual profits* are influenced by the industry's bargaining power with its suppliers and customers. On the input side, firms enter into transactions with suppliers of labor, raw materials and components, and finances. On the output side, firms either sell directly to the final customers or enter into contracts with intermediaries in the distribution chain. In all these transactions, the relative economic power of the two sides is important to the overall profitability of the industry firms.

Competitive Force 4: Bargaining Power of Buyers

Two factors determine the power of buyers: price sensitivity and relative bargaining power. Price sensitivity determines the extent to which buyers care to bargain on price; relative bargaining power determines the extent to which they will succeed in forcing the price down.[7]

Price Sensitivity Buyers are more price sensitive when the product is undifferentiated and there are few switching costs. For example, Windows-based personal computers are seen by customers as close substitutes of each other, and hence purchasing decisions among different brands of PCs is heavily influenced by price. The sensitivity of buyers to price also depends on the importance of the product to their own cost structure. When the product represents a large fraction of the buyers' cost (for example, the packaging material for soft drink producers), the buyer is likely to expend the resources necessary to shop for a lower cost alternative. In contrast, if the product is a small fraction of the buyers' cost (for example, windshield wipers for automobile manufacturers), it may not pay to expend resources to search for lower-cost alternatives. Further, the importance of the product to the buyers' own product quality also determines whether or not price becomes the most important determinant of the buying decision. The explosion in compensation paid to marquee sports figures can be seen as an example of this type of phenomenon because these players are viewed by teams as critical to their fan appeal and success as a franchise.

Relative Bargaining Power Even if buyers are price sensitive, they may not be able to achieve low prices unless they have a strong bargaining position. Relative bargaining power in a transaction depends, ultimately, on the cost to each party of not doing business with the other party. The buyers' bargaining power is determined by the number of buyers relative to the number of suppliers, volume of purchases by a single buyer, number of alternative products available to the buyer, buyers' costs of switching from one product to another, and the threat of backward integration by the buyers. For example, in the automobile industry, car manufacturers have considerable power over component manufacturers because auto companies are large buyers with several alternative suppliers to choose from, and switching costs are relatively low. In contrast, in the personal computer industry, computer makers have low bargaining power relative to the operating system software producers because of high switching costs.

Competitive Force 5: Bargaining Power of Suppliers

The analysis of the relative power of suppliers is a mirror image of the analysis of the buyer's power in an industry. Suppliers are powerful when there are only a few companies and few substitutes available to their customers. For example, in the soft drink industry, Coke and Pepsi are very powerful relative to the bottlers. In contrast, metal can suppliers to the soft drink industry are not very powerful because of intense competition among can producers and the threat of substitution by plastic bottles. Suppliers also have a great deal of power over buyers when the suppliers' product or service is critical to buyers' business. Microsoft's power in the personal computer industry is a good example of this. Suppliers also tend to be powerful when they pose a credible threat of forward integration. For example, IBM is powerful relative to mainframe computer leasing companies because of its unique position as a mainframe supplier and its own presence in the computer leasing business.

APPLYING INDUSTRY ANALYSIS: THE U.S. RETAIL DEPARTMENT STORE INDUSTRY

Let us consider the above concepts of industry analysis in the context of the U.S. retail department store industry. The growth of cities and mass production techniques spurred the emergence of retail clothing stores in the late 1800s. The rapid expansion of the market in the twentieth century fostered the development of regional and national chains that gave the industry its concentrated profile we see today. While the major players originally located in stand-alone flagship locations in urban centers, the population migration out of cities and the rise of the suburban shopping mall in the mid-twentieth century resulted in these players positioning themselves as "anchor stores"—large department stores selling a wide range of apparel, accessories, and other related goods that "anchored" the broader shopping mall and its selection of smaller specialty stores.

Broadly stated, the industry can be segmented into high-end, middle market, and discount department stores. Table 2-1 shows profitability of select competitors in these three segments. The overall department store industry has historically earned higher than average returns when compared to all U.S. industries (analysis described above), with the high-end and discount segments outperforming the middle market. What has accounted for this above average industry return? Looking forward, what is the department store industry's future profit potential?

Competition in the U.S. Retail Department Store Industry

Industry analysis can help to explain the above average profitability seen in the department store industry. Key elements of industry structure:

- The industry is concentrated, with the four largest players accounting for over 75 percent of the industry revenue in 2009.[8]
- Consumer demand grew along with the growth in U.S. affluence for most of the twentieth and early twenty-first century. This has meant that department stores have typically experienced growth without having to resort to high levels of price competition in an effort to steal market share from competitors.

TABLE 2-1	Retail Department store pre-tax profitability—select competitors 1991–2009
Company	**EBIT/Net Assets**
Neiman-Marcus Group, Inc.[a]	11.8%
Saks Inc / Saks Holdings, Inc.	5.2%
Nordstrom Inc.	13.8%
High-end segment average	10.3%
Sears Roebuck & Co / Sears Holding Group[b]	6.3%
Dillards Inc.	6.4%
R H Macy & Co / Macy's Inc.[c]	7.0%
J C Penney Co.	7.9%
Middle market segment average	6.8%
Wal-Mart Stores, Inc.	12.4%
Target Corp	11.3%
TJX Companies Inc.	22.1%
Discount segment average	12.5%
Average of all retail department store segments	9.9%[d]
Average of all U.S. companies	4.9%

Source: Financial statement data for noted companies, industry, and all publicly traded U.S.-based companies from 1991–2009, listed in Research Insight. Analysis completed November, 2011.
[a]Neiman-Marcus was taken private in 2006—results shown are through 2005.
[b]Includes Kmart beginning 2005 when the companies merged to form Sears Holding Group.
[c]Includes Bloomingdales, other brands, which make up about 10 percent of total revenues.
[d]Average of SIC codes 5311, 5331, and 5651 data 1991–2009. The representative group of competitors shown above mirrors the overall results of the department store industry with a return of 10.0 percent over the period.

- Competitors such as Nordstrom, Saks Fifth Avenue, and Neiman Marcus have successfully differentiated themselves on non-price parameters such as superior customer service, a differentiated product offering through the use of private label lines and exclusive designer relationships, loyalty programs, and an upscale shopping experience—all of which are designed to build customer loyalty and thus increase switching costs.
- There are significant economies of scale available to larger competitors, who have more power to obtain lower prices from their suppliers, to invest in sophisticated IT infrastructure to better understand customer needs and manage inventory, and to conduct national advertising campaigns. These economies of scale have been critical to the success of competitors pursuing a cost-leadership strategy (Wal-Mart, Target, TJX), who have been ruthless in streamlining their operations, reducing their cost from suppliers, and otherwise driving down their cost to bring product to market.
- Established competitors have strong brand recognition earned through years of effort, while a new competitor is faced with the need to expend large amounts of capital in order to gain this brand equity. This first mover advantage holds true not only in traditional physical stores but also in the realm of the Internet where consumers, lacking the ability to measure the quality of a store or product

by experiencing it firsthand, have tended to gravitate to established, "trusted" name brands.

- A new competitor in the industry would typically face a distribution constraint when seeking a prime retail location as established competitors have better access to prime retail locations and favorable terms since they are viewed as valuable "anchor" tenants that can ensure success of an entire development. With the increased use of the online channel, this barrier has been eased somewhat as a competitive factor in the industry.

- The rise of the online shopping channel as represented by online-only competitors such as Amazon.com has resulted in a large and growing threat of substitution for the traditional "bricks and mortar" stores. Competitors such as Nordstrom have aggressively developed their own online presence in an attempt to reduce this threat, while at the same time working to integrate their online and physical channels in order to leverage their physical presence to their advantage.

The Power of Buyers and Suppliers

Suppliers and buyers have limited power over firms in the industry for these reasons:

- Generally, buyers tend to have relatively low bargaining power with department stores—there is little or no "haggling" over price. Given the relative number of individual buyers to providers (high), buyers mainly are able to exert their ability to switch providers rather than to exert any relative strength in bargaining power.

- Suppliers to department stores also have low relative power due to their small size as compared to their clients. The expansion of the private label lines has also established a credible alternative to the designer lines, further reducing supplier power. Competitors in all segments of the department store industry have focused on building their power over suppliers. As an example, TJX added approximately 2,000 new suppliers in 2010 bringing their total global count to over 14,000.[9] Also, Nordstrom has no guaranteed supply arrangements with its vendors,[10] which allows it to maintain flexibility to adjust their products to meet current demand.

In recent years, industry dynamics have been shifting. First, growth in consumer demand slowed significantly during the recent global economic crisis, and there is speculation that it may not return to pre-crisis levels at least in the short term.[11] Also, the emergence of the Internet channel has begun to change consumer shopping behavior both online and off. The availability of price and product information has increased substitution as the consumer is able to make more informed buying decisions. The ease of shopping across multiple online outlets has reduced switching costs, and perhaps has served to reduce the value of the broad product offering of the retail department store model. In a similar offline shift, the rise of "lifestyle centers," which emphasize smaller specialty retailers clustered in an attractive center, has de-emphasized the role of the anchor store. In general, the trend toward specialization would seem to be against the department store model.[12]

While it is not clear what additional structural changes will take place in the industry, what is clear is that the competitors who adapt will be the ones to survive and thrive. Nordstrom's aggressive push to expand its online presence, TJX working to expand its global supplier base while pursuing a specialized offering strategy (Home Goods, Marshalls / TJ Maxx), and Wal-Mart's push into China and other high growth potential emerging markets are examples of actions competitors are taking to adapt to the changing dynamics of the marketplace.

Limitations of Industry Analysis

A potential limitation of the industry analysis framework discussed in this chapter is the assumption that industries have clear boundaries. In reality, it is often not easy to demarcate industry boundaries. For example, in analyzing Nordstrom's industry, should one limit the analysis to large department store competitors, or also include smaller specialty retailers which compete with Nordstrom for market share? With the rise of the discount and off-price retailers, should one include Wal-Mart and TJX? Where do online retailers such as Amazon.com fit? Inappropriate industry definition will result in incomplete analysis and inaccurate forecasts, and thus it is important to correctly scope the industry segment to be considered.

COMPETITIVE STRATEGY ANALYSIS

The profitability of a firm is influenced not only by its industry structure but also by the strategic choices it makes in positioning itself in the industry. While there are many ways to characterize a firm's business strategy, research has traditionally identified two generic competitive strategies, (1) cost leadership and (2) differentiation, that can potentially allow a firm to build a sustainable competitive advantage.[13] These strategies (shown in Figure 2-2) have broadly been seen as mutually exclusive—firms that straddle the two strategies are said to be "stuck in the middle" and expected to earn low profitability (the middle market department store competitors described in the last section are a good example of this).[14] These firms, the thinking goes, run the risk of not being able to attract price-conscious customers because their costs are too high; they are also unable to provide adequate differentiation to attract premium price customers.

FIGURE 2-2   Strategies for Creating Competitive Advantage

Source: © Cengage Learning

Additional research has attempted to explain the apparent exception of certain competitors, for instance, the Japanese automotive industry, which for many years offered both higher quality and lower cost than its competitors in the United States and Europe. Generally, though, this ability to compete successfully from the "middle" has been attributed to a focus on operational effectiveness—not strategy—that has allowed them to continuously push the "productivity frontier" ahead of their competitors. This advantage is only expected to be sustainable if it could not eventually be duplicated allowing competitors to "catch up."[15]

Sources of Competitive Advantage

Cost leadership enables a firm to supply the same product or service offered by its competitors at a lower cost. Differentiation strategy involves providing a product or service that is distinct in some important respect valued by the customer. We will illustrate both of these strategies using two companies in the U.S. retail department store industry. TJX Companies, Inc. (parent to stores such as T.J. Maxx and Marshalls) has been highly successful competing purely on a low-cost basis. Nordstrom, in contrast, has succeeded on the basis of differentiation by emphasizing exceptionally high customer service and broad, differentiated merchandise selection.

Competitive Strategy 1: Cost Leadership

Cost leadership is often the clearest way to achieve competitive advantage. In industries where the basic product or service is a commodity, cost leadership might be the only way to achieve superior performance. There are many ways to achieve cost leadership, including economies of scale and scope, economies of learning, efficient production, simpler product design, better sourcing and lower input costs, and efficient organizational processes. If a firm can achieve cost leadership, then it will be able to earn above-average profitability by merely charging the same price as its rivals. Conversely, a cost leader can force its competitors to cut prices and accept lower returns or to exit the industry.

Firms that achieve cost leadership focus on tight cost controls. They make investments in efficient scale plants, focus on product designs that reduce manufacturing costs, minimize overhead costs, capitalize on global sourcing opportunities, make little investment in risky research and development, and avoid serving marginal customers. They have organizational structures and control systems that focus on cost control.

Competitive Strategy 2: Differentiation

A firm following the differentiation strategy seeks to be unique in its industry along some dimension that is highly valued by customers. For differentiation to be successful, the firm has to accomplish three things. First, it needs to identify one or more attributes of a product or service that customers value. Second, it has to position itself to meet the chosen customer need in a unique manner. Finally, the firm has to achieve differentiation at a cost that is lower than the price the customer is willing to pay for the differentiated product or service.

Drivers of differentiation include providing superior intrinsic value via product quality, product variety, bundled services, or delivery timing. Differentiation can also be achieved by investing in signals of value such as brand image, product appearance, or reputation. Differentiated strategies require investments in research and development, engineering skills, and marketing capabilities. The organizational structures and control systems in firms with differentiation strategies need to foster creativity and innovation.

While successful firms choose between cost leadership and differentiation, they cannot completely ignore the dimension on which they are not primarily competing. Firms that target differentiation still need to focus on costs so that the differentiation can be achieved at an acceptable cost. Similarly, cost leaders cannot compete unless they achieve at least a minimum level on key dimensions on which competitors might differentiate, such as quality and service.

Achieving Competitive Advantage

The choice of competitive strategy does not automatically lead to the achievement of competitive advantage. To achieve competitive advantage, the firm has to have the capabilities needed to implement and sustain the chosen strategy. Both cost leadership and differentiation strategy require that the firm make the necessary commitments to acquire the core competencies needed and structure its value chain in an appropriate way. Core competencies are the economic assets that the firm possesses, whereas the value chain is the set of activities that the firm performs to convert inputs into outputs.

To evaluate whether a firm is likely to achieve its intended competitive advantage, the analyst should ask the following questions:

- What is the customer need that the company is focusing on?
- How does the company distinguish its customer value proposition from the alternative propositions available to the customers from its competitors?
- Does the firm currently have the key capabilities and processes to deliver its value proposition?

Sustaining Competitive Advantage

The uniqueness of a firm's core competencies and its value chain and the extent to which it is difficult for competitors to imitate them determine the sustainability of a firm's competitive advantage.[16] Very few companies are able to sustain their competitive advantage over a long period of time. There are a number of reasons for this. First, successful strategies are often copied by competitors. This can only be prevented or delayed if there are explicit barriers such as patents or other legal protections, or implicit barriers such as customer switching costs or first mover advantages. The second reason why firms lose their competitive advantage is due to changes in the environment. New technologies, changes in regulation, changes in customer requirements make current value propositions obsolete or enable creation of new, substitute propositions that might be more attractive for customers. As industries and markets evolve over time, it is critical that a firm's strategy evolve as well in response. The competitors who will win over time will be the ones who will continually be alert to the need to adapt to changing industry dynamics.

To evaluate whether or not a firm is likely to sustain its competitive advantage, an analyst should ask the following questions:

- Are there any barriers to imitation in this company's strategy? If so, what are they? How long are they likely to last?
- Are there any changes that potentially affect this company's industry and its strategic position in that industry? What are they? In what way are these changes likely to lead to lead to changes in the competitive dynamics in this industry?
- What actions, if any, can this company take to address these changes, and renew its competitive advantage? How likely is it that the company will be able to renew itself successfully?

Applying Competitive Strategy Analysis

Let us consider the concepts of competitive strategy analysis in the context of TJX and Nordstrom.

The TJX Companies, Inc.

TJX is the leading off-price apparel and home fashions retailer in the United States and worldwide. At the beginning of 2011, the company operated over 2,700 retail outlets through its T.J. Maxx, Marshalls, and HomeGoods brands in the United States; its Winners, Marshalls and HomeSense brands in Canada; and its T.K. Maxx and HomeSense brands in Europe.[17]

TJX pursues a cost leadership strategy, offering its customers a "rapidly changing assortment of quality, brand-name and designer merchandise at prices generally 20% to 60% below department and specialty store regular prices, every day."[18] In order to execute that strategy, the company has developed a low-cost, flexible business model that has at its core a focus on opportunistic buying of merchandise. Since TJX's philosophy of presenting its customers with a "treasure hunt atmosphere" is not dependent on offering complete product lines, having all sizes available, or presenting a set mix of merchandise, it has the ability to buy partial lots, discontinued items, or cancelled orders. This opportunistic positioning allows TJX to purchase very late in the merchandising cycle, enabling it to react quickly to market trends, to negotiate the best deals, and to adjust pricing to maintain its margin.[19] Key elements of this business model:

- Open store concept: The lack of set departments in its stores allows TJX to maintain an opportunistic product mix that targets current consumer tastes.[20]
- Global sourcing network: In order to source product opportunistically with maximum effectiveness, TJX maintains a global sourcing network, which in 2011 consisted of 700 buyers managing 14,000 vendors across 60 countries. As TJX noted in its 2009 Annual Report, "One way to think about our business model is as more of a sourcing machine than most other retailers."[21]
- Significant buying power: TJX quotes its "$20 billion buying pencil"[22] to describe the buying power its large scale gives it with vendors.
- Focus on efficient inventory management: True to its positioning as a low-cost competitor, TJX has an ongoing focus on increasing the efficiency of its supply chain.[23]

TJX sees itself as well positioned to take advantage of what it sees as a permanent shift in consumer spending behavior as a result of the global financial crisis: "We believe that there has been a paradigm shift among consumers to value and that our new customers will continue to be attracted to our great values even as the recession abates…. What sets this recession apart from previous ones is that we have seen positive business trends accelerate during the recession, underscoring our belief that there has been a fundamental shift in the consumer psyche toward value."[24]

During fiscal year 2010 (ending January 29, 2011), TJX results seemed to bear out management's viewpoint. Despite a challenging retail climate, sales increased by 8 percent to $21.9 billion, with same store sales increasing by 4 percent. Cost of sales fell, reflecting improved merchandise margins and increased cost leverage. Overall, net income grew 11 percent to $1.3 billion.[25] However, while TJX seemed to be executing its cost leadership strategy successfully, changes in the industry structure and moves by competitors had begun to raise questions about the long term sustainability of TJX's competitive position. Key questions:

- **Will there be enough merchandise available to purchase?** As competitors such as Nordstrom and Saks Fifth Avenue rapidly expand their own off-price chains, an ever-growing TJX could eventually face merchandise sourcing constraints as competitors increasingly retain product for their own off-price channels. TJX is cognizant of this potential issue and views its extensive global sourcing network and strong supplier relationships as key to its success in product procurement going forward.[26]

- **Can TJX expand successfully outside of the United States?** TJX views continued expansion as key to maintaining its low-cost position over the long term by ever-increasing purchasing and operational leverage. However, as it increasingly looks outside the United States for growth, it remains to be seen whether it can achieve the same success internationally.

- **Is the shift to value permanent?** It remains to be seen whether this consumer shift that TJX sees is permanent. TJX has undertaken a program of store remodeling and has made additional advertising expenditures in order to capitalize on this shift.[27] It is an open question whether this expenditure will result in a permanent increase in market share.

- **What about the Internet?** As of 2011, TJX had almost no online presence. While it is not clear at this point what threat online retailing represents to the TJX "treasure hunt" model, moves by competitors, such as the recent purchase of Haute-Look (an online apparel auction site) by Nordstrom and the increasing ubiquity of online retailing, raises the question of what TJX will need to do to defend itself against this substitute channel.

Nordstrom, Inc.

Nordstrom is a high-end department store offering a wide variety of apparel, shoes, and accessories. Founded as a shoe store in Seattle, Washington, in 1901, the company quickly became known for its broad selection of high-quality merchandise coupled with exceptional customer service. By 2011 the company had grown to be a leading retailer, operating 207 stores located in 28 states (both full-line Nordstrom and discount Nordstrom Rack stores) as well as a growing online presence. The company also offered a variety of private label credit and debit card products through Nordstrom fsb, its wholly-owned bank. The company posted 2010 annual earnings of $613 million against annual revenues of $9.7 billion.[28]

Nordstrom's success has historically been based on a competitive strategy of differentiation that has sought to build loyalty in consumers who have many retail purchase options. The key elements of that strategy:

- *Providing exceptional customer service:* From the beginning, Nordstrom has sought to differentiate itself in the market by providing exceptional customer service. A quote from the 2009 annual report sums up this customer-centric philosophy: "We follow, first and foremost, a customer strategy at Nordstrom—not a price, brand, technology or any other corporate strategy." [29]

- *Offering a broad selection of high-end, differentiated merchandise closely targeted to local tastes:* Nordstrom has sought to differentiate itself from competitors by low product overlap, which it has achieved with exclusive agreements with designers as well as by the development of an extensive private label line. In addition, Nordstrom prides itself on making buying decisions with local customer input, thus maximizing merchandising success and minimizing inventory investments.

While the above broad strategic elements have served it well for much of its 110-year history, in recent years Nordstrom has recognized that the rapid expansion of the online channel and the rise of the discount retail model represent shifts in the market that could threaten the long-term sustainability of its differentiation strategy. As such,

Nordstrom's current strategy is to stay true to its original precepts of superior customer service and product selection, while adding additional initiatives that it views as critical to remaining competitive in an evolving marketplace. Key initiatives being undertaken in response to this market shift:

- *Diversification into the discount segment*—In response to the market shift towards the discount segment, Nordstrom has rapidly expanded its Nordstrom Rack division of off-price stores. This has served several purposes. First, in establishing its own discount entrant, it has "created its own substitute" for customers that would otherwise potentially be lost to a TJX or other discount retailer. Also, the Rack division gives Nordstrom a channel to move slow-selling inventory from its full-line stores without needing to resort to more frequent sales or markdowns that might erode the brand. Finally, given that the discount segment tends to perform better in poor economic times, this can be seen as adding counter-cyclical balance to the full-line store segment.
- *Expansion and integration of a multichannel presence*—Responding to the changing shopping habits of consumers, Nordstrom has recently undertaken a number of initiatives designed to expand its online presence and fully integrate its systems across all channels. In 2010 the company launched a new version of the Nordstrom.com website designed to more effectively serve the online shopper. The integration of inventory systems across channels has enabled seamless multichannel customer services such as "Buy Online, Pick Up in Store" and rapid fulfillment of online orders from local stores. Recent initiatives designed to further enhance the multichannel offering include the addition of Wi-Fi to its full-line stores, development of mobile checkout, and the acquisition of online retailer HauteLook, Inc.—a provider of online private sales.[30] In general, Nordstrom views the development of a seamless multichannel shopping experience as an extension of its focus on providing superior customer service and as critical to its continued ability to compete successfully in an evolving marketplace.

As the United States slowly began to emerge from the deep downturn that began in 2008, Nordstrom was a company taking steps to adapt to changing industry dynamics. In early 2011, analysts seemed to think that it was on the right track:

"JWN remains one of our top picks in the department store space.... We believe Nordstrom is the most technologically savvy of the large cap department stores. The acquisition of HauteLook not only introduces a new revenue stream, but should help the company further expand its internet marketing capabilities and monetize the multi-channel customer (who spends 3-4x more than the store only customer)."[31]

"From its move in 2009/2010 to integrate its in-store and online inventory to its announcement yesterday of an acquisition of HauteLook, a leading online closeout channel, the Company remains well ahead of competitors in its online presence. Moreover, we think that this helps provide a long-term roadmap for growth..." [32]

"We continue to believe Nordstrom is a longer term share winner..." [33]

Analysts' opinions aside, it remains to be seen whether Nordstrom can maintain its superior competitive position going forward in the rapidly evolving industry landscape.

CORPORATE STRATEGY ANALYSIS

So far in this chapter we have focused on strategies at the individual business level. While some companies focus on only one business, many companies operate in multiple businesses. For example, the average number of business segments operated by the top

500 U.S. companies in 1992 was eleven industries.[34] In recent years, there has been an attempt by U.S. companies to reduce the diversity of their operations and focus on a relatively few "core" businesses. However, multi-business organizations continue to dominate the economic activity in most countries in the world.

When analyzing a multi-business organization, an analyst has to evaluate not only the industries and strategies of the individual business units but also the economic consequences—either positive or negative—of managing all the different businesses under one corporate umbrella. Some companies have viewed this multibusiness structure as a source of strength and have embraced it, while others have seen it as distracting and value dilutive and have moved to narrow their business focus. For example, General Electric has been very successful in creating significant value by managing a highly diversified set of businesses ranging from aircraft engines to light bulbs. In contrast, starting in 2000, the Swiss pharmaceutical giant Roche sold off its flavors and fragrances, vitamins, and fine chemicals businesses to focus on oncology and diagnostics.[35]

Sources of Value Creation at the Corporate Level

Economists and strategy researchers have identified several factors that influence an organization's ability to create value through a broad corporate scope. Economic theory suggests that the optimal scope of activity of a firm depends on the relative transaction cost of performing a set of activities inside the firm versus using the market mechanism.[36] Transaction cost economics implies that the multiproduct firm is an efficient choice of organizational form when coordination among independent, focused firms is costly due to market transaction costs.

Transaction costs can arise out of several sources. They may arise if the production process involves specialized assets such as human capital skills, proprietary technology, or other organizational know-how that is not easily available in the marketplace. Transaction costs also may arise from market imperfections such as information and incentive problems. If buyers and sellers cannot solve these problems through standard mechanisms such as enforceable contracts, it will be costly to conduct transactions through market mechanisms.

For example, as discussed in Chapter 1, capital markets may not work well when there are significant information and incentive problems, making it difficult for entrepreneurs to raise capital from investors. Similarly, if buyers cannot ascertain the quality of products being sold because of lack of information, or cannot enforce warranties because of poor legal infrastructure, entrepreneurs will find it difficult to break into new markets. Finally, if employers cannot assess the quality of applicants for new positions, they will have to rely more on internal promotions rather than external recruiting to fill higher positions in an organization. Emerging economies often suffer from these types of transaction costs because of poorly developed intermediation infrastructure.[37] Even in many advanced economies, examples of high transaction costs can be found. For example, in most countries other than the United States, the venture capital industry is not highly developed, making it costly for new businesses in high technology industries to attract financing. Even in the United States, transaction costs may vary across economic sectors. For example, electronic commerce continues to be hampered by consumer concerns regarding the security of credit card information sent over the Internet.[38]

Transactions inside an organization may be less costly than market-based transactions for several reasons. First, communication costs inside an organization are reduced because confidentiality can be protected and credibility can be assured through internal mechanisms. Second, the head office can play a critical role in reducing costs of enforcing agreements between organizational subunits. Third, organizational subunits can share valuable non-tradable assets (such as organizational skills, systems, and processes) or non-divisible assets (such as brand names, distribution channels, and reputation).

There are also forces that increase transaction costs inside organizations. Top management of an organization may lack the specialized information and skills necessary to manage businesses across several different industries. This lack of expertise reduces the possibility of actually realizing economies of scope, even when there is potential for such economies. This problem can be remedied by creating a decentralized organization, hiring specialist managers to run each business unit, and providing these managers with proper incentives. However, decentralization will also potentially decrease goal congruence among subunit managers, making it difficult to realize economies of scope.

Whether or not a multibusiness organization creates more value than a comparable collection of focused firms is, therefore, context dependent.[39] Analysts should ask the following questions to assess whether an organization's corporate strategy has the potential to create value:

- Are there significant imperfections in the product, labor, or financial markets in the industries (or countries) in which a company is operating? Is it likely that transaction costs in these markets are higher than the costs of similar activities inside a well-managed organization?
- Does the organization have special resources such as brand names, proprietary know-how, access to scarce distribution channels, and special organizational processes that have the potential to create economies of scope?
- Is there a good fit between the company's specialized resources and the portfolio of businesses in which the company is operating?
- Does the company allocate decision rights between the headquarters office and the business units optimally to realize all the potential economies of scope?
- Does the company have internal measurement, information, and incentive systems to reduce agency costs and increase coordination across business units?

Empirical evidence suggests that creating value through a multibusiness corporate strategy is difficult in practice. Several researchers have documented that diversified U.S. companies trade at a discount in the stock market relative to a comparable portfolio of focused companies.[40] Studies also show that acquisitions of one company by another, especially when the two are in unrelated businesses, often fail to create value for the acquiring companies.[41] Finally, there is considerable evidence that value is created when multibusiness companies increase corporate focus through divisional spin-offs and asset sales.[42]

There are several potential explanations for this diversification discount. First, managers' decisions to diversify and expand are frequently driven by a desire to maximize the size of their organization rather than to maximize shareholder value. Second, diversified companies often suffer from incentive misalignment problems leading to suboptimal investment decisions and poor operating performance. Third, capital markets find it difficult to monitor and value multibusiness organizations because of inadequate disclosure about the performance of individual business segments.

In summary, while companies can theoretically create value through innovative corporate strategies, there are many ways in which this potential fails to get realized in practice. Therefore, it pays to be skeptical when evaluating companies' corporate strategies.

Applying Corporate Strategy Analysis

Let's apply the concepts of corporate strategy analysis to the Tata Group, a diversified global company headquartered in India. Tata traces its beginnings to the founding of a private trading firm in 1868. In 2009-2010 the company reported revenues of

$67.4 billion, employed almost 400,000 people, and had operations in over 80 countries.[43] Its structure as a diversified conglomerate reflects its Indian roots as a legacy of the British colonial managing agency system, and also in the need to provide its own intermediary infrastructure in the absence of that infrastructure in the emerging Indian market.[44] Chairman Ratan Tata has worked since his appointment in 1991 to turn what was then a collection of highly independent companies spread across disparate industries into a modern global enterprise able to harness the value of multicompany synergy to successfully compete in India and beyond.

At the end of 2010, the Tata Group was organized into seven business sectors:[45]

- *Information Technology and Communications:* In 2009-2010 this sector represented about 16 percent of Tata's revenues. Tata Consultancy Services is India's most valuable IT company and its over 140,000 consultants provide IT services, business solutions, and outsourcing across 42 countries. This sector also includes companies engaged in product design and technology development services, interactive learning development, business support services, and telecommunications.
- *Engineering products and services:* This sector represented about 33 percent of Tata's revenues. Tata Motors, producer of the Nano, the world's least expensive car, is India's largest automobile company, and is also a significant player globally, being the world's fourth-largest truck manufacturer, the second-largest bus manufacturer, and the owner (since 2008) of Jaguar Land Rover. Other companies in this sector provide automotive, construction, and engineering products and services.
- *Materials:* Materials represented about 32 percent of Tata's revenues. Tata Steel, a Fortune Global 500 company in its own right,[46] employs over 80,000 people in nearly 50 countries. Other companies in the sector provide a wide range of materials production and services.
- *Services:* Services represented about 4 percent of Tata's revenues. The Taj Hotels Resorts and Palaces group offers 66 hotels across India as well as 16 international locations, while related companies provide additional rea-estate-focused services. Tata AIG Life Insurance Company and Tata AIG General Insurance Company provide insurance solutions to individuals and businesses. Additional companies provide asset management, management consulting, and other services.
- *Energy:* Energy represented about 6 percent of Tata's revenues. Tata Power is India's largest private-sector-integrated power utility. Tata BP Solar is the largest Indian maker of solar photovoltaic and solar water heating products.
- *Consumer Products:* Consumer products represented about 4 percent of Tata's revenues. Tata Beverage Group markets brands such as Tata Tea, Tata Coffee, Tetley (the leading UK market brand), Eight O'Clock Coffee, and Mount Everest Mineral Water. Other companies in the sector own retail stores, and also produce and market watches, jewelry, and eyewear.
- *Chemicals:* Chemicals represented about 3 percent of Tata's revenues. Tata Chemicals is the world's second largest producer of soda ash, and produces a variety of chemicals for the consumer, industrial, and farm sectors. Other companies in the sector pursue drug discovery and development and produce agrochemicals.

Given the conventional wisdom that multi-industry conglomerates will struggle to compete against their more-focused competitors, how has Tata managed to achieve its success thus far? The answer lies in the well-executed development of centralized functions applied across the group that support, connect, and elevate the individual companies on many different levels, while at the same time allowing them the independence to succeed on their own. Key elements of this model include:

- The primary connection between the Tata Group companies, and perhaps their biggest collective source of strength is the Tata Brand, which in 2011 was named one of the top 50 global brands by Brand Finance.[47] This recognition comes as the result of a well-planned and careful nurturing of the brand by Chairman Tata that began in 1995 when he introduced the Tata Brand Equity Scheme. This subscription plan establishes the criteria by which a subscriber company may use the Tata brand and also gain access to the resources of the broader group.[48] Subscribing companies sign the Brand Equity and Business Promotion (BEBP) agreement, which specifies a required code of conduct that helps to ensure high standards of quality and integrity across the company. A centralized organization, Tata Quality Management Services (TQMS), works to help Tata companies achieve their business objectives and meet the standards specified by the agreement. Companies who excel in quality management can be nominated for the JRD Quality Value Award, which is modeled after the Malcolm Baldrige Award.[49] Conversely, companies who fail to meet the standards set out in the BEBP agreement risk losing their right to use the Tata name. The value of the Tata brand is immense for a group company that is not well recognized in its market, and especially in emerging markets the brand can be a very powerful and important sign of quality and integrity.
- The Tata Group exploits its scale and the diversity of its collective companies in order to foster learning, leadership development, and the sharing of best practices across the group. Tata Administrative Services (TAS) coordinates a group-wide management recruitment and development program, recruiting at top Indian business schools and rotating new managers across group companies during a five-year development plan. The Tata Management Training Centre (TMTC) brings together senior executives, who share insights with their fellow executives from a huge diversity of industries.[50] The scale of the company is such that these programs can easily bring together 50 or more company CEOs, who share best practices, view problems from a multitude of perspectives, and build relationships that help facilitate cross-company communication and synergy.
- While Tata Group companies operate with a significant degree of independence, they have the financial, intellectual, and other resources of the broader group behind them. In many ways the central office acts as a venture capitalist—serving as a resource for investment funds, management expertise, and connections within the broader group, in industry, and in government. Much like venture capitalists, the Group Executive Office (GEO) members sit on the boards of Tata Group companies in order to facilitate communication between the central office and individual companies, and to bring the knowledge and experience of the broader group to each individual company.[51] This support allows group companies to act like a much larger company in making acquisitions, investing in new technologies, and making other strategic moves. The power of this backing can be seen in the acquisitions of Tetley Tea by Tata Tea in 2000, Corus by Tata Steel in 2007, and Jaguar Land Rover by Tata Motors in 2008, all of which represented an acquisition of a company much larger than the Tata company which acquired it. This would not have been possible without the backing of the broader group.[52]

As of 2010, almost 60 percent of Tata Group revenue came from outside the Indian market.[53] The increasingly global footprint of the company as well as the evolving global economy present several challenges to the effectiveness of its conglomerate model. First, the continued expansion into developed countries may reduce the importance of the internal intermediary infrastructure that Tata has worked to develop. Second, as the Indian economy continues to evolve, this same issue may eventually hold true in the home market.

Finally, the continued successful integration and coordination of the operating companies in a company with a strong tradition of independence will be made ever harder when spread across an increasingly broad geography. As the company works to identify a worthy successor to Ratan Tata (who is scheduled to retire in 2012),[54] how the Tata Group responds in the coming years to the challenges and opportunities presented by both globalization and the rapid development of its Indian home market will be closely watched as a test case for the viability of the multi-industry conglomerate in the modern global economy.

SUMMARY

Strategy analysis is an important starting point for the analysis of financial statements because it allows the analyst to probe the economics of the firm at a qualitative level. Strategy analysis also allows the identification of the firm's profit drivers and key risks, enabling the analyst to assess the sustainability of the firm's performance and make realistic forecasts of future performance.

Whether a firm is able to earn a return on its capital in excess of its cost of capital is determined by its own strategic choices: (1) the choice of an industry or a set of industries in which the firm operates (industry choice), (2) the manner in which the firm intends to compete with other firms in its chosen industry or industries (competitive positioning), and (3) the way in which the firm expects to create and exploit synergies across the range of businesses in which it operates (corporate strategy). Strategy analysis involves analyzing all three choices.

Industry analysis consists of identifying the economic factors which drive industry profitability. In general, an industry's average profit potential is influenced by the degree of rivalry among existing competitors, the ease with which new firms can enter the industry, the availability of substitute products, the power of buyers, and the power of suppliers. To perform industry analysis, the analyst has to assess the current strength of each of these forces in an industry and make forecasts of any likely future changes.

Competitive strategy analysis involves identifying the basis on which the firm intends to compete in its industry. In general, there are two potential strategies that could provide a firm with a competitive advantage: cost leadership and differentiation. Cost leadership involves offering at a lower cost the same product or service that other firms offer. Differentiation involves satisfying a chosen dimension of customer need better than the competition, at an incremental cost that is less than the price premium that customers are willing to pay. To perform strategy analysis, the analyst has to identify the firm's intended strategy, assess whether the firm possesses the competencies required to execute the strategy, and recognize the key risks that the firm has to guard against. The analyst also has to evaluate the sustainability of the firm's strategy.

Corporate strategy analysis involves examining whether a company is able to create value by being in multiple businesses at the same time. A well-crafted corporate strategy reduces costs or increases revenues from running several businesses in one firm relative to the same businesses operating independently and transacting with each other in the marketplace. These cost savings or revenue increases come from specialized resources that the firm has to exploit synergies across these businesses. For these resources to be valuable, they must be non-tradable, not easily imitated by competition, and non-divisible. Even when a firm has such resources, it can create value through a multibusiness organization only when it is managed so that the information and agency costs inside the organization are smaller than the market transaction costs.

The insights gained from strategy analysis can be useful in performing the remainder of the financial statement analysis. In accounting analysis, the analyst can examine whether a firm's accounting policies and estimates are consistent with its stated strategy. For example, a firm's choice of functional currency in accounting for its international operations should be consistent with the level of integration between domestic and international operations that the business strategy calls for. Similarly, a firm that mainly sells housing to high-risk customers should have higher-than-average bad debts expenses and a higher-than-average allowance for loan losses.

Strategy analysis is also useful in guiding financial analysis. For example, in a cross-sectional analysis, the analyst should expect firms with cost leadership strategy to have lower gross margins and higher asset turnover than firms that follow differentiated strategies. In a time series analysis, the analyst should closely monitor any increases in expense ratios and asset turnover ratios for low-cost firms, and any decreases in investments critical to differentiation for firms that follow differentiation strategy.

Business strategy analysis also helps in prospective analysis and valuation. First, it allows the analyst to assess whether, and for how long, differences between the firm's performance and its industry's (or industries') performance are likely to persist. Second, strategy analysis facilitates forecasting investment outlays the firm has to make to maintain its competitive advantage.

DISCUSSION QUESTIONS

1. Judith, an accounting major, states, "Strategy analysis seems to be an unnecessary detour in doing financial statement analysis. Why can't we just get straight to the accounting issues?" Explain to Judith why she might be wrong.

2. What are the critical drivers of industry profitability?

3. One of the fastest growing industries in the last 20 years is the memory chip industry, which supplies chips for personal computers and other electronic devices. Yet the average profitability for this industry has been very low. Using the industry analysis framework, list all the potential factors that might explain this apparent contradiction.

4. Rate the pharmaceutical and lumber industries as high, medium, or low on the following dimensions of industry structure:

	Pharmaceutical Industry	Lumber Industry
Rivalry		
Threat of new entrants		
Threat of substitute products		
Bargaining power of buyers		
Bargaining power of suppliers		

Given your ratings, which industry would you expect to earn the highest returns?

5. Joe Smith argues, "Your analysis of the five forces that affect industry profitability is incomplete. For example, in the banking industry, I can think of at least three other factors that are also important; namely, government regulation, demographic trends, and cultural factors." His classmate Jane Brown disagrees and says, "These three factors are important only to the extent that they influence one of the five forces." Explain how, if at all, the three factors discussed by Joe affect the five forces in the banking industry.

6. Coca-Cola and Pepsi are both very profitable soft drinks. Inputs for these products include corn syrup, bottles/cans, and soft drink syrup. Coca-Cola and Pepsi produce

the syrup themselves and purchase the other inputs. They then enter into exclusive contracts with independent bottlers to produce their products. Use the five forces framework and your knowledge of the soft drink industry to explain how Coca-Cola and Pepsi are able to retain most of the profits in this industry.

7. All major airlines offer frequent flier programs. Originally seen as a way to differentiate their providers in response to excess capacity in the industry, these programs have long since become ubiquitous. Many industry analysts believe that these programs have met with only mixed success in accomplishing their goal. Use the competitive advantage concepts to explain why.

8. What are the ways that a firm can create barriers to entry to deter competition in its business? What factors determine whether these barriers are likely to be enduring?

9. Explain why you agree or disagree with each of the following statements:
   a. It is better to be a differentiator than a cost leader, since you can then charge premium prices.
   b. It is more profitable to be in a high technology industry than a low technology one.
   c. The reason industries with large investments have high barriers to entry is that it is costly to raise capital.

10. There are very few companies that are able to be both cost leaders and differentiators. Why? Can you think of a company that has been successful at both?

11. Many consultants are advising diversified companies in emerging markets such as India, South Korea, Mexico, and Turkey to adopt corporate strategies proven to be of value in advanced economies such as the United States and the United Kingdom. What are the pros and cons of this advice?

NOTES

1. The discussion presented here is intended to provide a basic background in strategy analysis. For a more complete discussion of the strategy concepts, see, for example, *Contemporary Strategy Analysis* by Robert M. Grant (Cambridge, MA: Blackwell Publishers, 1991); *Economics of Strategy* by David Besanko, David Dranove, and Mark Shanley (New York: John Wiley & Sons, 1996); *Strategy and the Business Landscape* by Pankaj Ghemawat (Reading, MA: Addison Wesley Longman, 1999); and *Corporate Strategy: Resources and the Scope of the Firm* by David J. Collis and Cynthia Montgomery (Burr Ridge, IL: Irwin/McGraw-Hill, 1997).

2. Standard & Poor's Compustat data via Research Insight, accessed November 2010. The analysis here owes its logic to that presented in A. M. McGahan, "Do Competitors Perform Better When They Pursue Different Strategies?" working paper, Harvard Business School, May 12, 1999).

3. For a summary of this research, see F. M. Scherer, *Industrial Market Structure and Economic Performance*, second edition (Chicago: Rand McNally College Publishing, 1980).

4. See M. E. Porter, *Competitive Strategy* (New York: The Free Press, 1980).

5. The U.S. Department of Justice and the Federal Trade Commission use the Herfindahl-Hirschman Index (HHI) to measure concentration when evaluating horizontal mergers. The HHI is calculated by summing the squares of the individual market shares of all the participants. The Department of Justice considers a market with a result of less than 1,000 to be a competitive marketplace; a result of 1,000 to 1,800 to be a moderately concentrated marketplace; and a result of 1,800 or greater to be a highly concentrated marketplace. The four-firm concentration ratio is

another commonly used measure of industry concentration; it refers to the market share of the four largest firms in an industry.

6. Tesla Motors, Inc., Form S-1 (filed January 29, 2010), p. 17, http://www.sec.gov/Archives/edgar/data/1318605/000119312510017054/ds1.htm, accessed January, 2011.

7. While the discussion here uses *buyer* to connote industrial buyers, the same concepts also apply to buyers of consumer products. Throughout this chapter we use the terms *buyers* and *customers* interchangeably.

8. Standard & Poor's Compustat data via Research Insight, accessed April 2011. The department store industry is defined here as those firms contained in SIC codes 5311, 5331, and 5651.

9. The TJX Companies, Inc., 2010 Annual Report, via Thomson ONE, accessed August 2011.

10. Nordstrom, Inc., January 29, 2011, Form 10-K (filed March 18, 2011), p. 6, via Thomson ONE, accessed April 2011.

11. See for instance, C. Roche, P. Ducasse, C. Liao, and C. Grevler, "A New World Order of Consumption 2010 Report on Consumer Sentiment," The Boston Consulting Group, June 28, 2010, https://www.bcgperspectives.com/content/articles/consumer_products_retail_new_world_order_of_consumption/, accessed February 2011.

12. J. Weber and A. T. Palmer, "How The Net Is Remaking The Mall," *Bloomberg Businessweek*, May 9, 2005, http://www.businessweek.com/magazine/content/05_19/b3932105_mz057.htm, accessed April 2011; B. Boswell, "Investors Want to Know: What Defines a Lifestyle Center?" *Retail Traffic*, December 1, 2002, http://retailtrafficmag.com/mag/retail_investors_know_defines/, accessed April 6, 2011.

13. For a more detailed discussion of these two sources of competitive advantage, see M. E. Porter, *Competitive Advantage: Creating and Sustaining Superior Performance* (New York: The Free Press, 1985).

14. Ibid.

15. For a more detailed discussion of this theory, see Michael E. Porter, "What is Strategy," *Harvard Business Review* (November-December 1996).

16. See G. Hamel and C. K. Prahalad, *Competing for the Future* (Boston: Harvard Business School Press, 1994), for a more detailed discussion of the concept of core competencies and their critical role in corporate strategy.

17. The TJX Companies, Inc., January 29, 2011, Form 10-K (filed March 30, 2011), p. 2, via Morningstar Document Research, accessed February 2011.

18. Ibid.

19. Ibid., p. 4.

20. Ibid., p. 4.

21. The TJX Companies, Inc., 2009 Annual Report, p. 4, via Thomson ONE, accessed February 2011.

22. The TJX Companies, "Background Information 2010," The TJX Companies, Inc. website, http://www.tjx.com/files/pdf/TJXbackground_2011.pdf, accessed April 2011.

23. The TJX Companies, Inc., 2009 Annual Report, p. 6, via Thomson ONE, accessed February 2011.

24. Ibid., pp. 2–3.

25. The TJX Companies, Inc., January 29, 2011, Form 10-K (filed March 30, 2011), p. 30, via Morningstar Document Research, accessed February 2011.

26. The TJX Companies, Inc., "Why We Always Have Product Availability," The TJX Companies, Inc. website, http://www.tjx.com/investor_2.asp, accessed February 2011.

27. The TJX Companies, Inc., 2009 Annual Report, p. 4, http://thomson.mobular.net/thomson/7/2968/4250/, accessed February 2011.

28. Nordstrom, Inc., January 29, 2011, Form 10-K (filed March 18, 2011), p. 16, via Thomson ONE, accessed April 2011.

29. Nordstrom, Inc., 2009 Annual Report, p. 3, via Thomson ONE, accessed April 2011.

30. Nordstrom, Inc., 2010 Annual Report, pp. 4–5, via Thomson ONE, accessed May 2011.

31. M. L. Clark and C. Cuomo, "Nordstrom Highlights from Dinner with Management; Reiterate Overweight Rating," Morgan Stanley Research, March 16, 2011, via Thomson ONE, accessed April 2011.

32. E. Yruma and C. Sharma, "Nordstrom, Inc.: JWN: 4Q - Flow Through, Forward Thinking," KeyBanc Capital Markets, February 18, 2011, via Thomson ONE, accessed April 2011.

33. M. Exstein, C. Su, and T. Schorgi, "Full Price Selling Remains Strong Along with the Franchise Itself, Aggressively Expanding Its Presence in Both Physical Stores and E-Commerce," Credit Suisse Equity Research, February 17, 2011, via Thomson ONE, accessed April 2011.

34. C. Montgomery, "Corporate Diversification," *Journal of Economic Perspectives*, Summer 1994.

35. M. C. Mankins, D. Harding, and R. M. Weddigen, "How the Best Divest," *Harvard Business Review* (October 2008).

36. The following works are seminal to transaction cost economics: R. Coase, "The Nature of the Firm," *Economica* 4 (1937): 386–405; O. Williamson, *Markets and Hierarchies: Analysis and Antitrust Implications* (New York: The Free Press, 1975); and D. Teece, "Toward an Economic Theory of the Multi-product Firm," *Journal of Economic Behavior and Organization* 3 (1982): 39–63.

37. For a more complete discussion of these issues, see T. Khanna and K. Palepu, "Building Institutional Infrastructure in Emerging Markets," *Brown Journal of World Affairs*, Winter/Spring 1998, and T. Khanna and K. Palepu, "Why Focused Strategies May Be Wrong for Emerging Markets," *Harvard Business Review* (July-August 1997).

38. "E-commerce Held Back by Security Concerns," *Ecommerce Journal* (April 9, 2008), http://ecommerce-journal.com/news/e_commerce_held_back_by_security_concerns, accessed April 2011.

39. For an empirical study which illustrates this point, see T. Khanna and K. Palepu, "Is Group Affiliation Profitable in Emerging Markets? An Analysis of Diversified Indian Business Groups," *Journal of Finance* (April 2000): 867–891.

40. See L. Lang and R. Stulz, "Tobin's q, diversification, and firm performance," *Journal of Political Economy* 102 (1994): 1248–1280, and Phillip Berger and Eli Ofek, "Diversification's Effect on Firm Value," *Journal of Financial Economics* 37 (1994): 39–65.

41. See P. Healy, K. Palepu, and R. Ruback, "Which Takeovers Are Profitable: Strategic or Financial?" *Sloan Management Review* 38 (Summer 1997): 45–57.

42. See K. Schipper and A. Smith, "Effects of Recontracting on Shareholder Wealth: The Case of Voluntary Spin-offs," *Journal of Financial Economics* 12 (December 1983): 437–467, and L. Lang, A. Poulsen, and R. Stulz, "Asset Sales, Firm Performance, and the Agency Costs of Managerial Discretion," *Journal of Financial Economics* 37 (January 1995): 3–37.

43. The Tata Group, "Leadership with trust," The Tata Group website, http://www.tata.com/aboutus/sub_index.aspx?sectid=8hOk5Qq3EfQ=, accessed April 2011.

44. For a broader discussion of this topic, see Tarun Khanna and Krishna Palepu, "The Right Way to Restructure Conglomerates in Emerging Markets," *Harvard Business Review* (July-August 1999).

45. Information on Tata's business sectors from The Tata Group, "Tata group sector-wise operations," The Tata Group website, http://www.tata.com/htm/Group_Investor_pieChart.htm, accessed April 2011; The Tata Group, "Tata Group Brochure," The Tata Group website, http://www.tata.com/pdf/Tata_Group_Brochure.pdf, accessed April 2011.

46. "GLOBAL 500 Our annual ranking of the world's largest corporations," *Fortune Magazine*, http://money.cnn.com/magazines/fortune/global500/2009/snapshots/11459.html, accessed March 2011.

47. S. Sharma, "Worth its salt: Tata among top 50 global brands," The Financial Express, March 22, 2011, http://www.financialexpress.com/news/worth-its-salt-tata-among-top-50-global-brands/765653/1, accessed April 2011.

48. T. Khanna, K. Palepu, and D. M. Wu, "House of Tata, 1995: The Next Generation (A)," Case No. 9-798-037 (Boston: Harvard Business School Publishing, 1998, revised 2006), p. 6.

49. The Tata Group, "Business excellence," The Tata Group website, http://www.tata.com/article.aspx?artid=OMSlPyjJp68=, accessed April 2011.

50. The Tata Group, "Fan-TAS-tic fifty," The Tata Group website, http://www.tata.com/article.aspx?artid=qz8j1wqs3TU=, accessed April 2011.

51. T. Khanna and K. Palepu, "House of Tata—2000: The Next Generation (B)," Case No. 9-704-408 (Boston: Harvard Business School Publishing, 1998, revised 2006), p.1.

52. The Tata Group, "Mergers and acquisitions," The Tata Group website, http://www.tata.com/htm/Group_MnA_CompanyWise.htm, accessed May 2011.

53. The Tata Group, "Leadership with trust," The Tata Group website, http://www.tata.com/aboutus/sub_index.aspx?sectid=8hOk5Qq3EfQ=, accessed April 2011.

54. P. Mehra and J. Chakravort, "Ratan Tata to retire at end December 2012," Reuters, http://in.reuters.com/article/2010/08/04/idINIndia-50627320100804, accessed May 2011.

Chapter 3

OVERVIEW OF ACCOUNTING ANALYSIS

The purpose of accounting analysis is to evaluate the degree to which a firm's accounting captures its underlying business reality.[1] By identifying places where there is accounting flexibility, and by evaluating the appropriateness of the firm's accounting policies and estimates, analysts can assess the reliability of a firm's accounting numbers. Having identified any accounting distortions, analysts can then adjust a firm's accounting numbers using cash flow and footnote information to "undo" the distortions. Sound accounting analysis improves the reliability of conclusions from financial analysis, the next step in financial statement analysis.

THE INSTITUTIONAL FRAMEWORK FOR FINANCIAL REPORTING

There is typically a separation between ownership and management in public corporations. Financial statements serve as the vehicle through which owners keep track of their firms' financial situation. On a periodic basis, firms typically produce three primary financial reports: (1) an income statement that describes the operating performance during a time period, (2) a balance sheet that states the firm's assets and how they are financed, and (3) a cash flow statement (or in some countries, a funds flow statement) that summarizes the cash (or fund) flows of the firm. These statements are accompanied by footnotes that provide additional details on the financial statement line items, as well as by management's narrative discussion of the firm's performance in the Management Discussion and Analysis section.

To evaluate effectively the quality of a firm's financial statement data, the analyst needs to first understand the basic features of financial reporting and the institutional framework that governs them, as discussed in the following sections.

Accrual Accounting

One of the fundamental features of corporate financial reports is that they are prepared using accrual rather than cash accounting. Unlike cash accounting, accrual accounting distinguishes between the recording of costs and benefits associated with economic activities and the actual payment and receipt of cash. Net income is the primary periodic performance index under accrual accounting. To compute net income, the effects of economic transactions are recorded on the basis of *expected*, not necessarily *actual*, cash receipts and payments. Expected cash receipts from the delivery of products or services are recognized as revenues, and expected cash outflows associated with these revenues are recognized as expenses.

While there are many rules and conventions that govern the preparation of a firm's financial statements, there are only a few conceptual building blocks that form the foundation of accrual accounting. The following definitions are critical to the income statement, which summarizes a firm's revenues and expenses:[2]

- **Revenues** are economic resources earned during a time period. Revenue recognition is governed by the realization principle, which establishes that revenues should be recognized when (a) the firm has provided all, or substantially all, the goods or services to be delivered to the customer and (b) the customer has paid cash or is expected to pay cash with a reasonable degree of certainty.[3]
- **Expenses** are economic resources used up in a time period. Expense recognition is governed by the matching and the conservatism principles. Under these principles, expenses are resource costs (a) directly associated with revenues recognized in the same period, (b) associated with benefits that are consumed in this time period, or (c) whose future benefits are not reasonably certain.
- **Profit** is the difference between a firm's revenues and expenses in a time period.[4]

The following fundamental relationship is therefore reflected in a firm's income statement:

$$Profit = Revenues - Expenses$$

In contrast, the balance sheet is a summary at one point in time. The principles that define a firm's assets, liabilities, and equity are as follows:

- **Assets** are economic resources owned by a firm that are (a) likely to produce future economic benefits and (b) measurable with a reasonable degree of certainty.
- **Liabilities** are economic obligations of a firm arising from benefits received in the past that (a) are required to be met with a reasonable degree of certainty and (b) whose timing is reasonably well defined.
- **Equity** is the difference between a firm's assets and its liabilities.

The definitions of assets, liabilities, and equity lead to the fundamental relationship that governs a firm's balance sheet:

$$Assets = Liabilities + Equity$$

Delegation of Reporting to Management

While the basic definitions of the elements of a firm's financial statements are simple, their application in practice often involves complex judgments. For example, how should revenues be recognized when a firm sells land to customers and also provides customer financing? If revenue is recognized before cash is collected, how should potential defaults be estimated? Are the outlays associated with research and development activities, whose payoffs are uncertain, assets or expenses when incurred? Are contractual commitments under lease arrangements or post-retirement plans liabilities? If so, how should they be valued?

Because corporate managers have intimate knowledge of their firms' businesses, they are entrusted with the primary task of making the appropriate judgments in portraying myriad business transactions using the basic accrual accounting framework. The accounting discretion granted to managers is potentially valuable because it allows them to reflect inside information in reported financial statements. However, since investors view profits as a measure of managers' performance, managers have an incentive to use their accounting discretion to distort reported profits by making biased assumptions. Further, the use of accounting numbers in contracts between the firm and outsiders provides a motivation for management manipulation of accounting numbers.

This earnings management distorts financial accounting data, making it less valuable to external financial statement users. Therefore, the delegation of financial reporting decisions to managers has both costs and benefits. Accounting rules and auditing are mechanisms designed to reduce the cost and preserve the benefit of delegating financial reporting to corporate managers. The Sarbanes-Oxley Act increased the involvement of the audit committee of a firm's board of directors and required the personal certification of the CEO and CFO as to the appropriateness of financial reports as a way of reducing the costs of this delegation. The legal system is used to adjudicate disputes among managers, auditors, and investors.

Generally Accepted Accounting Principles

Given that it is difficult for outside investors to determine whether managers have used accounting flexibility to signal their proprietary information or merely to disguise reality, a number of accounting conventions have evolved to mitigate the problem. For example, in most countries financial statements are prepared using the historical cost convention, where assets and liabilities are recorded at historical exchange prices rather than fair values, replacement values, or values in use. This reduces managers' ability to overstate the value of the assets that they have acquired or developed, or to understate the value of liabilities. Of course, historical cost also limits the information that is available to investors about the potential of the firm's assets, since past exchange prices are usually different from fair values or values in use. In recognition of this, the world's major standard setters have increasingly required the use of fair value accounting in their respective standards.

INTRODUCTION OF FAIR VALUE ACCOUNTING

U.S. and international accounting standards require firms to use fair value accounting (FVA) to value certain financial assets. The rules specify which types of assets are to be recorded at fair values, and which are to be valued at cost. They also define how to record the unrealized gains and losses from using fair values, and how to measure fair values.

Under the rules, marketable securities and derivatives are required to be valued at their fair value. Financial instruments (such as debt securities) are reported at fair value if management anticipates that they will be traded in the future, or if they are potentially available to be traded. In contrast, debt instruments that managers anticipate holding to maturity are reported at cost.

The standards also specify whether gains or losses from revisions in fair values should appear in the income statement or be directly included in equity. Unrealized gains and losses on marketable securities, traded financial instruments, and derivatives that are not held for hedging purposes are included in net income. For financial instruments that are available for sale or derivatives held as part of a hedging arrangement, any unrealized gains or losses go directly to owners' equity and do not flow through the income statement.

Finally, standard setters have recognized that reporting financial assets at their fair values involves varying levels of subjectivity depending on the liquidity and transparency of the asset market in question. The standards have established a hierarchy for measuring the fair value of financial assets. Instruments that are traded in a liquid and orderly market are called Level One instruments and are valued using the latest market prices. Financial assets that are not traded in liquid markets, but which can be valued using financial models whose inputs are available from liquid markets, are called Level Two assets and are valued using the financial model and the market input prices. Finally, some instruments can be valued using financial models but require managers to estimate the inputs. These are termed Level Three assets, and require considerable management judgment to estimate their fair values.

The financial crisis of 2008 demonstrated the challenges in estimating fair values of financial instruments when markets for the securities in question are highly illiquid. Such was the case for mortgage-backed securities, which were claims on the cash flows from residential mortgage loans created through a process known as securitization. Many of these securities were owned by financial institutions throughout the world. As uncertainty about mortgage loan default rates and declines in the value of the underlying properties rose, the market for mortgage-backed securities became highly illiquid and there was wide variation in their values reported on the balance sheets of the banks and investment firms that owned the securities.

Accounting standards and rules also limit management's ability to misuse accounting judgment by regulating how particular types of transactions are recorded. For example, accounting standards for leases stipulate how firms are to record contractual arrangements to lease resources. Similarly, pension and other post-employment benefit standards describe how firms are to record commitments to provide pensions and other retirement benefits for employees. These accounting standards, which are designed to convey quantitative information on a firm's performance, are complemented by a set of disclosure principles. These disclosure principles guide the amount and kinds of information that is disclosed and require a firm to provide qualitative information related to the assumptions, policies, and uncertainties that underlie the quantitative data presented.

In the United States, the Securities and Exchange Commission (SEC) has the legal authority to set accounting standards. The SEC typically relies on private sector accounting bodies to undertake this task. Since 1973 accounting standards in the United States have been set by the Financial Accounting Standards Board (FASB); Generally Accepted Accounting Principles (GAAP) denote the standards, conventions, rules, and procedures that FASB requires firms to apply in preparing their financial statements.

Similar private or public sector accounting standard-setting bodies have developed locally based accounting standards in many other countries. More recently, the International Accounting Standards Board (IASB) and its predecessor, the International Accounting Standards Committee (IASC), have promoted worldwide accounting standards. Those standards, the International Financial Reporting Standards (IFRS), are gaining increasing acceptance worldwide.

U.S. GAAP / IFRS CONVERGENCE[5]

Local accounting standards arose independently over time in major capital markets with little regard for, or need of, cross-border consistency. The concept of convergence of these diverse standards first arose in the mid-twentieth century as post World War II economic integration and increased international capital flows began to create demand for greater comparability of financial information.

The IASC (International Accounting Standards Committee), established in 1973, was the first international standards setting body and issued its first standard in 1974. The IASC was reorganized in 2001 and renamed the IASB (International Accounting

Standards Board). Its goal is to "develop, in the public interest, a single set of high quality global accounting standards."[6] By 2011, IASB standards, known as IFRS (International Financial Reporting Standards) were required or permitted in almost 120 countries. In addition, by 2011 all remaining major economies had established timelines and programs to converge with or adopt IFRS.[7]

In 2002, the FASB in the United States and the IASB issued "The Norwalk Agreement" in which the two standard setters committed to the convergence of U.S. GAAP and IFRS. The agreement described a shared goal of developing accounting standards that could be used for both domestic and cross-border financial reporting and that would reduce complexity and the cost of business in global capital markets. Since then, there have been a number of important steps toward convergence. In 2007, the SEC eliminated the requirement that foreign issuers that used IFRS and listed in the United States provide financial statements reconciled to U.S. GAAP. During the same year, FASB and IASB completed their first major joint project and issued converged standards on business combinations. Subsequent discussions among the FASB, the IASB, and the SEC have reaffirmed a commitment to standard convergence and set 2011 as the horizon to determine whether it makes sense for U.S. companies to use IFRS.

In Chapter Four we discuss some of the remaining material differences between U.S. GAAP and IFRS, and how to compare the performance of companies using the two approaches.

Uniform accounting standards attempt to reduce managers' ability to record similar economic transactions in dissimilar ways, either over time or across firms. Thus they create a uniform accounting language and increase the credibility of financial statements by limiting a firm's ability to distort them. Increased uniformity from accounting standards, however, comes at the expense of reduced flexibility for managers to reflect genuine business differences in a firm's accounting decisions. Rigid accounting standards work best for economic transactions whose accounting treatment is not predicated on managers' proprietary information. However, when there is significant business judgment involved in assessing a transaction's economic consequences, rigid standards are likely to be dysfunctional for some companies because they prevent managers from using their superior knowledge of the business to determine how best to report the economics of key business events. Further, if accounting standards are too rigid, they may induce managers to expend economic resources to restructure business transactions to achieve a desired accounting result or to forgo transactions that may be difficult to report on.

External Auditing

External auditing, broadly defined as a verification of the integrity of the reported financial statements by someone other than the preparer, ensures that managers use accounting rules and conventions consistently over time, and that their accounting estimates are reasonable. In all public markets, listed companies are required to have their financial statements audited by an independent public accountant. In the United States, the standards and procedures to be followed by independent auditors are known as Generally Accepted Auditing Standards (GAAS). Under the Sarbanes-Oxley Act, the responsibility for overseeing audit firms and for ensuring that they are complying with GAAS resides with the Public Company Accounting Oversight Board (PCAOB), a regulatory body established by the Act. All public accounting firms are required to register with the PCAOB, which has the power to inspect and investigate audit work, and—if needed—to discipline auditors.

The Sarbanes-Oxley Act also specifies the relationship between a company and its external auditor, requiring auditors to report to, and be overseen by, a company's audit committee rather than its management. In addition, the Act prohibits public accounting firms from providing non-audit services, such as bookkeeping, information systems design and implementation, valuation and a range of other consulting services, to a company that it audits. Finally, the Act requires that audit firms rotate the lead and reviewing audit partner every five years.

While auditors issue an opinion on published financial statements, it is important to remember that the primary responsibility for the statements still rests with corporate managers. Auditing improves the quality and credibility of accounting data by limiting a firm's ability to distort financial statements to suit its own purposes. However, as audit failures at companies such as Enron and WorldCom, and more recently lawsuits that allege audit failures at companies such as AIG, Bear Stearns, Countrywide Financial Corp, Lehman Brothers, Washington Mutual,[8] New Century Financial,[9] and others suggest, auditing is imperfect. Audits cannot review all of a firm's transactions. They can also fail because of lapses in quality or in judgment by auditors who fail to challenge management for fear of losing future business.

Third-party auditing may also reduce the quality of financial reporting because it can constrain the kind of accounting rules and conventions that evolve over time. For example, the FASB considers the views of auditors in the standard-setting process. Auditors are likely to argue against accounting standards that produce numbers that are difficult to audit, even if the proposed rules provide relevant information for investors.

Legal Liability

The legal environment in which accounting disputes among managers, auditors, and investors are adjudicated can also have a significant effect on the quality of reported numbers. The threat of lawsuits and penalties has the beneficial effect of improving the accuracy of disclosure. However, the potential for significant legal liability might also discourage managers and auditors from supporting accounting proposals where management and auditor judgment and increased complexity or nuance come into play. In addition, the Sarbanes-Oxley Act enacted in 2002 has provisions that potentially increase this risk: managers must personally certify financial results, and auditors are subject to enhanced oversight and potential penalties from the PCAOB (Public Company Accounting Oversight Board) created by SOX. Also, as can be seen from the numerous lawsuits filed against auditing firms and management in the wake of the global financial crisis, the possibility of legal liability represents a very significant and real risk to both company managers and audit firms.

FACTORS INFLUENCING ACCOUNTING QUALITY

Because the mechanisms that limit managers' ability to distort accounting data themselves add noise, it is not optimal to use accounting regulation to completely eliminate managerial flexibility. Therefore, real-world accounting systems leave considerable room for managers to influence financial statement data. The net result is that information in corporate financial reports is noisy and biased, even in the presence of accounting regulation and external auditing.[10] The objective of accounting analysis is to evaluate the degree to which a firm's accounting captures its underlying business reality and to "undo" any accounting distortions. When potential distortions are large, accounting analysis can add considerable value.[11]

There are three potential sources of noise and bias in accounting data: (1) noise introduced by rigidity in accounting rules, (2) random forecast errors, and (3) systematic reporting choices made by corporate managers to achieve specific objectives. Each of these factors is discussed below.

Noise from Accounting Rules

Accounting rules introduce noise and bias because it is often difficult to restrict management discretion without reducing the information content of accounting data. For example, the Statement of Financial Accounting Standards (SFAS) No. 2 issued by the FASB requires firms to expense research and development outlays when they are incurred. Clearly, some of these expenditures have future value while others do not. However, because SFAS 2 does not allow firms to distinguish between the two types of expenditures, it leads to a systematic distortion of reported accounting numbers. Interestingly, the IASB allows firms to capitalize development expenditures, which are presumed to have future economic value, and like FASB requires research outlays to be expensed (IAS 38). Hence, broadly speaking, the degree of distortion introduced by accounting standards depends on how well uniform accounting standards capture the nature of a firm's transactions.

Forecast Errors

Another source of noise in accounting data arises from pure forecast error, because managers cannot predict future consequences of current transactions perfectly. For example, when a firm sells products on credit, accrual accounting requires managers to make a judgment about the probability of collecting payments from customers. If payments are deemed "reasonably certain," the firm treats the transactions as sales, creating accounts receivable on its balance sheet. Managers then make an estimate of the proportion of receivables that will not be collected. Because managers do not have perfect foresight, actual customer defaults are likely to be different from estimated defaults, leading to a forecast error. The extent of errors in managers' accounting forecasts depends on a variety of factors including the complexity of the business transactions, the predictability of the firm's environment, and unforeseen economy-wide changes.

Managers' Accounting Choices

Corporate managers also introduce noise and bias into accounting data through their own accounting decisions. Managers have a variety of incentives to exercise their accounting discretion to achieve certain objectives:[12]

- *Accounting-based debt covenants.* Managers may make accounting decisions to meet certain contractual obligations in their debt covenants. For example, firms' lending agreements with banks and other debt holders require them to meet covenants related to interest coverage, working capital ratios, and net worth, all defined in terms of accounting numbers. Violation of these agreements may be costly because lenders can trigger penalties including demanding immediate repayment of their loans. Managers of firms close to violating debt covenants have an incentive to select accounting policies and estimates to reduce the probability of covenant violation. The debt covenant motivation for managers' accounting decisions has been analyzed by a number of accounting researchers.[13]
- *Management compensation.* Another motivation for managers' accounting choice comes from the fact that their compensation and job security are often tied to reported profits. For example, many top managers receive bonus compensation if they exceed certain pre-specified profit targets. This provides motivation for managers to choose accounting policies and estimates to maximize their expected

compensation.[14] Stock option awards can also potentially induce managers to manage earnings. Options provide managers with incentives to understate earnings prior to option grants to lower the firm's current stock price and hence the option exercise price, and to inflate earnings and stock prices at the time of option exercise.[15]

- *Corporate control contests.* In corporate control contests, including hostile take-overs and proxy fights, competing management groups attempt to win over the firm's shareholders. Accounting numbers are used extensively in debating managers' performance in these contests. Therefore, managers may make accounting decisions to influence investor perceptions in corporate control contests.[16]

- *Tax considerations.* Managers may also make reporting choices to trade off between financial reporting and tax considerations. For example, U.S. firms are required to use LIFO inventory accounting for shareholder reporting in order to also use it for tax reporting. Under LIFO, when prices are rising, firms report lower profits, thereby reducing tax payments. Some firms may forgo the tax reduction in order to report higher profits in their financial statements.[17]

- *Regulatory considerations.* Since accounting numbers are used by regulators in a variety of contexts, managers of some firms may make accounting decisions to influence regulatory outcomes. Examples of regulatory situations where accounting numbers are used include antitrust actions, import tariffs to protect domestic industries, and tax policies.[18]

- *Capital market considerations.* Managers may make accounting decisions to influence the perceptions of capital markets. When there are information asymmetries between managers and outsiders, this strategy may succeed in influencing investor perceptions, at least temporarily.[19]

- *Stakeholder considerations.* Managers may also make accounting decisions to influence the perception of important stakeholders in the firm. For example, since labor unions can use healthy profits as a basis for demanding wage increases, managers may make accounting decisions to decrease income when they are facing union contract negotiations. In countries like Germany, where labor unions are strong, these considerations appear to play an important role in firms' accounting policy. Other important stakeholders that firms may wish to influence through their financial reports include suppliers and customers.[20]

- *Competitive considerations.* The dynamics of competition in an industry might also influence a firm's reporting choices. For example, a firm's segment disclosure decisions may be influenced by its concern that disaggregated disclosure may help competitors in their business decisions. Similarly, firms may not disclose data on their margins by product line for fear of giving away proprietary information. Finally, firms may discourage new entrants by making income-decreasing accounting choices.

In addition to accounting policy choices and estimates, the level of disclosure is also an important determinant of a firm's accounting quality. Corporate managers can choose disclosure policies that make it more or less costly for external users of financial reports to understand the true economic picture of their businesses. Accounting regulations usually prescribe minimum disclosure requirements, but they do not restrict managers from voluntarily providing additional disclosures. Managers can use various parts of the financial reports, including the Letter to the Shareholders, Management Discussion and Analysis, and footnotes, to describe the company's strategy, its accounting policies, and its current performance. There is wide variation across firms in how managers use their disclosure flexibility.[21]

STEPS IN PERFORMING ACCOUNTING ANALYSIS

In this section we discuss a series of steps that an analyst can follow to evaluate a firm's accounting quality.

Step 1: Identify Principal Accounting Policies

As discussed in the chapter on business strategy analysis, a firm's industry characteristics and its own competitive strategy determine its key success factors and risks. One of the goals of financial statement analysis is to evaluate how well these success factors and risks are being managed by the firm. In accounting analysis, therefore, the analyst should identify and evaluate the policies and the estimates the firm uses to measure its critical factors and risks.

Key success factors in the banking industry include interest rate and credit risk management; in the retail industry, inventory management is important; and for a manufacturer competing on product quality and innovation, research and development, and product defects after sale are major areas of concern. A significant success factor in the leasing business is to make accurate forecasts of residual values of the leased equipment at the end of the lease terms. In each of these cases, the analyst has to identify the accounting measures the firm uses to capture these business constructs, the policies that determine how the measures are implemented, and the important estimates embedded in these policies. For example, the accounting measure a bank uses to capture credit risk is its loan loss reserves, and the accounting measure that captures product quality for a manufacturer is its warranty expenses and reserves. For a firm in the equipment leasing industry, one of the most important accounting policies is the way residual values are recorded. Residual values influence the company's reported profits and its asset base. If residual values are overestimated, the firm runs the risk of having to take large write-offs in the future.

Step 2: Assess Accounting Flexibility

Not all firms have equal flexibility in choosing their accounting policies and estimates. Some firms' accounting choice is severely constrained by accounting standards and conventions. For example, even though research and development is a key success factor for biotechnology companies, managers in U.S. companies have no accounting discretion in reporting on this activity. Similarly, even though marketing and brand building are essential to the success of consumer goods firms, they are required to expense all their marketing outlays. In contrast, managing credit risk is one of the critical success factors for banks, and bank managers have the freedom to estimate expected defaults on their loans. Similarly, software developers have the flexibility to decide at what points in their development cycles the outlays can be capitalized.

If managers have little flexibility in choosing accounting policies and estimates related to their key success factors, accounting data are likely to be less informative for understanding the firm's economics. Such is likely to be the case for U.S. biotechnology firms that are required to expense research and development outlays. In contrast, if managers have flexibility in choosing the policies and estimates (as in the case for banks in reporting on credit risk), accounting numbers have the potential to be informative, depending upon how managers exercise this flexibility.

Regardless of the degree of accounting flexibility a firm's managers have in measuring their key success factors and risks, they have some flexibility with respect to other accounting policies. For example, firms have to make choices with respect to depreciation policy (straight-line or accelerated methods), inventory accounting policy (LIFO for U.S. firms, FIFO, or Average Cost), and policies regarding the estimation of pension and other post-employment benefits (expected return on plan assets, discount rate for liabilities, and rate of increase in wages and health care costs). Since all these policy choices can have a significant impact on the reported performance of a firm, they offer an opportunity for the firm to manage its reported numbers and should be the focus of analysis in this step.

Step 3: Evaluate Accounting Strategy

When managers have accounting flexibility, they can use it either to communicate their firm's economic situation or to hide true performance. Some of the questions one could ask in examining how managers exercise their accounting flexibility include the following:

- How do the firm's accounting policies compare to the norms in the industry? If they are dissimilar, is it because the firm's competitive strategy is unique? For example, consider a firm that reports a lower warranty allowance than the industry average. One explanation is that the firm competes on the basis of high quality and has invested considerable resources to reduce the rate of product failure. An alternative explanation is that the firm is merely understating its warranty liabilities.
- Do managers face strong incentives to use accounting discretion to manage earnings? For example, is the firm close to violating bond covenants? Or are the managers having difficulty meeting accounting-based bonus targets? Does management own significant stock? Is the firm in the middle of a proxy fight or union negotiations? Managers may also make accounting decisions to reduce tax payments or to influence the perceptions of the firm's competitors.
- Has the firm changed any of its policies or estimates? What is the justification? What is the impact of these changes? For example, if warranty expenses decreased, is it because the firm made significant investments to improve quality?
- Have the company's policies and estimates been realistic in the past? For example, firms may overstate their revenues and understate their expenses during the year by manipulating quarterly reports, which are not subject to a full-blown external audit. However, the auditing process at the end of the fiscal year forces such companies to make large fourth-quarter adjustments, providing an opportunity for the analyst to assess the quality of the firm's interim reporting. Similarly, firms that depreciate fixed assets too slowly will be forced to take a large write-off later. A history of write-offs may be, therefore, a sign of prior earnings management.
- Does the firm structure any significant business transactions so that it can achieve certain accounting objectives? For example, under current accounting standards, leasing firms can alter lease terms (the length of the lease or the bargain purchase option at the end of the lease term) so that the transactions qualify as sales-type leases for the lessors. Lehman Brothers used repurchase agreements called "Repo 105" transactions to window-dress its balance sheet. Under these agreements Lehman "sold" short-term loans immediately prior to its year-end and used the proceeds to pay down debt, making it appear less leveraged. After year-end, it borrowed cash and repurchased the loans.[22] Such behaviors suggest that the firm's managers are willing to expend economic resources merely to achieve an accounting objective.

Step 4: Evaluate the Quality of Disclosure

Managers can make it more or less easy for an analyst to assess the firm's accounting quality and to use its financial statements to understand business reality. While accounting rules require a certain amount of minimum disclosure, managers have considerable choice in the matter. Disclosure quality, therefore, is an important dimension of a firm's accounting quality.

In assessing a firm's disclosure quality, an analyst could ask the following questions:

- Does the company provide adequate disclosures to assess the firm's business strategy and its economic consequences? For example, some firms use the Letter to the Shareholders in their annual report to clearly lay out the firm's industry conditions, its competitive position, and management's plans for the future. Others use the letter to puff up the firm's financial performance and gloss over any competitive difficulties the firm might be facing.

- Do the footnotes adequately explain the key accounting policies and assumptions and their logic? For example, if a firm's revenue and expense recognition policies differ from industry norms, the firm can explain its choices in a footnote. Similarly, when there are significant changes in a firm's policies, footnotes can be used to disclose the reasons.

- Does the firm adequately explain its current performance? The Management Discussion and Analysis (MD&A) section of the annual report provides an opportunity to help analysts understand the reasons behind a firm's performance changes. Some firms use this section to link financial performance to business conditions. For example, if profit margins went down in a period, was it because of price competition or because of increases in manufacturing costs? If the selling and general administrative expenses went up, was it because the firm is investing in a differentiation strategy, or because unproductive overhead expenses were creeping up? Based on a review of the Fortune 500 companies, in 2003 the SEC released a circular indicating that companies should provide more discussion in MD&A about their critical accounting policies.[23] Companies were encouraged to disclose the most difficult and judgmental estimates and accounting policies they used, among other guidance.

- If accounting rules and conventions restrict the firm from measuring its key success factors appropriately, does the firm provide adequate additional disclosure to help outsiders understand how these factors are being managed? For example, if a firm invests in product quality and customer service, accounting rules do not allow the management to capitalize these outlays, even when the future benefits are certain. The firm's MD&A can be used to highlight how these outlays are being managed and their performance consequences. For example, the firm can disclose physical indexes of defect rates and customer satisfaction so that outsiders can assess the progress being made in these areas and the future cash flow consequences of these actions.

- If a firm is in multiple business segments, what is the quality of segment disclosure? Some firms provide excellent discussion of their performance by product segments and geographic segments. Others lump many different businesses into one broad segment. The level of competition in an industry and management's willingness to share desegregated performance data influence a firm's quality of segment disclosure.

- How forthcoming is the management with respect to bad news? A firm's disclosure quality is most clearly revealed by the way management deals with bad news. Does it adequately explain the reasons for poor performance? Does the company clearly articulate its strategy, if any, to address the company's performance problems?

- How good is the firm's investor relations program? Does the firm provide fact books with detailed data on the firm's business and performance? Is management accessible to analysts?

Step 5: Identify Potential Red Flags

In addition to the preceding steps, a common approach to accounting quality analysis is to look for "red flags" pointing to questionable accounting. These indicators suggest that the analyst should examine certain items more closely or gather more information on them. Some common red flags are the following:

- *Unexplained changes in accounting, especially when performance is poor.* This may suggest that managers are using their accounting discretion to "dress up" their financial statements.[24]

- *Unexplained transactions that boost profits.* For example, firms might undertake balance sheet transactions, such as asset sales or debt for equity swaps, to realize gains in periods when operating performance is poor.[25]

- *Unusual increases in accounts receivable in relation to sales increases.* This may suggest that the company is relaxing its credit policies or artificially loading up its distribution channels to record revenues during the current period, a practice commonly referred to as "channel stuffing." If credit policies are relaxed unduly, the firm may face receivable write-offs in subsequent periods as a result of customer defaults. If the firm accelerates shipments to its distributors, it may face either product returns or reduced shipments in subsequent periods.

- *Unusual increases in inventories in relation to sales increases.* If the inventory build-up is due to an increase in finished goods inventory, it could be a sign that demand for the firm's products is slowing down, suggesting that the firm may be forced to cut prices (and hence earn lower margins) or write down its inventory. A build-up in work-in-progress inventory tends to be good news on average, probably signaling that managers expect an increase in sales. If the build-up is in raw materials, it could suggest manufacturing or procurement inefficiencies, leading to an increase in cost of goods sold (and hence lower margins).[26]

- *An increasing gap between a firm's reported income and its cash flow from operating activities.* While it is legitimate for accrual accounting numbers to differ from cash flows, there is usually a steady relationship between the two if the company's accounting policies remain the same. Therefore, any *change* in the relationship between reported profits and operating cash flows might indicate subtle changes in the firm's accrual estimates. For example, a firm undertaking large construction contracts might use the percentage-of-completion method to record revenues. While earnings and operating cash flows are likely to differ for such a firm, they should bear a steady relationship to each other. Now suppose the firm increases revenues in a period through an aggressive application of the percentage-of-completion method. Then its earnings will go up, but its cash flow remains unaffected. This change in the firm's accounting quality will be manifested by a *change* in the relationship between the firm's earnings and cash flows.

- *An increasing gap between a firm's reported income and its tax income.* Once again, it is quite legitimate for a firm to follow different accounting policies for financial reporting and tax accounting as long as the tax law allows it.[27] However, the relationship between a firm's book and tax accounting is likely to remain stable over time unless there are significant changes in tax rules or accounting standards. Thus, an increasing gap between a firm's reported income and its tax income may indicate that financial reporting to shareholders has become more aggressive. For example, warranty expenses are estimated on an accrual basis for financial reporting, but they are recorded on a cash basis for tax reporting. Unless there is a big change in the firm's product quality, these two numbers bear a consistent relationship to each other. Therefore, a change in this relationship can be an indication either that product quality is changing significantly or that financial reporting estimates are changing.

- *A tendency to use financing mechanisms such as research and development partnerships, special-purpose entities, and the sale of receivables with recourse.* While these arrangements may have a sound business logic, they can also provide management with an opportunity to understate the firm's liabilities and/or overstate its assets.[28]
- *Unexpected large asset write-offs.* This may suggest that management is slow to incorporate changing business circumstances into its accounting estimates. Asset write-offs may also be a result of unexpected changes in business circumstances.[29]
- *Large fourth-quarter adjustments.* A firm's annual reports are audited by the external auditors, but its interim financial statements are usually only reviewed. If a firm's management is reluctant to make appropriate accounting estimates (such as provisions for uncollectible receivables) in its interim statements, it could be forced to make adjustments at the end of the year as a result of pressure from its external auditors. A consistent pattern of fourth-quarter adjustments, therefore, may indicate aggressive management of interim reporting.[30]
- *Qualified audit opinions or changes in independent auditors that are not well justified.* These may indicate a firm's aggressive attitude or a tendency to "opinion shop."
- *Related-party transactions or transactions between related entities.* These transactions may lack the objectivity of the marketplace, and managers' accounting estimates related to these transactions are likely to be more subjective and potentially self-serving.[31]
- *Unexplained increases in contingencies and off-balance sheet transactions.* These types of transactions could signify an attempt by management to window-dress the firm's balance sheet.

While the preceding list provides a number of red flags for potentially poor accounting quality, it is important to do further analysis before reaching final conclusions. Each of the red flags has multiple interpretations; some interpretations are based on sound business reasons, and others indicate questionable accounting. It is, therefore, best to use the red flag analysis as a starting point for further probing, not as an end point in itself.[32]

As we discussed in the previous chapter, it is important to also maintain a broad strategic view of the company's markets, customers, suppliers, and overall macroeconomic trends that may be influencing the company's performance. Keeping this perspective while identifying red flags in the company's financial statements can help to direct the analyst to areas of potential concern and provide an important context for further analysis.

Step 6: Undo Accounting Distortions

If the accounting analysis suggests that the firm's reported numbers are misleading, analysts should attempt to restate the reported numbers to reduce the distortion to the extent possible. It is, of course, virtually impossible to perfectly undo the distortion using outside information alone. However, some progress can be made in this direction by using the cash flow statement and the financial statement footnotes.

A firm's cash flow statement provides a reconciliation of its performance based on accrual accounting and cash accounting. If the analyst is unsure of the quality of the firm's accrual accounting, the cash flow statement provides an alternative benchmark of its performance. The cash flow statement also provides information on how individual line items in the income statement diverge from the underlying cash flows. For example, if an analyst is concerned that the firm is aggressively capitalizing certain costs that should be expensed, the information in the cash flow statement provides a basis to make the necessary adjustment.

Financial statement footnotes also provide information that is potentially useful in restating reported accounting numbers. For example, when a firm changes its accounting policies, it provides a footnote indicating the effect of that change if it is material. Similarly, some firms provide information on the details of accrual estimates such as the allowance for bad debts. The tax footnote usually provides information on the differences between a firm's accounting policies for shareholder reporting and tax reporting. Since tax reporting is often more conservative than shareholder reporting, the information in the tax footnote can be used to estimate what the earnings reported to shareholders would be under more conservative policies.

In Chapter 4, we show how to make accounting adjustments for some of the most common types of accounting distortions.

ACCOUNTING ANALYSIS PITFALLS

There are several potential pitfalls and common misconceptions in accounting analysis that an analyst should avoid.

1. Conservative Accounting Is Not "Good" Accounting

Some firms take the approach that it pays to be conservative in financial reporting and to set aside as much as possible for contingencies. This logic is commonly used to justify the expensing of R&D and advertising, and the rapid write-down of intangible assets. It is also used to support large loss reserves for insurance companies, for merger expenses, and for restructuring charges.

From the standpoint of a financial statement user, it is important to recognize that conservative accounting is not the same as "good" accounting. Financial statement users want to evaluate how well a firm's accounting captures business performance in an unbiased manner, and conservative accounting can be just as misleading as aggressive accounting in this respect.

It is certainly true that it can be difficult to estimate the economic benefits from many intangibles. However, the intangible nature of some assets does not mean that they do not have value. Indeed, for many firms these types of assets are their most valued. For example, the two most valuable assets for pharmaceutical companies, such as Pfizer, Merck, and Novartis, are the research capabilities that permit them to generate new drugs and their sales forces that enable them to sell those drugs to doctors. Yet neither is recorded on their balance sheets. From the investors' point of view, accountants' reluctance to value intangible assets does not diminish their importance. If they are not included in financial statements, investors must look to alternative sources of information on these assets.

Further, conservative accounting often provides managers with opportunities for "income smoothing," which may prevent analysts from recognizing poor performance in a timely fashion. Finally, over time investors are likely to figure out which firms are conservative and may discount their management's disclosures and communications.

2. Not All Unusual Accounting Is Questionable

It is easy to confuse unusual accounting with questionable accounting. While unusual accounting choices might make a firm's performance difficult to compare with other firms' performance, such an accounting choice might be justified if the company's business is unusual. For example, firms that follow differentiated strategies or firms that structure their business in an innovative manner to take advantage of particular market situations may make unusual accounting choices to properly reflect their business. Therefore, it is important to evaluate a company's accounting choices in the context of its business strategy.

Similarly, it is important not to automatically attribute all changes in a firm's accounting policies and accruals to earnings management motives.[33] Accounting changes can also reflect changed business circumstances. For example, as already discussed, a firm that shows unusual increases in its inventory might be preparing for a new product introduction. Similarly, unusual increases in receivables might merely be due to changes in a firm's sales strategy. Unusual decreases in the allowance for uncollectible receivables might reflect a firm's changed customer focus. It is therefore important for an analyst to consider all possible explanations for accounting changes and investigate them using the qualitative information available in a firm's financial statements.

VALUE OF ACCOUNTING DATA AND ACCOUNTING ANALYSIS

What is the value of accounting information and accounting analysis? Given the incentives and opportunities for managers to affect their firms' reported accounting numbers, some have argued that accounting data and accounting analysis are not likely to be useful for investors.

Researchers have examined the value of earnings and return on equity (ROE) by comparing stock returns that could be earned by a hypothetical investor who has perfect foresight of firms' earnings, return on equity (ROE), and cash flows for the following year.[34] To assess the importance of earnings, the hypothetical investor is assumed to buy stocks of firms that have earnings increases for the subsequent year and to sell stocks of firms with subsequent earnings decreases. If this strategy is followed consistently, the hypothetical investor would have earned over a 40-year period an average return of 37.5 percent per year. If a similar investment strategy is followed using ROE, buying stocks with subsequent increases in ROE and selling stocks with ROE decreases, an even higher annual return of 43 percent would be earned. In contrast, cash flow data appear to be considerably less valuable than earnings or ROE information. Annual returns generated from buying stocks with increased subsequent cash flows from operations and selling stocks with cash flow decreases would be only 9 percent. This suggests that next period's earnings and ROE performance are more relevant information for investors than cash flow performance.

Overall, this research suggests that the institutional arrangements and conventions created to mitigate potential misuse of accounting by managers are generally effective in providing assurance to investors. The research indicates that investors do not view earnings management as so pervasive as to make earnings data completely unreliable.

A number of research studies have examined whether accounting analysis is a valuable activity. By and large, this evidence indicates that there are opportunities for superior analysts to earn positive stock returns. Studies show that companies criticized in the financial press for misleading financial reporting subsequently suffered an average stock price drop of 8 percent.[35] Firms where managers appeared to inflate reported earnings prior to an equity issue and subsequently reported poor earnings performance had more negative stock performance after the offer than firms with no apparent earnings management.[36] Finally, firms subject to SEC investigation for earnings management showed an average stock price decline of 9 percent when the earnings management was first announced, and they continued to have poor stock performance for up to two years.[37]

These findings imply that analysts who are able to identify firms with misleading accounting are able to create value for investors. The findings also indicate that the stock market ultimately sees through earnings management. In most cases, earnings management is eventually uncovered and the stock price responds negatively to evidence that firms have inflated prior earnings through misleading accounting.

SUMMARY

In summary, accounting analysis is an important step in the process of analyzing corporate financial reports. The purpose of accounting analysis is to evaluate the degree to which a firm's accounting captures its underlying business reality. Sound accounting analysis improves the reliability of conclusions from financial analysis, the next step in financial statement analysis.

There are six principal steps in accounting analysis. The analyst begins by identifying the key accounting policies and estimates given the firm's industry and its business strategy. The second step is to evaluate the degree of flexibility available to managers given the accounting rules and conventions. Next, the analyst evaluates how managers exercise their accounting flexibility and the likely motivations behind managers' accounting strategy. The fourth step involves assessing the depth and quality of a firm's disclosures. The analyst should next identify any red flags, indicating a need for further investigation. The final step in accounting analysis is to restate accounting numbers to remove any noise and bias introduced by the accounting rules and management decisions.

The next chapter discusses how to implement these concepts and shows how to make some of the most common types of adjustments.

DISCUSSION QUESTIONS

1. A finance student states, "I don't understand why anyone pays any attention to accounting earnings numbers, given that a 'clean' number like cash from operations is readily available." Do you agree? Why or why not?
2. Fred argues, "The standards that I like most are the ones that eliminate all management discretion in reporting—that way I get uniform numbers across all companies and don't have to worry about doing accounting analysis." Do you agree? Why or why not?
3. Bill Simon says, "We should get rid of the FASB and SEC since free market forces will make sure that companies report reliable information." Do you agree? Why or why not?
4. Many firms recognize revenues at the point of shipment. This provides an incentive to accelerate revenues by shipping goods at the end of the quarter. Consider two companies, one of which ships its product evenly throughout the quarter, and the second, which ships all its products in the last two weeks of the quarter. Each company's customers pay 30 days after receiving shipment. Using accounting ratios, how can you distinguish these companies?
5. a. If management reports truthfully, what economic events are likely to prompt the following accounting changes?
   • Increase in the estimated life of depreciable assets
   • Decrease in the uncollectible allowance as a percentage of gross receivables
   • Recognition of revenues at the point of delivery rather than at the point cash is received
   • Capitalization of a higher proportion of software R&D costs
   b. What features of accounting, if any, would make it costly for dishonest managers to make the same changes without any corresponding economic changes?

6. The conservatism principle arises because of concerns about management's incentives to overstate the firm's performance. Joe Banks argues, "We could get rid of conservatism and make accounting numbers more useful if we delegated financial reporting to independent auditors rather than to corporate managers." Do you agree? Why or why not?

7. A fund manager states, "I refuse to buy any company that makes a voluntary accounting change, since it's certainly a case of management trying to hide bad news." Can you think of any alternative interpretation?

8. Fair value accounting attempts to make financial information more relevant to financial statement users, at the risk of greater subjectivity. What factors would you examine to evaluate the reliability of fair valued assets?

NOTES

1. Accounting analysis is sometimes also called "quality of earnings analysis." We prefer to use the term *accounting analysis* since we are discussing a broader concept than merely a firm's earnings quality.

2. These definitions paraphrase those of the Financial Accounting Standards Board (FASB), Statement of Financial Accounting Concepts No. 6, "Elements of Financial Statements" (1985). Our intent is to present the definitions at a conceptual, not technical, level. For a more complete discussion of these and related concepts, see the FASB's Statements of Financial Accounting Concepts (http://www.fasb.org).

3. SEC rules state that these criteria are satisfied when (i) there is persuasive evidence that an arrangement exists, (ii) delivery has occurred or services have been rendered, (iii) the selling price is fixed or determinable, and (iv) collectibility is reasonably assured (see SAB 104).

4. Strictly speaking, the comprehensive net income of a firm also includes gains and losses from increases and decreases in equity from non-operating activities or extraordinary items.

5. Background information on the history of U.S. GAAP / IFRS convergence from Financial Accounting Standards Board, "International Convergence of Accounting Standards—A Brief History," Financial Accounting Standards Board website, http://www.fasb.org/jsp/FASB/Page/SectionPage&cid=1176156304264, accessed February 2011.

6. IFRS Foundation website, http://www.ifrs.org/Home.htm, accessed January 2011.

7. *Who We Are and What We Do*, the IASB and IFRS Foundation brochure, January 2011, http://www.ifrs.org/NR/rdonlyres/9D0DE08C-C584-46EB-B36E-C4B9A8CB6A02/0/WhoWeAreJanuary2011English.pdf, accessed February 2011.

8. "FACTBOX-Auditor lawsuits in wake of credit crisis," January 21, 2011, Reuters, http://www.reuters.com/assets/print?aid=USN2122314420110121, accessed February 2011.

9. "Judge OKs $125 mln New Century lawsuit settlement," August 11, 2010, Reuters, http://www.reuters.com/article/2010/08/11/newcentury-settlement-idUSN1018298820100811, accessed February 2011.

10. Thus, although accrual accounting is theoretically superior to cash accounting in measuring a firm's periodic performance, the distortions it introduces can make accounting data less valuable to users. If these distortions are large enough, current cash flows may measure a firm's periodic performance better than accounting profits. The relative usefulness of cash flows and accounting profits in measuring performance, therefore, varies from firm to firm. For empirical evidence on this issue, see

P. Dechow, "Accounting Earnings and Cash Flows as Measures of Firm Performance: The Role of Accounting Accruals," *Journal of Accounting and Economics* 18 (July 1994): 3–42.

11. For example, Abraham Briloff wrote a series of accounting analyses of public companies in *Barron's* over several years. On average, the stock prices of the analyzed companies changed by about 8 percent on the day these articles were published, indicating the potential value of performing such analysis. For a more complete discussion of this evidence, see G. Foster, "Briloff and the Capital Market," *Journal of Accounting Research* 17 (Spring 1979): 262–74.

12. For a complete discussion of these motivations, see *Positive Accounting Theory*, by R. Watts and J. Zimmerman, (Englewood Cliffs, NJ: Prentice-Hall, 1986). A summary of this research is provided by T. Fields, T. Lys, and L. Vincent in "Empirical Research on Accounting Choice," *Journal of Accounting and Economics* 31 (September 2001): 255–307.

13. The most convincing evidence supporting the covenant hypothesis is reported in a study of the accounting decisions by firms in financial distress: A. Sweeney, "Debt-Covenant Violations and Managers' Accounting Responses," *Journal of Accounting and Economics* 17 (May 1994): 281–308.

14. Studies that examine the bonus hypothesis generally report evidence supporting the view that managers' accounting decisions are influenced by compensation considerations. See, for example, P. Healy, "The Effect of Bonus Schemes on Accounting Decisions," *Journal of Accounting and Economics* 7 (April 1985): 85–107; R. Holthausen, D. Larcker, and R. Sloan, "Annual Bonus Schemes and the Manipulation of Earnings," *Journal of Accounting and Economics* 19 (February 1995): 29–74; and F. Guidry, A. Leone, and S. Rock, "Earnings-Based Bonus Plans and Earnings Management by Business Unit Managers," *Journal of Accounting and Economics* 26 (January 1999): 113–42.

15. For empirical evidence that CEOs of firms with scheduled awards make opportunistic voluntary disclosures to maximize stock award compensation, see D. Aboody and R. Kasznik, "CEO Stock Option Awards and the Timing of Corporate Voluntary Disclosures, *Journal of Accounting and Economics* 29 (February 2000): 73–100.

16. L. DeAngelo, "Managerial Competition, Information Costs, and Corporate Governance: The Use of Accounting Performance Measures in Proxy Contests," *Journal of Accounting and Economics* 10 (January 1988): 3–36.

17. The trade-off between taxes and financial reporting in the context of manager's accounting decisions is discussed in detail in *Taxes and Business Strategy* by M. Scholes and M. Wolfson (Englewood Cliffs, NJ: Prentice-Hall, 1992). Many empirical studies have examined firm's LIFO/FIFO choices.

18. Several researchers have documented that firms affected by such situations have a motivation to influence regulators' perceptions through accounting decisions. For example, J. Jones documents that firms seeking import protections make income-decreasing accounting decisions in "Earnings Management During Import Relief Investigations," *Journal of Accounting Research* 29, no. 2 (Autumn 1991): 193–228.

A number of studies find that banks that are close to minimum capital requirements overstate loan loss provisions, understate loan write-offs, and recognize abnormal realized gains on securities portfolios. See S. Moyer, "Capital Adequacy Ratio Regulations and Accounting Choices in Commercial Banks," *Journal of Accounting and Economics* 12 (July 1990): 123–54; M. Scholes, G. P. Wilson, and M. Wolfson, "Tax Planning, Regulatory Capital Planning, and Financial Reporting Strategy for Commercial Banks," *Review of Financial Studies* 3 (1990): 625–50; A. Beatty, S. Chamberlain, and J. Magliolo, "Managing Financial Reports of

Commercial Banks: The Influence of Taxes, Regulatory Capital and Earnings," *Journal of Accounting Research* 33, no. 2 (1995): 231–61; and J. Collins, D. Shackelford, and J. Wahlen, "Bank Differences in the Coordination of Regulatory Capital, Earnings and Taxes," *Journal of Accounting Research* 33, no. 2 (Autumn 1995): 263–91. Finally, Kathy Petroni finds that financially weak property-casualty insurers that risk regulatory attention understate claim loss reserves: K. Petroni, "Optimistic Reporting in the Property Casualty Insurance Industry," *Journal of Accounting and Economics* 15 (December 1992): 485–508.

19. P. Healy and K. Palepu, "The Effect of Firms' Financial Disclosure Strategies on Stock Prices," *Accounting Horizons* 7 (March 1993): 1–11. For a summary of the empirical evidence, see P. Healy and J. Wahlen, "A Review of the Earnings Management Literature and Its Implications for Standard Setting," *Accounting Horizons* 13 (December 1999): 365–84.

20. R. Bowen, L. DuCharme, and D. Shores, in "Stakeholders' Implicit Claims and Accounting Method Choice," *Journal of Accounting and Economics* 20 (December 1995): 255–295, argue that, based on theory and anecdotal evidence, managers choose long-run income-increasing accounting methods as a result of ongoing implicit claims between a firm and its customers, suppliers, employees, and short-term creditors.

21. Financial analysts pay close attention to managers' disclosure strategies; the Association for Investment Management and Research publishes an annual report evaluating them for U.S. firms. For a discussion of these ratings, see M. Lang and R. Lundholm, "Cross-sectional Determinants of Analysts' Ratings of Corporate Disclosures," *Journal of Accounting Research* 31 (Autumn 1993): 246–71.

22. See Lehman Brothers Holding Inc. Chapter 11 Proceedings Examiners Report, Volume 3-Section III.A.4: Repo 105.)

23. Securities and Exchange Commission, "Summary by the Division of Corporation Finance of Significant Issues Addressed in the Review of the Periodic Reports of the Fortune 500 Companies," SEC website (accessed May 8, 2006).

24. For a detailed analysis of a company that made such changes, see "Anatomy of an Accounting Change" by K. Palepu in *Accounting & Management: Field Study Perspectives*, edited by W. Bruns, Jr., and R. Kaplan (Boston: Harvard Business School Press, 1987).

25. An example of this type of behavior is documented by John Hand in his study, "Did Firms Undertake Debt-Equity Swaps for an Accounting Paper Profit or True Financial Gain?" *The Accounting Review* 64 (October 1989): 587–623.

26. For an empirical analysis of inventory build-ups, see V. Bernard and J. Noel, "Do Inventory Disclosures Predict Sales and Earnings?" *Journal of Accounting, Auditing, and Finance* (Fall 1991).

27. This is true by and large in the United States and in several other countries. However, in some countries such as Germany and Japan, tax accounting and financial reporting have historically been closely tied together, so this particular red flag has not been very meaningful. With the adoption of international accounting standards and the development of public capital markets, financial reporting and tax accounting in these countries have begun to diverge.

28. For research on accounting and economic incentives in the formation of R&D partnerships, see A. Beatty, P. Berger, and J. Magliolo, "Motives for Forming Research and Development Financing Organizations," *Journal of Accounting and Economics* 19 (April 1995): 411–42. An overview of Enron's use of special purpose entities to manage earnings and window-dress its balance sheet is provided by P. Healy and K. Palepu, "The Fall of Enron," *Journal of Economic Perspectives* 17, no. 2 (Spring 2003): 3–26.

29. For an empirical examination of asset write-offs, see J. Elliott and W. Shaw, "Write-offs as Accounting Procedures to Manage Perceptions," *Journal of Accounting Research* 26, 1988: 91–119.

30. R. Mendenhall and W. Nichols report evidence consistent with managers taking advantage of their discretion to postpone reporting bad news until the fourth quarter. See R. Mendenhall and W. Nichols, "Bad News and Differential Market Reactions to Announcements of Earlier-Quarter versus Fourth-Quarter Earnings," *Journal of Accounting Research*, Supplement (1988): 63–86.

31. The role of insider transactions in the collapse of Enron is discussed by P. Healy and K. Palepu, "The Fall of Enron," *Journal of Economic Perspectives* 17, no. 2 (Spring 2003): 3–26.

32. This type of analysis is presented in the context of provisions for bad debts by M. McNichols and P. Wilson in their study, "Evidence of Earnings Management from the Provisions for Bad Debts," *Journal of Accounting Research*, Supplement (1988): 1–31.

33. This point has been made by several accounting researchers. For a summary of research on earnings management, see K. Schipper, "Earnings Management," *Accounting Horizons* (December 1989): 91–102.

34. See J. Chang, "The Decline in Value Relevance of Earnings and Book Values" (dissertation, Harvard University, 1998). Evidence is also reported by J. Francis and K. Schipper, "Have Financial Statements Lost Their Relevance?" *Journal of Accounting Research* 37, no. 2 (Autumn 1999): 319–52, and W. E. Collins, E. Maydew, and I. Weiss, "Changes in the Value-Relevance of Earnings and Book Value over the Past Forty Years," *Journal of Accounting and Economics* 24 (1997): 39–67.

35. See G. Foster, "Briloff and the Capital Market," *Journal of Accounting Research* 17, no. 1 (Spring 1979): 262–74.

36. See S. H. Teoh, I. Welch, and T. J. Wong, "Earnings Management and the Long-Run Market Performance of Initial Public Offerings," *Journal of Finance* 53 (December 1998): 1935–74; S. H. Teoh, I. Welch, and T. J. Wong, "Earnings Management and the Post-Issue Underperformance of Seasoned Equity Offerings," *Journal of Financial Economics* 50 (October 1998): 63–99; and S. Teoh, T. Wong, and G. Rao, "Are Accruals During Initial Public Offerings Opportunistic?" *Review of Accounting Studies* 3, nos. 1–2 (1998): 175–208.

37. See P. Dechow, R. Sloan, and A. Sweeney, "Causes and Consequences of Earnings Manipulation: An Analysis of Firms Subject to Enforcement Actions by the SEC," *Contemporary Accounting Research* 13, no. 1 (1996): 1–36, and M. D. Beneish, "Detecting GAAP Violation: Implications for Assessing Earnings Management among Firms with Extreme Financial Performance," *Journal of Accounting and Public Policy* 16 (1997): 271–309.

Chapter 4

IMPLEMENTING ACCOUNTING ANALYSIS

We learned in Chapter 3 that accounting analysis requires the analyst to adjust a firm's accounting numbers using cash flow and footnote information to "undo" any accounting distortions. This entails recasting a firm's financial statements using standard reporting nomenclature and formats. Firms frequently use somewhat different formats and terminology for presenting their financial results. Recasting the financial statements using a standard template, therefore, helps ensure that performance metrics used for financial analysis are calculated using comparable definitions across companies and over time.

Once the financial statements have been standardized, the analyst is ready to identify any distortions in financial statements. The analyst's primary focus should be on those accounting estimates and methods that the firm uses to measure its key success factors and risks. If there are differences in estimates and methods between firms or for the same firm over time, the analyst's job is to assess whether they reflect legitimate business differences or differences in managerial judgment or bias. Differences arising from managerial bias will require adjustment. In addition, even if accounting rules are adhered to consistently, accounting distortions can arise because the rules themselves do a poor job of capturing firm economics, creating opportunities for the analyst to adjust a firm's financials in a way that presents a more realistic picture of its performance.

In addition, in today's global business world, competitors frequently come from a diverse set of countries and report using different accounting standards, making it challenging for analysts to compare their financial performance. The two most widely used standards are U.S. GAAP and International Financial Reporting Standards (IFRS). In situations when these reporting differences are significant, the analyst can adjust the financials of the firms to put them on a level playing field.

This chapter begins by showing how to recast the firm's financial statements into a template that uses standard terminology and classifications. Next, we use discussion and examples to illustrate the most common types of accounting distortions that can arise and show how to make adjustments to the standardized financial statements to undo these distortions. We then identify some of the significant remaining differences between U.S. GAAP and IFRS and show how to adjust for these differences. Finally, we return to our TJX and Nordstrom comparison (first introduced in Chapter 2) in order to illustrate the adjustments we would make to more appropriately compare these two companies.

An analysis of the balance sheet is used to identify whether there have been any distortions to assets, liabilities, or owners' equity. Once an asset and liability misstatement has been identified, the analyst can make adjustments to the balance sheet at the beginning and/or end of the current year, as well as any needed adjustments to revenues and expenses in the latest income statement. This approach ensures that the financial ratios used to evaluate a firm's most recent results and forecast its future performance are based on financial data that appropriately reflect its business economics.

In some instances, information taken from a firm's footnotes and cash flow statement enables the analyst to make a precise adjustment for an accounting distortion. However, for many types of accounting adjustments, the company does not disclose all of the information needed to perfectly undo the distortion, requiring the analyst to make an approximate adjustment to the financial statements.

RECASTING FINANCIAL STATEMENTS

Firms sometimes use different nomenclature and formats to present their financial results. For example, the asset goodwill can be reported separately using such titles as Goodwill, Excess of Cost Over Net Assets of Acquired Companies, and Cost in Excess of Fair Value, or it can be included in the line item Other Intangible Assets. Interest Income can be reported either as a subcategory of Revenues, shown lower down the income statement as part of Other Income and Expenses, or sometimes as Interest Expense, Net of Interest Income.

These differences in financial statement terminology, classifications, and formats can make it difficult to compare performance across firms, and sometimes to compare performance for the same firm over time. The first task for the analyst in accounting analysis is, therefore, to recast the financial statements into a common format. This involves designing a template for the income statement, balance sheet, and cash flow statement that can be used to standardize financial statements for any company. Tables 4-1, 4-2, and 4-3 present the format used throughout the book to standardize the income statement, balance sheet, and cash flow statement, respectively.

TABLE 4-1	Standardized Income Statement Format
Standard Income Statement Accounts	**Sample Line Items in Reported Accounts**
Sales	Revenues
	Net sales
	Turnover
	Other non-interest income
	Other revenue
	Royalties and franchise-related fees
	Membership and service fees
	Services
	Commissions
	Licenses
Cost of Sales	Cost of goods sold
	Cost of merchandise sold
	Cost of products sold
	Cost of revenues
	Cost of services

(continued)

Standard Income Statement Accounts	Sample Line Items in Reported Accounts
	Financial services costs
	Depreciation on manufacturing facilities
SG&A	General and administrative
	Sales and marketing
	Salaries and benefits
	Servicing and maintenance
	Depreciation on selling and administrative facilities
Other Operating Expense	Amortization of intangibles
	Product development
	Research and development
	Provision for losses on credit sales
	Pre-opening costs
	Special charges
Investment Income	Equity income (from associates)
	Dividend income
	Rental income[1]
Other Income	Gains on sale of investments / long-term assets
	Foreign exchange gains
	Pre-tax gains from accounting changes
Other Expense	Losses on sale of investments / long-term assets
	Foreign exchange losses
	Pre-tax losses from accounting changes
	Restructuring charges
	Merger expenses
	Asset impairments
Interest Income	Interest income
Interest Expense	Interest on long-term debt
	Interest on short-term debt
Minority Interest	Minority interest
Tax Expense	Tax Expense
	Provision for taxes
Unusual Gains, Net of Unusual Losses	Any gains or losses reported on an after-tax basis, such as:
	Extraordinary items
	Non-recurring charges
	Effect of accounting changes
Preferred Dividends	Preferred dividends
Common Shares Outstanding	Common Shares Outstanding

Source: © Cengage Learning

TABLE 4-2   Standardized Balance Sheet Format

Standard Balance Sheet Accounts	Sample Line Items in Reported Accounts
Assets	
Cash and Marketable Securities	Cash
	Cash and cash equivalents
	Short-term investments
	Time deposits
Accounts Receivable	Accounts/trade receivables (net)
	Trade debtors
Inventory	Inventory
	Finished goods
	Raw materials
	Work-in-process
	Stocks
Other Current Assets	Prepaid expenses
	Taxes refundable
	Current assets of discontinued operations
	Due from affiliates
	Due from employees
	Prepaid income taxes

Standard Balance Sheet Accounts	Sample Line Items in Reported Accounts
Liabilities and Equity	
Short-Term Debt	Short-term debt
	Notes payable (bank)
	Bank overdraft
	Current portion of long-term debt
	Current portion of capital lease obligation
Accounts Payable	Accounts/trade payables
	Trade creditors
	Notes payable (trade)
Other Current Liabilities	Accrued expenses
	Accrued liabilities
	Taxes payable
	Dividends payable
	Deferred (unearned) revenue
	Customer advances
Long-Term Debt	Long-term debt
	Senior term notes
	Subordinated debt
	Capital lease obligations
	Convertible debt
	Pension/post-retirement benefit obligation

(continued)

Standard Balance Sheet Accounts	Sample Line Items in Reported Accounts	Standard Balance Sheet Accounts	Sample Line Items in Reported Accounts
Long-Term Tangible Assets	Plant, property, and equipment Land Non-current assets of discontinued operations	Deferred Taxes	Deferred income taxes
Long-Term Intangible Assets	Goodwill Software development costs Deferred financing costs Deferred subscriber acquisition costs Deferred charges Trademarks License rights	Other Long-Term Liabilities	Non-current deferred (unearned) revenues Other non-current liabilities
Other Long-Term Assets	Long-term investments Long-term receivables Investment in sales-type or direct-financing leases	Minority Interest	Minority interest
		Preferred Stock	Preferred stock Preferred convertible stock
		Common Shareholders' Equity	Common stock Additional paid-in capital Capital in excess of par Treasury stock Retained earnings Cumulative foreign currency gains and losses Accumulated other comprehensive income

Source: © Cengage Learning

TABLE 4-3	Standardized Cash Flow Statement Format
Standard Cash Flow Statement Accounts	**Sample Line Items in Reported Accounts**
Net Income	Net Income
After-tax interest expense (income)	Interest on long-term debt (calculated net of tax) Interest on short-term debt (calculated net of tax)
Non-operating Gains (Losses)	Gain (loss) on sale of investments / non-current assets Cumulative effect of accounting changes Gain (loss) on foreign exchange Extraordinary gains (losses)
Long-Term Operating Accruals — Depreciation and Amortization	Depreciation and amortization Amortization of subscriber acquisition costs Amortization of cost in excess of fair value of net assets acquired
Long-Term Operating Accruals — Other	Deferred revenues / costs Deferred income taxes Impairment of non-current assets Other non-cash charges to operations Equity earnings of affiliates / unconsolidated subs, net of cash received Minority interest Stock bonus awards
Net (Investments in) or Liquidation of Operating Working Capital	Changes in: Trade accounts receivable Other receivables Prepaid expenses Trade accounts payable Accrued expenses (liabilities) Due from affiliates Accounts payable and accrued expenses Refundable / payable income taxes Inventories Provision for doubtful accounts and bad debts Other current liabilities Other current assets
Net (Investment in) or Liquidation of Operating Long-Term Assets	Purchase / sale of non-current assets Acquisition of research and development Acquisition / sale of business Capital expenditures Equity investments Acquisition of subsidiary stock Capitalization of computer software development costs Cost in excess of the fair value of net assets acquired Investment in sales-type and direct financing leases

(continued)

Standard Cash Flow Statement Accounts	Sample Line Items in Reported Accounts
Net Debt (Repayment) or Issuance	Principal payments on debt Borrowings (repayments) under credit facility Issuance (repayment) of long-term debt Net increase (decrease) in short-term borrowings Notes payable
Dividend (Payments)	Cash dividends paid on common stock Cash dividends paid on preferred stock Distributions
Net Stock (Repurchase) or Issuance	Proceeds from issuance of common stock Issue of common stock for services Issue (redemption) of preferred securities Issue of subsidiary equity Purchase (issue) of treasury stock

Source: © Cengage Learning

To create standardized financials for a particular company, the analyst classifies each line item in that firm's financial statements using the appropriate account name from the above templates. This may require using information from the footnotes to ensure that accounts are classified appropriately. An example, applying the above template to standardize the financial statements for the year ending January 2011 for The TJX Companies, Inc., is shown in Appendix A at the end of this chapter.

MAKING ACCOUNTING ADJUSTMENTS

Once the financials have been standardized, the analyst can evaluate whether accounting adjustments are needed to correct any distortions in assets, liabilities, or equity, as discussed below.

Asset Distortions

Accountants define assets as resources that a firm owns or controls as a result of past business transactions, and which are expected to produce future economic benefits that can be measured with a reasonable degree of certainty. Assets can take a variety of forms, including cash, marketable securities, receivables from customers, inventory, fixed assets, long-term investments in other companies, and intangibles.

Distortions in asset values generally arise because there is ambiguity about whether

- The firm owns or controls the economic resources in question,
- The economic resources are likely to provide future economic benefits that can be measured with reasonable certainty, or
- The fair values of assets are lower or higher than their book values.

Who Owns or Controls Resources?

For most resources used by a firm, ownership or control is relatively straightforward—the firm using the resource owns the asset. However, some types of transactions make it difficult to assess who owns a resource. For example, does the lessor or the lessee own or control a resource that has been leased? Or consider a firm that discounts a customer receivable with a bank. If the bank has recourse against the firm should the customer default, is the real owner of the receivable the bank or the company?

Given the subjectivity of identifying when a company has control over an asset, accountants frequently use mechanical rules to define control. These rules make it easy for accountants to implement accounting standards, but they can result in differences in standards across countries. They also permit managers to "groom" transactions to satisfy their own financial reporting objectives. For example, both U.S. GAAP and IFRS currently permit lease transactions to be structured in such a way that the leased asset can be reported on the balance sheet of the lessee, the lessor, or on neither party's balance sheet.[2] Accounting analysis, therefore, involves assessing whether a firm's reported assets adequately reflect the key resources that are under its control, and whether adjustments are required to compare its performance with that of competitors.

Asset ownership issues also arise indirectly from the application of rules for revenue recognition. Firms are permitted to recognize revenues only when their product has been shipped or their service has been provided to the customer. Revenues are then considered "earned," and the customer has a legal commitment to pay for the product or service. As a result, for the seller, recognition of revenue frequently coincides with "ownership" of a receivable that is shown as an asset on its balance sheet. Therefore, accounting analysis that raises questions about whether or not revenues have been earned often affects the valuation of assets.

Ambiguity over whether a company owns an asset creates a number of opportunities for accounting analysis:

- Despite management's best intentions, financial statements sometimes do a poor job of reflecting the firm's economic assets since it is difficult for accounting rules to capture all of the subtleties associated with ownership and control.
- Because accounting rules on ownership and control permit managers to groom transactions such that essentially similar transactions are reported in very different ways, important assets may be omitted from the balance sheet even though the firm bears many of the economic risks of ownership.
- There may be legitimate differences in opinion between managers and analysts over residual ownership risks borne by the company, leading to differences in opinion over reporting for these assets.
- Aggressive revenue recognition, which boosts reported earnings, is likely to affect asset values.

Can Future Economic Benefits Be Measured with Reasonable Certainty?

It is almost always difficult to accurately forecast the future benefits associated with capital outlays because the world is uncertain. A company does not know whether a competitor will offer a new product or service that makes its own offering obsolete. It does not know whether the products manufactured at a new plant will be the type that customers want to buy. A company does not know whether changes in oil prices will make the oil drilling equipment that it manufactures less valuable.

Accounting rules deal with these challenges by stipulating the types of resources that can be recorded as assets and those that cannot. The judgment involved in creating these rules, however, can lead to reporting differences across firms and countries. For example, consider the treatment of the economic benefits from research and development (R&D), which is generally considered highly uncertain. Research projects may never deliver promised new products, the products they generate may not be economically viable, or products may be made obsolete by competitors' research. Under U.S. GAAP, R&D outlays are expensed, except for software development costs on products that satisfy technological feasibility standards (see SFAS 86). IFRS requires all research costs to be expensed but permits firms to capitalize development costs once standards of technical and market feasibility are satisfied (IAS 38).

Rules that require the immediate expensing of outlays for some key resources may be good accounting, but they create a challenge for the analyst—they make it more difficult to infer financial performance from the financial statements. If all U.S. firms expense R&D, financial statements will reflect differences in R&D success only when new products are commercialized rather than during the development process. Differences in R&D expensing for firms using U.S. GAAP and IFRS will also make it challenging for the analyst to assess how much of any differences in reported performance are due to reporting standards rather than economic performance. One way the analyst can attempt to correct for these distortions is by capitalizing key R&D outlays and adjusting the value of the intangible asset based on R&D updates.[3]

Have Fair Values of Assets Declined Below Book Value?

An asset is impaired when its fair value falls below its book value. Of course, markets for many long-term operating assets are illiquid and incomplete, making it highly subjective to infer their fair values. As the 2008 financial crisis demonstrated, asset valuation can also be subjective in markets that are typically highly liquid but which have temporarily frozen. Consequently, considerable management judgment is involved in deciding whether an asset is impaired and determining the value of any impairment loss.

For the analyst, this raises the possibility that asset values are misstated. In most countries, accounting standards require that a loss be recorded for permanent asset impairments. Once again, however, the specific rules differ across countries. For example, U.S. rules (SFAS 144) permit a certain amount of asset overstatement since the test for asset impairment compares the asset's book value to the expected value of *undiscounted* (rather than *discounted*) future cash flows expected to be generated from future use and sale of the asset. This can create situations where no financial statement loss is reported for an asset that is economically impaired. In contrast, IFRS requires the asset impairment test to be based on discounted (rather than undiscounted) cash flows.

The task of determining whether there has been an asset impairment and valuing the impairment is delegated to management with oversight by the firm's auditors. This leaves opportunities for potential management bias in valuing assets and for legitimate differences in opinion between managers and analysts over asset valuations. In most cases, management bias will lead to overstated assets since managers will prefer not to recognize an impairment. However, managers can also bias asset values downward by overstating the current level of impairment, thereby reducing future expenses and increasing future earnings.

Opportunities for accounting adjustments can therefore arise in the situations discussed above if

- Accounting rules do not do a good job of capturing the firm's economics,
- Managers use their discretion to distort the firm's performance, or
- There are legitimate differences in opinion between managers and analysts about economic uncertainties facing the firm that are reflected in asset values.

Overstated Assets

Asset overstatements are likely to arise when managers have incentives to increase reported earnings. Thus, adjustments to assets also typically require adjustments to the income statement in the form of either increased expenses or reduced revenues. The most common forms of asset (and earnings) overstatement are the following:

1. *Delayed asset write-downs.* If assets become impaired—that is, their realizable values fall below their book values—accounting rules generally require that they be written down to their fair values. Asset impairments affect earnings since write-downs are charged directly to earnings. Asset write-downs also increase a firm's leverage, potentially limiting its ability to access capital markets. However, determining an asset's fair value involves considerable judgment, potentially providing managers with an opportunity to defer asset impairments as a way to boost reported profits and to enhance their firms' financial position.[4]

    Analysts that cover firms where management of inventories and receivables is a key success factor (e.g., the fashion retail and consumer electronics industries) need to be particularly cognizant of this form of earnings management and its impact on assets. For example, if managers over-buy or over-produce in the current period, they are likely to have to offer customers discounts or attractive credit terms to get rid of surplus inventories. Significant customer discounts negatively impact earnings, while providing customers with credit carries the risk of default. Warning signs for delays in this type of asset write-down include growing inventory and receivables, write-downs of similar products by competitors, and business downturns for a firm's major customer.

    Deteriorating industry or firm economic conditions can also affect the value of long-term non-financial assets (such as plant and equipment) or intangible assets (such as goodwill). Although firms are required to recognize impairments in the values of these assets when they arise, second-hand markets for these asset types are often illiquid, incomplete, or nonexistent, making estimates of asset valuations and impairments inherently subjective. As a result, managers can use their reporting judgment to delay write-downs on the balance sheet and avoid showing impairment charges in the income statement.[5] This issue is particularly relevant for asset-intensive firms in volatile markets (e.g., airlines) or for firms that follow a strategy of aggressive growth through acquisitions (and thus have large amounts of goodwill on their balance sheet).[6] Warning signs for delays in impairments in long-term non-financial assets include declining long-term asset turnover, declines in return on assets to below the cost of capital for the firm, write-downs by other firms in the same industry that have also suffered deteriorating asset use, and overpayment for or unsuccessful integration of key acquisitions.

2. *Underestimated reserves (e.g., allowances for bad debts or loan losses).* Managers make estimates of expected customer defaults on accounts receivable and loans and create reserves to cover these anticipated costs. If managers underestimate the value of these reserves, assets and earnings will be overstated. Warning signs of inadequate allowances include growing receivables, business downturns for a firm's major clients, and growing loan delinquencies.

3. *Accelerated recognition of revenues (increasing receivables).* Managers typically have the best information on the uncertainties governing revenue recognition—whether a product or service has been provided to customers and whether cash collection is

reasonably likely. However, managers may also have incentives to accelerate the recognition of revenues, boosting reported earnings for the period. Accounts receivable and earnings will then be overstated. Aggressive revenue recognition is one of the most popular forms of earnings management cited by the SEC. Warning signs include receivables growth outpacing sales growth, and increasing days' receivable.

4. *Understated depreciation/amortization on long-term assets.* Managers make estimates of asset lives, salvage values, and amortization schedules for depreciable long-term assets. If these estimates are optimistic, long-term assets and earnings will be overstated. This issue is likely to be most pertinent for firms in asset-intensive businesses (e.g., airlines, utilities). A comparison of the firm's policies to those of its industry competitors with a similar asset base and strategy will help an analyst identify potential overstatements.

EXAMPLES OF HOW TO CORRECT FOR ASSET OVERSTATEMENT

The following examples illustrate some of the distortions that lead to overstated assets and the types of corrections that an analyst can make to reduce bias in the financial statements.

Delayed Write-Downs of Assets

In recent years, the portable MP3 player dominated the music delivery industry, influencing everything from format to record label strategy to how artists market and release their music. Apple has dominated the market with its iPod player—building a U.S. market share of over 75 percent since its introduction in 2001. Rivals such as Creative Technology, Sony, Microsoft, and Samsung have competed aggressively in an attempt to grab a share of this rapidly growing market. Key risks facing these firms include rapid changes in MP3 player technology and inventory management in the face of both relentless competition and potential technological obsolescence.

Singapore-based Creative Technology posted impressive revenue growth from the second half of 2003 through the first quarter of 2005, with predictable spikes in holiday season sales in both 2003 and 2004. However, gross margins steadily declined from 35 percent to 23 percent over this period. A more worrying trend was the firm's inventory management. Growth in inventory far outpaced growth in sales, leading to a 58 percent increase in days' inventory, from 100 days for the quarter ending September 30, 2003, to 158 days for the quarter ending March 31, 2005. Inventory at the end of March 2006 was valued at $451.2 million, up from $183.9 million nine months prior. This increase raises questions for analysts about Creative Technology's inventory value and potential obsolescence.

An analyst can assess whether inventory is impaired by talking with suppliers and customers, observing the speed of new product launches for MP3 players, benchmarking against the performance of other firms in the industry, and understanding the general sentiment about expected market growth. Based on this research, an analyst can judge whether Creative Technology's slowdown in inventory turnover is likely to persist, whether there are serious technological risks for the current inventory, and, if so, whether and how large an impairment charge is appropriate. Prior to the release of earnings for the June 31, 2005, quarter, several analysts raised questions about the growth in Creative Technology's inventory and anticipated that the company would be forced to record future inventory impairment charges.

Once an analyst concludes that inventory is overstated, the challenge is to estimate the magnitude of the write-down. For Creative Technology, this depends on the price discounts that are required to move slow-moving products. The after-tax cost of the impairment will reduce current and retained earnings. In addition, the tax effect of the impairment will lower the Tax Expense and reduce the Deferred Tax Liability since the inventory write-down is not recorded for tax purposes until the inventory is subsequently sold. Creative Technology enjoys a special status in Singapore that exempts certain elements of revenues from income tax. However, for illustrative purposes, using the local statutory tax rate of 20 percent, the financial statements could be modified as follows for an assumed inventory overstatement of $25 million:

	Adjustment	
($ Millions)	Assets	Liabilities & Equity
Balance Sheet		
Inventory	−25.0	
Deferred Tax Liability		−8.8
Common Shareholders' Equity		−16.2
Income Statement		
Cost of Sales		+25.0
Tax Expense		−8.8
Net Income		−16.2

In August 2005, Creative Technology announced that it would take a $20 million charge against inventory to reflect a decline in prices of certain components used to manufacture MP3 players. In the quarter ending March 31, 2006, the company took another inventory write-down due to a steep drop in the price of components such as flash memory and hard drives. Not surprisingly, Creative Technology's share price tumbled in response to news of the write-downs—from a high of close to $17 per share in early 2005, the stock traded at less than $5 per share in mid-2006.

Underestimated Reserves

In late 2006, Community Health Systems (CHS) was the leading operator of general and acute care hospitals in non-urban communities in the United States. The company owned 77 hospitals in 22 states, had a dominant market share in more than 85 percent of the markets it served, and in fiscal 2005 generated $3.7 billion in revenues.

CHS received payments for its services from governmental agencies, private insurers, and directly from the patients it served. Medicare was the single largest revenue provider, accounting for approximately 33 percent of net operating revenue in the quarter ended June 30, 2006. Managed care provided a further 25 percent of revenues, 10 percent came from Medicaid, and 13 percent was from self-pay sources (uninsured patients, patient deductibles, co-insurance payments not covered by the insurer, and patients whose insurance providers had failed to pay).

Prior to 2006, CHS estimated its allowance for doubtful accounts by reserving an amount equal to all receivables aged over 150 days, regardless of patient class. Based on this approach, CHS's quarterly filing for the quarter ended June 30, 2006, showed allowance for doubtful accounts at 32.5 percent of gross receivables. However, this approach did not differentiate among the risk characteristics of different classes of patients. In particular, it failed to recognize that collection rates were lowest for self-pay accounts and that there had been an increase in the proportion of revenues and receivables from these patients during the quarter.

An analyst who recognized the importance of the increase in the proportion of receivables from self-pay customers might decide that the June 2006 receivable allowances were understated, and that balance sheet adjustments needed to be made to Accounts Receivable (for the gross change in reserve), to the Deferred Tax Liability (for the tax impact of the increased expense), and to Retained Earnings (for the net effect). For example, if the analyst decided that allowances for doubtful accounts for CHS should be 36 percent rather than 32.5 percent of Accounts Receivable, to reflect the change in patient mix, Accounts Receivable would have to be reduced by $37.8 million (given the June 2006 Accounts Receivable balance of $1.08 billion and allowance for doubtful accounts of $351 million). Given the company's effective tax rate of 39 percent, this would reduce earnings and equity by $23.1 million and the Deferred Tax Liability by $14.7 million. The adjustment to the June 30, 2006, financial statements would, therefore, be as follows:

($ Millions)	Assets	Liabilities & Equity
Balance Sheet		
Accounts Receivable	−37.8	
Deferred Tax Liability		−14.7
Common Shareholders' Equity		−23.1
Income Statement		
Provision for Doubtful Accounts		+37.8
Tax Expense		−14.7
Net Income		−23.1

(table header spanning: **Adjustment**)

At the end of October 2006, CHS announced that it would change its methodology for estimating the allowance for doubtful accounts for the quarter ending September 30. Under the new method, the company estimated separate default rates for self-pay and other accounts receivable to reflect the differences in collection history. As a result, an incremental $65 million bad debt expense was recorded for the quarter and the estimate increased to 38 percent of gross receivables. Further allowance increases occurred in 2008 and 2009, to 40 percent and 42 percent of receivables respectively. CHS explained that the decline in collectability was primarily the result of the weak economy that had increased the number of patients qualifying for charity care, reduced enrollment in certain state Medicaid programs, and increased the number of non-resident aliens seeking indigent care.

Accelerated Recognition of Revenues

In 2006, the SEC announced an informal inquiry into the financials of Diebold Inc., a U.S. maker of voting equipment, automated teller machines, and bank security systems. In May 2007, Diebold announced that it had received a subpoena from the SEC seeking documents related to its revenue recognition practices. At issue was the recognition of certain North American revenues on "bill and hold" transactions, where the company billed its customers for sales and held the merchandise until later delivery. Under U.S. GAAP, these transactions could be recorded as revenue provided the customer requested that the seller hold the merchandise for legitimate business purposes, there was an agreed delivery schedule, the products were ready for shipment, and the seller did not have any future performance obligations.

From 2002 to 2003, Diebold's days' receivable had increased from 76 to 97 days—an increase of 28 percent. Upon investigation, the SEC detected a number of improper revenue transactions, including shipments from the factory to the warehouse that had been recorded as "bill and hold" sales. An analyst who had observed the increased days' receivable and the SEC interest in Diebold, and wanted to adjust the company's revenues could estimate the impact of the increase on sales and profits. To reduce days' receivable by 21 days, revenues and accounts receivable for 2003 would have to decline by $150 million, requiring the following changes to Diebold's 2003 financial reports:

1. Sales and Accounts Receivable would both decline by $150 million.
2. Cost of Sales would decline and Inventory would increase to reflect the reduction in sales. The value of the Cost of Sales / Inventory adjustment can be estimated by multiplying the sales adjustment by the ratio of cost of sales to sales (67 percent for Diebold in 2003), or $100.5 million (67 percent of $150 million).
3. The decline in pretax income would result in a lower Tax Expense in the company's financial reporting books (but presumably not in its tax books). Consequently, the Deferred Tax Liability would have to be reduced. Diebold's marginal tax rate was 35 percent, implying that the decline in the Tax Expense and Deferred Tax Liability would be $17.3 million [($150 − $100.5) × .35].

The full effect of the adjustment on the 2003 financial statements would therefore be as follows:

($ Millions)	Adjustment	
	Assets	Liabilities & Equity
Balance Sheet		
Accounts Receivable	−150.0	
Inventory	+100.5	
Deferred Tax Liability		−17.3
Common Shareholders' Equity		−32.2
Income Statement		
Sales		−150.0
Cost of Sales		−100.5
Tax Expense		−17.3
Net Income		−32.2

As a result of the SEC inquiry, Diebold launched an internal review of its accounting practices and in September of 2008 announced that it was restating its financial statements for the fiscal years 2003–2006 as well as the quarter ended March 31, 2007. In June 2010 the company agreed to pay a $25 million civil penalty to settle an SEC suit.

Source: © Cengage Learning

Understated Assets

Asset understatements typically arise when managers have incentives to deflate reported earnings. This may occur when the firm is performing exceptionally well and managers decide to store away some of the current strong earnings for a rainy day. Income smoothing, as it has come to be known, can be implemented by over-stating current period expenses (and understating the value of assets) during good times. Asset (and expense) understatements can also arise in a particularly bad year, when managers decide to "take a bath" by understating current period earnings to create the appearance of a turnaround in following years. Accounting analysis involves judging whether managers have understated assets (and also income) and, if necessary, adjusting the balance sheet and income statement accordingly.

Asset understatements can also arise because of accounting rules themselves. In many countries, accounting standards require firms to expense outlays for R&D and advertising because, even though they may create future value for owners, their outcomes are highly uncertain. Asset understatements can also arise when managers have incentives to understate liabilities. For example, if a firm records lease transactions as operating leases or if it discounts receivables with recourse, neither the assets nor the accompanying obligations are shown on its balance sheet. Yet, in some instances, this accounting treatment does not reflect the underlying economics of the transactions—the lessee may effectively own the leased assets, and the firm that sells receivables may still bear all of the risks associated with ownership. The analyst will then want to adjust the balance sheet (and also the income statement) for these effects.

The most common forms of asset (and earnings) understatement arise when there are the following:

1. *Overstated asset write-downs.* Managers potentially have an incentive to overstate asset write-downs either during years of exceptionally strong performance, or when the firm is financially distressed. By overstating asset impairments and overstating expenses in the current period, managers can show lower future expenses, boosting earnings in years of sub-par performance or when a turnaround is needed. Overstated asset write-downs can also arise when managers are less optimistic about the firm's future prospects than the analyst.

2. *Overestimated reserves (e.g., allowances for bad debts or loan losses).* If managers overestimate reserves for bad debts or loan losses, accounts receivable and loans will be understated.

3. *Overstated depreciation/amortization on long-term assets.* Firms that use tax depreciation estimates of asset lives, salvage values, or amortization rates are likely to amortize assets more rapidly than justifiable given the assets' economic usefulness, leading to long-term asset understatements.

4. *Lease assets off balance sheet.* Assessing whether a lease arrangement should be considered a rental contract (and hence recorded using the operating method) or equivalent to a purchase (and hence shown as a capital lease) is subjective. It depends on whether the lessee has effectively accepted most of the risks of ownership, such as obsolescence and physical deterioration. To standardize the reporting of lease transactions, accounting standards have created criteria for distinguishing between the two types. In the United States, SFAS 13 requires a lease transaction to be equivalent to an asset purchase if any of the following conditions hold: (1) ownership of the asset is transferred to the lessee at the end of the lease term, (2) the lessee has the option to purchase the asset for a bargain price at the end of the lease term, (3) the lease term is 75 percent or more of the asset's expected useful life, and (4) the present value of the lease payments is 90 percent or more of the fair value of the asset. Given these objective criteria, managers reporting under U.S. GAAP can structure lease contracts to circumvent the spirit of the distinction between capital and operating leases, potentially leading to the understatement of lease assets.[7] This is likely to be an important issue for the analysis of asset-intensive industries where there are options for leasing

(e.g., airlines and retail chains).[8] In contrast, IFRS standard IAS 17 focuses on transfer of risk and reward to indicate transfer of ownership rather than mandated numerical thresholds.

5. *Key intangible assets, such as R&D and trademarked brands, not reported on the balance sheet.* Some firms' most important assets are excluded from the balance sheet. Examples include investments in R&D, software development outlays, and brands and membership bases that are created through advertising and promotions. U.S. GAAP prohibits the capitalization of R&D outlays and membership acquisition costs (with an exception for certain software development costs), while countries reporting under IFRS are generally required to expense these costs as well (with some additional limited latitude in the area of development costs)—primarily because it is believed that the benefits associated with such outlays are too uncertain. New products may never reach the market due to technological infeasibility or to the introduction of superior products by competitors; and new members that sign up for a service as a result of a promotions campaign may subsequently quit. Expensing the cost of intangibles has two implications for analysts. First, the omission of intangible assets from the balance sheet inflates measured rates of return on capital (either return on assets or return on equity).[9] For firms with key omitted intangible assets, this omission has important implications for forecasting long-term performance; unlike firms with no intangibles, competitive forces will not cause their rates of return to fully revert to the cost of capital over time. For example, pharmaceutical firms have shown very high rates of return over many decades in part because of the impact of R&D accounting. A second effect of expensing outlays for intangibles is that it makes it more difficult for the analyst to assess whether the firm's business model works. Under the matching concept, operating profit is a meaningful indicator of the success of a firm's business model since it compares revenues and the expenses required to generate them. Immediately expensing outlays for intangible assets runs counter to matching and, therefore, makes it more difficult to judge a firm's operating performance. Consistent with this, research shows that investors view R&D and advertising outlays as assets rather than expenses.[10] Understated intangible assets are likely to be important for firms in pharmaceutical, software, branded consumer products, and subscription businesses.

EXAMPLES OF HOW TO CORRECT FOR ASSET UNDERSTATEMENT

The following examples illustrate some of the types of distortions that understate assets and show corrections that an analyst can make to ensure that assets are reflected appropriately.

Overstated Depreciation for Long-Term Assets

In 2009 Lufthansa, the German national airline, reported that it depreciated its aircraft over 12 years on a straight-line basis, with an estimated residual value of 15 percent of initial cost. Air France-KLM, an airline formed in 2004 by the merger of the French airline Air France and the Dutch airline KLM, is one of Lufthansa's main competitors. In contrast to Lufthansa, Air France-KLM reported that its aircraft depreciation was also estimated using the straight-line method but assuming an average life of 20 years and no residual value.[11]

For the analyst, these differences raise several questions. Do Lufthansa and Air France-KLM fly different types of routes, potentially explaining the differences in their depreciation policies? Alternatively, do they have different asset management strategies? For example, does Lufthansa use newer planes to attract more business travellers, to lower maintenance costs, or to lower fuel costs? If there do not appear to be operating differences that explain the differences in the two firms' depreciation rates, the analyst may well decide that it is necessary to adjust the depreciation rates for one or both firms to ensure that their performance is comparable.

To adjust for this effect, the analyst could choose to decrease Lufthansa's depreciation rates to match those of Air France-KLM. The following financial statement adjustments would then be required in Lufthansa's financial statements:

1. Increase the book value of the fleet at the beginning of the year to adjust for the relatively high depreciation rates that had been used in the past. This will also require an offsetting increase in equity (retained earnings) and in the deferred tax liability.
2. Reduce the depreciation expense (and increase the book value of the fleet) to reflect the lower depreciation for the current year, and increase the tax expense (in 2009, Lufthansa's tax rate was 25 percent). On the balance sheet, show an increase in equity and deferred tax liability.

Note that these changes are designed to show Lufthansa's results as if it had always used the same depreciation assumptions as Air France-KLM rather than to reflect a change in the assumptions for the current year going forward. This enables the analyst to compare ratios that use assets (e.g., return on assets) for the two companies.

Lufthansa reported in its 2009 Annual Report the total cost of its aircraft at the beginning of 2009 as €17,918 m, and that accumulated depreciation was €10,547 m. This implies that the average life of Lufthansa's fleet was 8.32 years, calculated as follows:

€ Millions (unless otherwise noted)

Aircraft cost, 01/01/09	17,918	Reported
Depreciable cost	15,230	Cost × (1 − .15)
Accumulated depreciation, 01/01/09	10,547	Reported
Accumulated depreciation / Depreciable cost	69.3%	
Depreciable life	12 years	Reported
Average age of aircraft	8.32	12 × .693 years

If Lufthansa used the same useful life and salvage estimates as Air France-KLM, Accumulated Depreciation would have been only €7,454 m, thereby increasing the company's Long-term Tangible Assets by €3,093 m and Common Shareholders' Equity by €2,320 m, while also increasing the Deferred Tax Liability by €773 m:

€ Millions (unless otherwise noted)

Aircraft cost at 01/01/09	17,918	Reported
Depreciable cost	17,918	No residual value
Depreciable life	20 years	Air France-KLM
Accumulated depreciation, 01/01/09	7,454	Over 8.32 years
Increase in Long-Term Tangible Assets	3,093	
Marginal Tax Rate	25.0%	Reported
Increase in Deferred Tax Liability	773	
Increase in Common Shareholders Equity	2,320	

Given its net investment in new aircraft of €2,055 m in 2009, Lufthansa's depreciation expense for 2009 (included in Cost of Sales) using the same useful life and salvage estimates as Air France-KLM, would have been €947 m [(17,918 + 2,055/2)/20] versus the €1,185 m reported by the company.[12] Thus, Cost of Sales would decline by €238 m, increasing the Tax Expense for the year by €60 m. On the balance sheet, these changes would increase Long-Term Tangible Assets by €238 m, increase Deferred Tax Liability by €60 m, and increase Common Shareholders' Equity by €178 m.

In summary, if Lufthansa were using the same depreciation method as Air France-KLM, its financial statements for the years ended December 31, 2009 and 2008, would have to be modified as follows:

(€ Millions)	Adjustment December 31, 2009		Adjustment December 31, 2008	
	Assets	Liabilities & Equity	Assets	Liabilities & Equity
Balance Sheet				
Long-Term Tangible Assets	+3,093 +238		+3,093	
Deferred Tax Liability		+773 + 60		+773
Shareholders' Equity		+2,320 + 178		+2,320
Total Impact	+3,331	+3,331	+3,093	+3,093
Income Statement				
Cost of Sales		−238		
Tax Expense		+60		
Net Income		+178		

Sales turnover (sales to average assets) comparisons for the two companies using reported data show that Lufthansa has higher turnover than Air France-KLM (0.91 versus 0.81). However, analysts that make the above adjustment would observe that the full amount of this difference is attributable to the different depreciation assumptions. After adjustment, Lufthansa's sales turnover declines to 0.81, identical to that of Air France-KLM.

Key Intangible Assets Off Balance Sheet

How should the analyst approach the omission of intangibles? One way is to leave the accounting as is but to recognize that forecasts of long-term rates of return will have to reflect the inherent biases that arise from this accounting method. A second approach is to capitalize intangibles and amortize them over their expected lives.

For example, consider the case of Microsoft, the largest software company in the world. Microsoft expenses its software R&D costs, arguing that all material research and development costs are incurred before technological feasibility is reached (U.S. GAAP allows capitalization of development costs once technical feasibility is established until the product is released to the market). What adjustment would be required if the analyst decided to capitalize Microsoft's software R&D and to amortize the intangible asset using the straight-line method over the expected life of software (approximately three years)? Assume that R&D spending occurs evenly throughout the year and that only half a year's amortization is taken on the latest year's spending. Given R&D outlays for the years 2007 to 2010, the R&D asset at the end of the 2010 fiscal year (06/30/10) is $13.2 billion, calculated as follows:

Year	R&D Outlay ($billions)	Proportion Capitalized 06/30/10 ($ billions)	Asset 06/30/10 ($ billions)	Proportion Capitalized 06/30/09 ($ billions)	Asset 06/30/09 ($ billions)
2010	$8.7	(1 − .33/2)	$7.3		
2009	9.0	(1 − .33/2 − .33)	4.5	(1 − .33/2)	$7.5
2008	8.2	(1 − .33/2 − .67)	1.4	(1 − .33/2 − .33)	4.1
2007	7.1			(1 − .33/2 − .67)	1.2
Total			$13.2		$12.8

The R&D amortization expenses (included in Other Operating Expenses) for 2009 and 2010 are $7.6 billion and $8.3 billion, respectively, and are calculated as follows:

Year	R&D Outlay ($billions)	Proportion Capitalized 06/30/10 ($ billions)	Expense 06/30/10 ($ billions)	Proportion Capitalized 06/30/09 ($ billions)	Expense 06/30/09 ($ billions)
2010	$8.7	.33/2	$1.4		
2009	9.0	.33	3.0	.33/2	$1.5
2008	8.2	.33	2.7	.33	2.7
2007	7.1	.33/2	1.2	.33	2.3
2006	6.6			.33/2	1.1
Total			$8.3		$7.6

Since Microsoft will continue to expense software R&D immediately for tax purposes, the change in reporting method will give rise to a Deferred Tax Liability. Given a marginal tax rate of 35 percent, this liability will equal 35 percent of the value of the Long-Term Intangible Assets reported, with the balance increasing Common Shareholders' Equity.

In summary, the adjustments required to capitalize software R&D for Microsoft for the years 2010 and 2009 are as follows:

($ Billions)	Adjustment June 30, 2010 Assets	Liabilities & Equity	Adjustment June 30, 2009 Assets	Liabilities & Equity
Balance Sheet				
Long-Term Intangible Assets	+13.2		+12.8	
Deferred Tax Liability		+4.6		+4.5
Common Shareholders' Equity		+8.6		+8.3
Income Statement				
Research and Development		−8.7		−9.0
		+8.3		+7.6
Tax Expense		+0.1		+0.5
Total Expenses		−0.3		−0.9
Net Income		+0.3		+0.9

Adjusting R&D in this way increases Microsoft's assets by 15 percent and lowers its return on average assets in 2010 from 18.8 percent to 16.4 percent, enabling analysts to understand the impact of the economic resources required to generate its earnings. Such adjustments can also allow analysts to compare the performance of companies that follow different R&D reporting standards or make different judgements on the treatment of these costs.

Source: © Cengage Learning

Liability Distortions

Liabilities are defined as economic obligations arising from benefits received in the past, and for which the amount and timing is known with reasonable certainty. Liabilities include obligations to customers that have paid in advance for products or services; commitments to public and private providers of debt financing; obligations to federal and local governments for taxes; commitments to employees for unpaid wages, pensions, and other retirement benefits; and obligations from court or government fines or environmental cleanup orders.

Distortions in liabilities generally arise because there is ambiguity about whether (1) an obligation has really been incurred and/or (2) the obligation can be measured.

Has an Obligation Been Incurred?

For most liabilities there is little ambiguity about whether an obligation has been incurred. For example, when a firm buys supplies on credit, it has incurred an obligation to the supplier. However, for some transactions it is more difficult to decide whether there is any such obligation. For example, if a firm announces a plan to restructure its business by laying off employees, has it made a commitment that would justify recording a liability? Or, if a software firm receives cash from its customers for a five-year software license, should the firm report the full cash inflow as revenues, or should some of it represent the ongoing commitment to the customer for servicing and supporting the license agreement?

Can the Obligation be Measured?

Many liabilities specify the amount and timing of obligations precisely. For example, a 20-year, $100 million bond issue with an 8 percent coupon payable semi-annually specifies that the issuer will pay the holders $100 million in 20 years, and it will pay out interest of $4 million every six months for the duration of the loan. However, for some liabilities it is difficult to estimate the amount of the obligation. For example, a firm that is responsible for an environmental cleanup clearly has incurred an obligation, but the amount is highly uncertain.[13] Similarly, firms that provide pension and post-retirement benefits for employees have incurred commitments that depend on uncertain future events, such as employee mortality rates and future inflation rates, making valuation of the obligation subjective. Future warranty and insurance claim obligations fall into the same category—the commitment is clear but the amount depends on uncertain future events.

Accounting rules frequently specify when a commitment has been incurred and how to measure the amount of the commitment. However, as discussed earlier, accounting rules are imperfect—they cannot cover all contractual possibilities and reflect all of the complexities of a firm's business relationships. They also require managers to make subjective estimates of future events to value the firm's commitments. Thus the analyst may decide that some important obligations are omitted from the financial statements or, if included, are understated, either because of management bias or because there are legitimate differences in opinion between managers and analysts over future risks and commitments. As a result, analysis of liabilities is usually with an eye to assessing whether the firm's financial commitments and risks are understated and/or its earnings overstated.

Understated Liabilities

Liabilities are likely to be understated when the firm has key commitments that are difficult to value and therefore not considered liabilities for financial reporting purposes. Understatements are also likely to occur when managers have strong incentives to overstate the soundness of the firm's financial position or to boost reported earnings. By understating leverage, managers present investors with a rosy picture of the firm's financial risks. Earnings management also understates liabilities (namely deferred or unearned revenues) when revenues are recognized upon receipt of cash, even though not all services have been provided.

The most common forms of liabilities understatements arise when the following conditions exist:

1. *Unearned revenues are understated through aggressive revenue recognition.* If cash has already been received but the product or service has yet to be provided, unearned or deferred revenues are created. This liability reflects the company's commitment to provide the service or product to the customer and is extinguished once that is accomplished. Firms that recognize revenues prematurely—after the receipt of cash but prior to fulfilling their product or service commitments to customers—understate deferred revenue liabilities and overstate earnings. Firms that bundle service contracts with the sale of a product are particularly prone to deferred revenue liability understatement since separating the price of the product from the price of the service is subjective.

2. *Loans from discounted receivables are off balance sheet.* As discussed earlier, receivables that are discounted with a financial institution are considered "sold" if the "seller" cedes control over the receivables to the financier. Yet if the sale permits the buyer to have recourse against the seller in the event of default, the seller continues to face collection risk. Given the management judgment involved in forecasting default and refinancing costs, as well as the incentives faced by managers to keep debt off the balance sheet, it is important for the analyst to evaluate the firm's estimates for default as well as the inherent commitments that it has for discounted receivables. Are the firm's estimates reasonable? Is it straightforward to forecast the costs of the default and prepayment risks? If not, does the analyst need to increase the value of the recourse liability? Or, in the extreme, does the analyst need to undo the sale and recognize a loan from the financial institution for the discounted value of the receivables?

3. *Long-term liabilities for leases are off balance sheet.* As discussed earlier in the chapter, key lease assets and liabilities can be excluded from the balance sheet if the company structures lease transactions to fit the accounting definition of an operating lease. Firms that groom transactions to avoid showing lease assets and obligations will have very different balance sheets from firms with virtually identical economics but which either use capital leases or borrow from the bank to actually purchase the equivalent resources. For firms that choose to structure lease transactions to fit the definition of an operating lease, the analyst can restate the leases as capital leases, as discussed in the Asset Understatement section. This will ensure that the firm's true financial commitments and risks will be reflected on its balance sheet, enabling comparison with peer firms.

EXAMPLES OF HOW TO CORRECT FOR LIABILITY UNDERSTATEMENT

The following examples illustrate some of these types of liability understatements and the corrections that an analyst can make to reduce bias in the financial statements.

Unearned Revenues Understated

Hansen Medical, Inc., is a U.S. provider of advanced medical robotics. Its Sensei Robotic Catheter System was designed to allow physicians to accurately position, manipulate, and control catheters, and had gained acceptance in hospitals globally. Typically, ownership of the Sensei system passed to customers upon shipment, at which point revenues were recognized. However, a large percentage of the sales contracts for systems included installation and training. In such instances, since these services were significant, Hansen deferred all system revenues until training and installation were completed.

The company went public in 2006 and raised funds through subsequent public offerings in 2008, 2009, and 2010. During this period it also formed key partnership agreements with larger medical device companies such as Philips Healthcare and GE Healthcare. However, following its IPO, Hansen consistently missed analyst expectations and generated losses.

In October 2009, a whistleblower alleged that Hansen had recognized revenues from the sale of some of its Sensei systems upon shipment, prior to completion of the system installation, setup, and training. After an investigation, the company determined that it would have to restate its financial results for 2007, 2008, and the first part of 2009, reducing revenues for these periods by $7.4 million, $6.8 million for 2008 alone. The adjustment required to correct Hansen's 2008 financials (as reported in its 10-K) would be as follows:

1. Sales would decline and unearned revenues (included in Other Current Liabilities) would increase by $6.8 million.
2. Cost of Sales would decline and Deferred Cost of Sales (included in Other Current Assets) would increase by $2.4 million to reflect the lower sales.
3. Since Hansen had reported losses since its inception, the restatement would not affect its tax position, requiring no adjustment to Tax Expense or to Deferred Taxes.

The full effect of the adjustment on the 2008 financial statements would therefore be as follows:

($ millions)	Adjustment	
	Assets	Liabilities & Equity
Balance Sheet		
Other Current Assets	+2.4	
Other Current Liabilities		+6.8
Common Shareholders' Equity		−4.4
Income Statement		
Sales	−6.8	
Cost of Sales	−2.4	
Net Income	−4.4	

The restatement reduced Hansen's previously reported revenues for 2008 by 22 percent and was accompanied by a drop in the firm's stock price of 9 percent on the announcement date, and 22 percent for the month (versus a 1 percent increase for the S&P 500 during that same period).

Equity Distortions

Accounting treats stockholders' equity as a residual claim on the firm's assets after paying off the other claimholders. Consequently, equity distortions arise primarily from distortions in assets and liabilities. For example, distortions in assets or liabilities that affect earnings also lead to distortions in equity. However, equity distortions can also arise that are not captured in an asset and liability analysis. One such distortion is for hybrid securities.

Hybrid securities include convertible debt and debt with warrants attached. These securities are partially pure debt and partially equity. Current U.S. accounting rules do not separate these components, typically implying that the balance sheet overstates firm debt and understates its equity. Without adjusting for this distortion, it can be difficult to understand the real financial risks and returns for firms with different types of hybrids. New accounting rules being considered in a joint FASB/IASB project are likely to address this issue by requiring securities such as convertible debt to be separated into two components on the balance sheet, a debt component and an equity component. Each would be valued at its fair value at the date of issue. This approach could be adopted by the analyst.

EXAMPLE OF HOW TO CORRECT FOR EQUITY DISTORTIONS

We illustrate the equity distortion arising from the issuance of hybrid securities and the corrections that the analyst can make to reduce bias in the financial statements.

Hybrid Securities

On October 27, 2009, Navistar International Corp. completed an offering of $550 million of 3.0 percent Convertible Senior Subordinated Notes due in 2014. At the same time, the company also issued $1.0 billion in Senior Unsecured Notes with an annual interest rate of 8.25 percent. The premium for conversion rights was therefore significant. The net present value of the $550 million convertible issue at an 8.25 percent discount rate is $434 million, implying that the convertibility premium was worth roughly $116 million. One way to adjust for this effect is to record the debt component at $434 million and to show the $116 million conversion premium as part of Common Shareholders' Equity. Interest on the debt would then be based on the 8.25 percent coupon rate of the straight note rather than the 3.0 percent (which reflects the conversion premium).

The effect of this adjustment on Navistar's financial statements at December 31, 2009, would be as follows:

($ millions)	Assets	Liabilities & Equity
Adjustment for December 31, 2009		
Balance Sheet		
Long-Term Debt		−116
Common Shareholders' Equity		+116

Given Navistar's high leverage, this change generates only a modest increase in its long-term debt to total capital ratio, from 107 percent to 110 percent.

Source: © Cengage Learning

COMPARING COMPANIES USING U.S. GAAP AND IFRS

In Chapter 3 we discussed the joint convergence project being undertaken by FASB and the IASB that has succeeded in reducing many of the differences between U.S. GAAP and IFRS. Many of the remaining differences are likely to have relatively minor effects on financial statement comparability, making it easier for analysts to compare the performance of companies using different standards.

Nonetheless, a few important differences remain. Some of these arise from differences in the way that U.S. and international standard setters have opted to trade-off the relevance and reliability of financial information. For example, in an effort to increase the relevance of financial information, IFRS permits companies to revalue long-term nonfinancial assets that have appreciated in value. In contrast, U.S. GAAP places a stronger weight on the reliability of financial information and precludes such upward revaluations. Differences can also reflect tax factors. For example, U.S. GAAP requires that firms that use the LIFO inventory valuation method for tax purposes follow the same method for financial reporting. LIFO is not used widely for tax purposes outside the United States and is not permitted under IFRS.

Table 4-4 shows some of the remaining important differences between U.S. GAAP and IFRS. The table also discusses the types of adjustments that analysts could make to ensure that performance comparisons of companies using the two standards are meaningful. This adjustment exercise can be challenging, particularly if information on the accounting effects is not disclosed. The adjustments we recommend take

TABLE 4-4	Adjusting for Key Differences between U.S. GAAP and IFRS	
Financial Statement Topic	Reporting Difference	Adjustment
Revenue Recognition		
Contracts with contingent payments (e.g., research contracts where payments are contingent on reaching milestones)	Under U.S. GAAP revenue cannot be recognized until the contingency is resolved; IFRS allows recognition when resolution of contingency is probable.	For IFRS firm, eliminate revenues and receivables recognized prior to the resolution of the contingency. Also adjust cost of sales/inventory and tax expense / deferred taxes.
Extraordinary Items	Can be reported separately under U.S. GAAP but not under IFRS, potentially affecting operating income.	Either (a) separate extraordinary items from operating income for IFRS firms, or (b) include extraordinary items in operating expenses for U.S. firms.
Receivables		
Factored (discounted) receivables with recourse	Under U.S. GAAP, factored receivables with recourse are recorded as a sale provided control over the receivables has been ceded to the financier and the seller has experience estimating the value of the recourse liability. IFRS typically does not permit factored receivables with recourse to be reported as a sale.	Either: (a) eliminate the gross value of factored receivables and loans on the balance sheet of IFRS firm and show the bad debt allowance as a recourse liability; or (b) add back the receivables and loans to the U.S. firm's balance sheet.

(continued)

Financial Statement Topic	Reporting Difference	Adjustment
Contracts where cash receipts are deferred	IFRS requires deferred receipts to be discounted to their present value; U.S. GAAP typically does not require deferred receipts to be discounted.	For short-term receivables, this effect should be modest. For long-term receivables, adjust financials of IFRS firm by (a) adding back discount to receivables and to revenues in year of sale; and (b) eliminating subsequent interest income and reducing receivables.
Inventory		
Inventory valuation method	IFRS does not permit use of LIFO as an inventory valuation method, which is permitted under U.S. GAAP.	Adjust U.S. company inventory balance to FIFO using LIFO reserve data. Adjust COGS for change in LIFO reserve. Also adjust for tax impact (tax expense and deferred taxes).
Reversal of impairments	Reversals of inventory impairments are allowed under IFRS, but are not permitted under U.S. GAAP.	Eliminate inventory reversal effect for IFRS company by deducting gain and reducing value of inventory.
Long-Lived Assets		
Plant, Property, and Equipment (PPE) Valuation	IFRS allows PPE to be valued at either historical cost or fair value; U.S. GAAP requires measurement at historical cost.	Eliminate asset revaluations for IFRS firms using revaluation reserve.
Impairment of long-lived tangible & finite lived intangible assets	Under U.S. GAAP, an impairment charge for the excess of carrying value over fair value is recorded when carrying value is greater than the value of *undiscounted* cash flows. IFRS records the impairment charge when the excess of carrying value exceeds the fair or realizable value.	Difficult to adjust.
Reversal of long-lived asset impairments	U.S. GAAP does not allow reversal of impairment; IFRS allows impairment reversals for assets other than goodwill.	Eliminate asset reversal effect for IFRS firms.
Capitalization of development costs	U.S. GAAP requires development costs to be expensed (except for software development costs); IFRS allows development costs to be capitalized if they meet specific criteria.	Either (a) expense development costs capitalized for IFRS firm, or (b) capitalize all R&D costs, with amortization over useful life for both U.S. and IFRS firms as illustrated earlier in this chapter.
Capitalization of direct response advertising costs	U.S. GAAP requires certain direct response advertising costs to be capitalized and amortized; all such costs are expensed immediately under IFRS.	Either (a) expense direct response advertising costs for U.S. firm, or (b) capitalize costs for IFRS firm with amortization over useful life.

(continued)

Financial Statement Topic	Reporting Difference	Adjustment
Debt and Equity		
Classification of compound instruments	U.S. GAAP generally requires compound instruments such as convertible bonds to be classified as liabilities. IFRS requires such instruments to be separated into debt and equity components.	Either (a) reclassify entire instrument as equity for IFRS firm, or (b) separate out the two components for U.S. firm.

Source: © Cengage Learning 2013

advantage of information that is likely to be publicly available, such as the asset revaluation reserve or the LIFO reserve, so that the financials of IFRS and U.S. GAAP firms are comparable.

EXAMPLES OF ADJUSTING FOR DIFFERENCES IN U.S. GAAP AND IFRS

The following illustrates some of the differences and the adjustments that an analyst can make to enhance the comparability of financial statements for firms using the competing standards.

Long-Term Asset Impairment Reversals

Consider the case of OZ Minerals, the third largest diversified mining company in Australia, the world's second largest producer of zinc, and a significant producer of copper, lead, gold, and silver. OZ Minerals reports under Australian Accounting Standards, which closely follow IFRS. In 2010 the firm announced that as a result of an improved outlook for the global economy, record copper prices, and the strong production of its Prominent Hill mine, it would increase pretax earnings by 201.1 million Australian dollars (approximately 172 million U.S. dollars) with the reversal of a 2008 impairment of the Prominent Hill PP&E asset. This impairment reversal increased pre-tax earnings for OZ Minerals by 44 percent for the year.

As shown in Table 4-4, reversals of impairments are permitted by IFRS but not by U.S. GAAP. An analyst comparing OZ Minerals' performance with that of U.S.-based mining companies such as Freeport-McMoRan Copper & Gold Inc., a major copper producer that also took a significant impairment charge in 2008, could therefore add back the reversal to OZ Minerals' earnings (with an adjustment for tax effects) as follows:

Millions of Australian Dollars	Assets	Liabilities & Equity
Balance sheet		
Long-Term Tangible Assets	−201.1	
Deferred Tax Liability		−60.0
Common Shareholders' Equity		−141.1
Income Statement		
Impairment reversal		−201.1
Tax Expense (reported by OZ)		−60.0
Net Income		−141.1

The add back of the impairment reversal reduces OZ Minerals' return on equity (ROE) from 18.4 percent to 13.9 percent.

LIFO Inventory Valuation

Caterpillar, Inc., is the world's leading manufacturer of construction and mining machines and related equipment. In 2010, Caterpillar used the last-in, first-out (LIFO) valuation method for approximately 70 percent of its inventories. An analyst wanting to compare Caterpillar with the European competitor CNH Global N.V. (which reports using IFRS) could adjust Caterpillar's inventory to approximate cost using the first-in, first-out (FIFO) method, since IFRS does not permit the use of LIFO. Caterpillar reports its LIFO reserve (the excess of estimated current costs over LIFO carrying value) as $2,575 million in 2010 and $3,022 million in 2009. The following adjustments to Caterpillar's financials reflect the cumulative effect of using LIFO at the end of FY 2009 and the incremental impact for FY 2010:

1) Add Caterpillar's LIFO reserve at the end of FY 2009, $3,022 million, to its inventory balance at the end of 2009, to revalue inventory to FIFO.
2) The cumulative inventory adjustment also increases equity at the end of FY 2009 and will require an adjustment to the Deferred Tax Liability. Given Caterpillar's tax rate of 35 percent, this effect is $1,058 million.
3) To make the incremental adjustment for FY 2010, the analyst will lower inventory by $447 million to reflect the decline in the LIFO reserve for the year ($2,575 million − $3,022 million) and increase cost of goods sold. This increase in expenses will be offset by a decline in the tax expense for $156 million ($447 million × the tax rate of 35 percent) and a decline in Deferred Tax Liability. The impact on net income and equity is therefore −$291 million (−$447 million + $156 million).

A summary of these entries is as follows:

Fiscal Year Ending ($ in millions)	December 31, 2010		December 31, 2009	
	Assets	Liabilities & Equity	Assets	Liabilities & Equity
Balance Sheet				
Inventory	−447		+3,022	
Deferred Tax Liability		−156		+1,058
Common Shareholders' Equity		−291		+1,964
Income Statement				
Cost of Goods Sold	+447			
Tax Expense	−156			
Total expense	+291			
Net Income	−291			

Caterpillar reports inventory turnover (cost of goods sold to average inventory) of 3.8 for 2010, the same as reported by its competitor CNH. However, after restating Caterpillar's financials to FIFO, its turnover declines to 2.9, indicating that it actually underperforms its rival.

Off Balance Sheet Discounted Receivables with Recourse

Tecumseh Products Company is a global manufacturer of compressors for residential and commercial air conditioning and refrigeration applications. It has manufacturing and assembly plants in the United States, Brazil, France, India, Canada, Mexico, Malaysia, and China. The company's Brazilian and Indian subsidiaries periodically factor their accounts receivables to financial institutions, both with and without recourse. The sale of receivables with recourse creates a contingent liability. Tecumseh reported that in 2010 receivables sold with "limited recourse liability" amounted to $19.4 million, 15 percent of reported receivables.

Since Tecumseh is a U.S. company, it will show the receivables factored with recourse as sold. The financing will therefore not appear on its balance sheet as a loan, and its receivables will be excluded from current assets. In contrast, other firms in the industry that use IFRS, such as Ingersoll-Rand PLC, a company headquartered in Ireland, and Sandvik AB from Sweden, show factored receivables and loans on their balance sheets. An analyst comparing Tecumseh with either of these competitors could therefore decide to restate Tecumseh's financials to add back the recourse receivables sold to Tecumseh's balance sheet as follows:

($ millions)	Adjustment for December 31, 2010	
	Assets	Liabilities & Equity
Balance Sheet		
Other Current Assets	+19.4	
Short-Term Debt		+19.4

On an unadjusted basis, Tecumseh appears to manage its receivables more closely than its European competitors, with days' receivable of 50.0, compared to 56.3 for Sandvik and 60.8 for Ingersoll-Rand. However, when factored receivables are added back to Tecumseh's ending 2010 accounts receivables, days' receivable increase to 57.5, comparable to its peers.

Source: © Cengage Learning 2013

APPLICATION TO TJX AND NORDSTROM

Let us return to the TJX and Nordstrom comparison discussed in Chapter 2. Are any of the accounting adjustments discussed in this chapter relevant to understanding the relative performance of TJX and Nordstrom? Would it make sense for an analyst covering the two companies to make any of the adjustments?

One potentially important accounting difference is that TJX Companies, Inc. leases virtually all of its stores using operating leases, whereas a significant portion of Nordstrom's stores are owned or leased under capital leases. As a result, TJX omits many more of its critical assets and lease obligations from its balance sheet than Nordstrom, making it challenging to compare the two firms asset intensity and financial leverage.

To evaluate how the difference in store ownership/leasing affects the financial performance of TJX and Nordstrom, the analyst can use information on lease commitments presented in the financial statement footnotes to estimate the value of the assets and liabilities that are omitted from the balance sheet. The leased property is subsequently depreciated over the life of the lease, and the lease payments are treated as interest and debt repayment. We show these computations for TJX below and present comparable adjustments for Nordstrom's operating leases in Appendix B.

To estimate the value of the operating lease assets and liabilities, we use information on the future minimum operating lease payments provided by TJX in its financial statement footnotes. For the years ending January 29, 2011, and January 30, 2010, these amounts were as follows:

Year Ended (in thousands)	January 29, 2011	January 30, 2010
Less than 1 year	$1,092,709	$1,005,366
1-3 years	1,938,020	1,771,055
3-5 years	1,464,690	1,307,773
More than 5 years	2,304,674	1,610,867
Total	$6,800,093	$5,695,061

TJX estimated the net present value of its minimum future lease obligations was $5,572.6 million on January 29, 2011, and $4,450.2 million on January 30, 2010. In addition, it reported that the average interest rate on its long-term debt was 5.5 percent. Based on the data on general lease terms given in the financial statements, we assume that the average lease term is 15 years. Given this information, the analyst can make the following adjustments to TJX's beginning and ending balance sheets, and to its income statement for the year ended January 29, 2011:

1. Capitalize the net present value of the minimum lease obligations as of January 30, 2010, increasing Long-Term Tangible Assets and Long-Term Debt by $4,450.2 million.[14]

2. Calculate the value of any change in lease assets and lease liabilities during the year from new lease transactions or terminations. On January 30, 2010, TJX's liability for operating lease commitments in 2011 and beyond was $4,450.2 million. During 2010, the company expected to repay $1,005.4 million (as per the schedule above), comprising $244.8 million of interest (5.5 percent of $4,450.2 million) and the remaining $760.6 million as retirement of the lease liability. If there had been no new lease commitments added during the year, the operating lease liability on January 29, 2011, would therefore have been $3,689.6 million ($4,450.2 million − $760.6 million). Yet TJX's actual lease commitment on January 29, 2011, was $5,572.6 million, indicating that it increased its leased store capacity by $1,883.0 million. TJX's Long-Term Tangible Assets and Long-Term Debt therefore increased by $1,883.0 million during 2010 as a result of net new lease commitments.

3. Record the change in lease asset value and expense from depreciation during the year. Using a fifteen-year life and straight-line depreciation, the depreciation expense for 2010 (included in Cost of Sales) is $359.4 m {[$4450.2 m + ($1,883.0 m/2)]/15}.

4. Add back the lease expense in the income statement, included in Cost of Sales, and apportion the payment between Interest Expense and repayment of Long-Term Debt. As previously mentioned, the lease expense is $1,005.4 million. As noted above, this reflects $244.8 million ($4,450.2 m × 5.5 percent) that is shown as Interest Expense and the remaining $760.6 million is allocated toward retiring the total operating lease liability.

5. Make changes to the Deferred Tax Liability to reflect differences in earnings under the capital and operating methods. If it capitalizes operating leases, TJX's expenses are $604.2 million ($359.4 million depreciation expense plus $244.8 million interest expense) versus $1,005.4 million under the operating method, a difference of $401.2 million. TJX will not change its tax books, but for financial reporting purposes it will show higher earnings before tax and thus a higher Tax Expense through deferred taxes. Given a corporate tax rate of 35 percent, Tax Expense will increase by $140.4 million ($401.2 million x .35) and the Deferred Tax Liability will increase by the same amount for the year ended January 29, 2011.

In summary, the adjustments to TJX's financial statements on January 30, 2010, and January 29, 2011, are as follows:

($ Billions)	Adjustment January 29, 2011		Adjustment January 30, 2010	
	Assets	Liabilities & Equity	Assets	Liabilities & Equity
Balance Sheet				
Long-term tangible assets	(1) +4,450.2 (2) +1,883.0 (3) −359.4		(1) +4,450.2	
Long-term debt		(1) +4,450.2 (2) +1,883.0 (4) −760.6		(1) +4,450.2
Deferred taxes		(5) +140.4		
Shareholders' equity		+260.8		
Income Statement				
Cost of sales		(3) +359.4 (4) −1005.4		
Net interest expense		(4) +244.8		
Tax expense		(5) +140.4		
Total increase in expense		−260.8		
Net Income		+260.8		

The increase in both TJX's long term asset and liability balances and related income statement impact resulting from the above adjustment significantly alters many of the financial ratios that an analyst uses to understand and categorize a firm's performance. In the next chapter we will look at these ratios in detail, comparing TJX and Nordstrom on both an unadjusted and adjusted basis.

SUMMARY

To implement accounting analysis, the analyst must first recast the financial statements into a common format so that financial statement terminology and formatting is comparable between firms and across time. A standard template for recasting the financials, presented in this chapter, is used throughout the remainder of the book.

Once the financial statements are standardized, the analyst can determine what accounting distortions exist in the firm's assets, liabilities, and equity. Common distortions that overstate assets include delays in recognizing asset impairments, underestimated reserves, aggressive revenue recognition leading to overstated receivables, and optimistic assumptions on long-term asset depreciation. Asset understatements can arise if managers overstate asset write-offs, use operating leases to keep assets off the balance sheet, or make conservative assumptions for asset depreciation. They can also arise because accounting rules require outlays for key assets (e.g., R&D and brands) to be immediately expensed. For liabilities, the primary concern for the analyst is whether the firm understates its real commitments. This can arise from off-balance liabilities (e.g., operating lease obligations), and from aggressive revenue recognition that understates unearned revenue obligations. Equity distortions frequently arise when there are distortions in assets and liabilities. However, they can also arise if firms issue hybrid securities.

Adjustments for distortions can, therefore, arise because accounting standards, although applied appropriately, do not reflect a firm's economic reality. They can also arise if the analyst has a different point of view from management about the estimates and assumptions made in preparing the financial statements. Finally, adjustments may be necessary for the analyst seeking to compare companies reporting under different accounting standards (broadly represented as U.S. GAAP and IFRS) in order to ensure that the data to be analyzed are comparable.

Once distortions have been identified, the analyst can use footnote and cash flow statement information to make adjustments to the balance sheet at the beginning and/ or end of the current year, as well as any needed adjustments to revenues and expenses in the latest income statement. This ensures that the most recent financial ratios used to evaluate a firm's performance and to forecast its future results are based on financial data that appropriately reflect its business economics.

Several points are worth remembering when doing accounting analysis. First, the bulk of the analyst's time and energy should be focused on evaluating and adjusting accounting policies and estimates that describe the firm's key strategic value drivers. Of course, this does not mean that management bias is not reflected in other accounting estimates and policies, and the analyst should certainly examine these. But given the importance of evaluating how the firm is managing its key success factors and risks, the bulk of the accounting analysis should be spent examining those policies that represent these key factors and risks.

It is also important to recognize that many accounting adjustments can only be approximations rather than precise calculations since much of the information necessary for making precise adjustments is not disclosed. The analyst should therefore try to avoid worrying about being overly precise in making accounting adjustments. By making even crude adjustments, it is usually possible to mitigate some of the limitations of accounting standards and problems of management bias in financial reporting.

DISCUSSION QUESTIONS

1. Use the templates shown in Tables 4-1, 4-2, and 4-3 to recast the following financial statements for Nordstrom, Inc.

Nordstrom, Inc. Consolidated Balance Sheets
(in millions)

	January 29, 2011	January 30, 2010
Assets		
Current assets:		
Cash and cash equivalents	$ 1,506	$795
Accounts receivable, net	2,026	2,035
Merchandise inventories	977	898
Current deferred tax assets, net	236	238
Prepaid expenses and other	79	88
Total current assets	4,824	4,054
Land, buildings and equipment (net of accumulated depreciation of $3,520 and $3,316)	2,318	2,242
Goodwill	53	53
Other assets	267	230
Total assets	$ 7,462	$ 6,579

Nordstrom, Inc. Consolidated Balance Sheets
(in millions)

	January 29, 2011	January 30, 2010
Liabilities and Shareholders' Equity		
Current liabilities:		
Accounts payable	$ 846	$ 726
Accrued salaries, wages and related benefits	375	336
Other current liabilities	652	596
Current portion of long-term debt	6	356
Total current liabilities	1,879	2,014
Long-term debt, net	2,775	2,257
Deferred property incentives, net	495	469
Other liabilities	292	267
Commitments and contingencies		
Shareholders' equity:		
Common stock, no par value: 1,000 shares authorized; 218.0 and 217.7 share issued and outstanding	1,168	1,066
Retained earnings	882	525
Accumulated other comprehensive loss	(29)	(19)
Total shareholders' equity	2,021	1,572
Total liabilities and shareholders' equity	**$ 7,462**	**$ 6,579**

Source: Nordstrom, Inc. SEC 10-K filed March 18, 2011.

Nordstrom, Inc. Consolidated Statements of Earnings
(in millions)

Fiscal Year	2010	2009	2008
Net sales	$ 9,310	$ 8,258	$ 8,272
Credit card revenues	390	369	301
Total revenues	9,700	8,627	8,573
Cost of sales and related buying and occupancy costs	(5,897)	(5,328)	(5,417)
Selling, general and administrative expenses:			
Retail	(2,412)	(2,109)	(2,103)
Credit	(273)	(356)	(274)
Earnings before interest and income taxes	1,118	834	779
Interest expense, net	(127)	(138)	(131)
Earnings before income taxes	991	696	648
Income tax expense	(378)	(255)	(247)
Net earnings	**$ 613**	**$ 441**	**$ 401**

Source: Nordstrom, Inc. SEC 10-K filed March 18, 2011.

Nordstrom, Inc. Consolidated Statements of Cash Flows
(in millions)

Fiscal Year	2010	2009	2008
Operating Activities			
Net earnings	$ 613	$ 441	$ 401
Adjustments to reconcile net earnings to net cash provided by operating activities:			
Depreciation and amortization of buildings and equipment	327	313	302
Amortization of deferred property incentives and other, net	(54)	(42)	(21)
Deferred income taxes, net	2	(58)	(36)
Stock-based compensation expense	42	32	28
Tax benefit from stock-based compensation	15	6	3
Excess tax benefit from stock-based compensation	(16)	(7)	(4)
Provision for bad debt expense	149	251	173
Change in operating assets and liabilities:			
Accounts receivable	(74)	(159)	(93)
Merchandise inventories	(80)	(1)	53
Prepaid expenses and other assets	1	(38)	38
Accounts payable	72	168	16
Accrued salaries, wages and related benefits	37	120	(54)
Other current liabilities	42	81	(48)
Deferred property incentives	95	96	119
Other liabilities	6	48	(29)
Net cash provided by operating activities	1,177	1,251	848
Investing activities			
Capital expenditures	(399)	(360)	(563)
Change in credit card receivables originated at third parties	(66)	(182)	(232)
Other, net	3	1	3
Net cash used in investing activities	(462)	(541)	(792)
Financing activities			
(Repayments) proceeds from commercial paper borrowings	–	(275)	275
Proceeds from long-term borrowings, net of discounts	498	399	150
Principal payments on long-term borrowings	(356)	(25)	(410)
Increase in cash book overdrafts	37	9	20
Cash dividends paid	(167)	(139)	(138)
Repurchase of common stock	(84)	–	(264)
Proceeds from exercise of stock options	35	21	13
Proceeds from employee stock purchase plan	13	13	17
Excess tax benefit from stock-based compensation	16	7	4
Other, net	4	3	(9)
Net cash (used in) provided by financing activities	(4)	13	(342)
Net increase (decrease) in cash and cash equivalents	711	723	(286)
Cash and cash equivalents at beginning of year	795	72	358
Cash and cash equivalents at end of year	$1,506	$ 795	$ 72

Source: Nordstrom, Inc. SEC 10-K filed March 18, 2011.

2. Refer to the Creative Technology example on delaying write-downs of current assets. How much excess inventory do you estimate Creative Technology is holding in March 2005 if the firm's optimal days' inventory is 100 days? Calculate the inventory impairment charge for Creative Technology if 50 percent of this excess inventory is deemed worthless? Record the changes to Creative Technology's financial statements from adjusting for this impairment.

3. U.S.-based American International Group, Inc. (AIG) is one of the world's largest insurance companies, offering property, casualty, life insurance, and retirement services to customers in more than 130 countries. In its 2010 10-K report to the SEC, it discloses the following information on the loss reserves created for claims originating in 2000:

	(in millions)
Net reserves held in 2000:	$ 26,971
Cumulative net liability paid as of:	
One year later	$ 9,709
Two years later	17,149
Three years later	21,930
Four years later	26,090
Five years later	29,473
Six years later	32,421
Seven years later	34,660
Eight years later	36,497
Nine years later	38,943
Ten years later	40,153
Net reserves for 2000 re-estimated as of:	
One year later	$26,979
Two years later	30,696
Three years later	32,732
Four years later	36,210
Five years later	41,699
Six years later	43,543
Seven years later	44,475
Eight years later	45,767
Nine years later	47,682
Ten years later	50,422
Net redundancy (deficiency)	$(23,451)

Was the initial estimate for loss reserves originating in 2000 too low or too high? How has the firm updated its estimate of this obligation over time? What percentage of the original liability remains outstanding for 2000 claims at the end of 2010? As a financial analyst, what questions would you have for the CFO on its 2000 liability?

4. AMR, the parent of American Airlines, provides the following footnote information on its capital and operating leases:

AMR's subsidiaries lease various types of equipment and property, primarily aircraft and airport facilities. The future minimum lease payments required under capital leases, together with the present value of such payments, and future minimum lease payments required under operating leases that have initial or remaining non-cancellable lease terms in excess of one year as of December 31, 2010, were (in millions):

Year Ending December 31	Capital Leases	Operating Leases
2011	$186	$1,254
2012	136	1,068
2013	120	973
2014	98	831
2015	87	672
2016 and thereafter	349	6,006
	$976	$10,804
Less amount representing interest	$372	
Present value of net minimum lease payments	$604	

AMR further disclosed that "lease terms vary but are generally six to 25 years for aircraft and seven to 40 years for other leased property and equipment." Assuming that all leases are for aircraft with an average lease term of 15 years, what interest rate does AMR use to capitalize its capital leases? Use this rate to capitalize AMR's operating leases at December 31, 2010. Record the adjustment to AMR's balance sheet to reflect the capitalization of operating leases. How would this reporting change affect AMR's Income Statement in 2011?

5. In 2011, Tata became the first Indian brand to be named in the top 50 global brands in Brand Finance's 2011 Global 500 report, which assigned the Tata brand a value of $15.8 billion. What approaches would you use to estimate the value of brands? What assumptions underlie these approaches? As a financial analyst, what would you use to assess whether the brand value assigned by Brand Finance was a reasonable reflection of the future benefits from this brand? What questions would you raise with the firm's CFO about the firm's brand assets?

6. As the CFO of a company, what indicators would you look at to assess whether your firm's long-term assets were impaired? What approaches could be used, either by management or an independent valuation firm, to assess the dollar value of any asset impairment? As a financial analyst, what indicators would you look at to assess whether a firm's long-term assets were impaired? What questions would you raise with the firm's CFO about any charges taken for asset impairment?

7. The cigarette industry is subject to litigation for health hazards posed by its products. The industry has been in an ongoing process of negotiating a settlement of these claims with state and federal governments. As the CFO for Altria Group, the parent company of Philip Morris, one of the larger firms in the industry, what information would you report to investors in the annual report on the firm's litigation risks? How would you assess whether the firm should record a liability for this risk, and if so, what approach would you use to assess the value of this liability? As a financial analyst following Altria, what questions would you raise with the CEO over the firm's litigation liability?

8. Refer to the Lufthansa example on asset depreciation estimates. What adjustments would be required if Lufthansa's aircraft depreciation were computed using an average life of 25 years and salvage value of 5 percent (instead of the reported values of 12 years and 15 percent)? Show the adjustments to the 2008 and 2009 balance sheets, and to the 2009 income statement.

9. In early 2003, Bristol-Myers Squibb announced that it would have to restate its financial statements as a result of stuffing as much as $3.35 billion worth of products into wholesalers' warehouses from 1999 through 2001. The company's sales and cost of sales during this period was as follows:

($ millions)	2001	2000	1999
Net sales	$18,139	$17,695	$16,502
Cost of products sold	5,454	4,729	4,458

The company's marginal tax rate during the three years was 35 percent. What adjustments are required to correct Bristol-Myers Squibb's balance sheet for December 31, 2001? What assumptions underlie your adjustments? How would you expect the adjustments to affect Bristol-Myers Squibb's performance in the coming few years?

NOTES

1. If a firm's primary business income is from rentals, rental income will be classified as Sales, rather than Investment Income.
2. The IASB and FASB are currently considering a proposal for all lease commitments to be capitalized and shown as an asset and liability on the lessee's balance sheet.
3. See P. Healy, S. Myers, and C. Howe, "R&D Accounting and the Tradeoff Between Relevance and Objectivity," *Journal of Accounting Research* 40 (June 2002): 677–711, for an analysis of the value of capitalizing R&D and then annually assessing impairment.
4. J. Elliott and D. Hanna find that the market anticipates large write-downs by about one quarter, consistent with managers' reluctance to take write-downs on a timely basis. See "Repeated Accounting Write-Offs and the Information Content of Earnings," *Journal of Accounting Research* 34, Supplement, 1996.
5. J. Francis, D. Hanna, and L. Vincent find that management is more likely to exercise judgment in its self-interest for goodwill write-offs and restructuring charges than for inventory or PP&E write-offs. See "Causes and Effects of Discretionary Asset Write-Offs," *Journal of Accounting Research* 34, Supplement, 1996.
6. P. Healy, K. Palepu, and R. Ruback find that acquisitions added value for only one-third of the 50 largest acquisitions during the early 1980s, suggesting that acquirers frequently do not recover goodwill. See "Which Takeovers Are Profitable—Strategic or Financial?" *Sloan Management Review*, Summer 1997.
7. Managers can avoid capitalizing leases by assuming long asset lives (that get around the 75 percent of asset life rule) and high discount rates (to avoid violating the 90 percent of present value rule). Research indicates that some firms responded to the adoption of SFAS 13, which changed the rules for lease capitalization, by grooming transactions to avoid having to capitalize leases. See E. Imhoff and J. Thomas, "Economic Consequences of Accounting Standards: The Lease Disclosure Rule Change," *Journal of Accounting & Economics* 10 (December 1988): 277–311, and S. El-Gazzar, S. Lilien, and V. Pastena, "Accounting for Leases by Lessees," *Journal of Accounting & Economics* 8 (October 1986): 217–238. FASB has responded by issuing ten standards on leases, five interpretations, ten technical bulletins, and 27 EITFs, many designed to reduce managers' ability to avoid capitalizing leases.

8. E. Imhoff, R. Lipe, and D. Wright show that adjustments to capitalize operating leases have a significant impact on leverage and other key financial ratios. See "Operating Leases: Impact of Constructive Capitalization," *Accounting Horizons* 5 (March 1991): 51–64.

9. P. Healy, S. Myers, and C. Howe, "R&D Accounting and the Tradeoff Between Relevance and Objectivity," *Journal of Accounting Research* 40 (June 2002): 677–711, show that the magnitude of this bias is sizable.

10. See B. Bublitz and M. Ettredge, "The Information in Discretionary Outlays: Advertising, Research and Development," *The Accounting Review* 64 (1989): 108–124; S. Chan, J. Martin, and J. Kensinger, "Corporate Research and Development Expenditures and Share Value," *Journal of Financial Economics* 26 (1990): 255–276; R. Dukes," An Investigation of the Effects of Expensing Research and Development Costs on Security Prices," in proceedings of the conference on topical research in accounting (New York University, 1976); J. Elliott, G. Richardson, T. Dyckman, and R. Dukes," The Impact of SFAS No. 2 on Firm Expenditures on Research and Development: Replications and Extensions," *Journal of Accounting* 22 (1984): 85–102; M. Hirschey and J. Weygandt," Amortization Policy for Advertising and Research and Development Expenditures," *Journal of Accounting Research* 23 (1985): 326–335; C. Wasley and T. Linsmeier, "A Further Examination of the Economic Consequences of SFAS No. 2," *Journal of Accounting Research* 30 (1992): 156–164; E. Eccher, "Discussion of the Value Relevance of Intangibles: The Case of Software Capitalization," *Journal of Accounting Research* 36 (1998): 193–198; B. Lev and T. Sougiannis, "The Capitalization, Amortization, and Value-Relevance of R&D," *Journal of Accounting and Economics* 21 (1996): 107–138; and D. Aboody and B. Lev, "The Value-Relevance of Intangibles: The Case of Software Capitalization" (working paper, University of California, 1998).

11. See Lufthansa, Annual Report 2009 (Cologne, Germany: Deutsche Lufthansa AG, 2010) and Air France-KLM 2009–10 Reference Document (Paris, France: Air France-KLM, 2010).

12. Lufthansa, Annual Report 2009 (Cologne, Germany: Deutsche Lufthansa AG, 2010).

13. M. Barth and M. McNichols discuss ways for investors to estimate the value of environmental liabilities. See "Estimation and Market Valuation of Environmental Liabilities Relating to Superfund Sites," *Journal of Accounting Research* 32, Supplement, 1994.

14. When a firm records a capital lease, the Long-Term Tangible Asset equals the Long-Term Debt only at inception. Thereafter, the two numbers are unequal because the asset is reduced by depreciation expense while the debt is reduced by the lease payment net of interest expense. For most companies it is not possible to learn the book value of the asset, requiring the analyst to record the asset at the same value as the debt.

APPENDIX A Recasting Financial Statements into Standardized Templates

The following tables show the financial statements for The TJX Companies, Inc. for the year ended January 2011, both as reported by the company and as standardized using the classifications discussed in this chapter. The first column in each reported financial statement presents the classifications that are used for each line item to standardize the statements. Note that the classifications are not applied to subtotal lines such as Total current assets or Net income. The recast financial statements for TJX are prepared by simply totalling the balances of line items with the same standard classifications. For example, on the balance sheet there are two line items classified as *Other Current Assets – Prepaid expenses and other current assets* and *Current deferred income taxes, net*.

The TJX Companies, Inc. Reported Consolidated Balance Sheet
(In thousands)

Fiscal Year Ended		January 29, 2011	January 30, 2010
Classifications:	**Assets**		
	Current assets:		
Cash and Marketable Securities	Cash and cash equivalents	$1,741,751	$1,614,607
Cash and Marketable Securities	Short-term investments	76,261	130,636
Accounts Receivable	Accounts receivable, net	200,147	148,126
Inventory	Merchandise inventories	2,765,464	2,532,318
Other Current Assets	Prepaid expenses and other current assets	249,832	255,707
Other Current Assets	Current deferred income taxes, net	66,072	122,462
	Total current assets	5,099,527	4,803,856
	Property at cost:		
Long-Term Tangible Assets	Land and buildings	320,633	281,527
Long-Term Tangible Assets	Leasehold costs and improvements	2,112,151	1,930,977
Long-Term Tangible Assets	Furniture, fixtures and equipment	3,256,446	3,087,419
	Total property at cost	5,689,230	5,299,923
Long-Term Tangible Assets	Less accumulated depreciation and amortization	3,239,429	3,026,041
	Net property at cost	2,449,801	2,273,882
Long-Term Tangible Assets	Property under capital lease, net of accumulated amortization of $21,591 and $19,357, respectively	10,981	13,215
Other Long-Term Assets	Other assets	231,518	193,230
Long-Term Intangible Assets	Goodwill and trademark, net of amortization	179,936	179,794
	Total assets	**$ 7,971,763**	**$ 7,463,977**
	Liabilities		
	Current liabilities:		
Short-Term Debt	Obligation under capital lease due within one year	$ 2,727	$ 2,355
Accounts Payable	Accounts payable	1,683,929	1,507,892
Other Current Liabilities	Accrued expenses and other current liabilities	1,347,951	1,248,002
Other Current Liabilities	Federal, foreign, and state income taxes payable	98,514	136,737
	Total current liabilities	3,133,121	2,894,986
Other Long-Term Liabilities	Other long-term liabilities	709,321	697,099

(continued)

Fiscal Year Ended		January 29, 2011	January 30, 2010
Deferred Taxes	Non-current deferred income taxes, net	241,905	192,447
Long-Term Debt	Obligation under capital lease, less portion due within one year	13,117	15,844
Long-Term Debt	Long-term debt, exclusive of current installments	774,400	774,325
Other Long-Term Liabilities	Commitments and contingencies	–	–
	Shareholders' equity		
Common Shareholders' Equity	Common stock, authorized 1,200,000,000 shares, par value $1, issued and out-standing 389, 657, 340, and 409,386,126 respectively	389,657	409,386
Common Shareholders' Equity	Additional paid in capital	–	–
Common Shareholders' Equity	Accumulated other compre-hensive income (loss)	(91,755)	(134,124)
Common Shareholders' Equity	Retained earnings	2,801,997	2,614,014
	Total shareholders' equity	3,099,899	2,889,276
	Total liabilities and shareholders' equity	$ 7,971,763	$ 7,463,977

Source: The TJX Companies, Inc. SEC 10-K filed March 30, 2011.

The TJX Companies, Inc. Reported Consolidated Statements of Income
(in thousands)

Fiscal Year Ended		January 29, 2011	January 30, 2010	January 31, 2009
Classifications:				(53 weeks)
Sales	Net sales	$ 21,942,193	$ 20,288,444	$ 18,999,505
Cost of Sales	Cost of sales, including buying and occupancy costs	16,040,461	14,968,429	14,429,185
SG&A	Selling, general and administrative expenses	3,710,053	3,328,944	3,135,589
Other Operating Expense	Provision (credit) for computer intru-sion related costs	(11,550)	–	(30,500)

(continued)

The TJX Companies, Inc. Reported Consolidated Statements of Income
(in thousands)

Fiscal Year Ended		January 29, 2011	January 30, 2010	January 31, 2009
Net Interest Expense (Income)	Interest expense, net	39,137	39,509	14,291
	Income from continuing Operations before provision for income taxes	2,164,092	1,951,562	1,450,940
Tax Expense	Provision for income taxes	824,562	737,990	536,054
	Income from continuing Operations	1,339,530	1,213,572	914,886
Unusual Gains, Net of Unusual Losses	Gain (loss) from discontinued operations, net of income taxes	3,611	–	(34,269)
	Net income	$ 1,343,141	$ 1,213,572	$ 880,617

Source: The TJX Companies, Inc. SEC 10-K filed March 30, 2011.

The TJX Companies, Inc. Reported Consolidated Statements of Cash Flows
(in thousands)

Fiscal Year Ended		January 29, 2011	January 30, 2010	January 31, 2009
Classifications:				
	Cash flows from operating activities:			
Net Income	Net income Adjustments to reconcile net income to net cash provided by operating activities:	$1,343,141	$1,213,572	$880,617
Long-Term Operating Accruals – Depreciation and Amortization	Depreciation and amortization	458,052	435,218	401,707
Long-Term Operating Accruals – Other	Assets of discontinued operations sold	–	–	31,328
Long-Term Operating Accruals – Other	Loss on property disposals and impairment charges	96,073	10,270	23,903

(continued)

Fiscal Year Ended		January 29, 2011	January 30, 2010	January 31, 2009
Long-Term Operating Accruals – Other	Deferred income tax Provision	50,641	53,155	132,480
Long-Term Operating Accruals – Other	Share-based compensation	58,804	55,145	51,229
Long-Term Operating Accruals – Other	Excess tax benefits from share-based compensation	(28,095)	(17,494)	(18,879)
	Changes in assets and liabilities:			
Net (Investments in) or Liquidation of Operating Working Capital	(Increase) in accounts Receivable	(23,587)	(1,862)	(8,245)
Net (Investments in) or Liquidation of Operating Working Capital	Decrease (increase) in Merchandise inventories	(211,823)	147,805	(68,489)
Net (Investments in) or Liquidation of Operating Working Capital	Decrease (increase) in prepaid expenses and other current assets	495	21,219	(118,830)
Net (Investments in) or Liquidation of Operating Working Capital	Increase (decrease) in accounts payable	163,823	197,496	(141,580)
Net (Investments in) or Liquidation of Operating Working Capital	Increase (decrease) in accrued expenses and other liabilities	77,846	31,046	(34,525)
Net (Investments in) or Liquidation of Operating Working Capital	(Decrease) increase in income taxes payable	(11,801)	152,851	(10,488)
Long-Term Operating Accruals – Other	Other	2,912	(26,495)	34,344
	Net cash provided by operating activities	$ 1,976,481	$ 2,271,926	$ 1,154,572
	Cash flow from investing activities:			
Net (Investments in) or Liquidation of Operating Long-Term Assets	Property additions	(707,134)	(429,282)	(582,932)

(*continued*)

The TJX Companies, Inc. Reported Consolidated Statements of Cash Flows
(in thousands)

Fiscal Year Ended		January 29, 2011	January 30, 2010	January 31, 2009
Net (Investments in) or Liquidation of Operating Long-Term Assets	Proceeds to settle net investment hedges	–	–	14,379
Net (Investments in) or Liquidation of Operating Long-Term Assets	Purchase of short-term investments	(119,530)	(278,692)	–
Net (Investments in) or Liquidation of Operating Long-Term Assets	Sales and maturities of short-term investments	180,116	153,275	–
Net (Investments in) or Liquidation of Operating Long-Term Assets	Other	(1,065)	(5,578)	(34)
	Net cash (used in) investing activities	$ (647,613)	$ (560,277)	$ (568,587)
	Cash flows from financing activities:			
Net Debt (Repayment) or Issuance	Proceeds from issuance of long-term debt	–	774,263	–
Net Debt (Repayment) or Issuance	Principal payments on current portion of long-term debt	–	(393,573)	–
Net Debt (Repayment) or Issuance	Cash payments for debt issuance expenses	(3,118)	(7,202)	–
Net Debt (Repayment) or Issuance	Payments on capital lease obligation	(2,355)	(2,174)	(2,008)
Net Stock (Repurchase) or Issuance	Cash payments for repurchase of common stock	(1,193,380)	(944,762)	(751,097)
Net Stock (Repurchase) or Issuance	Proceeds from issuance of common stock	176,159	169,862	142,154
Net Stock (Repurchase) or Issuance	Excess tax benefits from share-based compensation	28,095	17,494	18,879
Dividend (payments)	Cash dividends paid	(229,329)	(197,662)	(176,749)
	Net cash (used in) financing activities	$ (1,223,928)	$ (583,754)	$ (768,821)
Non-operating Losses (Gains)	Effect of exchange rate changes on cash	22,204	33,185	(96,249)

(continued)

Fiscal Year Ended		January 29, 2011	January 30, 2010	January 31, 2009
	Net increase (decrease) in cash and cash equivalents	127,144	1,161,080	(279,085)
	Cash and cash equivalents at beginning of year	1,614,607	453,527	732,612
	Cash and cash equivalents at end of year	$ 1,741,751	$ 1,614,607	$ 453,527

Source: The TJX Companies, Inc. SEC 10-K filed March 30, 2011.

TJX Standardized Consolidated Balance Sheet
(in thousands)

Fiscal Year Ended	January 29, 2011	January 30, 2010
ASSETS		
Cash and Marketable Securities	$1,818,012	$1,745,243
Accounts Receivable	200,147	148,126
Inventory	2,765,464	2,532,318
Other Current Assets	315,904	378,169
Total Current Assets	5,099,527	4,803,856
Long-Term Tangible Assets	2,460,782	2,287,097
Long-Term Intangible Assets	179,936	179,794
Other Long-Term Assets	231,518	193,230
Total Long-Term Assets	2,872,236	2,660,121
Total Assets	$ 7,971,763	$ 7,463,977
LIABILITIES		
Accounts Payable	$1,683,929	$1,507,892
Short-Term Debt	2,727	2,355
Other Current Liabilities	1,446,465	1,384,739
Total Current Liabilities	3,133,121	2,894,986
Long-Term Debt	787,517	790,169
Deferred Taxes	241,905	192,447
Other Long-Term Liabilities	709,321	697,099
Total Long-Term Liabilities	1,738,743	1,679,715
Total Liabilities	$ 4,871,864	$ 4,574,701
Minority Interest	–	–
SHAREHOLDER'S EQUITY		
Preferred Stock	–	–
Common Shareholder's Equity	3,099,899	2,889,276
Total Shareholders' Equity	3,099,899	2,889,276
Total Liabilities and Shareholders' Equity	$ 7,971,763	$ 7,463,977

TJX Standardized Consolidated Statements of Income
(In thousands)

Fiscal Year Ended	January 29, 2011	January 30, 2010	January 31, 2009
Sales	$21,942,193	$20,288,444	$18,999,505
Cost of sales	16,040,461	14,968,429	14,429,185
Gross profit	5,901,732	5,320,015	4,570,320
SG&A	3,710,053	3,328,944	3,135,589
Other operating expense	(11,550)	–	(30,500)
Operating income	2,203,229	1,991,071	1,465,231
Net interest expense (income)	39,137	39,509	14,291
Pre-tax income	2,164,092	1,951,562	1,450,940
Tax expense	824,562	737,990	536,054
Unusual gains, net of unusual losses	3,611	–	(34,269)
Net income	$ 1,343,141	$ 1,213,572	$ 880,617

TJX Standardized Consolidated Statements of Cash Flows
(In thousands)

Fiscal Year Ended	January 29, 2011	January 30, 2010	January 31, 2009
Cash Flows from Operating Activities			
Net Income	$1,343,141	$1,213,572	$880,617
After-tax interest expense (income)	24,200	26,120	9,020
Non-operating Losses (Gains)	22,204	33,185	(96,249)
Long-term operating accruals	638,387	509,799	656,112
Depreciation and Amortization	458,052	435,218	401,707
Other	180,335	74,581	254,405
Operating cash flow before working capital investments	2,027,932	1,782,676	1,449,500
Net (Investments in) or Liquidation of Operating Working Capital	(5,047)	548,555	(382,157)
Operating cash flow before investment in long-term assets	2,022,885	2,331,231	1,067,343
Cash Flows Used for Investing Activities			
Net (Investments in) or Liquidation of Operating Long-term Assets	(647,613)	(560,277)	(568,587)
Free cash flow available to debt and equity	1,375,272	1,770,954	498,756
Cash Flows from (used for) Financing Activities			
After-tax net interest (expense) income	(24,200)	(26,120)	(9,020)

(continued)

Fiscal Year Ended	January 29, 2011	January 30, 2010	January 31, 2009
Net Debt (Repayment) or Issuance	(5,473)	371,314	(2,008)
Free cash flow available to equity	1,345,599	2,116,148	487,728
Dividend (payments)	(229,329)	(197,662)	(176,749)
Net Stock (Repurchase) or Issuance	(989,126)	(757,406)	(590,064)
Net increase (decrease) in cash	127,144	1,161,080	(279,085)

Note: The cash flow statement shows the cash flows from operating activities attributable to all capital providers (debt and equity). Consequently, Net after-tax interest expense (income) is added back to Net Income in the Operating cash flow segment and reported in the Financing segment. Net after-tax interest expense (income) is Net interest expense (income) × (1 − Average tax rate).

APPENDIX B Nordstrom, Inc. Operating Lease Adjustment

To estimate the value of Nordstrom's operating lease assets and liabilities, we use footnote information on the future minimum operating lease payments provided by Nordstrom in the financial statement footnotes included in its 2010 10-K. For the years ending January 29, 2011, and January 30, 2010, these amounts were as follows:

Year ended (in thousands)	January 29, 2011	January 30, 2010
Less than 1 year	$ 111	$ 98
1-2 years	108	101
2-3 years	100	89
3-4 years	96	82
4-5 years	92	78
More than 5 years	524	406
Total	$ 1,031	$ 854

Whereas in the TJX adjustment shown earlier in the chapter TJX provides an estimate of the net present value of its minimum future lease obligations, Nordstrom does not provide such an estimate. However, using Nordstrom's reported average interest rate on its long-term debt of 6.3 percent, and estimating an average lease term of 18 years using data on general lease terms given in the 10-K, we can estimate the present value of Nordstrom's minimum lease obligations for the year ended January 29, 2011, as $685 million and for the year ended January 30, 2010, as $578 million.[15] With those estimates, we can now make the following adjustments to Nordstrom's beginning and ending balance sheets and to its income statement for the year ended January 29, 2011:

1. Capitalize the estimated net present value of the minimum lease obligations as of January 30, 2010, increasing Long-Term Tangible Assets and Long-Term Debt by $578 million.
2. Calculate the value of any change in lease assets and lease liabilities during the year from new lease transactions or terminations. On January 30, 2010, the estimated present value of Nordstrom's liability for operating lease commitments in 2011

[15]The net present value of Nordstrom's reported future operating lease obligation is calculated using 6.3 percent as a discount rate, which represents the average of Nordstrom's long-term debt at the time, and an 18 year assumed average lease term. The first 5 years are discounted by year as reported, with the remaining obligation (reported as a lump sum due beyond year 5) spread on a straight line basis across years 6–18 and discounted.

and beyond was $578 million. During 2010, the company expected to repay $98 million (as per the schedule above), comprising $36.4 million of interest (6.3 percent of $578 million) and the remaining $61.6 million as retirement of the lease liability. If there had been no new lease commitments added during the year, the operating lease liability on January 29, 2011, would therefore have been $516.4 million ($578 million − $61.6 million). Yet Nordstrom's actual lease commitment on January 29, 2011, was $685 million, indicating that it increased its leased store capacity by $168.6 million. Nordstrom's Long-Term Tangible Assets and Long-Term Debt therefore increased by $168.6 million during 2010 as a result of net new lease commitments.

3. Record the change in lease asset value and expense from depreciation during the year. Using an eighteen-year life and straight-line depreciation, the depreciation expense for 2010 (included in Cost of Sales) is $36.8 million {[$578 m + ($168.6 m/2)]/18}.
4. Add back the lease expense in the income statement, included in Cost of Sales, and apportion the payment between Interest Expense and repayment of Long-Term Debt. As previously mentioned, the lease expense is $98 million. As noted above, this reflects $36.4 million ($578 m × 6.3 percent) that is shown as Interest Expense and the remaining $61.6 million is allocated toward retiring the total operating lease liability.
5. Make changes to the Deferred Tax Liability to reflect differences in earnings under the capital and operating methods. If it capitalizes operating leases, Nordstrom's expenses are $73.2 million ($36.8 million depreciation expense plus $36.4 million interest expense) versus $98 million under the operating method, a difference of $24.8 million. Nordstrom will not change its tax books, but for financial reporting purposes it will show higher earnings before tax and thus a higher Tax Expense through deferred taxes. Given a corporate tax rate of 35 percent, Tax Expense will increase by $8.7 million ($24.8 million × .35) and the Deferred Tax Liability will increase by the same amount for the year ended January 29, 2011.

In summary, the adjustments to Nordstrom's financial statements on January 30, 2010, and January 29, 2011, are as follows:

($ Billions)	Adjustment January 29, 2011 Assets	Liabilities & Equity	Adjustment January 30, 2010 Assets	Liabilities & Equity
Balance Sheet				
Long-term tangible assets	(1) +578.0 (2) +168.6 (3) −36.8		(1) +578.0	
Long-term debt		(1) +578.0 (2) +168.6 (4) −61.6		(1) +578.0
Deferred taxes		(5) +8.7		
Shareholders' equity		+16.1		
Income Statement				
Cost of sales		(3) +36.8 (4) −98.0		
Net interest expense		(4) +36.4		
Tax expense		(5) +8.7		
Total increase in expense		−16.1		
Net Income		+16.1		

As noted in the TJX example above, we will be examining the impact of these adjustments in the next chapter.

Chapter 5

FINANCIAL ANALYSIS

The goal of financial analysis is to assess the performance of a firm in the context of its stated goals and strategy. There are two principal tools of financial analysis: ratio analysis and cash flow analysis. Ratio analysis involves an assessment of how various line items in a firm's financial statements relate to one another. Cash flow analysis allows the analyst to examine the firm's liquidity and to assess the management of operating, investment, and financing cash flows.

Financial analysis is used in a variety of contexts. Ratio analysis that compares a company's present performance to its past performance and/or to the performance of its peers provides the foundation for making forecasts of future performance. As we will discuss in later chapters, financial forecasting is useful in company valuation, credit evaluation, financial distress prediction, security analysis, and mergers and acquisitions analysis.

RATIO ANALYSIS

The value of a firm is determined by its profitability and growth. As shown in Figure 5-1, the firm's growth and profitability are influenced by its product market and financial market strategies. The product market strategy is implemented through the firm's competitive strategy, operating policies, and investment decisions. Financial market strategies are implemented through financing and dividend policies.

Thus, the four levers managers can use to achieve their growth and profit targets are (1) operating management, (2) investment management, (3) financing strategy, and (4) dividend policy. The objective of ratio analysis is to evaluate the effectiveness of the firm's policies in each of these areas. Effective ratio analysis involves relating the financial numbers to the underlying business factors in as much detail as possible. While ratio analysis may not give an analyst all the answers regarding the firm's performance, it will help the analyst frame questions for further probing.

In ratio analysis, the analyst can (1) compare ratios for a firm over several years (a time-series comparison), (2) compare ratios for the firm and other firms in the industry (cross-sectional comparison), and/or (3) compare ratios to some absolute benchmark. In a time-series comparison, the analyst can hold firm-specific factors constant and examine the effectiveness of a firm's strategy over time. Cross-sectional comparison facilitates examining the relative performance of a firm within its industry, holding industry-level factors constant. For most ratios there are no absolute benchmarks. The exceptions

FIGURE 5-1   Drivers of a Firm's Profitability and Growth

Source: © Cengage Learning

are measures of rates of return, which can be compared to the cost of the capital associated with the investment. For example, subject to distortions caused by accounting, the rate of return on equity (ROE) can be compared to the cost of equity capital. In the discussion below, we will illustrate two of these approaches using the examples of TJX and Nordstrom, the retailers introduced in Chapter 2. As we discussed in Chapter 2, TJX is an off-price competitor that pursues a cost-leadership strategy. Nordstrom has established itself as a high-end competitor that pursues a differentiation strategy by providing superior customer service and broad, differentiated merchandise selection. Our comparison will allow us to examine the impact of these two strategies on the financial ratios of the companies.

In addition to pursuing different competitive strategies, TJX and Nordstrom also follow very different strategies when it comes to financing their stores. TJX leases virtually all of its stores using off–balance sheet operating leases. In contrast, while Nordstrom also utilizes operating leases to some extent, the company owns at least a portion of more than two-thirds of its store square footage (land, buildings, or both), and finances the owned portion with long term debt. These financing strategies impact many of the ratios that we will calculate in this chapter.

In order to fully explore the above choices made by the two companies, we will focus in on two types of cross-sectional comparison—comparing TJX and Nordstrom's ratios for the fiscal year ending January 29, 2011, both on an "As Reported" and "As Adjusted" basis, with the adjustments in the second comparison taking into account the differing use of off–balance sheet operating leases mentioned above. Comparison of TJX with Nordstrom on an "As Reported" basis allows us to see the impact of the different strategic, financial, and operational decisions on the financial ratios of the two companies. Comparison on an "As Adjusted" basis removes the distortion caused by the differing magnitude of their operating lease usage so that we can more clearly compare their true operating performance.

While in certain cases companies being compared will make differing strategic choices that strongly impact their financial performance and ratios, the analyst will not always choose to make adjustments to their financials in order to compare them. In the comparison of TJX and Nordstrom, a major difference between the competitors relates to how each executes its branded credit card offering. TJX has chosen to outsource its credit card operations, giving up operational control and potential earnings but also insulating itself from potential losses due to bad debt. Nordstrom, on the other hand, views its in-house credit card operations as a strategic advantage and part of its broader strategy of providing superior customer service. The result of these business decisions is seen primarily in Nordstrom's much higher accounts receivables balance as compared to TJX, and impacts many of the ratio calculations that we will discuss later in this chapter. Given that Nordstrom views this segment as an integral part of its operations, we choose not to remove it when comparing Nordstrom to TJX. However, it pays to be aware of the choices being made here and to understand the resultant impact on any comparative analysis, and as such we highlight this impact in the ratio analysis where appropriate.

As a final consideration, it is important to ensure that the financial statements of the company being analyzed do not include any additional data that will distort the analysis. Since the purpose of financial statement analysis is to better understand the performance of the firm as it relates to its strategy, care needs to be taken that any operations and events that are extraneous to that strategy do not change the picture that the analyst forms of the firm. The major categories of such distortions include one-time write-offs of assets and results from discontinued operations, including the gain or loss on the disposal of such operations. In such instances, it is useful to look at financial results of the core operations of the firm by adjusting the presented financial statements to exclude the impact of one-time effects. For example, TJX sold its interest in Bob's Stores in 2008. As a result, its 2008 income statement contains a $34 million loss on the discontinued operations. Without adjusting for this effect it would have been difficult to meaningfully use TJX's 2008 results as a benchmark for performance in 2009 and beyond, or to compare it to a competitor such as Nordstrom. For the same reason, we have excluded a $3.6 million gain due to discontinued operations for TJX in 2010, with this adjustment being included in the "As Adjusted" financial statements for TJX.

In order to facilitate replication of the ratio calculations presented below, we present in the appendix to this chapter two versions of the 2010 financial statements of TJX and Nordstrom.[1] The first set of financial statements is presented in the standardized format described in Chapter 4. These "Standardized" financial statements put both companies' reported financials in one standard format to facilitate direct comparison.[2] The second, "Condensed" financial statements recast the standardized financial statements to facilitate the calculation of several ratios discussed in the chapter. We will discuss later in the chapter how this recasting process works. These two statement formats are presented on both an "As Reported" and "As Adjusted" basis as described above.

Measuring Overall Profitability

The starting point for a systematic analysis of a firm's performance is its return on equity (ROE), defined as

$$\text{ROE} = \frac{\text{Net income}}{\text{shareholders' equity}}$$

ROE is a comprehensive indicator of a firm's performance because it provides an indication of how well managers are employing the funds invested by the firm's

TABLE 5-1	Return of Equity for TJX and Nordstrom			
Year ended January 29, 2011	**As Reported**		**As Adjusted**	
	TJX	**Nordstrom**	**TJX**	**Nordstrom**
Return on Equity	46.5%	39.0%	55.4%	40.0%

Source: © Cengage Learning 2013

shareholders to generate returns. On average over the twenty-year period 1991–2010, publicly traded firms in the United States generated ROEs of a little over 10 percent.[3]

In the long run, the value of the firm's equity is determined by the relationship between its ROE and its cost of equity capital.[4] That is, those firms that are expected over the long run to generate ROEs in excess of the cost of equity capital should have market values in excess of book value, and vice versa. (We will return to this point in more detail in Chapters 7 and 8.)

A comparison of ROE with the cost of capital is useful not only for analyzing the value of the firm but also in considering the path of future profitability. The generation of consistent supernormal profitability will, absent significant barriers to entry, attract competition. For that reason ROEs tend over time to be driven by competitive forces toward a "normal" level—the cost of equity capital. Thus, one can think of the cost of equity capital as establishing a benchmark for the ROE that would be observed in a long-run competitive equilibrium. Deviations from this level arise for two general reasons. One is the industry conditions and competitive strategy that cause a firm to generate supernormal (or subnormal) economic profits, at least over the short run. The second is distortions due to accounting.

Table 5-1 shows the ROE based on reported and adjusted earnings for TJX and Nordstrom.

TJX outperformed Nordstrom in 2010, which on the surface is perhaps not surprising given that the difficult financial climate at the time tended to favor discount retailers. While Nordstrom's unadjusted ROE of 39.0 percent trails the 46.5 percent earned by TJX in 2010, the performance of both companies exceeded both historical trends of ROE in the economy and reasonable estimates of the cost of equity capital for the firms.[5] When ROE is calculated using adjusted financials the differential grows significantly, reflecting the greater impact of the adjustment to TJX due to its much larger use of operating leases. We will examine the drivers behind these adjustments as we deconstruct ROE below.

TJX's superior profitability performance relative to Nordstrom is reflected in the difference between the market value of equity to book value ratios for the two firms. As we will discuss in Chapter 7, ROE is a key determinant of a company's market to book ratio. As of January 29, 2011, which represented the end of both companies' fiscal year 2010, TJX's market to book ratio was 6.0 and Nordstrom's ratio was 4.4. This differential in market valuation could be an indication that investors expected TJX to continue to outperform Nordstrom in the coming years and to earn a superior return for its shareholders.

Decomposing Profitability: Traditional Approach

A company's ROE is affected by two factors: how profitably it employs its assets and how big the firm's asset base is relative to shareholders' investment. To understand the effect of these two factors, ROE can be decomposed into return on assets (ROA) and a measure of financial leverage, as follows:

$$\textbf{ROE} = \textbf{ROA} \times \textbf{Financial leverage}$$
$$= \frac{\text{Net income}}{\text{Assets}} \times \frac{\text{Assets}}{\text{Shareholders' equity}}$$

ROA tells us how much profit a company is able to generate for each dollar of assets invested. Financial leverage indicates how many dollars of assets the firm is able to deploy for each dollar invested by its shareholders.

The return on assets itself can be decomposed into a product of two factors:

$$\text{ROA} = \frac{\text{Net income}}{\text{Sales}} \times \frac{\text{Sales}}{\text{Assets}}$$

The ratio of net income to sales is called net profit margin or return on sales (ROS); the ratio of sales to assets is known as asset turnover. The profit margin ratio indicates how much the company is able to keep as profits for each dollar of sales it makes. Asset turnover indicates how many sales dollars the firm is able to generate for each dollar of its assets.

Table 5-2 displays the three drivers of ROE for our retail firms: net profit margins, asset turnover, and financial leverage. In comparing TJX to Nordstrom on an As Reported basis, a significantly higher asset turnover is key to explaining how TJX, even with a slightly lower net profit margin and a much lower financial leverage than Nordstrom, was able to post an overall higher return on equity of 46.5 percent against 39.0 percent for Nordstrom in FY 2010.

This preliminary decomposition of ROE begins to show us how an examination of the building blocks of these ratios can yield a deeper understanding of how strategic, investment, and financing decisions made by the firm affect its ratios. For instance, in noting that higher asset turnover is a key driver of TJX's higher ROE when compared to Nordstrom, an analyst would recall TJX's decision to outsource its credit card operations (resulting in a much lower Accounts Receivable balance when compared to Nordstrom, who maintains its credit card operations in house), and TJX's more extensive use of off–balance sheet operating leases to finance its stores (which reduces both overall reported asset and debt level). While adjusting for the operating lease impact for both firms brings the asset turnover of TJX closer to that of Nordstrom, the difference in credit card strategies continues to drive a higher ROA for TJX. The greatly increased ROE for TJX of 55.4 percent on an As Adjusted basis is the result primarily of increased financial leverage resulting from the addition of long-term debt to TJX's balance sheet as part of the operating lease adjustment. Finally, the higher adjusted ROS for TJX is the result of lower current expense incurred as a result of the operating lease adjustment.

TABLE 5-2	Traditional Decomposition of ROE			
Year ended January 29, 2011	As Reported		As Adjusted	
	TJX	Nordstrom	TJX	Nordstrom
Net profit margin (ROS)	6.1%	6.3%	7.3%	6.5%
× Asset turnover	2.94	1.47	1.84	1.36
= Return on assets (ROA)	18.0%	9.3%	13.4%	8.8%
× Financial leverage	2.58	4.19	4.12	4.55
= Return on equity (ROE)	46.5%	39.0%	55.4%	40.0%

Source: © Cengage Learning 2013

Decomposing Profitability: Alternative Approach

Even though the above approach is popularly used to decompose a firm's ROE, it has several limitations. In the computation of ROA, the denominator includes the assets claimed by all providers of capital to the firm, but the numerator includes only the earnings available to equity holders. The assets themselves include both operating assets and financial assets such as cash and short-term investments. Further, net income includes income from operating activities as well as interest income and expense, which are consequences of financing decisions. Often it is useful to distinguish between these two drivers of performance. Finally, the financial leverage ratio used above does not recognize the fact that a firm's cash and short-term investments are in essence "negative debt" because they can be used to pay down the debt on the company's balance sheet.[6] These issues are addressed by an alternative approach to decomposing ROE.[7]

Before discussing this alternative ROE decomposition approach, we define in Table 5-3 some terminology used in this section as well as in the rest of this chapter.

We use the terms defined above to recast the financial statements of TJX and Nordstrom. These recast financial statements, which are shown in the appendix as condensed statements, are used to decompose ROE in the following manner:

$$
\begin{aligned}
\text{ROE} &= \frac{\text{NOPAT}}{\text{Equity}} - \frac{(\text{Net interest expense after tax})}{\text{Equity}} \\[2mm]
&= \frac{\text{NOPAT}}{\text{Net assets}} \times \frac{\text{Net assets}}{\text{Equity}} - \frac{\text{Net interest expense after tax}}{\text{Net debt}} \times \frac{\text{Net debt}}{\text{Equity}} \\[2mm]
&= \frac{\text{NOPAT}}{\text{Net assets}} \times \left(1 + \frac{\text{Net debt}}{\text{Equity}}\right) - \frac{\text{Net interest expense after tax}}{\text{Net debt}} \times \frac{\text{Net debt}}{\text{Equity}} \\[2mm]
&= \text{Operating ROA} + (\text{Operating ROA} - \text{Effective interest rate after tax}) \\
&\quad \times \text{Net financial leverage} \\[2mm]
&= \text{Operating ROA} + \text{Spread} \times \text{Net financial leverage}
\end{aligned}
$$

Operating ROA is a measure of how profitably a company is able to deploy its operating assets to generate operating profits. This would be a company's ROE if it were financed

TABLE 5-3	Definitions of Accounting Items Used in Ratio Analysis
Item	**Definition**
Net interest expense after tax	(Interest expense − Interest income) × (1 − Tax rate)[a]
Net operating profit after taxes (NOPAT)	Net income + Net interest expense after tax
Operating working capital	(Current assets − Cash and marketable securities) − (Current liabilities − Short-term debt and current portion of long-term debt)
Net long-term assets	Total long-term assets − Non-interest-bearing long-term liabilities
Net debt	Total interest-bearing liabilities − Cash and marketable securities
Net assets	Operating working capital + Net long-term assets
Net capital	Net debt + Shareholders' equity

[a]The calculation of net interest expense treats interest expense and interest income as absolute values, independent of how these figures are reported in the income statement.
Source: © Cengage Learning 2013

entirely with equity. Spread is the incremental economic effect from introducing debt into the capital structure. This economic effect of borrowing is positive as long as the return on operating assets is greater than the cost of borrowing. Firms that do not earn adequate operating returns to pay for interest cost reduce their ROE by borrowing. Both the positive and negative effect is magnified by the extent to which a firm borrows relative to its equity base. The ratio of net debt to equity provides a measure of this net financial leverage. A firm's spread times its net financial leverage, therefore, provides a measure of the financial leverage gain to the shareholders.

Operating ROA can be further decomposed into NOPAT margin and operating asset turnover as follows:

$$\text{Operating ROA} = \frac{\text{NOPAT}}{\text{Sales}} \times \frac{\text{Sales}}{\text{Net assets}}$$

NOPAT margin is a measure of how profitable a company's sales are from an operating perspective. Operating asset turnover measures the extent to which a company is able to use its operating assets to generate sales.

Table 5-4 presents the alternative decomposition of ROE for TJX and Nordstrom. The ratios in this table show that on an As Reported basis TJX's 2010 operating ROA was almost four times higher than its traditional ROA, with 2010 operating ROA of 70.6 percent compared to traditional ROA of 18.0 percent. The difference between TJX's operating ROA and traditional ROA is driven by a much higher net operating asset turnover (11.33 in 2010) when compared to its traditionally defined asset turnover (2.94 in 2010) shown in Table 5-2—a result of TJX's large cash balance and use of non interest-bearing liabilities (such as accounts payable) to finance a significant portion of its net operating assets.

Nordstrom also had a higher As Reported operating ROA than traditional ROA (20.4 percent compared to 9.3 percent). While a higher net operating asset turnover as compared to traditional asset turnover (2.86 as compared to 1.47) was the primary driver of Nordstrom's higher operating ROA, a higher net operating profit margin as compared to traditional net profit margin (7.1 percent as compared to 6.3 percent) also was a factor.

Comparing the two firms on an As Reported basis, TJX's dramatically higher operating asset turnover as compared to Nordstrom's is driven (as was asset turnover discussed previously) by its relatively low net assets that result from its strategy of outsourcing its branded credit card (and thus not carrying a high accounts receivable balance) and leasing virtually all of its stores (thus carrying low net long-term assets relative to Nordstrom).

TABLE 5-4	**Distinguishing Operating and Financing Components in ROE Decomposition**			
Year ended January 29, 2011	As Reported		As Adjusted	
	TJX	Nordstrom	TJX	Nordstrom
Net operating profit margin	6.2%	7.1%	8.1%	7.5%
× Net operating asset turnover	11.33	2.86	3.44	2.44
= Operating ROA	70.6%	20.4%	27.8%	18.4%
Spread	73.1%	16.1%	22.8%	14.2%
× Net financial leverage	−0.33	1.16	1.21	1.52
= Financial leverage gain	−24.1%	18.6%	27.6%	21.6%
ROE = Operating ROA + Financial leverage gain	46.5%	39.0%	55.4%	40.0%

Source: © Cengage Learning 2013

Continuing on an As Reported basis, Nordstrom is able to create shareholder value through its financing strategy. In 2010, the spread between Nordstrom's operating ROA and its after-tax interest cost was 16.1 percent, and its net financial leverage (net debt as a percentage of equity) was 116 percent. These factors combined to contribute a financial leverage gain of 18.6 percent in 2010, which is the incremental difference between Nordstrom's operating ROA of 20.4 percent and its ROE of 39.0 percent.

TJX, on the other hand, while it had a 73.1 percent spread between operating ROA and its after-tax interest cost (which actually calculates at a negative rate due to its negative net debt position; that is, the company had more cash than debt), had a negative financial leverage gain resulting from that negative net debt position. As a result, its operating ROA at 70.6 percent is actually higher than its ROE of 46.5 percent in 2010. Remembering once more TJX's use of off–balance sheet financing for its stores (which results in TJX having artificially low reported financial leverage) will help the analyst understand the impact of that decision on the financing component of its ROE.

As noted above, TJX shows an adjusted ROE of 55.4 percent—a significant increase over its As Reported ROE of 46.5 percent, and well above Nordstrom's As Adjusted ROE of 40.0 percent (Nordstrom as a whole generally sees minor impact from the operating lease adjustment given its more limited use of operating leases). The impact of the operating lease adjustment can be seen most strongly in net operating asset turnover for TJX, which falls from 11.33 to 3.44 due to the greatly increased asset base, bringing operating ROA down from 70.6 percent to 27.8 percent. This in turn reduces the spread between TJX's operating ROA and after tax interest cost from 73.1 percent to 22.8 percent. Even so, the change in net financial leverage from −0.33 on an As Reported basis to 1.21 on an As Adjusted basis creates a positive financial leverage gain of 27.6 percent, as compared to a −24.1 percent gain on an As Reported basis. What this says is that TJX's use of additional leverage (as simulated with the adjustments made for the operating leases) has actually helped—through an increase in net operating profit margin, but primarily by reversing a negative financial leverage gain, to create additional shareholder return as seen in the higher As Adjusted ROE.

The appropriate benchmark for evaluating operating ROA is the weighted average cost of debt and equity capital, or WACC. In the long run, the value of a firm's assets is determined by how its operating ROA compares to this norm. Moreover, over the long run and absent some barrier to competitive forces, operating ROA will tend to be pushed toward the weighted average cost of capital. Since the WACC is typically lower than the cost of equity capital, operating ROA over time tends to be pushed to a level lower than that to which ROE tends. We will discuss further the use and calculation of the WACC in Chapter 8.

The average operating ROA for public firms in the United States in the twenty-year period 1991–2010 was 9 percent.[8] In 2010 both TJX and Nordstrom significantly exceeded this benchmark. The impressive operating performance of both firms would have been obscured by using the simple ROA measure.[9]

Assessing Operating Management: Decomposing Net Profit Margins

A firm's net profit margin, or return on sales (ROS), shows the profitability of the company's operating activities. Further decomposition of a firm's ROS allows an analyst to assess the efficiency of the firm's operating management. A popular tool used in this analysis is the common-sized income statement in which all the line items are expressed as a percentage of sales revenues.

Common-sized income statements make it possible to compare trends in income statement relationships over time for the firm and trends across different firms in the industry. To illustrate how the income statement analysis can be used, common-sized income

TABLE 5-5	Common-Sized Income Statement and Profitability Ratios			
Year ended January 29, 2011	As Reported		As Adjusted	
	TJX	**Nordstrom**	**TJX**	**Nordstrom**
Line Items as a Percent of Sales				
Sales	100.0%	100.0%	100.0%	100.0%
Cost of Sales	71.0%	57.4%	68.1%	56.8%
SG&A	16.9%	27.7%	16.9%	27.7%
Other operating expense	2.1%	3.4%	2.1%	3.4%
Other income, net of other expense	0.0%	0.0%	0.0%	0.0%
Net interest expense (income)	0.2%	1.3%	1.3%	1.7%
Tax expense	3.8%	3.9%	4.4%	4.0%
Unusual gains, net of unusual losses	0.0%[a]	0.0%	0.0%	0.0%
Net income	6.1%	6.3%	7.3%	6.5%
Key Profitability Ratios				
Gross profit margin	29.0%	42.6%	32.0%	43.2%
EBITDA margin	12.1%	14.9%	15.1%	15.5%
NOPAT margin	6.23%	7.13%	8.10%	7.53%
Recurring NOPAT margin	6.19%	7.13%	8.10%	7.53%

[a]This figure is rounded to zero although there was actually a gain of $3.6 million here (which is reflected in the difference in NOPAT and recurring NOPAT margin below).
Source: © Cengage Learning 2013

statements for TJX and Nordstrom are shown in Table 5-5. The table also shows some commonly used profitability ratios. We will use the information in Table 5-5 to investigate the drivers behind TJX and Nordstrom's net income margins (ROS) in 2010.

In this section we focus primarily on an analysis of As Reported numbers. As can be seen in Table 5-5, the operating lease adjustment results in revised As Adjusted numbers for both companies, with TJX showing the larger change due to its greater use of operating leases. The impact of the adjustment is straightforward on the income statement, in that both companies show an increase in profitability metrics (gross profit, EBITDA, NOPAT, and ROS) due to a lower cost of goods sold (due to the depreciation component of COGS being only a portion of the previously utilized lease expense), and show increased interest expense (due to the added debt component) and tax expense (due to higher net income). We will point out a few of the more interesting results of the adjustment where warranted.

Gross Profit Margins

The difference between a firm's sales and cost of sales is gross profit. Gross profit margin is an indication of the extent to which revenues exceed direct costs associated with sales, and it is computed as

$$\text{Gross profit margin} = \frac{\text{Sales} - \text{Cost of sales}}{\text{Sales}}$$

Gross margin is influenced by two factors: (1) the price premium that a firm's products or services command in the marketplace and (2) the efficiency of the firm's procurement and production process. The price premium a firm's products or services can command is influenced by the degree of competition and the extent to which its products are unique. The firm's cost of sales can be low when it can purchase its inputs at a lower cost than competitors and/or run its production processes more efficiently. This is generally the case when a firm has a low-cost strategy.

Table 5-5 indicates that consistent with Nordstrom's premium price strategy, its gross margin on an As Reported basis of 42.6 percent in 2010 was significantly higher than that of TJX.

Selling, General, and Administrative Expenses

A company's selling, general, and administrative (SG&A) expenses are influenced by the operating activities it has to undertake to implement its competitive strategy. As discussed in Chapter 2, firms with differentiation strategies have to undertake activities to achieve that differentiation. A company competing on the basis of quality and rapid introduction of new products is likely to have higher R&D costs relative to a company competing purely on a cost basis. Similarly, a company that attempts to build a brand image, distribute its products through full-service retailers, and provide significant customer service is likely to have higher selling and administration costs relative to a company that sells through warehouse retailers or direct mail and does not provide much customer support.

A company's SG&A expenses are also influenced by the efficiency with which it manages its overhead activities. The control of operating expenses is likely to be especially important for firms competing on the basis of low cost. However, even for differentiators, it is important to assess whether the cost of differentiation is commensurate with the price premium earned in the marketplace.

Several ratios in Table 5-5 allow us to evaluate the effectiveness with which TJX and Nordstrom manage their SG&A expenses. First, the ratio of SG&A expense to sales shows how much a company is spending to generate each sales dollar. We see that TJX has a significantly lower ratio of SG&A to sales than does Nordstrom. This should not be surprising given that TJX pursues a low-cost strategy whereas Nordstrom pursues an intensively customer-service-focused strategy. Given that TJX and Nordstrom are pursuing radically different pricing, merchandising, and service strategies, it is not surprising that they have very different cost structures: TJX's lower gross margins and lower SG&A to sales are reflective of its low cost strategy, while Nordstrom's higher margins and also higher SG&A expenses reflect its focus on providing a high service, differentiated offering to more affluent customers. A key question is, when both these costs are netted out, which company performed better? Two ratios provide useful signals here: net operating profit margin (NOPAT margin) and EBITDA margin:

$$\text{NOPAT margin} = \frac{\text{NOPAT}}{\text{Sales}}$$

$$\text{EBITDA margin} = \frac{\text{Earnings before interest, taxes, depreciation, and amortization}}{\text{Sales}}$$

NOPAT margin provides a comprehensive indication of the operating performance of a company because it reflects all operating costs and eliminates the effects of debt policy. EBITDA margin provides similar information, except that it excludes depreciation and amortization expense, a significant non-cash operating expense. Some analysts prefer to use EBITDA margin because they believe that it focuses on "cash" operating items. While this is to some extent true, it can be potentially misleading for two reasons. EBITDA is not a strictly cash concept because sales, cost of sales, and SG&A expenses often include non-cash items. Also, depreciation is a real operating expense, and it reflects to some extent the consumption of resources. Therefore, ignoring it can be misleading.

Table 5-5 shows that TJX was able to earn 6.2 cents in operating profits out of every dollar of sales it generated, whereas Nordstrom earned 7.1 cents per sales dollar. It is interesting to note that on an As Adjusted basis TJX actually earns a higher operating profit to sales than Nordstrom.

Recall that in Table 5-3 we define NOPAT as net income plus net interest expense after tax. Therefore, NOPAT is influenced by any unusual or non-operating income (expense) items included in net income. We can calculate a "recurring" NOPAT margin by eliminating these items. Nordstrom's recurring and traditional NOPAT margins are the same, indicating no unusual or non-operating income or expense items impacting net income in 2010. For TJX as well the major portion of its profits came from its core business. TJX's recurring NOPAT margin is slightly lower than its traditional NOPAT margin in 2010 (6.19 percent compared to 6.23 percent) due to the small gain on discontinued operations in 2010 (mentioned at the beginning of the chapter) related to the reduction of a reserve related to settling lease-related obligations of former businesses.[10] While in this particular example there was only a minor difference between recurring and traditional NOPAT margin, in general, recurring NOPAT may be a better benchmark to use when extrapolating current performance into the future since it reflects margins from the core business activities of a firm, especially if in the particular years analyzed the firm generated significant income from non-core or discontinued operations. The alternate approach that we take, of course, is to adjust the financials to remove this non-recurring item entirely as we do in As Adjusted numbers.

Nordstrom also has a better EBITDA margin than TJX on an As Reported basis, although the difference narrows when comparing As Adjusted numbers, since on an As Reported basis TJX's use of operating leases results in much higher leasing expense, which is included in EBITDA, while Nordstrom's higher depreciation expense resulting from its store ownership strategy is excluded.

Tax Expense

Taxes are an important element of a firm's total expenses. Through a wide variety of tax planning techniques, firms can attempt to reduce their tax expenses.[11] There are two measures one can use to evaluate a firm's tax expense. One is the ratio of tax expense to sales, and the other is the ratio of tax expense to earnings before taxes (also known as the average tax rate). The firm's tax footnote provides a detailed account of why its average tax rate differs from the statutory tax rate.

Table 5-5 shows that Nordstrom had a slightly higher income tax expense as a percent of sales than TJX. Given that the two companies had the same average tax rate in 2010 at 38 percent, this difference can be attributed to Nordstrom's higher pretax profits as a percent of sales, although the situation is reversed on an As Adjusted basis.

In summary, an examination of common-sized income statement ratios can illuminate strategic and operational differences among competitors. While Nordstrom's positioning as a high-end retailer allows it to earn a larger gross margin on sales than TJX, it is a tight control over expenses that helps TJX to compensate for its lower gross margin and to ultimately earn a similar net income margin.

Key Analysis Questions

A number of business questions will be useful to an analyst assessing the various elements of operating management:

- *Are the company's margins consistent with its stated competitive strategy?* For example, a differentiation strategy should usually lead to higher gross margins than a low-cost strategy.
- *Are the company's margins changing? Why? What are the underlying business causes—changes in competition, changes in input costs, or poor overhead cost management?*
- *Is the company managing its overhead and administrative costs well? What are the business activities driving these costs? Are these activities necessary?*
- *Are the company's tax policies sustainable, or is the current tax rate influenced by one-time tax credits?*
- *Do the firm's tax planning strategies lead to other business costs?* For example, if the operations are located in tax havens, how does this affect the company's profit margins and asset utilization? Are the benefits of tax planning strategies (reduced taxes) greater than the increased business costs?

Evaluating Investment Management: Decomposing Asset Turnover

Asset turnover is the second driver of a company's return on equity. Since firms invest considerable resources in their assets, using them productively is critical to overall profitability. A detailed analysis of asset turnover allows the analyst to evaluate the effectiveness of a firm's investment management. There are two primary areas of investment management: (1) working capital management and (2) management of long-term assets, both of which are discussed in further detail below.

Working Capital Management

Working capital is defined as the difference between a firm's current assets and current liabilities. However, this definition does not distinguish between operating components (such as accounts receivable, inventory, and accounts payable) and financing components (such as cash, marketable securities, and notes payable). An alternative measure that makes this distinction is operating working capital, defined in Table 5-3 as

Operating working capital = (Current assets − cash and marketable securities)
− (Current liabilities − Short-term and current portion of long-term debt)

The components of operating working capital that analysts primarily focus on are accounts receivable, inventory, and accounts payable. A certain amount of investment in working capital is generally necessary for the firm to run its normal operations. For example, a firm's credit policies and distribution policies determine its optimal level of accounts receivable. The nature of the production process and the need for buffer stocks determine the optimal level of inventory. Finally, accounts payable is a routine source of financing for the firm's working capital, and payment practices in an industry determine the normal level of accounts payable.

The following ratios are useful in analyzing a firm's working capital management: operating working capital as a percent of sales, operating working capital turnover, accounts receivable turnover, inventory turnover, and accounts payable turnover. The turnover ratios can also be expressed in number of days of activity that the operating working capital (and its components) can support. These ratios are defined below:

$$\text{Operating working capital to sales ratio} = \frac{\text{Operating working capital}}{\text{Sales}}$$

$$\text{Operating working capital turnover} = \frac{\text{Sales}}{\text{Operating working capital}}$$

$$\text{Accounts receivable turnover} = \frac{\text{Sales}}{\text{Accounts receivable}}$$

$$\text{Inventory turnover} = \frac{\text{Cost of goods sold}^{12}}{\text{Inventory}}$$

$$\text{Accounts payable turnover} = \frac{\text{Purchases}}{\text{Accounts payable}} \ or \ \frac{\text{Cost of goods sold}}{\text{Accounts payable}}$$

$$\text{Days' receivables} = \frac{\text{Accounts receivable}}{\text{Average sales per day}}$$

$$\text{Days' inventory} = \frac{\text{Inventory}}{\text{Average cost of goods sold per day}}$$

$$\text{Days' payables} = \frac{\text{Accounts payable}}{\text{Average purchases (or cost of goods sold) per day}}$$

Operating working capital turnover indicates how many dollars of sales a firm is able to generate for each dollar invested in operating working capital. Accounts receivable turnover, inventory turnover, and accounts payable turnover allow the analyst to examine how productively the three principal components of working capital are being used. Days' receivables, days' inventory, and days' payables are another way to evaluate the efficiency of a firm's working capital management.[13]

Long-Term Assets Management

Another area of investment management concerns the utilization of a firm's long-term assets. It is useful to define again a firm's investment in long-term assets:

$$\text{Net long-term assets} = (\text{Total long-term assets} - \text{Non-interest-bearing long-term liabilities})$$

Long-term assets generally consist of net property, plant, and equipment (PP&E), intangible assets such as goodwill, and other assets. Non-interest-bearing long-term liabilities include items such as deferred taxes. We define net long-term assets and net working capital in such a way that their sum, net operating assets, is equal to the sum of net debt and equity, or net capital. This is consistent with the way we defined operating ROA earlier in the chapter.

The efficiency with which a firm uses its net long-term assets is measured by the following two ratios: net long-term assets as a percent of sales and net long-term asset turnover, defined as

$$\text{Net long-term asset turnover} = \frac{\text{Sales}}{\text{Net long-term assets}}$$

Property plant and equipment (PP&E) is the most important long-term asset in a firm's balance sheet. The efficiency with which a firm's PP&E is used is measured either by the ratio of PP&E to sales or by the PP&E turnover ratio:

$$\text{PP\&E turnover} = \frac{\text{Sales}}{\text{Net property, plant, and equipment}}$$

Key Analysis Questions

The ratios discussed in the two preceding sections allow the analyst to explore a number of business questions:

- *How well does the company manage its inventory? Does the company use modern manufacturing techniques? Does it have good vendor and logistics management systems? If inventory ratios are changing, what is the underlying business reason? Are new products being planned? Is there a mismatch between the demand forecasts and actual sales?*
- *How well does the company manage its credit policies? Are these policies consistent with its marketing strategy? Is the company artificially increasing sales by loading the distribution channels?*
- *Is the company taking advantage of trade credit? Is it relying too much on trade credit? If so, what are the implicit costs?*
- *Is the company's investment in plant and equipment consistent with its competitive strategy? Does the company have a sound policy of acquisitions and divestitures?*

Table 5-6 shows the asset turnover ratios for TJX and Nordstrom on an As Reported and As Adjusted basis. The major impact of the operating lease adjustment comes in long-term asset ratios, with small secondary impacts in the ratios that use cost of goods sold. Due to the narrow impact of the operating lease adjustment in this section, we will focus here on an analysis of As Reported numbers and quickly summarize the key changes due to the adjustments at the end of the section.

TJX is extremely efficient at managing its working capital needs, with operating working capital representing less than 1 percent of total sales in 2010. Tight inventory management, a slightly slow payment policy (seen in a 35.3 days payable), low short-term debt, and the small accounts receivable balance (reflective of TJX's decision to outsource its branded credit card) contribute to TJX's low operating working capital levels.

Nordstrom is using its vendors to provide operating working capital even more effectively (and is more willing perhaps to stretch out payments to vendors) than TJX with days accounts payable in 2010 of 47.6. The primary driver of Nordstrom's much higher ratio of operating working capital to sales (and thus lower operating working capital turnover) of 16.5 percent in 2010 (as compared to 0.76 percent for TJX) is its large accounts receivable balance that results from its previously discussed strategy of financing its customers through its in-house credit card operations (which results in a lengthy days accounts receivable of 76.6 in 2010 compared to 2.5 for TJX). Nordstrom is quite efficient in managing its inventory with inventory turnover of 6.2 times in 2010, the same as TJX. This is interesting in that intuitively, one would expect that TJX (as a company pursuing a low-cost, efficient supply chain strategy) would be

TABLE 5-6	Asset Management Ratios			
Year ended January 29, 2011	As Reported		As Adjusted	
	TJX	Nordstrom	TJX	Nordstrom
Operating working capital/Sales	0.76%	16.5%	0.76%	16.5%
Net long-term assets/Sales	8.1%	18.4%	28.4%	24.4%
PP&E/Sales	11.3%	25.5%	31.3%	31.3%
Operating working capital turnover	132.2	6.1	132.2	6.1
Net long-term assets turnover	12.4	5.4	3.5	4.1
PP&E turnover	8.9	3.9	3.2	3.2
Accounts receivable turnover	148.2	4.8	148.2	4.8
Inventory turnover	6.2	6.2	5.9	6.1
Accounts payable turnover	10.3	7.7	9.9	7.6
Days' accounts receivable	2.5	76.6	2.5	76.6
Days' inventory	59.3	58.9	61.9	59.5
Days' accounts payable	35.3	47.6	36.9	48.1

Source: © Cengage Learning 2013

much more successful at efficient inventory management than a company such as Nordstrom, which prides itself on a broad and differentiated selection. The ratios show that Nordstrom appears to achieve both a broad selection and efficient inventory management at the same time.

TJX shows significantly better net long-term asset and PP&E utilization than Nordstrom as seen in its higher net long-term asset and PP&E turnover ratios. This is reflective of the difference in store financing strategies discussed previously. When this difference is adjusted for, these ratios are much more comparable, as seen in the comparison of As Adjusted numbers for net long-terms assets/sales, PP&E/sales, net long-term asset turnover, and PP&E turnover (which are just the inverse of the first two ratios). There are small differences between As Reported and As Adjusted figures for inventory turnover and accounts payable turnover and their inverse days' inventory and days' accounts payable, but these differences are minor and can be attributed to the adjustment made to cost of goods sold.

Evaluating Financial Management: Analyzing Financial Leverage

Financial leverage enables a firm to have an asset base larger than its equity. The firm can augment its equity through borrowing and the creation of other liabilities such as accounts payable, accrued liabilities, and deferred taxes. Financial leverage increases a firm's ROE as long as the cost of the liabilities is less than the return from investing these funds. In this respect, it is important to distinguish between interest-bearing liabilities such as notes payable, other forms of short-term and long-term debt that carry an explicit interest charge, and other liabilities. Some of these other forms of liability, such as accounts payable or deferred taxes, do not carry any interest charge at all. Others, such as capital lease obligations and pension obligations, carry an implicit interest charge. Finally, some firms carry large cash balances or investments in marketable securities. These balances reduce a firm's net debt because conceptually the firm can pay down its debt using its cash and short-term investments.

While financial leverage can potentially benefit a firm's shareholders, it can also increase their risk. Unlike equity, liabilities have predefined payment terms, and the firm faces risk of financial distress if it fails to meet these commitments. There are a number of ratios to evaluate the degree of risk arising from a firm's financial leverage.

Current Liabilities and Short-Term Liquidity

The following ratios are useful in evaluating the risk related to a firm's current liabilities:

$$\text{Current ratio} = \frac{\text{Current assets}}{\text{Current liabilities}}$$

$$\text{Quick ratio} = \frac{\text{Cash} + \text{Short-term investments} + \text{Accounts receivable}}{\text{Current liabilities}}$$

$$\text{Cash ratio} = \frac{\text{Cash} + \text{Marketable securities}}{\text{Current liabilities}}$$

$$\text{Operating cash flow ratio} = \frac{\text{Cash flow from operations}}{\text{Current liabilities}}$$

All the above ratios attempt to measure the firm's ability to repay its current liabilities. The first three compare a firm's current liabilities with its short-term assets that can be used to repay those liabilities. The fourth ratio focuses on the ability of the firm's operations to generate the resources needed to repay its current liabilities.

Since both current assets and current liabilities have comparable duration, the current ratio is a key index of a firm's short-term liquidity. Analysts view a current ratio of more than one to be an indication that the firm can cover its current liabilities from the cash realized from its current assets. However, the firm can face a short-term liquidity problem even with a current ratio exceeding one when some of its current assets are not easy to liquidate. Quick ratio and cash ratio capture the firm's ability to cover its current liabilities from liquid assets. Quick ratio assumes that the firm's accounts receivable are liquid. This is true in industries where the creditworthiness of the customers is beyond dispute, or when receivables are collected in a very short period. When these conditions do not prevail, cash ratio, which considers only cash and marketable securities, is a better indication of a firm's ability to cover its current liabilities in an emergency. Operating cash flow is another measure of the firm's ability to cover its current liabilities from cash generated from operations of the firm.

The liquidity ratios for TJX and Nordstrom are shown in Table 5-7. Nordstrom's significantly higher accounts receivable balances drive its higher current and quick ratios

TABLE 5-7	Liquidity Ratios			
Year ended January 29, 2011	As Reported		As Adjusted	
	TJX	Nordstrom	TJX	Nordstrom
Current ratio	1.66	2.01	1.66	2.01
Quick ratio	0.65	1.41	0.65	1.41
Cash ratio	0.60	0.39	0.60	0.39
Operating cash flow ratio	0.73	0.62	0.73	0.62

Source: © Cengage Learning 2013

relative to TJX. The cash ratios are somewhat more comparable given that accounts receivable is not included in this calculation and both companies have a healthy cash balance in 2010. TJX's operating cash flow ratio was slightly ahead of that of Nordstrom, indicating overall stronger cash flow from operations relative to its current liabilities. In general, both firms' liquidity situations are comfortable and are not likely to be a point of concern for short-term creditors. Finally, it can be noted that the operating lease adjustment had no impact on these ratios.

Debt and Long-Term Solvency

A company's financial leverage is also influenced by its debt financing policy. There are several potential benefits from debt financing. First, debt is typically cheaper than equity because the firm promises predefined payment terms to debt holders. Second, in most countries interest on debt financing is tax deductible whereas dividends to shareholders are not tax deductible. Third, debt financing can impose discipline on the firm's management and motivate it to reduce wasteful expenditures. Fourth, for non-public debt, it is likely to be easier for management to communicate their proprietary information on the firm's strategies and prospects to private lenders than to public capital markets. Such communication can potentially reduce a firm's cost of capital. For all these reasons, it is advantageous for firms to use at least some debt in their capital structure. Too much reliance on debt financing, however, is potentially costly to the firm's shareholders. The firm will face financial distress if it defaults on the interest and principal payments. Debt holders also impose covenants on the firm, restricting the firm's operating, investment, and financing decisions.

The optimal capital structure for a firm is determined primarily by its business risk. A firm's cash flows are highly predictable when there is little competition or there is little threat of technological changes. Such firms have low business risk; hence they can rely heavily on debt financing. In contrast, if a firm's operating cash flows are highly volatile and its capital expenditure needs are unpredictable, it may have to rely primarily on equity financing. Managers' attitudes toward risk and financial flexibility also often determine a firm's debt policies.

There are a number of ratios that help the analyst in this area. To evaluate the mix of debt and equity in a firm's capital structure, the following ratios are useful:

$$\text{Liabilities to equity ratio} = \frac{\text{Total liabilities}}{\text{Shareholders' equity}}$$

$$\text{Debt-to-equity ratio} = \frac{\text{Short-term debt} + \text{Long-term debt}}{\text{Shareholders' equity}}$$

Net-debt-to-equity ratio

$$= \frac{\text{Short-term debt} + \text{Long-term debt} - \text{Cash and marketable securities}}{\text{Shareholders' equity}}$$

Debt-to-capital ratio

$$= \frac{\text{Short-term debt} + \text{Long-term debt}}{\text{Short-term debt} + \text{Long-term debt} + \text{Shareholders' equity}}$$

Net-debt-to-net-capital ratio

$$= \frac{\text{Interest bearing liabilities} - \text{Cash and marketable securities}}{\text{Interest bearing liabilities} - \text{Cash and marketable securities} + \text{Shareholders' equity}}$$

The first ratio reformulates one of the three primary ratios underlying ROE, the assets-to-equity ratio (it is the assets-to-equity ratio minus one). The second ratio provides an indication of how many dollars of debt financing the firm is using for each dollar invested by its shareholders. The third ratio uses net debt, which is total debt minus cash and marketable securities, as the measure of a firm's borrowings. The fourth and fifth ratios measure debt as a proportion of total capital. In calculating all the above ratios, it is important to include all interest-bearing obligations, whether the interest charge is explicit or implicit. Recall that examples of line items that carry an implicit interest charge include capital lease obligations and pension obligations.

Analysts sometimes include any potential off-balance-sheet obligations that a firm may have, such as non-cancellable operating leases, in the definition of a firm's debt. We show that (as previously described) in the As Adjusted numbers in our TJX and Nordstrom example.

The ease with which a firm can meet its interest payments is an indication of the degree of risk associated with its debt policy. The interest coverage ratio provides a measure of this construct:

$$\text{Interest coverage (earnings basis)} = \frac{\text{Net income} + \text{Interest expense} + \text{Tax expense}}{\text{Interest expense}}$$

$$\text{Interest coverage (cash flow basis)}$$
$$= \frac{\text{Cash flow from operations} + \text{Interest expense} + \text{Taxes paid}}{\text{Interest expense}}$$

The earnings-based coverage ratio indicates the dollars of earnings available for each dollar of required interest payment; the cash-flow-based coverage ratio indicates the dollars of cash generated by operations for each dollar of required interest payment. In both these ratios, the denominator is the interest expense. In the numerator we add taxes back because taxes are computed only after interest expense is deducted. A coverage ratio of one implies that the firm is barely covering its interest expense through its operating activities, which is a very risky situation. The larger the coverage ratio, the greater the cushion the firm has to meet interest obligations.

Key Analysis Questions

Some of the business questions to ask when the analyst is examining a firm's debt policies follow:

- *Does the company have enough debt? Is it exploiting the potential benefits of debt—interest tax shields, management discipline, and easier communication?*
- *Does the company have too much debt given its business risk? What type of debt covenant restrictions does the firm face? Is it bearing the costs of too much debt, risking potential financial distress and reduced business flexibility?*
- *What is the company doing with the borrowed funds? Investing in working capital? Investing in fixed assets? Are these investments profitable?*
- *Is the company borrowing money to pay dividends? If so, what is the justification?*

We show debt and coverage ratios for TJX and Nordstrom in Table 5-8. On an As Reported basis, TJX carries a much lower debt load than Nordstrom, which is reflected

TABLE 5-8	Debt and Coverage Ratios			
Year ended January 29, 2011	**As Reported**		**As Adjusted**	
	TJX	Nordstrom	TJX	Nordstrom
Liabilities to equity	1.58	3.19	3.12	3.55
Debt to equity	0.27	1.66	1.81	2.03
Net debt to equity	−0.33	1.16	1.21	1.52
Debt to capital	0.22	0.62	0.64	0.67
Net debt to net capital	−0.49	0.54	0.55	0.60
Interest coverage (earnings based)	45.2	8.5	9.7	7.0
Interest coverage (cash flow based)	60.1	13.3	14.1	11.2

Source: © Cengage Learning 2013

in the As Reported debt ratios shown in Table 5-8. As discussed, this makes sense given that Nordstrom finances its ownership of a large proportion of its stores with long-term debt, while TJX avoids this debt with the use of operating leases. In addition, TJX shows extraordinarily high interest coverage ratios, but this picture changes when one again considers TJX's store leasing strategy. When both companies are adjusted for the impact of their operating lease usage, the debt ratios align much more closely, as seen in the As Adjusted ratios in Table 5-8.

If the present value of minimum lease rental obligations is added to TJX's net debt, its net debt to equity ratio increases dramatically—which can be seen in the As Adjusted net debt to equity. The impact of the operating lease adjustment is similar but of much less magnitude for Nordstrom given its more limited use of operating leases. Also, notice how the additional interest expense added as part of the operating lease adjustment brings the interest coverage ratios of the companies much closer together (seen in As Adjusted interest coverage). These items illustrate the importance of considering off-balance sheet obligations in analyzing a company's financial management. In general, both companies are in a relatively comfortable situation relative to their fixed obligations, even after factoring in operating lease commitments.

Ratios of Disaggregated Data

So far we have discussed how to compute ratios using information in the financial statements. Analysts often probe the above ratios further by using disaggregated financial and physical data. For example, for a multibusiness company, one could analyze the information by individual business segments. Such an analysis can reveal potential differences in the performance of each business unit, allowing the analyst to pinpoint areas where a company's strategy is working and where it is not. It is also possible to probe financial ratios further by computing ratios of physical data pertaining to a company's operations. The appropriate physical data to look at varies from industry to industry. As an example in retailing, one could compute productivity statistics such as sales per store, sales per square foot, customer transactions per store, and average amount of sale per customer transaction. In the hotel industry, room occupancy rates provide important information; in the cellular telephone industry, acquisition cost per new subscriber and subscriber retention rate are important. These disaggregated ratios are particularly useful for young firms and young industries such as Internet firms, where accounting data may not fully capture the business economics due to conservative accounting rules.

Putting It All Together: Assessing Sustainable Growth Rate

Analysts often use the concept of sustainable growth as a way to evaluate a firm's ratios in a comprehensive manner. A firm's sustainable growth rate is defined as

$$\text{Sustainable growth rate} = \text{ROE} \times (1 - \text{Dividend payout ratio})$$

We already discussed the analysis of ROE in the previous four sections. The dividend payout ratio is defined as

$$\text{Divided payout ratio} = \frac{\text{Cash dividends paid}}{\text{Net income}}$$

A firm's dividend payout ratio is a measure of its dividend policy. Firms pay dividends for several reasons. They provide a way to return to shareholders any cash generated in excess of the firm's operating and investment needs. When there are information asymmetries between a firm's managers and its shareholders, dividend payments can serve as a signal to shareholders about managers' expectations of the firm's future prospects. Firms may also pay dividends to attract a certain type of shareholder base.

Sustainable growth rate is the rate at which a firm can grow while keeping its profitability and financial policies unchanged. A firm's return on equity and its dividend payout policy determine the pool of funds available for growth. Of course the firm can grow at a rate different from its sustainable growth rate if its profitability, payout policy, or financial leverage changes. Therefore, the sustainable growth rate provides a benchmark against which a firm's growth plans can be evaluated. Figure 5-2 shows how a firm's sustainable growth rate can be linked to all the ratios discussed in this chapter.

FIGURE 5-2	Sustainable Growth Rate Framework for Financial Ratio Analysis

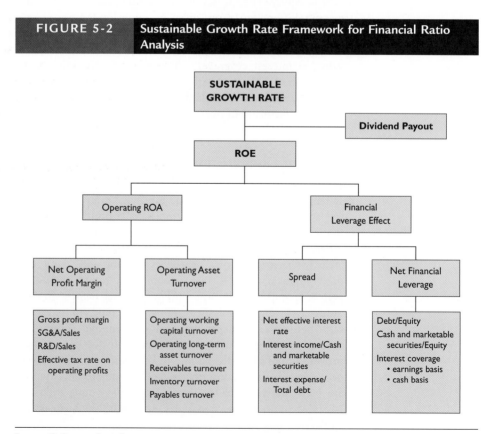

Source: © Cengage Learning

These linkages allow an analyst to examine the drivers of a firm's current sustainable growth rate. If the firm intends to grow at a higher rate than its sustainable growth rate, one could assess which of the ratios are likely to change in the process.

Key Analysis Questions

Analysis of sustainable growth can lead to asking the following types of business questions:

- *How quickly can the firm grow its business by keeping its profitability and financial policies unchanged?*
- *If it intends growing faster, where is the growth going to come from? Is management expecting profitability to increase? Or asset productivity to improve? Are these expectations realistic? Is the firm planning for these changes?*
- *If the firm is planning to increase its financial leverage or cut dividends, what is the likely impact of these financial policy changes?*

Table 5-9 shows the sustainable growth rate and its components for TJX and Nordstrom. TJX had a significantly higher sustainable growth rate relative to Nordstrom on both an As Reported and As Adjusted basis, due to both its higher ROEs and a lower dividend payout ratio. TJX's actual sales, asset, and liability growth rates in 2010 were considerably lower than implied by its sustainable growth rate, reflecting management's balanced approach to growth, investment, and returning funds to shareholders in the form of dividends and stock repurchase.

Historical Patterns of Ratios for U.S. Firms

To provide a benchmark for analysis, Table 5-10 reports historical values of the key ratios discussed in this chapter. These ratios are calculated using financial statement data for all publicly listed U.S. companies. The table shows the values of ROE, its key components, and the sustainable growth rate for each of the years 1991 to 2010, and the average for this twenty year period. The data show that the average ROE over this time frame has been 10.3 percent, average operating ROA has been 9.0 percent, and the average spread between operating ROA and net borrowing costs after tax has been 2.5 percent. The average sustainable growth rate for U.S. companies during this period has been 4.9 percent. Of course, an individual company's ratios might depart from these economy-wide averages for a number of reasons, such as industry effects, company strategies, and management effectiveness. Nonetheless, the average values in the table serve as useful benchmarks in financial analysis.

TABLE 5-9	Sustainable Growth Rate			
Year ended January 29, 2011	**As Reported**		**As Adjusted**	
	TJX	**Nordstrom**	**TJX**	**Nordstrom**
Return on equity	46.5%	39.0%	55.4%	40.0%
Dividend payout ratio	17.1%	27.2%	17.1%	27.2%
Sustainable growth rate	38.6%	28.4%	45.9%	29.1%

Source: © Cengage Learning 2013

TABLE 5-10	Historical Values of Key Financial Ratios						
Year	ROE	NOPAT Margin	Operating Asset Turnover	Operating ROA	Spread	Net Financial Leverage	Sustainable Growth Rate
1991	6.6%	6.3%	1.55	7.2%	−0.1%	1.20	0.5%
1992	4.4%	4.4%	1.60	6.1%	−0.6%	1.14	−1.6%
1993	8.8%	5.0%	1.67	6.5%	0.7%	1.17	2.6%
1994	14.0%	7.1%	1.77	11.0%	3.9%	1.16	7.9%
1995	13.8%	6.1%	1.83	8.3%	6.8%	1.11	7.3%
1996	14.8%	6.6%	1.83	9.4%	7.5%	1.14	8.7%
1997	13.8%	7.5%	1.83	10.4%	3.7%	1.11	8.2%
1998	13.1%	7.9%	1.76	9.7%	2.3%	1.22	7.4%
1999	13.5%	7.8%	1.69	9.9%	3.8%	1.25	8.4%
2000	10.1%	7.0%	1.71	8.0%	1.8%	1.31	5.2%
2001	1.4%	4.0%	1.47	3.0%	−3.0%	1.34	−2.7%
2002	−2.2%	1.7%	1.31	−2.7%	−7.9%	1.51	−4.4%
2003	13.3%	8.3%	1.57	9.5%	3.5%	1.58	8.7%
2004	13.3%	8.0%	1.70	10.1%	3.4%	1.49	8.3%
2005	13.8%	9.0%	1.78	11.9%	3.7%	1.21	8.2%
2006	16.7%	10.3%	1.88	14.1%	7.4%	1.23	11.1%
2007	12.1%	8.8%	1.75	12.4%	5.2%	1.23	6.6%
2008	0.1%	3.4%	1.68	6.8%	−0.7%	1.33	−4.7%
2009	8.9%	7.6%	1.49	9.8%	3.3%	1.31	4.4%
2010	12.4%	10.3%	1.65	12.9%	5.6%	1.04	7.9%
Average	10.3%	6.9%	1.68	9.0%	2.5%	1.23	4.9%

Ratios are based on beginning balance sheet data.

Source: Financial statement data for all publicly traded U.S. companies between 1991 and 2010, listed in Standard & Poor's Compustat database.

CASH FLOW ANALYSIS

The ratio analysis discussion focused on analyzing a firm's income statement (net profit margin analysis) or its balance sheet (asset turnover and financial leverage). The analyst can get further insights into the firm's operating, investing, and financing policies by examining its cash flows. Cash flow analysis also provides an indication of the quality of the information in the firm's income statement and balance sheet. As before, we will illustrate the concepts discussed in this section using TJX's and Nordstrom's cash flows.

Cash Flow and Funds Flow Statements

All U.S. companies are required to include a statement of cash flows in their financial statements under Statement of Financial Accounts Standard No. 95 (SFAS 95). In the cash flow statement, firms report their cash flows in three categories: cash flow from operations, cash flow related to investments, and cash flow related to financing activities. Cash flow from operations is the cash generated by the firm from the sale of goods and services after paying for the cost of inputs and operations. Cash flow related to investment activities shows the cash paid for capital expenditures, intercorporate investments, acquisitions, and cash received from the sales of long-term assets.

Cash flow related to financing activities shows the cash raised from (or paid to) the firm's stockholders and debt holders.

Firms use two cash flow statement formats: the direct format and the indirect format. The key difference between the two formats is the way they report cash flow from operating activities. In the direct cash flow format, which is used by only a small number of firms, operating cash receipts and disbursements are reported directly. In the indirect format, firms derive their operating cash flows by making adjustments to net income. Because the indirect format links the cash flow statement with the firm's income statement and balance sheet, many analysts and managers find this format more useful. As a result, the FASB requires firms using the direct format to report operating cash flows in the indirect format as well.

Recall from Chapter 3 that net income differs from operating cash flows because revenues and expenses are measured on an accrual basis. There are two types of accruals embedded in net income. First, there are current accruals like credit sales and unpaid expenses. Current accruals result in changes in a firm's current assets (such as accounts receivable, inventory, prepaid expenses) and current liabilities (such as accounts payable and accrued liabilities). The second type of accruals included in the income statement is noncurrent accruals such as depreciation, deferred taxes, and equity income from unconsolidated subsidiaries. To derive cash flow from operations from net income, adjustments have to be made for both these types of accruals. In addition, adjustments must be made for nonoperating gains included in net income such as profits from asset sales.

Some firms outside the United States report a funds flow statement rather than a cash flow statement of the type described above. Prior to SFAS 95, U.S. firms also reported a similar statement. Funds flow statements show working capital flows, not cash flows. It is useful for analysts to know how to convert a funds flow statement into a cash flow statement.

Funds flow statements typically provide information on a firm's working capital from operations, defined as net income adjusted for noncurrent accruals, and gains from the sale of long-term assets. As discussed above, cash flow from operations essentially involves a third adjustment, the adjustment for current accruals. Thus it is relatively straightforward to convert working capital from operations to cash flow from operations by making the relevant adjustments for current accruals related to operations.

Information on current accruals can be obtained by examining changes in a firm's current assets and current liabilities. Typically, operating accruals represent changes in all the current asset accounts other than cash and cash equivalents, and changes in all the current liabilities other than notes payable and the current portion of long-term debt.[14] Cash from operations can be calculated as follows:

> Working capital from operations
> − Increase (or + decrease) in accounts receivable
> − Increase (or + decrease) in inventory
> − Increase (or + decrease) in other current assets excluding cash and
>   cash equivalents
> + Increase (or − decrease) in accounts payable
> + Increase (or − decrease) in other current liabilities excluding debt.

Funds flow statements also often do not classify investment and financing flows. In such a case, the analyst has to classify the line items in the funds flow statement into these two categories by evaluating the nature of the business transactions that give rise to the flow represented by the line items.

Analyzing Cash Flow Information

Cash flow analysis can be used to address a variety of questions regarding a firm's cash flow dynamics:

- How strong is the firm's internal cash flow generation? Is the cash flow from operations positive or negative? If it is negative, why? Is it because the company is growing? Is it because its operations are unprofitable? Or is it having difficulty managing its working capital properly?
- Does the company have the ability to meet its short-term financial obligations, such as interest payments, from its operating cash flow? Can it continue to meet these obligations without reducing its operating flexibility?
- How much cash did the company invest in growth? Are these investments consistent with its business strategy? Did the company use internal cash flow to finance growth, or did it rely on external financing?
- Did the company pay dividends from internal free cash flow, or did it have to rely on external financing? If the company had to fund its dividends from external sources, is the company's dividend policy sustainable?
- What type of external financing does the company rely on? Equity, short-term debt, or long-term debt? Is the financing consistent with the company's overall business risk?
- Does the company have excess cash flow after making capital investments? Is it a long-term trend? What plans does management have to deploy the free cash flow?

While the information in reported cash flow statements can be used to answer the above questions directly in the case of some firms, it may not be easy to always do so for a number of reasons. First, even though SFAS 95 provides broad guidelines on the format of a cash flow statement, there is still significant variation across firms in how cash flow data are disclosed. Therefore, to facilitate a systematic analysis and comparison across firms, analysts often recast the information in the cash flow statement using their own cash flow model. Second, firms include interest expense and interest income in computing their cash flow from operating activities. However, these two items are not strictly related to a firm's operations. Interest expense is a function of financial leverage, and interest income is derived from financial assets rather than operating assets. Therefore it is useful to restate the cash flow statement to take this into account.

Analysts use a number of different approaches to restate the cash flow data. One such model is shown in Table 5-11. This presents cash flow from operations in two stages. The first step computes cash flow from operations before operating working capital investments. In computing this cash flow, the model excludes interest expense and interest income. To compute this number starting with a firm's net income, an analyst adds back three types of items: (1) after-tax net interest expense because this is a financing item that will be considered later; (2) non-operating gains or losses typically arising out of asset disposals or asset write-offs because these items are investment related and will be considered later; and (3) long-term operating accruals such as depreciation and deferred taxes because these are non-cash operating charges.

Several factors affect a firm's ability to generate positive cash flow from operations. Healthy firms that are in a steady state should generate more cash from their customers than they spend on operating expenses. In contrast, growing firms—especially those with heavy outlays for research and development, advertising and marketing, or building an organization to sustain future growth—may experience negative operating cash flow. Firms' working capital management also affects whether they generate positive cash flow from operations. Firms in the growing stage typically use cash flow for

TABLE 5-11	Cash Flow Analysis			
Year ended January 29, 2011	**As Reported**		**As Adjusted**	
	TJX	Nordstrom	TJX	Nordstrom
Net Income	**1,343.1**	**613.0**	**1,600.3**	**629.1**
After-tax net interest expense (income)	24.2	78.6	176.0	101.2
Non-operating losses (gains)	158.4	0.0	162.0	0.0
Long-term operating accruals	587.8	465.0	1,087.6	510.5
Operating cash flow before working capital investments	**2,113.5**	**1,156.6**	**3,025.9**	**1,240.8**
Net (investments in) or liquidation of operating working capital	(5.0)	99.0	(5.0)	99.0
Operating cash flow before investment in long-term assets	**2,108.5**	**1,255.6**	**3,020.9**	**1,339.8**
Net (investment in) or liquidation of operating long-term assets	(708.2)	(462.0)	(2,591.2)	(630.6)
Free cash flow available to debt and equity	**1,400.3**	**793.6**	**429.7**	**709.2**
After-tax net interest income (expense)	(24.2)	(78.6)	(176.0)	(101.2)
Net debt (repayment) or issuance	(2.4)	179.0	1,120.0	286.0
Free cash flow available to equity	**1,373.7**	**894.0**	**1,373.7**	**894.0**
Dividend (payments)	(229.3)	(167.0)	(229.3)	(167.0)
Net stock issuance (repurchase), and other equity changes	(1,017.2)	(16.0)	(1,017.2)	(16.0)
Net increase (decrease) in cash balance	**127.2**	**711.0**	**127.2**	**711.0**

Source: © Cengage Learning 2013

operating working capital items such as funding customers (accounts receivable) and purchasing inventories (net of accounts payable financing from suppliers). Net investments in working capital are a function of firms' credit policies (accounts receivable), payment policies (payables, prepaid expenses, and accrued liabilities), and expected growth in sales (inventories). Thus, in interpreting firms' cash flow from operations after working capital, it is important to keep in mind their growth strategy, industry characteristics, and credit policies.

The cash flow analysis model next focuses on cash flows related to long-term investments. These investments take the form of capital expenditures, intercorporate investments, and mergers and acquisitions. Any positive operating cash flow after making operating working capital investments allows the firm to pursue long-term growth opportunities. If the firm's operating cash flows after working capital investments are not sufficient to finance its long-term investments, it has to rely on external financing to fund its growth. Such firms have less flexibility to pursue long-term investments than those that can fund their growth internally. There are both costs and benefits from being able to fund growth internally. The cost is that managers can use the internally generated free cash flow to fund unprofitable investments. Such wasteful capital expenditures are less likely if managers are forced to rely on external capital suppliers. However, reliance on external capital markets may make it difficult for managers to undertake long-term risky investments if it is not easy to communicate to the capital markets the benefits from such investments.

Any excess cash flow after these long-term investments is free cash flow that is available for both debt holders and equity holders. Debt cash transactions include interest payments and principal payments as well as new borrowing. Cash flow after payments to debt holders is free cash flow available to equity holders. Cash transactions involving shareholders include dividend payments and stock repurchases, as well as issues of new equity.

Firms with negative free cash flow to both debt and equity have to borrow additional funds to meet their interest and debt repayment obligations, cut dividend payments, or issue additional equity. Managers of firms in this situation are often reluctant to cut dividends for fear that it will be viewed negatively by investors. While this may be feasible in the short term, it is not prudent for a firm to continue to pay dividends to equity holders unless it has a positive free cash flow on a sustained basis. In contrast, firms with large positive free cash flow to debt and equity run the risk of making unproductive investments to pursue growth for its own sake. An analyst, therefore, should carefully examine the investment plans of such firms.

The model in Table 5-11 suggests that the analyst should focus on a number of cash flow measures: (1) cash flow from operations before investment in working capital and interest payments, to examine whether or not the firm is able to generate a cash surplus from operations; (2) cash flow from operations after investment in working capital, to assess how the firm's working capital is being managed and whether or not it has the flexibility to invest in long-term assets for future growth; (3) free cash flow available to debt and equity holders, to assess a firm's ability to meet its interest and principal payments; and (4) free cash flow available to equity holders, to assess the firm's financial ability to sustain its dividend policy and to identify potential agency problems from excess free cash flow. These measures have to be evaluated in the context of the company's business, its growth strategy, and its financial policies. Further, changes in these measures from year to year provide valuable information on the stability of the cash flow dynamics of the firm.

Key Analysis Questions

The cash flow model in Table 5-11 can also be used to assess a firm's earnings quality. The reconciliation of a firm's net income with its cash flow from operations facilitates this exercise. Following are some of the questions an analyst can probe in this respect:

- *Are there significant differences between a firm's net income and its operating cash flow? Is it possible to clearly identify the sources of this difference? Which accounting policies contribute to this difference? Are there any one-time events contributing to this difference?*
- *Is the relationship between cash flow and net income changing over time? Why? Is it because of changes in business conditions or because of changes in the firm's accounting policies and estimates?*
- *What is the time lag between the recognition of revenues and expenses and the receipt and disbursement of cash flows? What type of uncertainties need to be resolved in between?*
- *Are the changes in receivables, inventories, and payables normal? If not, is there adequate explanation for the changes?*

Finally, as we will discuss in Chapter 7, free cash flow available to debt and equity and free cash flow available to equity are critical inputs into the cash-flow-based valuation of firms' assets and equity, respectively.

Analysis of TJX's and Nordstrom's Cash Flow

Both TJX and Nordstrom reported their cash flows using the indirect cash flow statement. Table 5-11 recasts these statements using the approach discussed above so that we can analyze the two companies' cash flow dynamics.

The cash flow analysis presented in Table 5-11 shows that on an As Reported basis TJX had an operating cash flow before working capital investments of $2.114 billion in 2010. The difference between its earnings and this cash flow is attributable primarily to depreciation and amortization charges, which is a non-cash expense that is included in the company's income statement. TJX made a small net investment in operating working capital (the result of increases in accounts receivable and inventory netted out against increases in accounts payable, income taxes payable, and inventory) resulting in an operating cash flow before investment in long-term assets of $2.109 billion for 2010. Investment in store renovations and improvements, fit ups for new stores, and expansion of office and distribution centers comprised the bulk of net investment in operating long-term assets of $708.2 million, resulting in a free cash flow available to debt and equity of $1.4 billion in 2010. Netting out a small amount of after-tax net interest income and debt repayment resulted in a free cash flow available to equity of $1.37 billion. As part of an ongoing share repurchase program, TJX repurchased roughly $1.0 billion in shares. That, combined with a dividend of $229.3 million resulted in a net increase of cash of $127.2 million in 2010. Generally, TJX had a strong cash flow situation in 2010, as it was able to fund its rapid expansion, an increasing dividend to shareholders, and an aggressive share repurchase program while increasing its cash balance.

Nordstrom's As Reported operating cash flow before working capital investments was $1.16 billion in 2010. By liquidating $99 million of operating capital mainly through increases in accounts payable and other liabilities (partially offset by increases in accounts receivable and inventory), Nordstrom was able to generate $1.26 billion in operating cash flow before investment in long-term assets. Like TJX, Nordstrom invested heavily in its expansion, leaving free cash flow available to debt and equity of $793.6 million in 2010. Net proceeds from a $500 million debt issue, an increase in short-term borrowings, and the reduction in after-tax net interest expense resulted in free cash flow available to equity of $894 million. Like TJX, Nordstrom issued a dividend and bought back a small amount of stock, resulting in a net increase in its cash balance of $711 million.

As discussed in Chapter 4 and shown in Table 5-11, bringing the operating leases onto the balance sheet as capital leases boosts net income. It also increases operating cash flows as adjustments for depreciation and the increase in deferred tax liability are included in long-term operating accruals. In the investments segment, investments in long-term assets increase as new lease agreements are entered and capitalized. Finally, in the financing section, net debt issuance increases as debt is added from newly capitalized leases and annual payments are made for principal and interest (after-tax).

SUMMARY

This chapter presents two key tools of financial analysis: ratio analysis and cash flow analysis. Both these tools allow the analyst to examine a firm's performance and its financial condition given its strategy and goals. Ratio analysis involves assessing the firm's income statement and balance sheet data. Cash flow analysis relies on the firm's cash flow statement. In this chapter we applied these tools to TJX and Nordstrom in order to compare the two firms' performance on both an As Reported and As Adjusted (for the use of off–balance sheet operating leases) basis.

The starting point for ratio analysis is the company's ROE. The next step is to evaluate the three drivers of ROE, which are net profit margin, asset turnover, and financial leverage. Net profit margin reflects a firm's operating management, asset turnover reflects its investment management, and financial leverage reflects its financing policies. Each of these areas can be further probed by examining a number of ratios. For example, common-sized income statement analysis allows a detailed examination of a firm's net margins. Similarly, turnover of key working capital accounts such as accounts receivable, inventory, and accounts payable, and turnover of the firm's fixed assets, allow further examination of a firm's asset utilization. Finally, short-term liquidity ratios, debt policy ratios, and coverage ratios provide a means of examining a firm's financial leverage.

A firm's sustainable growth rate—the rate at which it can grow without altering its operating, investment, and financing policies—is determined by its ROE and its dividend policy. The concept of sustainable growth provides a way to integrate the different elements of ratio analysis and to evaluate whether or not a firm's growth strategy is sustainable. If a firm's plans call for growing at a rate above its current sustainable rate, then one can analyze which of the firm's ratios is likely to change in the future.

Cash flow analysis supplements ratio analysis in examining a firm's operating activities, investment management, and financial risks. Firms in the United States are currently required to report a cash flow statement summarizing their operating, investment, and financing cash flows. Firms in other countries typically report working capital flows, but it is possible to use this information to create a cash flow statement.

Since there are wide variations across firms in the way cash flow data are reported, analysts often use a standard format to recast cash flow data. We discussed one such cash flow model in this chapter. This model allows the analyst to assess whether a firm's operations generate cash flow before investments in operating working capital, and how much cash is being invested in the firm's working capital. It also enables the analyst to calculate the firm's free cash flow after making long-term investments, which is an indication of the firm's ability to meet its debt and dividend payments. Finally, the cash flow analysis shows how the firm is financing itself, and whether its financing patterns are too risky.

The insights gained from analyzing a firm's financial ratios and its cash flows are valuable in forecasting the firm's future prospects.

DISCUSSION QUESTIONS

1. Which of the following types of firms do you expect to have particularly high or low asset turnover? Explain why.
   - a supermarket
   - a pharmaceutical company
   - a jewelry retailer
   - a steel company
2. Which of the following types of firms do you expect to have high or low sales margins? Why?
   - a supermarket
   - a pharmaceutical company
   - a jewelry retailer
   - a software company

3. James Broker, an analyst with an established brokerage firm, comments: "The critical number I look at for any company is operating cash flow. If cash flows are less than earnings, I consider a company to be a poor performer and a poor investment prospect." Do you agree with this assessment? Why or why not?

4. In 2005 IBM had a return on equity of 26.7 percent, whereas Hewlett-Packard's return was only 6.4 percent. Use the decomposed ROE framework to provide possible reasons for this difference based on the data below:

	IBM	HP
NOPAT/Sales	9.0%	2.7%
Sales/Net Assets	2.16	2.73
Effective After Tax Interest Rate	2.4%	1.1%
Net Financial Leverage	0.42	−0.16

Source: Thomson One

5. Joe Investor asserts, "A company cannot grow faster than its sustainable growth rate." True or false? Explain why.

6. What are the reasons for a firm having lower cash from operations than working capital from operations? What are the possible interpretations of these reasons?

7. ABC Company recognizes revenue at the point of shipment. Management decides to increase sales for the current quarter by filling all customer orders. Explain what impact this decision will have on
   - Days' receivable for the current quarter
   - Days' receivable for the next quarter
   - Sales growth for the current quarter
   - Sales growth for the next quarter
   - Return on sales for the current quarter
   - Return on sales for the next quarter

8. What ratios would you use to evaluate operating leverage for a firm?

9. What are the potential benchmarks that you could use to compare a company's financial ratios? What are the pros and cons of these alternatives?

10. In a period of rising prices, how would the following ratios be affected by the accounting decision to select LIFO, rather than FIFO, for inventory valuation?
    - Gross margin
    - Current ratio
    - Asset turnover
    - Debt-to-equity ratio
    - Average tax rate

NOTES

1. Both TJX and Nordstrom end their fiscal years on the last Saturday in January. TJX calls the fiscal year ending January 30, 2011, fiscal year 2011, while Nordstrom calls that same time period fiscal year 2010. For clarity, we will call the fiscal year ending January 30, 2010, as fiscal year 2009, and the fiscal year ending January 29, 2011, as fiscal year 2010.

2. TJX and Nordstrom financial statements used as the source for creating the standardized statements accessed via Thomson ONE.

3. Financial statement data for all publicly traded U.S. companies between 1991 and 2010, listed in Standard & Poor's Compustat database, accessed October 2011.

4. In computing ROE, one can either use the beginning equity, ending equity, or an average of the two. Conceptually, the average equity is appropriate, particularly for rapidly growing companies. However, for most companies, this computational choice makes little difference as long as the analyst is consistent. Therefore, in practice most analysts use ending balances for simplicity. This comment applies to all ratios discussed in this chapter where one of the items in the ratio is a flow variable (items in the income statement or cash flow statement) and the other item is a stock variable (items in the balance sheet). Throughout this chapter we use the beginning balances of the stock variables.

5. We discuss in greater detail in Chapter 8 how to estimate a company's cost of equity capital.

6. Strictly speaking, part of a cash balance is needed to run the firm's operations, so only the excess cash balance should be viewed as negative debt. However, firms do not provide information on excess cash, so we subtract all cash balances in our definitions and computations. An alternative possibility is to subtract only short-term investments and ignore the cash balance completely.

7. See D. Nissim and S. Penman, "Ratio Analysis and Valuation: From Research to Practice," *Review of Accounting Studies* 6 (2001): 109–154, for a more detailed description of this approach.

8. Financial statement data for all publicly traded U.S. companies between 1991 and 2010, listed in Standard & Poor's Compustat database, accessed October 2011.

9. Both TJX and Nordstrom have a solid credit rating and a relatively low cost of debt. We will discuss in Chapter 8 how to estimate a company's weighted average cost of capital.

10. TJX Companies, Inc., January 29, 2011, Form 10-K (filed March 30, 2011), p. 25, http://www.tjx.com/investor_landing.asp, accessed May 2011.

11. See *Taxes and Business Strategy* by M. Scholes and M. Wolfson (Englewood Cliffs, NJ: Prentice-Hall, 1992).

12. If firms that are analyzed use different inventory methods, the analyst can adjust to a common method for computing inventory turnover and days' inventory. This can be accomplished by adjusting LIFO inventory and LIFO cost of sales to FIFO values using disclosures on the effect of LIFO inventory valuation in the inventory footnote disclosure.

13. There are a number of issues related to the calculation of these ratios in practice. First, in calculating all the turnover ratios, the assets used in the calculations can either be beginning of the year values, year-end values, or an average of the beginning and ending balances in a year. We use the beginning of the year values in our calculations. Second, strictly speaking, one should use credit sales to calculate accounts receivable turnover and days' receivables. But since it is usually difficult to obtain data on credit sales, total sales are used instead. Similarly, in calculating accounts payable turnover or days' payables, cost of goods sold is substituted for purchases for data availability reasons.

14. Changes in cash and marketable securities are excluded because this is the amount being explained by the cash flow statement. Changes in short-term debt and the current portion of long-term debt are excluded because these accounts represent financing flows, not operating flows.

APPENDIX A   THE TJX COMPANIES, INC. FINANCIAL STATEMENTS

We present here for reference Standardized and Condensed financial statements for TJX, on both an As Reported and As Adjusted (as detailed in the chapter) basis. It is important to note that "As Reported" and "As Adjusted" refers to the numbers included in the statements—as noted previously, the Standardized and Condensed financial statement formats have been developed as a way to facilitate comparison and forecasting, and differ from the format presented by a specific company in its filings. Also note that the standardized statements shown below are generated by the BAV software tool and based on data reported by the Thomson ONE database, which makes minor modifications to the data as reported by the firm. As a consequence, the standardized statements shown below will not be an exact match to the standardized statements shown in the appendix to Chapter 4, which were manually compiled to illustrate the general methodology of creating standardized statements. Finally, As Adjusted statements show differences from As Reported statements only in the years (FY 2010 for income and cash flow statements, FY 2011 and 2010 for beginning balance sheets) where adjustments have been made.

The TJX Companies, Inc.
Standardized Statements of Income ($ millions)

AS REPORTED

Fiscal Year	2010	2009	2008
Sales	**21,942.2**	**20,288.4**	**18,999.5**
Cost of Sales	15,5768	14,538.2	13,993.0
Gross Profit	**6,365.4**	**5,750.2**	**5,006.5**
SG&A	3,712.6	3,319.7	3,170.0
Other Operating Expense	458.1	435.2	371.2
Operating Income	**2,194.7**	**1,995.3**	**1,465.3**
Investment Income	0.0	0.0	0.0
Other Income, net of Other Expense	8.5	(1.7)	0.0
Other Income	15.3	7.5	0.0
Other Expense	6.8	9.2	0.0
Net Interest Expense (Income)	39.1	42.0	14.3
Interest Income	9.9	9.8	22.2
Interest Expense	49.0	51.8	36.5
Minority Interest	0.0	0.0	0.0
Pre-Tax Income	**2,164.1**	**1,951.6**	**1,451.0**
Tax Expense	824.6	738	536.1
Unusual Gains, Net of Unusual Losses (after tax)	3.6	0.0	(34.3)
Net Income	**1,343.1**	**1,213.6**	**880.6**
Preferred Dividends	0.0	0.0	0.0
Net Income to Common	**1,343.1**	**1,213.6**	**880.6**

Source: Thomson ONE database and Business Analysis and Valuation (BAV) Model V.5.

The TJX Companies, Inc.
Standardized Beginning Balance Sheet ($ millions)
AS REPORTED

Fiscal Year	2011	2010	2009
Assets			
Cash and Marketable Securities	1,821.5	1,745.2	453.5
Accounts Receivable	200.1	148.1	143.5
Inventory	2,765.5	2,532.3	2,619.3
Other Current Assets	312.4	378.2	409.8
Total Current Assets	**5,099.5**	**4,803.8**	**3,626.1**
Long-Term Tangible Assets	2,689.9	2,478.4	2,372.6
Long-Term Intangible Assets	182.3	181.7	179.5
Other Long-Term Assets	0.0	0.0	0.0
Total Long-Term Assets	**2,872.2**	**2,660.1**	**2,552.1**
Total Assets	**7,971.8**	**7,464.0**	**6,178.2**
Liabilities			
Accounts Payable	1,683.9	1,507.9	1,276.1
Short-Term Debt	2.7	2.4	395.0
Other Current Liabilities	1,446.4	1,384.7	1,096.8
Total Current Liabilities	**3,133.0**	**2,895.0**	**2,767.9**
Long-Term Debt	787.5	790.2	383.8
Deferred Taxes	241.9	192.4	127.0
Other Long-Term Liabilities (non-interest bearing)	709.3	697.1	765.0
Total Long-Term Liabilities	**1,738.7**	**1,679.7**	**1,275.8**
Total Liabilities	**4,871.9**	**4,574.7**	**4,043.7**
Minority Interest	0.0	0.0	0.0
Shareholders' Equity			
Preferred Stock	0.0	0.0	0.0
Common Shareholders' Equity	3,099.9	2,889.3	2,134.6
Total Shareholders' Equity	**3,099.9**	**2,889.3**	**2,134.6**
Total Liabilities and Shareholders' Equity	**7,971.8**	**7,464.0**	**6,178.2**

Balance sheet items are shown as beginning of period balances.
Source: Thomson ONE database and Business Analysis and Valuation (BAV) Model V.5.

The TJX Companies, Inc.
Standardized Statements of Cash Flows ($ millions)
AS REPORTED

Fiscal Year	2010	2009	2008
Net Income	**1,343.1**	**1,213.6**	**880.6**
After-tax net interest expense (income)	24.2	26.1	9.0
Non-operating losses (gains)	158.4	(21.5)	55.2
Long-term operating accruals	587.8	456.6	489.3
Depreciation and amortization	458.1	435.2	401.7
Other	129.7	21.4	87.6

(continued)

Fiscal Year	2010	2009	2008
Operating cash flow before working capital investments	**2,113.5**	**1,674.8**	**1,434.1**
Net (investments in) or liquidation of operating working capital	(5.0)	548.6	(347.8)
Operating cash flow before investment in long-term assets	**2,108.5**	**2,223.4**	**1,086.3**
Net (investment in) or liquidation of operating long-term assets	(708.2)	(434.9)	(568.6)
Free cash flow available to debt and equity	**1,400.3**	**1,788.5**	**517.7**
After-tax net interest income (expense)	(24.2)	(26.1)	(9.0)
Net debt (repayment) or issuance	(2.4)	371.4	(2.0)
Free cash flow available to equity	**1,373.7**	**2,133.8**	**506.7**
Dividend (payments)	(229.3)	(197.7)	(176.7)
Net stock issuance (repurchase), and other equity changes	(1017.2)	(774.9)	(608.9)
Net increase (decrease) in cash balance	**127.2**	**1,161.2**	**(278.9)**

Source: Thomson ONE database and Business Analysis and Valuation (BAV) Model V.5.

The TJX Companies, Inc.
Condensed Statements of Income ($ millions)
AS REPORTED

Fiscal Year	2010	2009	2008
Sales	**21,942.2**	**20,288.4**	**18,999.5**
Net Operating Profit after Tax	1,367.3	1,239.7	889.6
Net Income	1,343.1	1,213.6	880.6
+ Net Interest Expense after Tax	24.2	26.1	9.0
= Net Operating Profit after Tax	**1,367.3**	**1,239.7**	**889.6**
− Net Interest Expense after Tax	24.2	26.1	9.0
Interest Expense	49.0	51.8	36.5
− Interest Income	9.9	9.8	22.2
= Net Interest Expense (Income)	39.1	42.0	14.3
× (1 − Tax Expense/Pre-Tax Income)	0.62	0.62	0.63
= Net Interest Expense after Tax	**24.2**	**26.1**	**9.0**
= Net Income	**1,343.1**	**1,213.6**	**880.6**
− Preferred Stock Dividends	0.0	0.0	0.0
= Net Income to Common	**1,343.1**	**1,213.6**	**880.6**

Source: Thomson ONE database and Business Analysis and Valuation (BAV) Model V.5.

The TJX Companies, Inc.
Condensed Beginning Balance Sheet ($ millions)
AS REPORTED

Fiscal Year	2011	2010	2009
Beginning Net Working Capital	147.7	166.0	799.7
Accounts Receivable	200.1	148.1	143.5
+ Inventory	2,765.5	2,532.3	2,619.3

(continued)

Fiscal Year	2011	2010	2009
+ Other Current Assets	312.4	378.2	409.8
− Accounts Payable	1,683.9	1,507.9	1,276.1
− Other Current Liabilities	1,446.4	1,384.7	1,096.8
= **Beginning Net Working Capital**	**147.7**	**166.0**	**799.7**
+ **Beginning Net Long-Term Assets**	1,921.0	1,770.6	1,660.1
Long-Term Tangible Assets	2,689.9	2,478.4	2,372.6
+ Long-Term Intangible Assets	182.3	181.7	179.5
+ Other Long-Term Assets	0.0	0.0	0.0
− Minority Interest	0.0	0.0	0.0
− Deferred Taxes	241.9	192.4	127.0
− Other Long-Term Liabilities (non-interest bearing)	709.3	697.1	765.0
= **Beginning Net Long-Term Assets**	**1,921.0**	**1,770.6**	**1,660.1**
= **Total Beginning Net Assets**	**2,068.7**	**1,936.6**	**2,459.8**
Beginning Net Debt	**(1,031.3)**	**(952.6)**	**325.3**
Short-Term Debt	2.7	2.4	395.0
+ Long-Term Debt	787.5	790.2	383.8
− Cash	1,821.5	1,745.2	453.5
= **Beginning Net Debt**	**(1,031.3)**	**(952.6)**	**325.3**
+ **Beginning Preferred Stock**	0.0	0.0	0.0
+ **Beginning Shareholders' Equity**	3,099.9	2,889.3	2,134.6
= **Total Net Capital**	**2,068.6**	**1,936.7**	**2,459.9**

Source: Thomson ONE database and Business Analysis and Valuation (BAV) Model V.5.

The TJX Companies, Inc.
Standardized Statements of Income ($ millions)

AS ADJUSTED

Fiscal Year	2010	2009	2008
Sales	**21,942.2**	**20,288.4**	**18,999.5**
Cost of Sales	14,930.8	14,538.2	13,993.0
Gross Profit	**7,011.4**	**5,750.2**	**5,006.5**
SG&A	3,712.6	3,319.7	3,170.0
Other Operating Expense	458.1	435.2	371.2
Operating Income	**2,840.7**	**1,995.3**	**1,465.3**
Investment Income	0.0	0.0	0.0
Other Income, net of Other Expense	8.5	(1.7)	0.0
Other Income	15.3	7.5	0.0
Other Expense	6.8	9.2	0.0
Net Interest Expense (Income)	283.9	42.0	14.3
Interest Income	9.9	9.8	22.2
Interest Expense	293.8	51.8	36.5
Minority Interest	0.0	0.0	0.0
Pre-Tax Income	**2,565.3**	**1,951.6**	**1,451.0**
Tax Expense	965.0	738	536.1
Unusual Gains, Net of Unusual Losses (after tax)	0.0	0.0	(34.3)
Net Income	**1,600.3**	**1,213.6**	**880.6**
Preferred Dividends	0.0	0.0	0.0
Net Income to Common	**1,600.3**	**1,213.6**	**880.6**

Source: Thomson ONE database and Business Analysis and Valuation (BAV) Model V.5.

The TJX Companies, Inc.
Standardized Beginning Balance Sheet ($ millions)
AS ADJUSTED

Fiscal Year	2011	2010	2009
Assets			
Cash and Marketable Securities	1,821.5	1,745.2	453.5
Accounts Receivable	200.1	148.1	143.5
Inventory	2,765.5	2,532.3	2,619.3
Other Current Assets	312.4	378.2	409.8
Total Current Assets	**5,099.5**	**4,803.8**	**3,626.1**
Long-Term Tangible Assets	8,663.7	6,928.6	2,372.6
Long-Term Intangible Assets	182.3	181.7	179.5
Other Long-Term Assets	0.0	0.0	0.0
Total Long-Term Assets	**8,846.0**	**7,110.3**	**2,552.1**
Total Assets	**13,945.5**	**11,914.1**	**6,178.2**
Liabilities			
Accounts Payable	1,683.9	1,507.9	1,276.1
Short-Term Debt	2.7	2.4	395.0
Other Current Liabilities	1,450.0	1,384.7	1,096.8
Total Current Liabilities	**3,136.6**	**2,895.0**	**2,767.9**
Long-Term Debt	6,360.1	5,240.4	383.8
Deferred Taxes	382.3	192.4	127.0
Other Long-Term Liabilities (non-interest bearing)	709.3	697.1	765.0
Total Long-Term Liabilities	**7,451.7**	**6,129.9**	**1,275.8**
Total Liabilities	**10,588.3**	**9,024.9**	**4,043.7**
Minority Interest	0.0	0.0	0.0
Shareholders' Equity			
Preferred Stock	0.0	0.0	0.0
Common Shareholders' Equity	3,357.1	2,889.3	2,134.6
Total Shareholders' Equity	**3,357.1**	**2,889.3**	**2,134.6**
Total Liabilities and Shareholders' Equity	**13,945.5**	**11,914.1**	**6,178.2**

Balance sheet items are shown as beginning of period balances.
Source: Thomson ONE database and Business Analysis and Valuation (BAV) Model V.5.

The TJX Companies, Inc.
Standardized Statements of Cash Flows ($ millions)
AS ADJUSTED

Fiscal Year	2010	2009	2008
Net Income	**1,600.3**	**1,213.6**	**880.6**
After-tax net interest expense (income)	176.0	26.1	9.0
Non-operating losses (gains)	162.0	(21.5)	55.2
Long-term operating accruals	1,087.6	456.6	489.3
Depreciation and amortization	817.5	435.2	401.7
Other	270.1	21.4	87.6
Operating cash flow before working capital investments	**3,025.9**	**1,674.8**	**1,434.1**

(continued)

Fiscal Year	2010	2009	2008
Net (investments in) or liquidation of operating working capital	(5.0)	548.6	(347.8)
Operating cash flow before investment in long-term assets	**3,020.9**	**2,223.4**	**1,086.3**
Net (investment in) or liquidation of operating long-term assets	(2,591.2)	(434.9)	(568.6)
Free cash flow available to debt and equity	**429.7**	**1,788.5**	**517.7**
After-tax net interest income (expense)	(176.0)	(26.1)	(9.0)
Net debt (repayment) or issuance	1,120.0	371.4	(2.0)
Free cash flow available to equity	**1,373.7**	**2,133.8**	**506.7**
Dividend (payments)	(229.3)	(197.7)	(176.7)
Net stock issuance (repurchase), and other equity changes	(1,017.2)	(774.9)	(608.9)
Net increase (decrease) in cash balance	**127.2**	**1,161.2**	**(278.9)**

Source: Thomson ONE database and analyst calculation.

The TJX Companies, Inc.
Condensed Statements of Income ($ millions)
AS ADJUSTED

Fiscal Year	2010	2009	2008
Sales	**21,942.2**	**20,288.4**	**18,999.5**
Net Operating Profit after Tax	**1,777.4**	**1,239.7**	**889.6**
Net Income	1,600.3	1,213.6	880.6
+ Net Interest Expense after Tax	177.1	26.1	9.0
= Net Operating Profit after Tax	**1,777.4**	**1,239.7**	**889.6**
− Net Interest Expense after Tax	177.1	26.1	9.0
Interest Expense	293.8	51.8	36.5
− Interest Income	9.9	9.8	22.2
= Net Interest Expense (Income)	283.9	42.0	14.3
× (1 − Tax Expense/Pre-Tax Income)	0.62	0.62	0.63
= Net Interest Expense after Tax	**177.1**	**26.1**	**9.0**
= Net Income	**1,600.3**	**1,213.6**	**880.6**
− Preferred Stock Dividends	0.0	0.0	0.0
= Net Income to Common	**1,600.3**	**1,213.6**	**880.6**

Source: Thomson ONE database and Business Analysis and Valuation (BAV) Model V.5.

The TJX Companies, Inc.
Condensed Beginning Balance Sheet ($ millions)
AS ADJUSTED

Fiscal Year	2011	2010	2009
Beginning Net Working Capital	144.1	166.0	799.7
Accounts Receivable	200.1	148.1	143.5
+ Inventory	2,765.5	2,532.3	2,619.3
+ Other Current Assets	312.4	378.2	409.8
− Accounts Payable	1,683.9	1,507.9	1,276.1

(continued)

Fiscal Year	2011	2010	2009
− Other Current Liabilities	1,450.0	1,384.7	1,096.8
= **Beginning Net Working Capital**	**144.1**	**166.0**	**799.7**
+ **Beginning Net Long-Term Assets**	7,754.4	6,220.8	1,660.1
Long-Term Tangible Assets	8,663.7	6,928.6	2,372.6
+ Long-Term Intangible Assets	182.3	181.7	179.5
+ Other Long-Term Assets	0.0	0.0	0.0
− Minority Interest	0.0	0.0	0.0
− Deferred Taxes	382.3	192.4	127.0
− Other Long-Term Liabilities (non-interest bearing)	709.3	697.1	765.0
= **Beginning Net Long-Term Assets**	**7,754.4**	**6,220.8**	**1,660.1**
= **Total Beginning Net Assets**	**7,898.5**	**6,386.9**	**2,459.8**
Beginning Net Debt	4,541.3	3,497.6	325.3
Short-Term Debt	2.7	2.4	395.0
+ Long-Term Debt	6,360.1	5,240.4	383.8
− Cash	1,821.5	1,745.2	453.5
= **Beginning Net Debt**	**4,541.3**	**3,497.6**	**325.3**
+ **Beginning Preferred Stock**	0.0	0.0	0.0
+ **Beginning Shareholders' Equity**	3,357.1	2,889.3	2,134.6
= **Total Net Capital**	**7,898.4**	**6,386.9**	**2,459.9**

Source: Thomson ONE database and Business Analysis and Valuation (BAV) Model V.5.

APPENDIX B   NORDSTROM, INC. FINANCIAL STATEMENTS

We present here for reference Standardized and Condensed financial statements for Nordstrom, on both an As Reported and As Adjusted (as detailed in the chapter) basis. A reminder that "As Reported" and "As Adjusted" refers to the numbers presented in the statements, not the format, which is used to facilitate comparison and forecasting, and is not specifically representative of the format presented in company filings. Finally, As Adjusted statements show differences from As Reported statements only in the years (FY 2010 for income and cash flow statements, FY 2011 and 2010 for beginning balance sheets) where adjustments have been made.

Nordstrom, Inc.
Standardized Statements of Income ($ millions)
AS REPORTED

Fiscal Year	2010	2009	2008
Sales	**9,700.0**	**8,627.0**	**8,573.0**
Cost of Sales	5,570.0	5,015.0	5,115.0
Gross Profit	**4,130.0**	**3,612.0**	**3,458.0**
SG&A	2,685.0	2,465.0	2,386.0
Other Operating Expense	327.0	313.0	302.0
Operating Income	**1,118.0**	**834.0**	**770.0**
Investment Income	0.0	0.0	0.0
Other Income, net of Other Expense	0.0	0.0	9.0
Other Income	0.0	0.0	9.0

(continued)

Fiscal Year	2010	2009	2008
Other Expense	0.0	0.0	0.0
Net Interest Expense (Income)	127.0	138.0	131.0
Interest Income	6.0	10.0	14.0
Interest Expense	133.0	148.0	145.0
Minority Interest	0.0	0.0	0.0
Pre-Tax Income	**991.0**	**696.0**	**648.0**
Tax Expense	378.0	255.0	247.0
Unusual Gains, Net of Unusual Losses (after tax)	0.0	0.0	0.0
Net Income	**613.0**	**441.0**	**401.0**
Preferred Dividends	0.0	0.0	0.0
Net Income to Common	**613.0**	**441.0**	**401.0**

Source: Thomson ONE database and Business Analysis and Valuation (BAV) Model V.5.

Nordstrom, Inc.
Standardized Beginning Balance Sheet ($ millions)
AS REPORTED

Fiscal year	2011	2010	2009
Assets			
Cash and Marketable Securities	1,506.0	795.0	72.0
Accounts Receivable	2,026.0	2,035.0	1,942.0
Inventory	977.0	898.0	900.0
Other Current Assets	315.0	326.0	303.0
Total Current Assets	**4,824.0**	**4,054.0**	**3,217.0**
Long-Term Tangible Assets	2,585.0	2,472.0	2,391.0
Long-Term Intangible Assets	53.0	53.0	53.0
Other Long-Term Assets	0.0	0.0	0.0
Total Long-Term Assets	**2,638.0**	**2,525.0**	**2,444.0**
Total Assets	**7,462.0**	**6,579.0**	**5,661.0**
Liabilities			
Accounts Payable	846.0	726.0	563.0
Short-Term Debt	6.0	356.0	299.0
Other Current Liabilities	1,027.0	932.0	739.0
Total Current Liabilities	**1,879.0**	**2,014.0**	**1,601.0**
Long-Term Debt	2,775.0	2,257.0	2,214.0
Deferred Taxes	0.0	0.0	0.0
Other Long-Term Liabilities (non-interest bearing)	787.0	736.0	636.0
Total Long-Term Liabilities	**3,562.0**	**2,993.0**	**2,850.0**
Total Liabilities	**5,441.0**	**5,007.0**	**4,451.0**
Minority Interest	0.0	0.0	0.0
Shareholders' Equity			
Preferred Stock	0.0	0.0	0.0
Common Shareholders' Equity	2,021.0	1,572.0	1,210.0
Total Shareholders' Equity	**2,021.0**	**1,572.0**	**1,210.0**
Total Liabilities and Shareholders' Equity	**7,462.0**	**6,579.0**	**5,661.0**

Source: Thomson ONE database and Business Analysis and Valuation (BAV) Model V.5.

Nordstrom, Inc.
Standardized Statements of Cash Flows ($ millions)
AS REPORTED

Fiscal year	2010	2009	2008
Net Income	**613.0**	**441.0**	**401.0**
After-tax net interest expense (income)	78.6	87.4	81.1
Non-operating losses (gains)	0.0	0.0	0.0
Long-term operating accruals	465.0	495.0	445.0
Depreciation and amortization	327.0	313.0	302.0
Other	138.0	182.0	143.0
Operating cash flow before working capital investments	**1,156.6**	**1,023.4**	**927.1**
Net (investments in) or liquidation of operating working capital	99.0	315.0	2.0
Operating cash flow before investment in long-term assets	**1,255.6**	**1,338.4**	**929.1**
Net (investment in) or liquidation of operating long-term assets	(462.0)	(541.0)	(792.0)
Free cash flow available to debt and equity	**793.6**	**797.4**	**137.1**
After-tax net interest income (expense)	(78.6)	(87.4)	(81.1)
Net debt (repayment) or issuance	179.0	108.0	35.0
Free cash flow available to equity	**894.0**	**818.0**	**91.0**
Dividend (payments)	(167.0)	(139.0)	(138.0)
Net stock issuance (repurchase), and other equity changes	(16.0)	44.0	(239.0)
Net increase (decrease) in cash balance	**711.0**	**723.0**	**(286.0)**

Source: Thomson ONE database and Business Analysis and Valuation (BAV) Model V.5.

Nordstrom, Inc.
Condensed Statements of Income ($ millions)
AS REPORTED

Fiscal year	2010	2009	2008
Sales	**9,700.0**	**8,627.0**	**8,573.0**
Net Operating Profit after Tax	691.6	528.4	482.1
Net Income	613.0	441.0	401.0
+ Net Interest Expense after Tax	78.6	87.4	81.1
= Net Operating Profit after Tax	**691.6**	**528.4**	**482.1**
− Net Interest Expense after Tax	78.6	87.4	81.1
Interest Expense	133.0	148.0	145.0
− Interest Income	6.0	10	14.0
= Net Interest Expense (Income)	127.0	138.0	131.0
× (1 − Tax Expense/Pre-Tax Income)	0.62	0.63	0.62
= Net Interest Expense after Tax	**78.6**	**87.4**	**81.1**
= Net Income	**613.0**	**441.0**	**401.0**
− Preferred Stock Dividends	0.0	0.0	0.0
= Net Income to Common	**613.0**	**441.0**	**401.0**

Source: Thomson ONE database and Business Analysis and Valuation (BAV) Model V.5.

Nordstrom, Inc.
Condensed Beginning Balance Sheet ($ millions)
AS REPORTED

Fiscal year	2011	2010	2009
Beginning Net Working Capital	1,445.0	1,601.0	1,843.0
Accounts Receivable	2,026.0	2,035.0	1,942.0
+ Inventory	977.0	898.0	900.0
+ Other Current Assets	315.0	326.0	303.0
− Accounts Payable	846.0	726.0	563.0
− Other Current Liabilities	1,027.0	932.0	739.0
= **Beginning Net Working Capital**	**1,445.0**	**1,601.0**	**1,843.0**
+ **Beginning Net Long-Term Assets**	**1,851.0**	**1,789.0**	**1,808.0**
Long-Term Tangible Assets	2,585.0	2,472.0	2,391.0
+ Long-Term Intangible Assets	53.0	53.0	53.0
+ Other Long-Term Assets	0.0	0.0	0.0
− Minority Interest	0.0	0.0	0.0
− Deferred Taxes	0.0	0.0	0.0
− Other Long-Term Liabilities (non-interest bearing)	787.0	736.0	636.0
= **Beginning Net Long-Term Assets**	**1,851.0**	**1,789.0**	**1,808.0**
= **Total Beginning Net Assets**	**3,296.0**	**3,390.0**	**3,651.0**
Beginning Net Debt	1,275.0	1,818.0	2,441.0
Short-Term Debt	6.0	356.0	299.0
+ Long-Term Debt	2,775.0	2,257.0	2,214.0
− Cash	1,506.0	795.0	72.0
= **Beginning Net Debt**	**1,275.0**	**1,818.0**	**2,441.0**
+ **Beginning Preferred Stock**	**0.0**	**0.0**	**0.0**
+ **Beginning Shareholders' Equity**	**2,021.0**	**1,572.0**	**1,210.0**
= **Total Net Capital**	**3,296.0**	**3,390.0**	**3,651.0**

Source: Thomson ONE database and Business Analysis and Valuation (BAV) Model V.5.

Nordstrom, Inc.
Standardized Statements of Income ($ millions)
AS ADJUSTED

Fiscal Year	2010	2009	2008
Sales	9,700.0	8,627.0	8,573.0
Cost of Sales	5,508.0	5,015.0	5,115.0
Gross Profit	4,191.2	3,612.0	3,458.0
SG&A	2,685.0	2,465.0	2,386.0
Other Operating Expense	327.0	313.0	302.0
Operating Income	1,179.2	834.0	770.0
Investment Income	0.0	0.0	0.0
Other Income, net of Other Expense	0.0	0.0	9.0
Other Income	0.0	0.0	9.0
Other Expense	0.0	0.0	0.0
Net Interest Expense (Income)	163.4	138.0	131.0
Interest Income	6.0	10.0	14.0
Interest Expense	169.4	148.0	145.0

(*continued*)

Fiscal Year	2010	2009	2008
Minority Interest	0.0	0.0	0.0
Pre-Tax Income	**1,015.8**	**696.0**	**648.0**
Tax Expense	386.7	255.0	247.0
Unusual Gains, Net of Unusual Losses (after tax)	0.0	0.0	0.0
Net Income	**629.1**	**441.0**	**401.0**
Preferred Dividends	0.0	0.0	0.0
Net Income to Common	**629.1**	**441.0**	**401.0**

Source: Thomson ONE database and Business Analysis and Valuation (BAV) Model V.5.

Nordstrom, Inc.
Standardized Beginning Balance Sheet ($ millions)
AS ADJUSTED

Fiscal year	2011	2010	2009
Assets			
Cash and Marketable Securities	1,506.0	795.0	72.0
Accounts Receivable	2,026.0	2,035.0	1,942.0
Inventory	977.0	898.0	900.0
Other Current Assets	315.0	326.0	303.0
Total Current Assets	**4,824.0**	**4,054.0**	**3,217.0**
Long-Term Tangible Assets	3,294.8	3,050.0	2,391.0
Long-Term Intangible Assets	53.0	53.0	53.0
Other Long-Term Assets	0.0	0.0	0.0
Total Long-Term Assets	**3,347.8**	**3,103.0**	**2,444.0**
Total Assets	**8,171.8**	**7,157.0**	**5,661.0**
Liabilities			
Accounts Payable	846.0	726.0	563.0
Short-Term Debt	6.0	356.0	299.0
Other Current Liabilities	1,027.0	932.0	739.0
Total Current Liabilities	**1,879.0**	**2,014.0**	**1,601.0**
Long-Term Debt	3,460.0	2,835.0	2,214.0
Deferred Taxes	8.7	0.0	0.0
Other Long-Term Liabilities (non-interest bearing)	787.0	736.0	636.0
Total Long-Term Liabilities	**4,255.7**	**3,571.0**	**2,850.0**
Total Liabilities	**6,134.7**	**5,585.0**	**4,451.0**
Minority Interest	0.0	0.0	0.0
Shareholders' Equity			
Preferred Stock	0.0	0.0	0.0
Common Shareholders' Equity	2,037.1	1,572.0	1,210.0
Total Shareholders' Equity	**2,037.1**	**1,572.0**	**1,210.0**
Total Liabilities and Shareholders' Equity	**8,171.8**	**7,157.0**	**5,661.0**

Source: Thomson ONE database and Business Analysis and Valuation (BAV) Model V.5.

Nordstrom, Inc.
Standardized Statements of Cash Flows ($ millions)
AS ADJUSTED

Fiscal year	2010	2009	2008
Net Income	629.1	441.0	401.0
After-tax net interest expense (income)	101.2	87.4	81.1
Non-operating losses (gains)	0.0	0.0	0.0
Long-term operating accruals	510.5	495.0	445.0
Depreciation and amortization	363.8	313.0	302.0
Other	146.7	182.0	143.0
Operating cash flow before working capital investments	1,240.8	1,023.4	927.1
Net (investments in) or liquidation of operating working capital	99.0	315.0	2.0
Operating cash flow before investment in long-term assets	1,339.8	1,338.4	929.1
Net (investment in) or liquidation of operating long-term assets	(630.6)	(541.0)	(792.0)
Free cash flow available to debt and equity	709.2	797.4	137.1
After-tax net interest income (expense)	(101.2)	(87.4)	(81.1)
Net debt (repayment) or issuance	286.0	108.0	35.0
Free cash flow available to equity	894.0	818.0	91.0
Dividend (payments)	(167.0)	(139.0)	(138.0)
Net stock issuance (repurchase), and other equity changes	(16.0)	44.0	(239.0)
Net increase (decrease) in cash balance	711.0	723.0	(286.0)

Source: Thomson ONE database and analyst calculation.

Nordstrom, Inc.
Condensed Statements of Income ($ millions)
AS ADJUSTED

Fiscal year	2010	2009	2008
Sales	9,700.0	8,627.0	8,573.0
Net Operating Profit after Tax	730.3	528.4	482.1
Net Income	629.1	441.0	401.0
+ Net Interest Expense after Tax	101.2	87.4	81.1
= Net Operating Profit after Tax	730.3	528.4	482.1
− Net Interest Expense after Tax	101.2	87.4	81.1
Interest Expense	169.4	148.0	145.0
− Interest Income	6.0	10	14.0
= Net Interest Expense (Income)	163.4	138.0	131.0
× (1 − Tax Expense/Pre-Tax Income)	0.62	0.63	0.62
= Net Interest Expense after Tax	101.2	87.4	81.1
= Net Income	629.1	441.0	401.0
− Preferred Stock Dividends	0.0	0.0	0.0
= Net Income to Common	629.1	441.0	401.0

Source: Thomson ONE database and Business Analysis and Valuation (BAV) Model V.5.

Nordstrom, Inc.
Condensed Beginning Balance Sheet ($ millions)
AS ADJUSTED

Fiscal year	2011	2010	2009
Beginning Net Working Capital	1,445.0	1,601.0	1,843.0
Accounts Receivable	2,026.0	2,035.0	1,942.0
+ Inventory	977.0	898.0	900.0
+ Other Current Assets	315.0	326.0	303.0
− Accounts Payable	846.0	726.0	563.0
− Other Current Liabilities	1,027.0	932.0	739.0
= **Beginning Net Working Capital**	**1,445.0**	**1,601.0**	**1,843.0**
+ **Beginning Net Long-Term Assets**	**2,552.1**	**2,367.0**	**1,808.0**
Long-Term Tangible Assets	3,294.8	3,050.0	2,391.0
+ Long-Term Intangible Assets	53.0	53.0	53.0
+ Other Long-Term Assets	0.0	0.0	0.0
− Minority Interest	0.0	0.0	0.0
− Deferred Taxes	8.7	0.0	0.0
− Other Long-Term Liabilities (non–interest bearing)	787.0	736.0	636.0
= **Beginning Net Long-Term Assets**	**2,552.1**	**2,367.0**	**1,808.0**
= **Total Beginning Net Assets**	**3,997.1**	**3,968.0**	**3,651.0**
Beginning Net Debt	1,960.0	2,396.0	2,441.0
Short-Term Debt	6.0	356.0	299.0
+ Long-Term Debt	3,460.0	2,835.0	2,214.0
− Cash	1,506.0	795.0	72.0
= **Beginning Net Debt**	**1,960.0**	**2,396.0**	**2,441.0**
+ **Beginning Preferred Stock**	**0.0**	**0.0**	**0.0**
+ **Beginning Shareholders' Equity**	**2,037.1**	**1,572.0**	**1,210.0**
= **Total Net Capital**	**3,997.1**	**3,968.0**	**3,651.0**

Source: Thomson ONE database and Business Analysis and Valuation (BAV) Model V.5.

PROSPECTIVE ANALYSIS: FORECASTING

Most financial statement analysis tasks are undertaken with a forward-looking decision in mind—and much of the time it is useful to summarize the view developed in the analysis with an explicit forecast. Managers need forecasts to formulate business plans and provide performance targets; analysts need forecasts to help communicate their views of the firm's prospects to investors; and bankers and debt market participants need forecasts to assess the likelihood of loan repayment. Moreover, there are a variety of contexts (including but not limited to security analysis) where the forecast is usefully summarized in the form of an estimate of the firm's value. This estimate can be viewed as an attempt to best reflect in a single summary statistic the manager's or analyst's view of the firm's prospects.

Prospective analysis includes two tasks—forecasting and valuation—that together represent approaches to explicitly summarizing the analyst's forward-looking views. In this chapter we focus on forecasting; valuation is the topic of the next two chapters. Forecasting is not so much a separate analysis as it is a way of summarizing what has been learned through business strategy analysis, accounting analysis, and financial analysis. However, there are certain techniques and knowledge that can help a manager or analyst to structure the best possible forecast based on what has been learned in the previous steps. Below we summarize an approach to structuring the forecast, offer information useful in getting started, explore the relationship between the other analytical steps and forecasting, and give detailed steps to forecast earnings, balance sheet data, and cash flows. The key concepts discussed in this chapter are illustrated using a forecast for TJX, the off-price retailer examined in Chapter 5.

THE OVERALL STRUCTURE OF THE FORECAST

The best way to forecast future performance is to do it comprehensively—producing not only an earnings forecast, but also a forecast of cash flows and the balance sheet. A comprehensive approach is useful, even in cases where one might be interested primarily in a single facet of performance, because it guards against unrealistic implicit assumptions. For example, if an analyst forecasts growth in sales and earnings for several years without explicitly considering the required increases in working capital and plant assets and the associated financing, the forecast might possibly imbed unreasonable assumptions about asset turnover, leverage, or equity capital infusions.

A comprehensive approach involves many forecasts, but in most cases they are all linked to the behavior of a few key "drivers." The drivers vary according to the type of business, but for businesses outside the financial services sector, the sales forecast is nearly always one of the key drivers; profit margin is another. When asset turnover is expected to remain stable—often a realistic assumption—working capital accounts and investment in plants should track the growth in sales closely. Most major expenses also track sales, subject to expected shifts in profit margins. By linking forecasts of such amounts to the sales forecast, one can avoid internal inconsistencies and unrealistic implicit assumptions.

In some contexts the manager or analyst is interested ultimately in a forecast of cash flows, not earnings per se. Nevertheless, in practice even forecasts of cash flows tend to be grounded on forecasts of accounting numbers, including sales, earnings, assets, and liabilities. Of course it would be possible in principle to move directly to forecasts of cash flows—inflows from customers, outflows to suppliers and laborers, and so forth—and in some businesses this is a convenient way to proceed. In most cases, however, the growth prospects, profitability, and investment and financing needs of the firm are more readily framed in terms of accrual-based sales, operating earnings, assets, and liabilities. These amounts can then be converted to cash flow measures by adjusting for the effects of non-cash expenses and expenditures for working capital and plant, property, and equipment.

A Practical Framework for Forecasting

The most practical approach to forecasting a company's financial statements is to focus on projecting "condensed" financial statements, as used in the ratio analysis in Chapter 5, rather than attempting to project detailed financial statements at the level that the company reports. There are several reasons for this recommendation. Forecasting condensed financial statements involves a relatively small set of assumptions about the future of the firm, so the analyst will have more ability to think about each of the assumptions carefully. A detailed line-item forecast is likely to be very tedious, and an analyst may not have a good basis to make all the assumptions necessary for such forecasts. Further, for most purposes, condensed financial statements are all that are needed for analysis and decision making. We therefore approach the task of financial forecasting with this framework.

Recall that the condensed income statement that we used in Chapter 5 consists of the following elements: sales, net operating profits after tax (NOPAT), net interest expense after tax, taxes, and net income. The condensed balance sheet consists of net operating working capital, net long-term assets, net debt, and equity. Also recall that we start with a balance sheet at the beginning of the forecasting period. Assumptions about how we use the beginning balance sheet and run the firm's operations will lead to the income statement for the forecasting period; assumptions about investment in working capital and long-term assets, and how we finance these assets, results in a balance sheet at the end of the forecasting period.

To forecast the condensed income statement, one needs to begin with an assumption about next period's sales. Beyond that, assumptions about NOPAT margin, interest rate on beginning debt, and tax rate are all that are needed to prepare the condensed income statement for the period.

To forecast the condensed balance sheet for the end of the period (or the equivalent, the beginning of the next period), we need to make the following additional assumptions: (1) the ratio of net operating working capital to sales, to estimate the level of working capital needed to support those sales; (2) the ratio of net operating long-term assets to the following year's sales, to calculate the expected level of net operating long-term assets; and (3) the ratio of net debt to capital to estimate the levels of debt and equity needed to finance the estimated amount of assets on the balance sheet.

Once we have the condensed income statement and balance sheet, it is relatively straightforward to compute the condensed cash flow statement, including cash flow from operations before working capital investments, cash flow from operations after working capital investments, free cash flow available to debt and equity, and free cash flow available to equity.

We discuss how best to make the necessary assumptions to forecast the condensed income statement, balance sheet, and cash flow statements below.

PERFORMANCE BEHAVIOR: A STARTING POINT

Every forecast has, at least implicitly, an initial benchmark—some notion of how a particular amount, such as sales or earnings, would be expected to behave in the absence of detailed information. For example, in beginning to contemplate fiscal 2011 profitability for TJX, 2010 performance might be a starting point. Another potential place to begin might be 2010 performance adjusted for recent trends. A third possibility that might seem reasonable—but one that generally turns out not to be very useful—is the average performance over several prior years.

By the time one has completed a business strategy analysis, an accounting analysis, and a detailed financial analysis, the resulting forecast might differ significantly from the original point of departure. Nevertheless, for purposes of having a starting point that can help anchor the detailed analysis, it is also useful to know how certain financial statistics behave "on average" for all firms.

In the case of some key statistics, such as earnings, a point of departure based only on prior behavior of the number is more powerful than one might expect. Research demonstrates that some such benchmarks for earnings are almost as accurate as the forecasts of professional security analysts, who have access to a rich information set (we return to this point in more detail later). Thus, the benchmark is often not only a good starting point but also close to the amount forecast after detailed analysis. Large departures from the benchmark could be justified only in cases where the firm's situation is demonstrably unusual.

Reasonable points of departure for forecasts of key accounting numbers can be based on the evidence summarized next. Such evidence may also be useful for checking the reasonableness of a completed forecast.

Sales Growth Behavior

Sales growth rates tend to be "mean-reverting": firms with above-average or below-average rates of sales growth tend to revert over time to a "normal" level (historically in the range of 7 to 9 percent for U.S. firms) within three to ten years. Figure 6-1 documents this mean-reverting effect for the period 1993 through 2010 for all the publicly traded U.S. firms covered by the Compustat database. All firms are ranked in terms of their sales growth in 1993 (year 1) and formed into five portfolios based on the relative ranking of their sales growth in that year. Firms in portfolio 1 are in the top 20 percent of rankings in terms of their sales growth in 1993, those in portfolio 2 fall into the next 20 percent, while those in portfolio 5 are in the bottom 20 percent when ranked by sales growth. The sales growth rates of firms in each of these five portfolios are traced from 1993 through the subsequent nine years (years 2 to 10). The same experiment is repeated with 1997 and then 2001 as the base year (year 1). The results are averaged over the three experiments, and the resulting sales growth rates of each of the five portfolios for years 1 through 10 are plotted in Figure 6-1.

The figure shows that the group of firms with the highest growth initially—sales growth rates of a little over 70 percent—experience a decline to about an 8 percent

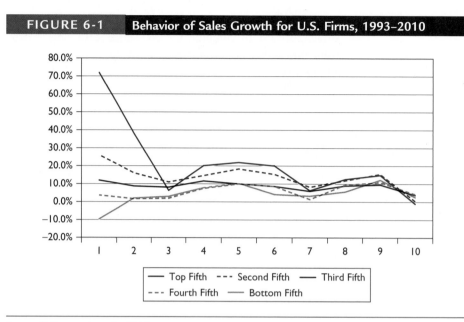

FIGURE 6-1   Behavior of Sales Growth for U.S. Firms, 1993–2010

Source: © Cengage Learning 2013

growth rate within three years and are never much above 20 percent in the next seven years. Those with the lowest initial sales growth rates, negative 10 percent, improve immediately to a marginally positive sales growth in year 2 and show positive growth through year 10. One explanation for the pattern of sales growth seen in Figure 6-1 is that as industries and companies mature, their growth rate slows down due to demand saturation and intra-industry competition. Therefore, even when a firm is growing rapidly at present, it is generally unrealistic to assume that the current high growth will persist indefinitely. Of course, how quickly a firm's growth rate reverts to the average depends on the characteristics of its industry and its own competitive position within an industry.

Earnings Behavior

Earnings have been shown on average to follow a process that can be approximated by a "random walk" or "random walk with drift." This implies that the prior year's earnings is a good starting point in considering future earnings potential. Even a simple random walk forecast—one that predicts next year's earnings will be equal to last year's earnings—is surprisingly useful. One study documents that professional analysts' year-ahead forecasts are only 22 percent more accurate, on average, than a simple random walk forecast.[1] Thus a final earnings forecast will usually not differ dramatically from a random walk benchmark. In addition, it is reasonable to adjust this simple benchmark for the earnings changes of the most recent quarter, i.e., changes relative to the comparable quarter of the prior year after controlling for the long-run trend in the series.

Although the average level of earnings over several prior years is not useful, long-term trends in earnings tend to be sustained on average, and so they are also worthy of consideration. If quarterly data are also included, then some consideration should usually be given to any departures from the long-run trend that occurred in the most recent quarter. For most firms, these most recent changes tend to be partially repeated in subsequent quarters.[2]

Return on Equity Behavior

Given that prior earnings serve as a useful benchmark for future earnings, one might expect the same to be true of measures of return on investment such as ROE. That, however, is not the case for two reasons. First, even though the average firm tends to sustain the current earnings level, this is not true of firms with unusual levels of ROE. Firms with abnormally high (low) ROE tend to experience earnings declines (increases).[3]

Second, firms with higher ROEs tend to expand their investment bases more quickly than others, which causes the denominator of the ROE to increase. Of course, if firms could earn returns on the new investments that match the returns on the old ones, then the level of ROE would be maintained. However, firms have difficulty continuing to generate those impressive ROEs. Firms with higher ROEs tend to find that, as time goes by, their earnings growth does not keep pace with growth in their investment base, and ROE ultimately falls.

The resulting behavior of ROE and other measures of return on investment is characterized as mean-reverting, a pattern similar to that observed for sales growth rates earlier. Firms with above-average or below-average rates of return tend to revert over time to a "normal" level (historically in the range of 10 to 15 percent for U.S. firms) within no more than ten years.[4] Figure 6-2 documents this mean-reverting effect for U.S. firms from 1993 through 2010. All firms are ranked in terms of their ROE in 1993 (year 1) and formed into five portfolios in a similar fashion to the sales growth analysis above. Firms in portfolio 1 have the top 20 percent ROE rankings in 1993, those in portfolio 2 fall into the next 20 percent, and those in portfolio 5 have the bottom 20 percent. The average ROE of firms in each of these five portfolios is then traced through nine subsequent years (years 2 to 10). The same experiment is repeated with 1997 and 2001 as the base year (year 1). Figure 6-2 plots the average ROE of each of the five portfolios in years 1 to 10 averaged across these three experiments.

Though the five portfolios start out in year 1 with a wide range of ROEs (−60 percent to +30 percent), by year 10 the pattern of mean-reversion is clear. The most profitable group of firms initially—with average ROEs of 30 percent—experience a decline to below 20 percent

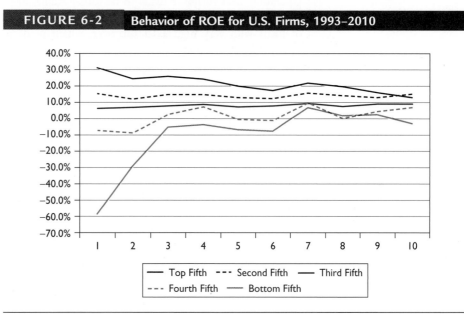

FIGURE 6-2   **Behavior of ROE for U.S. Firms, 1993–2010**

within five years. By year 10 this group of firms has an ROE of 12 percent. Those with the lowest initial ROEs (−60 percent) experience a dramatic increase in ROE in the first three years and are marginally profitable or at least close to breakeven by the final four years.

The pattern in Figure 6-2 is not a coincidence—it is exactly what the economics of competition would predict. The tendency of high ROEs to fall is a reflection of high profitability attracting competition; the tendency of low ROEs to rise reflects the mobility of capital away from unproductive ventures toward more profitable ones.[5] Despite the general tendencies documented in Figure 6-2, there are some firms whose ROEs may remain above or below normal levels for long periods of time. In some cases the phenomenon reflects the strength of a sustainable competitive advantage, but in other cases it is purely an artifact of conservative accounting methods. A good example of the latter phenomenon in the United States is pharmaceutical firms, whose major economic asset, the intangible value of research and development, is not recorded on the balance sheet and is therefore excluded from the denominator of ROE. For these firms, one could reasonably expect high ROEs—in excess of 20 percent—over the long run, even in the face of strong competitive forces.

The Behavior of Components of ROE

The behavior of rates of return on equity can be analyzed further by looking at the behavior of its key components. Recall from Chapter 5 that ROEs and profit margins are linked as follows:

$$\begin{aligned} \text{ROE} &= \text{Operating ROA} + (\text{Operating ROA} - \text{Net interest rate after tax}) \\ &\quad \times \text{Net financial leverage} \\ &= \text{NOPAT margin} \times \text{Opearting asset turnover} + \text{Spread} \\ &\quad \times \text{Net financial leverage} \end{aligned}$$

The time-series behaviors of the primary components of ROE for U.S. companies for 1993 through 2010 are shown in a series of figures in the appendix to this chapter. Some major conclusions can be drawn from these figures:

(1) Operating asset turnover tends to be rather stable, in part because it is largely a function of the technology of the industry. The only exception to this is the set of firms with very high asset turnover, which tends to decline somewhat over time before stabilizing;

(2) Net financial leverage also tends to be stable, simply because management policies on capital structure are not often changed; and

(3) NOPAT margin stands out as the most variable component of ROE. If the forces of competition drive abnormal ROEs toward more normal levels, the change is most likely to arrive in the form of changes in profit margins. The change in NOPAT margin will drive changes in the spread, since the cost of borrowing is likely to remain stable because leverage tends to be stable.

To summarize, profit margins and ROEs tend to be driven by competition to normal levels over time. What constitutes normal varies widely according to the technology employed within an industry and the corporate strategy pursued by the firm, both of which influence turnover and leverage.[6] In a fully competitive equilibrium, profit margins should remain high for firms that must operate with a low turnover, and vice versa.

The above discussion of rates of return and margins implies that a reasonable starting point for forecasting such statistics should consider more than just the most recent observation. One should also consider whether that rate or margin is above or below a normal level. If so, then absent detailed information to the contrary, one would expect some movement over time toward that norm. Of course this central tendency might be overcome in some cases—for example, where the firm has erected barriers to competition that can protect margins, even for extended periods. The lesson from the evidence, however, is that such cases are unusual.

In contrast to rates of return and margins, it is reasonable to assume that asset turnover, financial leverage, and net interest rate remain relatively constant over time. Unless there is an explicit change in technology or financial policy being contemplated for future periods, a reasonable starting point for assumptions for these variables is the current period level. The only exceptions to this appear to be firms with either very high asset turns that experience some decline in this ratio before stabilizing, or those firms with very low (usually negative) net debt to capital that appear to increase leverage before stabilizing. In addition, firms with very high levels of leverage tend to survive at a lower rate than more conservatively financed firms, driving down averages over time.

As we proceed with the steps involved in producing a detailed forecast, the reader will note that we draw on knowledge of the behavior of accounting numbers to some extent. However, it is important to keep in mind that a knowledge of average behavior will not fit all firms well. The art of financial statements analysis requires not only knowing what the "normal" patterns are but also having expertise in identifying those firms that will not follow the norm.

OTHER FORECASTING CONSIDERATIONS

In general, the mean-reverting behavior of sales growth and return on equity that is demonstrated by the broader market should hold for individual companies over time. The starting point for any forecast should therefore be the time-series behavior of the various measures of firm performance, as discussed. However, there are several other factors that the analyst should consider in making forecasts. These include an understanding of implications of the three levels of analysis that precede prospective analysis—strategy, accounting, and financial performance—and of macroeconomic considerations.[7]

Strategy, Accounting, and Financial Analysis and Forecasting

The analysis of a firm's strategy, accounting, and financial performance discussed throughout this book can generate important questions and insights about a firm's future performance. A projection of the future performance of any company must therefore be grounded in an understanding of the questions raised by these analyses, such as:

- From business strategy analysis: What are the characteristics of the industry in which a firm operates? Are there significant barriers to entry that are likely to deter future competition? If so, how long are they expected to last? What are the industry's growth prospects? How are they likely to affect future competition? And, does the company in question have a clear strategy that positions it for future success? For example, following up on the discussion of TJX's business strategy in Chapter 2, the analyst might ask whether TJX has succeeded in creating a retailing infrastructure that will allow it to continue to succeed in the U.S. market? Will it be able to replicate this market success internationally? At what rate will TJX be able to grow its sales, both in the short term and the long term, without sacrificing its margins? Will competitors be able to replicate TJX's efficiency while competing with a differentiated product offering?
- From accounting analysis: The accounting analysis discussed in Chapters 3 and 4 provide the analyst with an understanding of how a company's accounting affects its reported financial performance. Are assets overstated, requiring a future

write-down? Does the firm have off–balance sheet assets, such as R&D, that over-state reported rates of return? If so, what are the implications for future accounting statements? For TJX, we pointed out that the firm's accounting resulted in the value and associated liabilities of operating leases being excluded from the firm's assets and liabilities.

• From financial analysis: What are the sources of a firm's poor or strong recent performance? Is this performance sustainable? Are there any discernible patterns in the firm's past performance? If so, are there any reasons why this trend is likely to continue or to change?

These insights assist the analyst in answering questions of whether and for how long the firm will be able to maintain any competitive advantage and current performance levels, which are critical to forecasting. The answers to these questions determine the speed with which the firm's performance follows the general mean-reverting trends discussed above.

Macroeconomic Factors and Forecasting

For companies whose financial performance is highly sensitive to the economic cycle, the analyst will also want to consider macroeconomic conditions when making forecasts. Such is likely to be the case for TJX, which in the first half of 2011 faced a slow U.S. economic recovery following the economic crisis of 2008. Despite increased consumer spending, overall spending had not yet recovered to pre-recession levels. TJX's focus on value had helped it to maintain growth during the difficult economic time, with sales growing at average of 5 percent per year from FY 2007 through FY 2010.[8]

However, several factors are likely to affect TJX's growth prospects. High gas prices could temper consumer enthusiasm for driving to suburban stores and reduce consumer spending. Further, the slow pace of the economic recovery, with unemployment continuing to hover near the 10 percent level and a weak housing market, combined with concerns over U.S. government debt levels and legislative gridlock, raised concerns of the potential for a "double-dip" recession in the United States. Such economic conditions generally favor discount retailers such as TJX but also lead to reduced overall consumer spending.[9] Finally, TJX's expansion plans in Europe are likely to be affected by a deteriorating economic climate arising from the financial crises in Greece, Portugal, Spain, Ireland, and Italy.

While macroeconomic factors certainly will have an impact on TJX's performance in the short, medium, and long term, these factors cannot be forecast with a high degree of certainty. Consequently, for forecasting purposes it is generally advisable to assume that the impact of changes in the business cycle will even out in the long run.

MAKING FORECASTS

The analysis of TJX's performance in Chapter 5, and preceding discussions about general market behavior and TJX's strategic positioning, leads us to the conclusion that while TJX has consistently generated above-normal returns for its stakeholders, in the long run it is likely that a portion of the firm's abnormal profits will be competed away. The performance of the firm will revert toward the mean, as has been the general trend that we have seen earlier in the chapter.

Table 6-1 shows the forecasting assumptions we have made for TJX for years 2011 to 2020. We use as our base the adjusted financial statements detailed in Chapter 5 so that we can fully incorporate the impact of TJX's off–balance sheet operating leases into our forecasts. We have chosen a ten-year forecasting period because we believe that the firm

TABLE 6-1	Forecasting Assumptions for TJX									
Forecast Year	2011	2012	2013	2014	2015	2016	2017	2018	2019	2020
Sales growth rate	5.7%	6.6%	7.1%	6.9%	6.7%	6.5%	6.3%	6.1%	5.9%	5.7%
NOPAT margin	7.9%	7.5%	7.1%	6.7%	6.3%	5.9%	5.5%	5.0%	4.5%	4.0%
Beginning net operating working capital/sales	0.6%	1.0%	1.0%	1.0%	1.0%	1.0%	1.0%	1.0%	1.0%	1.0%
Beginning net operating long-term assets/sales	33.4%	34.0%	34.3%	34.5%	34.8%	35.0%	35.3%	35.5%	35.8%	36.0%
Beginning net debt to capital ratio	57.5%	57.5%	57.5%	57.5%	57.5%	57.5%	57.5%	57.5%	57.5%	57.5%
After-tax cost of debt	2.73	2.73	2.73	2.73	2.73	2.73	2.73	2.73	2.73	2.73

Source: © Cengage Learning 2013

should reach a relatively steady state of performance by then (discussed in further detail in Chapter 8). We discuss the forecasting assumptions below.

The forecasts for TJX for the first two or three years of the forecast period are a straightforward extrapolation of recent performance, which are heavily influenced by the company's strategic positioning, existing financials, and other company-specific metrics. This is generally a valid approach for an established company such as TJX for a few reasons. First, the company's management gives no indication of any major restructurings or changes to its operating and financing policies in the short term. Second, the beginning balance sheet for any forecast period places constraints on operating activities during that forecast period. For example, inventories at the beginning of the year will determine to some extent the sales activities during the year; stores in operation at the beginning of the year also determine to some extent the level of sales achievable during the year. To put it another way, since our discussion above shows that asset turns for a company do not usually change significantly in a short time, sales in any period are to some extent constrained by the beginning of the period assets in place in the company's balance sheet (although a company like TJX with explicit plans to expand assets through new store openings will be able to achieve some flexibility in this regard).

In contrast, when the analysis shifts focus to the later years of the forecast, the analyst should increasingly incorporate the influence of mean-reverting behavior demonstrated by the time-series analyses behavior discussed earlier.

Developing a Sales Growth Forecast

Despite the intense competition in retailing, TJX has built an impressive track record of steady earnings and sales growth, with 15 consecutive years of earnings per share growth as of 2010 and with annual consolidated comparable store sales increasing every year except one in its 34 years of business.[10] Given this history, it is reasonable to expect that TJX will continue to deliver growth over the forecast period. TJX has three geographic segments—the domestic market in the United States, which shows signs of stagnating as a result of the intensity of competition and market saturation; the Canadian market, which at this point seems to be behaving in a similar manner to the U.S. market; and the European market, where TJX's initial expansion out of North America into the markets of the U.K., Ireland, Germany, and Poland are critical components to continued expansion as the U.S. and Canadian markets approach saturation.

At the beginning of 2011, TJX operated over 2,000 stores in the United States with its T.J. Maxx, Marshalls, and Home Goods formats, with U.S. sales accounting for roughly 77 percent of total TJX revenue. Sales for T.J. Maxx and Marshalls stores (referred to collectively as Marmaxx) grew 6 percent in the year ending January 2011, compared to 7.4 percent in the previous year. Comparable store sales grew by 4 percent. Home Goods store sales (which made up about 12 percent of total U.S. sales) grew 9 percent in the year ending January 2011, with same store sales increasing 6 percent. Given that TJX has a fairly comprehensive U.S. retail network (the company estimated that it had achieved roughly 70 percent market penetration in the U.S. market by 2011), new store openings would be expected to increasingly cannibalize sales from existing stores in the same area as full market penetration is approached, reducing growth in comparable store sales.[11] New store openings are also likely to slow as unique attractive locations become increasingly scarce. At the same time, TJX viewed the recent economic downturn as an opportunity to broaden its customer base, perceiving a permanent consumer "shift to value," and has worked to attract and retain more affluent customers with store upgrades and targeted advertising.[12] However, it is unclear whether this shift in consumer sentiment will be permanent and whether this initiative will be successful in offsetting a coming slowdown in same store sales. TJX also faces increasing competition from high-end department stores that have established their own off-price formats (Nordstrom Rack, Off 5th), as well as from the growing online channel. Thus, it is reasonable to expect that TJX's overall U.S. sales growth will trend downward, though probably at a slower pace than would be implied by the mean-reverting tendency of sales growth for the overall market.

TJX Canada sales (which accounted for about 12 percent of total TJX sales) increased 16 percent for the year ended January 2011 as compared to the previous year, although roughly 9 percent of that was due to currency translation—previous year's sales growth had been only 1 percent, including currency translation impact, which reduced that level by 3 percent. Same store sales increased by 4 percent for the year ended January 2011 and 2 percent for the previous year. Absent currency translation effect, TJX Canada seems to be behaving in a similar manner to the U.S. segment. TJX estimates market penetration in Canada at about 70 percent in early 2011, and thus it is reasonable to expect that TJX Canada will exhibit similar sales growth characteristics as the U.S. market discussed above.[13]

TJX's European operation presents a more interesting forecasting challenge. The subtleties of local tastes and bureaucratic complexities in local real estate markets have made it extremely challenging for nondomestic retailing companies to establish market leadership outside their home markets. Since its entry into the U.K. in 1994, TJX has worked to establish its position as the only major off-price retailer in Europe, with operations in 2011 in the U.K., Germany, and Poland. Sales grew by 10 percent from 2009 to 2010, and 13 percent when a negative currency translation impact is excluded.[14] While TJX continues to see strong growth potential in Europe, early in 2011 it actually announced plans to slow its expansion in order to address execution concerns that in the year ended January 2011, resulted in a decrease in segment profit and a decline in same store sales.[15] Given TJX's estimate of 41 percent penetration in its European segment, it is reasonable to assume that once the company sorts out its operational issues, it will experience a rate of growth that may surpass that of its more penetrated markets

TABLE 6-2	Forecasted Sales Growth for TJX									
Forecast Year	2011	2012	2013	2014	2015	2016	2017	2018	2019	2020
TJX U.S./Canada	5.7%	6.4%	6.7%	6.5%	6.2%	6.0%	5.8%	5.7%	5.5%	5.3%
TJX Europe	5.0%	8.0%	10.0%	10.0%	10.0%	10.0%	10.0%	9.0%	8.5%	8.0%
Overall Sales Growth	5.7%	6.6%	7.1%	6.9%	6.7%	6.5%	6.3%	6.1%	5.9%	5.7%

Source: © Cengage Learning 2013

in the United States and Canada. However, on an overall basis, a higher growth rate in Europe will likely not be enough to overcome slowing growth in the United States and Canada, given that as of 2011 the European segment contributed only about 11 percent of total TJX sales revenue and, in our ten year forecast period, rises only to about 14 percent of total TJX sales revenue.

The projections in Table 6-2 reflect the analysis of TJX's three geographic segments discussed above. We have combined the U.S. and Canada segments given that they appear to have similar growth and saturation characteristics. For TJX overall we show a gradual improvement in sales growth over the next couple of years, followed by a slow decline in growth as the impact of mean-reversion pressures are felt. While this pattern is based on a mixture of business intelligence and a knowledge of long-term trends in the market, it is important to note that an analyst could capture much of the dynamics of the projections merely by assuming that TJX will not be immune to the long-run forces of competition and mean reversion.

Developing a NOPAT Margin Forecast

In the U.S. and Canadian markets, TJX is likely to face increasing direct competitive pressure from the high-end department stores such as Nordstrom and Saks as they expand their off-price brands in the United States, and from U.S. and domestic competitors such as Target, Wal-Mart, Nordstrom, and Hudson's Bay Company as they establish or expand their Canadian presence. In addition, an improving economy in the United States would be expected to shift some portion of the more affluent end of TJX's customer base back toward the high-end department stores as consumer sentiment improves. TJX believes that its program of store upgrades and targeted advertising will be successful in retaining its broader customer base as the economy rebounds. In addition, it expects its global supply chain infrastructure to help it continue to increase inventory turns and reduce the need for markdowns by purchasing later in the sales cycle. This improved merchandising and affluent customer retention, if successfully executed, could lead to a narrowing of the margin gap seen in the comparison of TJX and Nordstrom in Chapter 5. However, over time it is likely that competitive pressures will have a greater impact, leading to a steady decline in NOPAT margins, although perhaps at a slower rate than that of less successful competitors.

Slow customer acceptance, start-up costs, and less-developed infrastructure has resulted in TJX's European operations generating lower margins than its U.S./Canadian businesses. In addition, European execution problems and accompanying weak financial results in 2011 led the company to slow expansion plans until the issues had been resolved.[16] We anticipate that in the short term TJX's European margins will continue to be lower than those in the United States and Canada as the company sorts out its execution issues and establishes a larger presence in the market. Thereafter, margins in

TABLE 6-3	Forecasted NOPAT Margins for TJX									
Forecast Year	2011	2012	2013	2014	2015	2016	2017	2018	2019	2020
Overall NOPAT margin	7.9%	7.5%	7.1%	6.7%	6.3%	5.9%	5.5%	5.0%	4.5%	4.0%

Source: © Cengage Learning 2013

Europe will show slow improvement as customer acceptance grows and operational effi-ciencies are achieved. However, given the costs of managing expected higher growth in Europe and continued lower levels of consumer acceptance versus the United States, we expect that margins in Europe will remain lower than those of the U.S. and Canadian markets throughout the forecast period, further lowering the company's overall NOPAT margins. Table 6-3 shows our forecast of TJX's average NOPAT margins going forward. While we would have preferred to forecast NOPAT margins by segment, TJX does not provide fully allocated segment data in order for us to do so. As a result, our overall NOPAT margin forecast takes into account the analysis above.

Developing a Working Capital to Sales Forecast

As discussed in Chapter 5, TJX had an operating working capital ratio to sales of less than 1.0 in the year ended January 2011. The primary drivers of this low ratio were its focus on driving higher inventory turnover and its low accounts receivable levels result-ing from the strategic decision to outsource the TJX branded credit card operations. While TJX prides itself in prompt payment to vendors, as reflected in its reasonable 35.3 days accounts payable in 2010, this low ratio implies that TJX is able to fund its working capital needs—primarily for inventory—through its trade and other short-term creditors and accruals.

TJX continues to view its opportunistic buying strategy as critical to its success at maintaining low inventory levels, and it has built its global supplier network to facilitate this strategy.[17] Working capital needs are also likely to decline as TJX improves opera-tions in Europe and takes advantage of its growing international presence to negotiate more favorable terms with its suppliers. Therefore, it is reasonable to expect that its net operating working capital to sales ratio will remain at or near its current level as the firm's market power grows and it continues to invest in its supply chain.

Developing a Long-Term Assets to Sales Forecast

As the pace of TJX's new store openings in the United States and Canada slows, compa-rable store sales growth should improve as fewer new stores will open up near existing stores, reducing the risk of customer cannibalization. This should have a beneficial impact on the firm's long-term asset use in the United States and Canada. Counteracting this improvement is TJX's recent focus on attracting and retaining more affluent custo-mers with enhanced stores. Also, with growth in the asset-intensive European segment outpacing that of the North American businesses, TJX's ratio of long-term assets to sales is likely to gradually deteriorate over the forecast horizon.

Developing a Capital Structure Forecast

As we discussed previously (and as can be seen in the historical data on capital structure found in the appendix), a company's capital structure would typically be expected to remain constant over the forecast period, simply because management policies on capital structure are slow to change. We would expect this to be true of TJX as well after looking at recent actions related to capital structure taken by the company. For instance, TJX's Board of Directors authorized a $1.0 billion share repurchase program in February 2010, of which $594 million had yet to be repurchased as of January 2011. In addition, the Board of Directors approved a new stock repurchase program in February 2011 authorizing the repurchase of an additional $1.0 billion of TJX common stock. However, there was no time limit within which these purchases needed to be completed, and decisions on share repurchases were based on the firm's assessment of "various factors including anticipated excess cash flow, liquidity, market conditions, the economic environment and prospects for the business and other factors."[18] Thus, we expect that it is unlikely that TJX will make any fundamental change in its capital structure so that the firm's leverage and debt yield (5.5 percent before tax and 3.4 percent after tax) remain relatively stable.

Having made the set of key assumptions detailed above, it is a straightforward task to derive the forecasted income statements and beginning balance sheets for years 2011 through 2020 as shown in Table 6-4. Under these forecasts, TJX's sales will grow to $40.6 billion, almost double the level in 2010. By 2020, the firm will have a net operating asset base of $15.0 billion and shareholders' equity of $6.4 billion. Consistent with market-wide patterns of mean-reversion in returns, TJX's return on equity and operating return on assets will decline steadily—ROE from 55.4 percent in 2010 to 21.7 percent by 2020, and Operating ROA from 27.8 percent to 10.8 percent over the same period.

Cash Flow Forecasts

Once we have forecasted income statements and balance sheets, we can derive cash flows for the years 2011 through 2020. Note that we need to forecast the beginning balance sheet for 2021 to compute the cash flows for 2020. This balance sheet is not shown in Table 6-4. For the purpose of illustration, we assume that the sales growth and the balance sheet ratios remain the same in 2021 as in 2020. Based on this, we project a beginning balance sheet for 2021 and compute the cash flows for 2020. Cash flow to capital is equal to NOPAT minus increases in net working capital and net long-term assets. As Table 6-4 shows, the free cash flow to all providers of capital decreases from $1.1 billion in 2011 to $0.8 billion by 2020, while cash flow to equity, which adds/deducts cash inflows/outflows to debt holders, decreases from $1.4 billion to $1.0 billion over the same period.

SENSITIVITY ANALYSIS

The projections discussed thus far represent nothing more than an estimation of a most likely scenario for TJX. Managers and analysts are typically interested in a broader range of possibilities. An analyst estimating the value of TJX would typically consider the sensitivity of projections to the key assumptions about sales growth, profit margins, and asset utilization. What if TJX is able to retain more of its competitive advantage in the United States than assumed in the above forecasts? Alternatively, what if it is unable to successfully address its operational issues in Europe and is unable to replicate its success in the United States in other markets? It is wise to also generate projections based on a variety of assumptions to determine the sensitivity of the forecasts to these assumptions.

There is no limit to the number of possible scenarios that can be considered. One systematic approach to sensitivity analysis is to start with the key assumptions underlying a set of forecasts, and then examine the sensitivity to the assumptions with greatest uncertainty in a given situation. For example, if a company has experienced a variable pattern of gross margins in the past, it is important to make projections using a range

TABLE 6-4 Forecasted Financial Statements for TJX

Forecast Year	2011	2012	2013	2014	2015	2016	2017	2018	2019	2020
Beginning Balance Sheet										
Beg. net working capital	144.1	247.2	264.8	283.1	302.0	321.7	341.9	362.8	384.2	406.1
+ Beg. net long-term assets	7,754.4	8,406.0	9,069.1	9,765.6	10,495.4	11,258.0	12,052.7	12,878.7	13,734.5	14,618.9
= net operating assets	**7,898.5**	**8,653.3**	**9,333.9**	**10,048.7**	**10,797.4**	**11,579.7**	**12,394.7**	**13,241.4**	**14,118.7**	**15,025.0**
Net Debt	4,541.4	4,975.3	5,366.6	5,777.6	6,208.1	6,657.9	7,126.5	7,613.4	8,117.8	8,638.9
+ Preferred stock	0.0	0.0	0.0	0.0	0.0	0.0	0.0	0.0	0.0	0.0
+ Shareholders' equity	3,357.1	3,677.6	3,967.2	4,271.0	4,589.3	4,921.8	5,268.2	5,628.1	6,001.0	6,386.2
= Net capital	**7,898.5**	**8,653.3**	**9,333.9**	**10,048.7**	**10,797.4**	**11,579.7**	**12,394.7**	**13,241.4**	**14,118.7**	**15,025.0**
Income Statement										
Sales	23,192.9	24,723.6	26,479.0	28,306.1	30,202.6	32,165.7	34,192.2	36,277.9	38,418.3	40,608.2
Net operating profits after tax	1,832.2	1,854.3	1,880.0	1,896.5	1,902.8	1,897.8	1,880.6	1,813.9	1,728.8	1,624.3
− Net interest expense after tax	123.9	135.7	146.4	157.6	169.4	181.6	194.4	207.7	221.5	235.7
= Net income	1,708.4	1,718.6	1,733.6	1,738.9	1,733.4	1,716.2	1,686.2	1,606.2	1,507.4	1,388.7
− Preferred dividends	0	0	0	0	0	0	0	0	0	0
= Net income to common	**1,708.4**	**1,718.6**	**1,733.6**	**1,738.9**	**1,733.4**	**1,716.2**	**1,686.2**	**1,606.2**	**1,507.4**	**1,388.7**
Operating return on assets	23.2%	21.4%	20.1%	18.9%	17.6%	16.4%	15.2%	13.7%	12.2%	10.8%
Return on common equity	50.9%	46.7%	43.7%	40.7%	37.8%	34.9%	32.0%	28.5%	25.1%	21.7%
Book value of assets growth rate	23.7%	9.6%	7.9%	7.7%	7.5%	7.2%	7.0%	6.8%	6.6%	6.4%
Book value of common equity	16.2%	9.6%	7.9%	7.7%	7.5%	7.2%	7.0%	6.8%	6.6%	6.4%
Growth rate										
Net operating asset turnover	2.9	2.9	2.8	2.8	2.8	2.8	2.8	2.7	2.7	2.7
Cash Flow Data										
Net income	1,708.4	1,718.6	1,733.6	1,738.9	1,733.4	1,716.2	1,686.2	1,606.2	1,507.4	1,388.7
− Change in net working capital	103.1	17.6	18.3	19.0	19.6	20.3	20.9	21.4	21.9	23.2
− Change in net long-term assets	651.6	663.0	696.5	729.8	762.6	794.7	825.9	855.9	884.4	833.3
+ Change in net debt	434.0	391.3	411.0	430.5	449.8	468.6	486.9	504.4	521.1	492.4
= Free cash flow to equity	1,387.6	1,429.3	1,429.8	1,420.6	1,400.9	1,369.8	1,326.3	1,233.3	1,122.2	1,024.7
Net operating profit after tax	1,832.2	1,854.3	1,880.0	1,896.5	1,902.8	1,897.8	1,880.6	1,813.9	1,728.8	1,624.3
− Change in net working capital	103.1	17.6	18.3	19.0	19.6	20.3	20.9	21.4	21.9	23.2
− Change in net long-term assets	651.6	663.0	696.5	729.8	762.6	794.7	825.9	855.9	884.4	833.3
= Free cash flow to capital	1,077.5	1,173.7	1,165.2	1,147.7	1,120.5	1,082.8	1,033.8	936.6	822.5	767.9

Source: © Cengage Learning 2013

of margins. Alternatively, if a company has announced a significant change in its expansion strategy, asset utilization assumptions might be more uncertain. In determining where to invest one's time in performing sensitivity analysis, it is therefore important to consider historical patterns of performance, changes in industry conditions, and changes in a company's competitive strategy.

In the case of TJX, two likely alternatives to the forecast can be readily envisioned. The forecast presented above expects that TJX's above average success in the U.S. market gradually diminishes, while the European division addresses its operational issues and contributes stronger growth and improvement in performance. An upside case for TJX would have the firm continuing to achieve strong results in the United States and resisting the mean-reverting trends that characterize the market in general, in addition to the increased contribution from European operations. On the downside, the projected improvement in the European business could fail to materialize, hastening the decline in TJX's overall performance toward the market averages.

Seasonality and Interim Forecasts

Thus far, we have concerned ourselves with annual forecasts. However, especially for security analysts in the United States, forecasting is very much a quarterly exercise. Forecasting quarter-by-quarter raises a new set of questions. How important is seasonality? What is a useful starting point—the most recent quarter's performance? The comparable quarter of the prior year? Some combination of the two? How should quarterly data be used to produce an annual forecast? Does the item-by-item approach to forecasting used for annual data apply equally well to quarterly data? Full consideration of these questions lies outside the scope of this chapter, but we can begin to answer some of them.

Seasonality is a more important phenomenon in sales and earning behavior than one might guess. It is present for more than just the retail sector firms that benefit from holiday sales. Seasonality also results from weather-related phenomena (e.g., for electric and gas utilities, construction firms, and motorcycle manufacturers), new product introduction patterns (e.g., for the automobile industry), and other factors. Analysis of the time series behavior of earnings for U.S. firms suggests that at least some seasonality is present in nearly every major industry.

The implication for forecasting is that one cannot focus only on performance of the most recent quarter as a starting point. In fact, the evidence suggests that, in forecasting earnings, if one had to choose only one quarter's performance as a basis for forecasting, it would be the comparable quarter of the prior year, not the most recent quarter. Note how this finding is consistent with the reports of analysts or the financial press; when they discuss a quarterly earnings announcement, it is nearly always evaluated relative to the performance of the comparable quarter of the prior year, not the most recent quarter.

Research has produced models that forecast sales, earnings, or EPS based solely on prior quarters' observations. These models are not used by many analysts since they have access to much more information than such simple models contain. However, the models are useful for helping those unfamiliar with the behavior of earnings data to understand how it tends to evolve over time. Such an understanding can provide useful general background, a point of departure in forecasting that can be adjusted to reflect details not revealed in the history of earnings, or a "reasonableness" check on a detailed forecast.

One model of the earnings process that fits well across a variety of industries is the so-called Foster model.[19] Using Q_t to denote earnings (or EPS) for quarter t, and $E(Q_t)$ as its expected value, the Foster model predicts that

$$E(Q_t) = Q_{t-4} + \delta + \varphi(Q_{t-1} - Q_{t-5})$$

Foster shows that a model of the same form also works well with quarterly sales data.

The form of the Foster model confirms the importance of seasonality because it shows that the starting point for a forecast for quarter t is the earnings four quarters ago, Q_{t-4}. It states that, when constrained to using only prior earnings data, a reasonable forecast of earnings for quarter t includes the following elements:

- the earnings of the comparable quarter of the prior year (Q_{t-4});
- a long-run trend in year-to-year quarterly earnings increases (δ); and
- a fraction (φ) of the year-to-year increase in quarterly earnings experienced most recently ($Q_{t-1} - Q_{t-5}$).

The parameters δ and φ can easily be estimated for a given firm with a simple linear regression model available in most spreadsheet software.[20] For most firms the parameter φ tends to be in the range of .25 to .50, indicating that 25 to 50 percent of an increase in quarterly earnings tends to persist in the form of another increase in the subsequent quarter. The parameter δ reflects in part the average year-to-year change in quarterly earnings over past years, and it varies considerably from firm to firm.

Research indicates that the Foster model produces one quarter ahead forecasts that vary from actual results by $.30 to $.35 per share, on average. Such a degree of accuracy stacks up surprisingly well with that of security analysts, who obviously have access to much information ignored in the model. As one would expect, most of the evidence supports analysts' forecasts being more accurate, but the models are good enough to be a reasonable approximation in most circumstances. While it would certainly be unwise to rely completely on such a mechanistic model, an understanding of the typical earnings behavior reflected by the model is useful.

SUMMARY

Forecasting represents the first step of prospective analysis and serves to summarize the forward-looking view that emanates from business strategy analysis, accounting analysis, and financial analysis. Although not every financial statement analysis is accompanied by such an explicit summarization of a view of the future, forecasting is still a key tool for managers, consultants, security analysts, investment bankers, commercial bankers, and other credit analysts, among others.

The best approach to forecasting future performance is to do it comprehensively—producing not only an earnings forecast but also a forecast of cash flows and the balance sheet as well. Such a comprehensive approach provides a guard against internal inconsistencies and unrealistic implicit assumptions. The approach described here involves a condensed, line-by-line analysis, so as to recognize that different items on the income statement and balance sheet are influenced by different drivers. Nevertheless, it remains the case that a few key projections—such as sales growth and profit margin—usually drive most of the projected numbers.

The forecasting process should be embedded in an understanding of how various financial statistics tend to behave on average and what might cause a firm to deviate from that average. Absent detailed information to the contrary, one would expect sales and earnings numbers to persist at their current levels, adjusted for overall trends of recent years. However, rates of return on investment (ROEs) tend, over several years, to move from abnormal to normal levels—close to the cost of equity capital—as the forces of competition come into play. Profit margins also tend to shift to normal levels, but for this statistic "normal" varies widely across firms and industries, depending on the levels of asset turnover and leverage. Some firms are capable of creating barriers to entry that enable them to fight these tendencies toward normal returns, even for many years, but such firms are the unusual cases.

Forecasting should be preceded by a comprehensive business strategy, accounting, and financial analysis. It is important to understand the dynamics of the industry in which the firm operates and its competitive positioning within that industry. Therefore, while general market trends provide a useful benchmark, it is critical that the analyst incorporate the views developed about the firm's prospects to guide the forecasting process.

For some purposes, including short-term planning and security analysis, forecasts for quarterly periods are desirable. One important feature of quarterly data is seasonality; at least some seasonality exists in the sales and earnings data of nearly every industry. An understanding of a firm's intra-year peaks and valleys is a necessary ingredient of a good forecast of performance on a quarterly basis.

Forecasts provide the input for estimating a firm's value, which can be viewed as the best attempt to reflect in a single summary statistic the manager's or analyst's view of the firm's prospects. The process of converting a forecast into a value estimate is labeled valuation and is discussed in the next chapter.

DISCUSSION QUESTIONS

1. Merck is one of the largest pharmaceutical firms in the world, and over an extended period of time in the recent past, it consistently earned higher ROEs than the pharmaceutical industry as a whole. As a pharmaceutical analyst, what factors would you consider to be important in making projections of future ROEs for Merck? In particular, what factors would lead you to expect Merck to continue to be a superior performer in its industry, and what factors would lead you to expect Merck's future performance to revert to that of the industry as a whole?

2. John Right, an analyst with Stock Pickers, Inc., claims, "It is not worth my time to develop detailed forecasts of sales growth, profit margins, et cetera, to make earnings projections. I can be almost as accurate, at virtually no cost, using the random walk model to forecast earnings." What is the random walk model? Do you agree or disagree with John Right's forecast strategy? Why or why not?

3. Which of the following types of businesses do you expect to show a high degree of seasonality in quarterly earnings? Explain why.
   - a supermarket
   - a pharmaceutical company
   - a software company
   - an auto manufacturer
   - a clothing retailer

4. What factors are likely to drive a firm's outlays for new capital (such as plant, property, and equipment) and for working capital (such as receivables and inventory)? What ratios would you use to help generate forecasts of these outlays?

5. How would the following events (reported this year) affect your forecasts of a firm's future net income?
   - an asset write-down
   - a merger or acquisition
   - the sale of a major division
   - the initiation of dividend payments

6. Consider the following two earnings forecasting models:

Model 1:
$$E(EPS_{t+1}) = EPS_t$$

$$E(EPS_{t+1}) = \frac{1}{5}\sum_{t=1}^{5} EPS_t$$

$E(EPS_{t+1})$ is the expected forecast of earnings per share for year $t+1$, given information available at t. Model 1 is usually called a random walk model for earnings, whereas Model 2 is called a mean-reverting model. The earnings per share for TJX for the fiscal years ending January 2006 (FY2005) through January 2010 (FY2009) are as follows:

Fiscal Year	2005	2006	2007	2008	2009
EPS	$1.40	$1.60	$1.70	$2.00	$2.80

a. What would the forecast for earnings per share in FY2010 be for each model?
b. Actual earnings per share for TJX in FY2010 were $3.30. Given this information, what would be the FY2011 forecast for earnings per share for each model? Why do the two models generate quite different forecasts? Which do you think would better describe earnings per share patterns? Why?

7. Joe Fatcat, an investment banker, states, "It is not worth my while to worry about detailed long-term forecasts. Instead, I use the following approach when forecasting cash flows beyond three years: I assume that sales grow at the rate of inflation, capital expenditures are equal to depreciation, and that net profit margins and working capital to sales ratios stay constant." What pattern of return on equity is implied by these assumptions? Is this reasonable?

NOTES

1. See P. O'Brien, "Analysts' Forecasts as Earnings Expectations," *Journal of Accounting and Economics* (January 1988): 53–83.
2. See G. Foster, "Quarterly Accounting Data: Time Series Properties and Predictive Ability Results," *The Accounting Review* (January 1977): 1–21.
3. See R. Freeman, J. Ohlson, and S. Penman, "Book Rate-of-Return and Prediction of Earnings Changes: An Empirical Investigation," *Journal of Accounting Research* (Autumn 1982): 639–53.
4. See S. Penman, "An Evaluation of Accounting Rate-of-Return," *Journal of Accounting, Auditing, and Finance* (Spring 1991): 233–56; E. Fama and K. French, "Size and Book-to-Market Factors in Earnings and Returns," *Journal of Finance* (March 1995): 131–56; and V. Bernard, "Accounting-Based Valuation Methods: Evidence on the Market-to-Book Anomaly and Implications for Financial Statements Analysis," (working paper, University of Michigan, 1994). Ignoring the effects of accounting artifacts, ROEs should be driven in a competitive equilibrium to a level approximating the cost of equity capital.
5. The pattern of ROE mean reversion is not just a U.S. phenomenon. It is also common among non-U.S. firms. Research finds that the pattern persists across a wide range of countries, and that mean reversion is faster in countries with more competitive product and capital markets, and with less efficient governments. See P. Healy, G. Serafeim, S. Srinivasan, and G. Yu, "Market Competition, Government Efficiency, and Profitability Around the World," HBS Working Paper, No. 12-010, 2011.

6. A "normal" profit margin is that which, when multiplied by the turnover achievable within an industry and with a viable corporate strategy, yields a return on investment that just covers the cost of capital. However, as mentioned above, accounting artifacts can cause returns on investment to deviate from the cost of capital for long periods, even in a competitive equilibrium.

7. A recent paper by B. Groysberg, P. Healy, N. Nohria, and G. Serafeim, "What Factors Drive Analyst Forecasts?" *Financial Analysts Journal* 67, no. 4 (July–August 2011) finds that, controlling for prior year performance, the most important factors explaining analysts' revenue and earnings forecasts are their assessments of its industry's growth prospects, followed by their evaluations of the quality of its top management, the firm's ability to execute its strategy, whether its judged to have a performance-driven culture, and the competitiveness of its industry.

8. Thomson ONE, accessed May 2011.

9. For instance, see Tim Fernholz, "With Debt Ceiling Reached, Tensions Rise First in Washington," *National Journal*, May 26, 2011, http://www.nationaljournal.com/budget/with-debt-limit-reached-tensions-rise-first-in-washington-20110516, accessed May 2011, and Simon Constable, "Economist Shiller Sees Potential for "Double Dip' Recession," *Wall Street Journal*, August 28, 2010, http://online.wsj.com/article/SB10001424052748704147804575455370525902224.html, accessed May 2011.

10. TJX Companies, Inc., 2010 Annual Report, p. 1, http://www.tjx.com/investor_landing.asp, accessed May 2011.

11. TJX Companies, Inc., January 29, 2011, Form 10-K (filed March 30, 2011), pp. 5–6, http://www.tjx.com/investor_landing.asp, accessed May 2011.

12. TJX Companies, Inc., 2009 Annual Report, pp. 3–4, http://www.tjx.com/investor_landing.asp, accessed May 2011.

13. TJX Companies, Inc., January 29, 2011, Form 10-K (filed March 30, 2011), pp. 27–28, http://www.tjx.com/investor_landing.asp, accessed May 2011.

14. TJX Companies, Inc., 2009 Annual Report, p. 8, http://www.tjx.com/investor_landing.asp, accessed May 2011.

15. TJX Companies, Inc., January 29, 2011, Form 10-K (filed March 30, 2011), p. 28, http://www.tjx.com/investor_landing.asp, accessed May 2011.

16. Ibid, p. 28.

17. TJX Companies, Inc., 2009 Annual Report, http://www.tjx.com/investor_landing.asp, accessed May 2011.

18. TJX Companies, Inc., 2010 Annual Report, p. 31, http://www.tjx.com/investor_landing.asp, accessed May 2011.

19. See Foster, op. cit. A somewhat more accurate model is furnished by Brown and Rozeff, but it requires interactive statistical techniques for estimation. See L. Brown and M. Rozeff, "Univariate Time Series Models of Quarterly Accounting Earnings per Share," *Journal of Accounting Research* (Spring 1979): 179–89.

20. To estimate the model, we write in terms of realized earnings (as opposed to expected earnings) and move Q_{t-4} to the left-hand side:

$$Q_t - Q_{t-4} = \delta + \phi(Q_{t-1} - Q_{t-5}) + e_t$$

We now have a regression where $(Q_t - Q_{t-4})$ is the dependent variable, and its lagged value—$(Q_{t-1} - Q_{t-5})$—is the independent variable. Thus, to estimate the equation, prior earnings data must first be expressed in terms of year-to-year changes; the change for one quarter is then regressed against the change for the most recent quarter. The intercept provides an estimate of δ, and the slope is an estimate of φ. The equation is typically estimated using 24 to 40 quarters of prior earnings data.

APPENDIX The Behavior of Components of ROE

In Figure 6-2 we show that ROEs tend to be mean-reverting. In this appendix we show the behavior of the key components of ROE—operating ROA, operating margin, operating asset turnover, and net financial leverage. These ratios are computed using the same portfolio approach described in the chapter, based on the data for all publicly listed U.S. firms for the time period 1993 through 2010 as listed in the Compustat database.

FIGURE A-1 Behavior of Operating ROA for U.S. Firms, 1993–2010

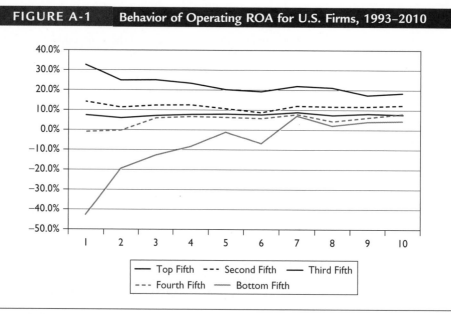

Source: © Cengage Learning 2013

FIGURE A-2 Behavior of NOPAT Margin for U.S. Firms, 1993–2010

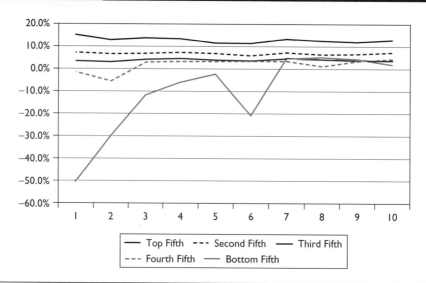

Source: © Cengage Learning 2013

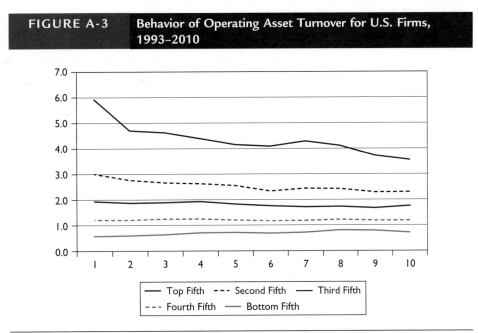

FIGURE A-3   Behavior of Operating Asset Turnover for U.S. Firms, 1993–2010

Source: © Cengage Learning 2013

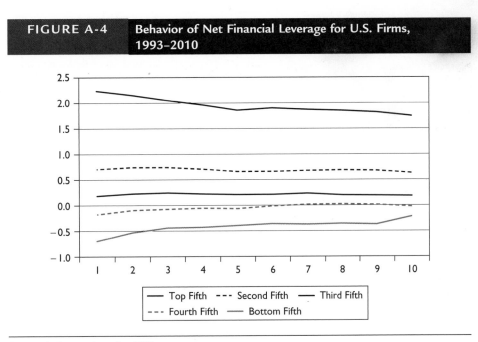

FIGURE A-4   Behavior of Net Financial Leverage for U.S. Firms, 1993–2010

Source: © Cengage Learning 2013

Chapter 7

PROSPECTIVE ANALYSIS: VALUATION THEORY AND CONCEPTS

The previous chapter introduced forecasting, the first stage of prospective analysis. In this and the following chapter we describe valuation, the second and final stage of prospective analysis. This chapter focuses on valuation theory and concepts, and the following chapter discusses implementation issues.

Valuation is the process of converting forecasts into an estimate of the value of the firm's assets or equity. At some level, nearly every business decision involves valuation, at least implicitly. Within the firm, capital budgeting involves considering how a particular project will affect firm value. Strategic planning focuses on how value is influenced by larger sets of actions. Outside the firm, security analysts conduct valuation to support their buy/sell recommendations, and potential acquirers (often with the assistance of investment bankers) estimate the value of target firms and the synergies they might offer. Even credit analysts, who typically do not explicitly estimate firm value, must at least implicitly consider the value of the firm's equity "cushion" if they are to maintain a complete view of the risk associated with lending activity.

In practice, a wide variety of valuation approaches are employed. For example, in evaluating the fairness of a takeover bid, investment bankers commonly use five to ten different methods of valuation. Among the available methods are the following:

- *Valuation based on price multiples.* Under this approach, a current measure of performance or single forecast of performance is converted into value by applying an appropriate price multiple derived from the value of comparable firms. For example, firm value can be estimated by applying a price-to-earnings ratio to a forecast of the firm's earnings for the coming year. Other commonly used multiples include price-to-book ratios and price-to-sales ratios.
- *Discounted dividends.* This approach expresses the value of the firm's equity as the present value of forecasted future dividends.
- *Discounted abnormal earnings.* Under this approach, the value of the firm's equity is expressed as the sum of its current book value and present value of forecasted abnormal earnings.
- *Discounted cash flow (DCF) analysis.* This approach involves the production of detailed, multiple-year forecasts of cash flows. The forecasts are then discounted at the firm's estimated cost of capital to arrive at an estimated value.

These methods are developed throughout the chapter, and their pros and cons discussed. To simplify our discussion, we illustrate valuation for a firm that is exclusively equity-financed. Chapter 8 discusses valuation implementation challenges, including valuing firms that are financially leveraged.

VALUATION USING PRICE MULTIPLES

Valuations based on price multiples are widely used by analysts. The primary reason for their popularity is their simplicity. The approach typically involves the following steps:

Step 1: Select a measure of performance or value (e.g., earnings, sales, cash flows, book equity, book assets) as the basis for the multiple. The two most commonly used performance measures are earnings and book equity.

Step 2: For firms that are comparable to the firm analyzed, deflate their stock prices by their selected performance measure to generate multiples, such as price-earnings multiples or the price-to-book multiples.

Step 3: Apply the average multiple for the comparable firms to the performance or value measure of the firm being analyzed.

Under this approach, the analyst relies on the market to undertake the difficult task of considering the short- and long-term prospects for growth and profitability and their implications for the values of the comparable firms. Then the analyst *assumes* that the pricing of the comparable firms is applicable to the firm at hand.

Key Issues with Multiples-Based Valuation

On the surface, using multiples seems straightforward. Unfortunately, in practice it is not as simple as it would appear. Identification of "comparable" firms is often quite difficult. There are also some choices to be made concerning how multiples will be calculated. Finally, explaining why multiples vary across firms, and how applicable another firm's multiple is to the one at hand, requires a sound understanding of the determinants of each multiple.

Selecting Comparable Firms

Ideally, price multiples used in a comparable firm analysis are those for firms with similar operating and financial characteristics. Firms within the same industry are the most obvious candidates. But even within narrowly defined industries, it is often difficult to identify comparable firms. Many firms are in multiple industries, making it difficult to identify representative benchmarks. In addition, firms within the same industry frequently have different strategies, growth opportunities, and profitability, creating comparability problems.

One way of dealing with these issues is to average across *all* firms in the industry. The analyst implicitly hopes that the various sources of non-comparability cancel each other out, so that the firm being valued is comparable to a "typical" industry member. Another approach is to focus on only those firms within the industry that are most similar.

For example, consider using multiples to value TJX. Business databases such as OneSource and Hoover's classify TJX as belonging to sectors such as retail apparel, department stores, and family clothing stores. As we discussed in Chapter 2, given its broad demographic customer base, its competitors include Neiman Marcus, Saks Fifth Avenue, and Nordstrom on the high end, Sears, Dillards, Macy's, and J.C. Penney in the mid-market, and Wal-Mart and Target at the discount level. The average price-earnings ratio for TJX's publicly listed competitors in 2010 was 23.7 and the average price-to-book ratio was 2.1. However, it is unclear whether these multiples are useful benchmarks for valuing TJX. TJX attracts a broader demographic than the full-line stores of its more narrowly focused high-end competitors, offers a more targeted value proposition (high-end merchandise at discount prices) than mid-market players such as Sears and

J.C. Penney, and presents a more specific product offering (apparel and home goods) than its discount competitors Wal-Mart and Target. In addition, it competes against specialized apparel and home goods retailers both online and off.

Multiples for Firms with Poor Performance

Price multiples can be affected when the denominator variable is temporarily performing poorly. This is especially common when the denominator is a flow measure, such as earnings or cash flows. For example, Sears Holding Corp., one of TJX's mid-market competitors, was barely profitable in the fiscal years ended January 2009, 2010, and 2011. Its 2010 price-earnings ratio of 63.9, which was well above the industry average, indicated that investors expected the company to experience a performance turnaround. Consequently, including Sears as one of the benchmark firms in computing an industry price-earnings multiple for TJX would probably be misleading.

Analysts have numerous options for handling the problems for multiples created by transitory shocks to the denominator. One option is to simply exclude firms with large transitory effects from the set of comparable firms. If Sears Holding Corp. were excluded from TJX's peer group, the average price-earnings ratio for the industry grouping used declines from 23.7 to 17.9, which is much closer to the industry median ratio of 15.0. The magnitude of this effect illustrates how sensitive price-earnings multiples can be to transitory shocks. If transitory poor performance is due to a one-time write-down or special item, analysts can simply exclude the effect from their computation of the comparable multiple. Finally, analysts can reduce the effect of temporary problems in past performance on multiples by using a denominator that is a forecast of future performance rather than the past measure itself. Multiples based on forecasts are termed *leading* multiples, whereas those based on historical data are called *trailing* multiples. Leading multiples are less likely to include one-time gains and losses in the denominator, simply because such items are difficult to anticipate.

Adjusting Multiples for Leverage

Price multiples should be calculated in a way that preserves consistency between the numerator and denominator. Consistency is an issue for those ratios where the denominator reflects performance *before* servicing debt. Examples include the price-to-sales multiple and any multiple of operating earnings or operating cash flows. When calculating these multiples, the numerator should include not just the market value of equity but the value of debt as well.

THE DISCOUNTED DIVIDEND VALUATION METHOD

Finance theory holds that the value of any financial claim is the present value of the cash payoffs that its claimholders receive. Since shareholders receive cash payoffs from a company in the form of dividends, the value of their equity is the present value of future dividends (including any liquidating dividend).

$$\text{Equity value} = \text{PV(Expected future dividends)}$$

The present value concept is used to make it possible to sum up future dividends received in different time periods. A dollar of dividends received today is worth more than a dollar received in the future because the dollar received today can be reinvested, enabling the investor to receive the reinvested dollar plus a return on that investment in the future. For example, suppose a dollar received today can be invested to earn an annual return of 10 percent. After one year, the original dollar is worth $1.10 ($1 + $1 * 10%), and after two years it is worth $1.21 ($1.10 + $1.10 * 10%). This process of converting dollars today into future dollars is called compounding.

The conversion of future dollars into today's dollars is called discounting. Using the above example, $1 received in one year's time is equivalent to $0.909 today ($1/$1.10). One dollar received in two years is worth $0.826 ($1/$1.21). Appendix A provides a more comprehensive review of the present value concept.

To better understand how the discounted dividend approach works, consider the following simplified example. At the beginning of year 1, Down Under Company raises $60 million of equity and uses the proceeds to buy a fixed asset. Operating profits before depreciation (all received in cash) are expected to be $40 million in year 1, $50 million in year 2, and $60 million in year 3. The firm pays out all operating profits as dividends and pays no taxes. At the end of year 3, the company terminates and has no remaining value. If the firm's shareholders expect to earn a 10 percent return, the value of the firm's equity (after the initial equity has been raised and the fixed asset purchased) is $122.8 million, computed as follows:

Year	Dividend (1)	PV Factor (2)	PV of Dividend (1 × 2)
1	$40 m	0.909	$36.4 m
2	50 m	0.826	41.3 m
3	60 m	0.751	45.1 m
Equity value			$122.8 m

Of course, in reality firms' lives are not three years but indefinite. How does the dividend discount model capture an indefinite stream of future dividends? The typical way is to assume that after some time the owner sells the stock, generating a terminating dividend or terminal value. But what would the terminating value of the stock be worth? Several simplifying assumptions can be used to answer this question and are discussed in the following chapter.

In summary, the dividend discount model is the basis for most of the popular theoretical approaches for stock valuation. It resolves many of the limitations discussed for multiples. But it also has its own shortcomings, particularly for firms that pay no dividends or very low dividends, where it is difficult to forecast future dividends. We therefore turn to modifications of the dividend discount model.

THE DISCOUNTED ABNORMAL EARNINGS VALUATION METHOD

There is a direct link between dividends and earnings. If all equity (other than capital transactions) flows through the income statement,[1] the ending book value of equity for existing shareholders is simply the beginning book value plus net income less dividends.[2] This relation can be rewritten as follows:

Dividends = Net Income + Beginning book equity − Ending book equity

By using this identity, we can rewrite the dividend discount formula so that the equity value is as follows:[3]

Equity value = Book equity + PV (Expected abnormal earnings)

Book equity is simply the latest book value of equity. Abnormal earnings are net income less a capital charge and are computed as follows:

Abnormal earnings = Net income − (Expected return * Beginning book equity)

The capital charge recognizes that shareholders have an opportunity cost for the equity funds invested in the business. At the beginning of a year (or quarter) on a book basis funds equal to the beginning book equity are invested in the firm on the shareholders' behalf. They expect to earn a return on this investment, their expected return. Abnormal earnings arise when the firm is able to produce earnings that exceed this capital charge.

The earnings-based formulation has intuitive appeal. If a firm can earn only the required rate of return on its book value, then investors should be willing to pay no more than book value for the stock. Investors should pay more or less than book value if earnings are above or below this normal level. Thus, the deviation of a firm's market value from book value depends on its ability to generate "abnormal earnings." The formulation also implies that a firm's stock value reflects the cost of its existing net assets (i.e., its book equity) plus the present value of future growth options (represented by cumulative abnormal earnings).

To illustrate the earnings-based valuation approach, let us return to the Down Under Company three-year example. Assuming the company depreciates its fixed assets using the straight-line method, its accounting-based earnings will be $20 million lower than dividends in each of the three years. Year 1 earnings are therefore expected to be $20 million (the projected cash inflows/dividends of $40 million net of depreciation). The capital charge is $6 million, representing investors' required return of 10 percent times the book value of assets at the beginning of year 1 ($60 million, the cost of fixed assets). Consequently, expected abnormal earnings for year 1 are $14 million ($20 million less the $6 million capital charge). The firm's beginning book equity, earnings, capital charges, abnormal earnings, and valuation will be as follows:

Year	Expected Beginning Book Value	Expected Earnings	Capital Charge	Expected Abnormal Earnings	PV Factor	PV of Expected Abnormal Earnings
1	$60 m	$20 m	$6 m	$14 m	0.909	$12.7 m
2	40 m	30 m	4 m	26 m	0.826	21.5 m
3	20 m	40 m	2 m	38 m	0.751	28.6 m
Cumulative PV of abnormal earnings						62.8 m
+ Beginning book value						60.0 m
= Equity value						$122.8 m

This stock valuation of $122.8 million is identical to the value estimated when the expected future dividends are discounted directly.

Accounting Methods and Discounted Abnormal Earnings

One question that arises when valuation is based directly on earnings and book values is how the estimate is affected by managers' choice of accounting methods and accrual estimates. Would estimates of value differ for two otherwise identical firms if one used more conservative accounting methods than the other? We will see that, provided analysts recognize the impact of differences in accounting methods on future earnings (and hence their earnings forecasts), the accounting effects *per se* should have no influence on their value estimates. There are two reasons. First, double-entry bookkeeping is self-correcting. Inflated earnings for one period ultimately have to be reversed in subsequent periods. Second, accounting choices that affect a firm's current earnings also affect its book value, and therefore affect the capital charges used to estimate future abnormal earnings. For example, conservative accounting lowers a firm's current earnings and book equity, but also reduces future capital charges and inflates its future abnormal earnings.

To see how these two effects undo the effect of differences in accounting methods or accrual estimates let us return to Down Under Company and see what happens if its managers choose to be conservative and expense some unusual costs that could have been capitalized as inventory at year 1. This accounting decision causes earnings and ending book value to be lower by $10 million. The inventory is then sold in year 2. For the time being, let us say the accounting choice has no influence on the analyst's view of the firm's real performance.

Management's choice reduces abnormal earnings in year 1 and book value at the beginning of year 2 by $10 million. However, future earnings will be higher, for two reasons. First, future earnings will be higher by $10 million when the inventory is sold in year 2. Second, the capital charge for normal earnings in year 2 will be $1 million lower, representing 10 percent (investors' required return) times $10 million decline in book value of equity at the beginning of year 2. The $10 million decline in abnormal earnings in year 1 is therefore perfectly offset (on a present value basis) by the $11 million higher abnormal earnings in year 2. As a result, the value of Down Under Company under conservative reporting is identical to the value under the earlier accounting method ($122.8 million).

Year	Expected Beginning Book Value	Expected Earnings	Expected Abnormal Earnings	PV Factor	PV of Expected Abnormal Earnings
1	$60 m	$10 m	$4 m	0.909	$3.6 m
2	30 m	40 m	37 m	0.826	30.6 m
3	20 m	40 m	38 m	0.751	28.6 m
Cumulative PV of abnormal earnings					62.8 m
+ Beginning book value					60.0 m
= Equity value					$122.8 m

Provided the analyst is aware of biases in accounting data that arise from managers' using aggressive or conservative accounting choices, abnormal earnings-based valuations are unaffected by variation in accounting decisions. This shows that strategic and accounting analyses are critical precursors to abnormal earnings valuation. The strategic and accounting analysis tools help the analyst to identify whether abnormal earnings arise from sustainable competitive advantage or from unsustainable accounting manipulations. For example, consider the implications of failing to understand the reasons for a decline in earnings from a change in inventory policy for Down Under Company. If an analyst mistakenly interpreted the decline as indicating that the firm was having difficulty moving its inventory, rather than that it had used conservative accounting, the analyst might reduce expectations of future earnings. The estimated value of the firm *would* then be lower than that reported in our example.

Key Analysis Questions

Valuation of equity under the discounted abnormal earnings method requires the analyst to answer the following questions:

- Is the firm reporting using conservative or aggressive accounting that will be reversed in subsequent years, and which should be reflected in the analyst's forecasts of net income and book equity?
- What are expected future net income, book values of equity, and therefore abnormal earnings over a finite forecast horizon (usually 5 to 10 years) given

the firm's industry competitiveness, the firm's positioning, and its accounting conservatism?

- What is expected future abnormal net income beyond the final year of the forecast horizon (called the "terminal year") based on some simplifying assumption? If abnormal returns are expected to persist, what are the barriers to entry that deter competition?
- What is the firm's cost of equity used to compute the present value of abnormal earnings?

REVISITING PRICE MULTIPLE VALUATIONS

As noted earlier in this chapter, despite their relative simplicity and popularity, valuation multiples are difficult to implement given wide differences in multiples even for firms that are in the same industry. The abnormal earnings valuation method provides insight into factors that lead to differences in the leading multiples, value-to-book and value-to-earnings, across firms.

Value-to-Book Equity Multiple

If the abnormal earnings valuation formula is scaled by book value, the left-hand side becomes the equity value-to-book ratio as opposed to the equity value itself. The right-hand side variables can be rearranged to reflect three multiple drivers (i) expected future earnings deflated by beginning book value, or our old friend return on equity (ROE), discussed in Chapter 5; (ii) the expected growth in equity book value over time; and (iii) the return required by equity investors. The actual valuation formula is as follows:

$$\frac{\text{Equity value}}{\text{Book equity}} = 1 + \text{PV}(\text{Expected abnormal ROE} \times \text{Expected beginning book equity growth})$$

Abnormal ROE is the firm's ROE less the return required by equity investors. As discussed in financial analysis (Chapter 5), ROEs can be expressed as the product of three components (profit margins, sales turnover, and leverage). The ROE projections used to compute the equity value-to-book ratio, therefore, reflect these same components.

Firms with positive abnormal ROEs are able to invest their net assets to create value for shareholders and will have equity value-to-book ratios greater than one. In contrast, firms with negative abnormal ROEs are unable to invest shareholder funds at a rate greater than shareholders' required return and have ratios below one.

The magnitude of a firm's value-to-book multiple also depends on its expected book equity growth, defined as forecasted beginning book equity deflated by the current book equity. Firms can grow their equity base by issuing new equity or by reinvesting profits. If this new equity is invested in positive valued projects for shareholders, that is, projects with ROEs that exceed the cost of capital, the firm will boost its equity value-to-book multiple. Conversely, for firms with ROEs that are less than the cost of capital, equity growth further lowers the multiple.

The valuation task can now be framed in terms of two key questions about the firm's "value drivers":

- Will the firm be able to generate ROEs that exceed its shareholders' required return, and if so, for how long?
- How quickly will the firm's investment base (book value) grow?

Returning to the three-year Down Under Company example, the implied equity value-to-book multiple can be estimated as follows:

	Year 1	Year 2	Year 3
Beginning book value	$60 m	$40 m	$20 m
Earnings	$20 m	$30 m	$40 m
ROE	0.33	0.75	2.00
− Cost of capital	0.10	0.10	0.10
= Abnormal ROE	0.23	0.65	1.90
× (Beg. Book equity growth)	1.00	0.67	0.33
= Abnormal ROE scaled by book value growth	0.23	0.43	0.63
× PV factor	0.909	0.826	0.751
= PV of abnormal ROE scaled by book value growth	0.212	0.358	0.476
Cumulative PV of abnormal ROE scaled by book value growth	1.046		
+ 1.00	1.000		
= Equity value-to-book multiple	2.046		

There are several points to note from these calculations. First, ROE is earnings deflated by beginning, not ending or average equity. Year 1 ROE is therefore 33 percent, computed as earnings of $20 million deflated by beginning book value of $60 million. The ROE grows over time, reflecting increasing earnings and declining beginning book equity. Second, beginning book equity growth is forecasted beginning book equity deflated by current book equity. For Down Under, the current book equity and beginning book equity for year 1 are both $60 million, implying that the year 1 growth multiple is 1. Year 2 beginning book equity is $40 million, 67 percent of the current $60 million. And in year 3, it is $20 million, 33 percent of current book equity. The decline in beginning book equity growth over time reflects the finite life of the project. Finally, the equity value-to-book multiple for Down Under of 2.046 implies that the stock value is $122.8 (current book equity of $60 times 2.046), once again identical to the dividend discount model value.

Value-to-Earnings Multiple

The equity value-to-book formulation can also be used to construct the equity value-earnings multiple as follows:

$$\text{Equity value-to-earnings multiple} = \text{Equity value-to-book multiple} \times \frac{\text{Book value of equity}}{\text{Earnings}}$$

$$= \frac{\text{Equity value-to-book multiple}}{\text{ROE}}$$

In other words, the same factors that drive a firm's equity value-to-book multiple also explain its equity value-earnings multiple. The key difference between the two multiples is that the value-earnings multiple is affected by the firm's current level of ROE performance, whereas the value-to-book multiple is not. Firms that have low current ROEs relative to investor expectations reflected in the equity value-to-book multiple, that is firms predicted to have strong increases in ROE, will have very high value-earnings multiples and vice versa. If a firm has a zero or negative ROE, its PE multiple is not defined. Value-earnings multiples are therefore more volatile than value-to-book multiples.

The following data for a subset of firms in the retail apparel/department store industry illustrate the relation among return on beginning equity (ROE), book equity growth, the price-to-book ratio, and the price-earnings ratio:

Company	ROE	Book Equity Growth	Price-to-Book Ratio	Price-Earnings Ratio
TJX Companies, Inc.	46.5%	10.5%	6.0	14.5
Nordstrom, Inc.	39.0%	28.6%	4.4	14.9
Sears Holding Corp.	1.5%	−1.2%	1.0	63.9
Target Corp.	19.0%	6.3%	2.5	13.6

TJX and Nordstrom have high price-to-book multiples, both relative to their peers and to other listed U.S. firms, implying that investors expect the two firms will continue to generate ROEs that exceed their required return and to show strong growth. Target has a respectable price-to-book multiple that exceeds one, indicating that it is also expected to continue to generate positive abnormal ROEs and growth, albeit lower than for TJX and Nordstrom. The comparable price-earnings ratios for the three firms imply that investors do not anticipate any major differences in their future ROE growth relative to current ROE.

In contrast, Sears has by far the lowest price-to-book multiple. Its value of one indicates that investors expect it to generate future ROEs that just meet their required return. Sears' very high price-to-earnings multiple of 63.9 implies that investors expect that the current ROE of 1.5 percent (certainly lower than the required return) will likely increase in the future to match their required return.

Key Analysis Questions

To value a firm using multiples, an analyst has to assess the quality of the variable used as the multiple basis, and to determine the appropriate peer firms to include in the benchmark multiple. Analysts are therefore likely to be interested in answering the following questions:

- How well does the denominator used in the multiple reflect the firm's performance? For example, if earnings or book equity are used as the denominator, has the firm made conservative or aggressive accounting choices that affect these variables and that are likely to unwind in the coming years? Is the firm likely to show strong growth in earnings or book equity? If earnings are the denominator, does the firm have temporarily poor or strong performance?
- What is the sustainability of the firm's growth and ROE based on the competitive dynamics of its industry and product market and its own competitive position?

> • Which are the most suitable peer companies to include in the benchmark multiple computation? Have these firms had comparable growth (earnings or book values), profitability, and quality of earnings to the firm being analyzed? Do they have the same risk characteristics?

SHORTCUT FORMS OF EARNINGS-BASED VALUATION

The discounted abnormal earnings valuation formula can be simplified by making assumptions about the relation between a firm's current and future abnormal earnings. Similarly, the equity value-to-book formula can be simplified by making assumptions about long-term ROEs and growth.

Abnormal Earnings Simplification

Several assumptions about the relation between current and future net income are popular for simplifying the abnormal earnings model. First, abnormal earnings can be assumed to follow what is known as a random walk. This implies that an analyst's best guess about future expected abnormal earnings are current abnormal earnings. The model assumes that past shocks to abnormal earnings continue forever, but that future shocks are random or unpredictable. The random walk model can be written as follows:

$$\text{Forecasted abnormal earnings} = \text{Current abnormal earnings}$$

Under the model, the best guess of abnormal earnings in any future year is just current abnormal earnings. It is also possible to include a drift term in the model, allowing abnormal earnings to grow or decline by a constant amount, or at a constant rate in each period.

How does the above assumption about future abnormal earnings simplify the discounted abnormal earnings valuation model? If abnormal earnings follow a random walk, all future forecasts of abnormal earnings are simply current abnormal earnings. Consequently, the present value of future abnormal earnings can be calculated by valuing the current level of abnormal earnings as a perpetuity. It is then possible to rewrite value as follows:

$$\text{Equity value} = \text{Book equity} + \frac{\text{Current abnormal earnings}}{\text{Expected return}}$$

The equity value is the current book value of equity plus current abnormal earnings divided by the expected return for equity investors. The perpetuity formula can be adjusted to incorporate expectations of constant growth in future abnormal earnings.

In reality, of course, shocks to abnormal earnings are unlikely to persist forever. Firms that have positive shocks are likely to attract competitors that will reduce opportunities for future abnormal performance. Firms with negative abnormal earnings shocks are likely to fail or to be acquired by other firms that can manage their resources more effectively. The persistence of abnormal performance will therefore depend on strategic factors such as barriers to entry and switching costs, discussed in Chapter 2. To reflect this, analysts frequently assume that current shocks to abnormal earnings decay over time. Under this assumption, abnormal earnings are said to follow an autoregressive model. Forecasted abnormal earnings are then:

$$\text{Forecasted abnormal earnings} = \beta \, \text{Current abnormal earnings}$$

β is a parameter that captures the speed with which abnormal earnings decay over time. If there is no decay, β is one and abnormal earnings follow a random walk. If β is zero, abnormal earnings decay completely within one year. Estimates of β using actual company data indicate that for a typical U.S. firm, β is approximately 0.6, implying that on average abnormal ROEs decline by around 40 percent per year. However, the rate of decline varies by industry and is smaller for firms with large accruals and one-time accounting charges.[4]

The autoregressive model implies that stock values can again be written as a function of current abnormal earnings and book values:[5]

$$\text{Equity value} = \text{Book equity} + \frac{\beta \, \text{Current abnormal earnings}}{\text{Expected return} - (1 - \beta)}$$

This formulation implies that stock values are simply the sum of current book value plus current abnormal earnings weighted by the cost of equity capital and persistence in abnormal earnings.

ROE and Growth Simplifications

It is also possible to make simplifications about long-term ROEs and equity growth to reduce forecast horizons for estimating the equity value-to-book multiple. Firms' long-term ROEs are affected by such factors as barriers to entry in their industries, change in production or delivery technologies, and quality of management. As discussed in Chapter 6, these factors tend to force abnormal ROEs to decay over time. One way to model this decay is to assume that ROEs revert to the mean. Forecasted ROE after one period then takes the following form:

$$\text{Forecast ROE} = \text{Current ROE} + \beta(\text{Current ROE} - \text{Steady State ROE})$$

Steady state ROE could either be the firm's required return for equity investors or its long-term industry ROE. β is a "speed of adjustment factor" that reflects how quickly it takes the ROE to revert to its steady state.[6]

Growth rates in the book value of equity are driven by several factors. First, the size of the firm is important. Small firms can sustain very high growth rates for an extended period, whereas large firms find it more difficult to do so. Second, firms with high rates of growth are likely to attract competitors, which reduces their growth rates. As a result, steady-state rates of growth in book equity are likely to be similar to rates of growth in the overall economy, which in the United States have averaged 3 to 4 percent per year.

The long-term patterns in ROE and book equity growth rates imply that for most companies there is limited value in making forecasts for valuation beyond a relatively short horizon, generally five to ten years. Powerful economic forces tend to lead firms with superior or inferior performance early in the forecast horizon to revert to a level that is comparable to that of other firms in the industry or the economy. For a firm in steady state, that is, expected to have a stable ROE and book equity growth rate, the value-to-book multiple formula simplifies to the following:

$$\frac{\text{Equity value}}{\text{Book equity}} = 1 + \frac{\text{Expected ROE} - \text{Required return}}{\text{Required return} - \text{book growth}}$$

Consistent with this simplified model, there is a strong relationship between price-to-book ratios and current ROEs. Figure 7-1 shows the relation between these variables for firms in the retail apparel/department store industry we discussed earlier. The correlation between the two variables is 0.97.

Of course, analysts can make a variety of simplifying assumptions about a firm's ROE and growth. For example, they can assume that they decay slowly or rapidly to the cost of capital and the growth rate for the economy. They can assume that the rates decay to

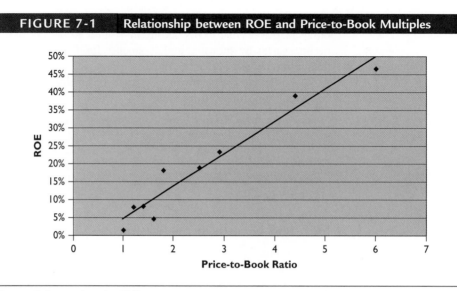

FIGURE 7-1   Relationship between ROE and Price-to-Book Multiples

Source: © Cengage Learning 2013

the industry or economy average ROEs and book value growth rates. The valuation formula can easily be modified to accommodate these assumptions.

THE DISCOUNTED CASH FLOW MODEL

The final valuation method discussed here is the discounted cash flow approach. This is the valuation method taught in most finance classes. Like the abnormal earnings approach, it is derived from the dividend discount model. It is based on the insight that dividends can be recast as free cash flows:[7]

Dividends = Operating cash flow − Capital outlays + Net cash flows from debt owners

As discussed in Chapter 5, operating cash flows to equity holders are simply net income plus depreciation less changes in working capital accruals. Capital outlays are capital expenditures less asset sales. Finally, net cash flows from debt owners are issues of new debt less retirements less the after-tax cost of interest.[8]

The dividend discount model can therefore be written as the present value of free cash flows to equity. Under this formulation, value to shareholders is estimated as follows:

Equity value = PV(Expected free cash flows to equity)

Valuation under the discounted cash flow method therefore involves the following steps:

Step 1: Forecast free cash flows available to equity holders over a finite forecast horizon (usually 5 to 10 years),

Step 2: Forecast free cash flows beyond the terminal year based on some simplifying assumption, and

Step 3: Discount free cash flows to equity holders at the cost of equity. The discounted amount represents the estimated value of free cash flows available to equity.

Returning to the Down Under Company example, there is no debt, so that the free cash flows to owners are simply the operating profits before depreciation. Since the company's required return for shareholders is assumed to be 10 percent, the present value of the free cash flows is calculated as follows:

Year	Expected Free Cash Flows	PV Factor	PV of Expected Free Cash Flows
1	$40 m	0.909	$36.4 m
2	50 m	0.826	41.3 m
3	60 m	0.751	45.1 m
Equity value			$122.8 m

Notice that the value of Down Under's equity is exactly the same as that estimated using the discounted abnormal earnings method. This should not be surprising. Both methods are derived from the dividend discount model. And in estimating value under the two approaches, we have used the same underlying assumptions to forecast earnings and cash flows.

COMPARING VALUATION METHODS

We have discussed three methods of valuation derived from the dividend discount model: discounted dividends, discounted abnormal earnings (or abnormal ROEs), and discounted cash flows. Since the methods are all derived from the same underlying model, no one version can be considered superior to the others. As long as analysts make the same assumptions about firm fundamentals, value estimates under all three methods will be identical. However, there are important differences between the models that are discussed below:

Differences in Focus

The methods frame the valuation task differently and can in practice focus the analyst's attention on different issues. The earnings-based approaches frame the issues in terms of accounting data such as earnings and book values rather than cash flows. Analysts spend considerable time analyzing historical income statements and balance sheets, and their primary forecasts are typically for these accounting variables.

Defining values in terms of ROEs has the advantage that it focuses analysts' attention on ROE, the same key measure of performance that is decomposed in a standard financial analysis. Furthermore, because ROEs control for firm scale, it is likely to be easier for analysts to evaluate the reasonableness of their forecasts by benchmarking them with ROEs of other firms in the industry and the economy. This type of benchmarking is more challenging for free cash flows and abnormal earnings.

Differences in Required Structure

The methods differ in the amount of analysis and structure required for valuation. The discounted abnormal earnings and ROE methods require analysts to construct both pro forma income statements and balance sheets to forecast future earnings and book values. In contrast, the discounted cash flow method requires analysts to forecast income statements and changes in working capital and long-term assets to generate free cash flows. Finally, the discounted dividend method requires analysts to forecast dividends.

The discounted abnormal earnings, ROE, and free cash flow models all require more structure for analysis than the discounted dividend approach. They therefore help analysts avoid structural inconsistencies in their forecasts of future dividends by specifically requiring a prediction of firms' future performance and investment opportunities.

Similarly, the discounted abnormal earnings/ROE method requires more structure and work than the discounted cash flow method to build full pro forma balance sheets. This permits analysts to avoid inconsistencies in the firm's financial structure.

Differences in Terminal Value Implications

A third difference between the methods is in the effort required for estimating terminal values. Terminal value estimates for the abnormal earnings and ROE methods tend to represent a much smaller fraction of total value than under the discounted cash flow or dividend methods. On the surface, this would appear to mitigate concerns about the aspect of valuation that leaves the analyst most uncomfortable. Is this apparent advantage real? As explained below, the answer turns on how well value is already reflected in the accountant's book value.

The abnormal earnings valuation does not eliminate the discounted cash flow terminal value problem, but it does reframe it. Discounted cash flow terminal values include the present value of *all* expected cash flows beyond the forecast horizon. Under abnormal earnings valuation, that value is broken into two parts: the present values of *normal* earnings and *abnormal* earnings beyond the terminal year. The terminal value in the abnormal earnings technique includes only the *abnormal* earnings. The present value of *normal* earnings is already reflected in the original book value.

The abnormal earnings approach, then, recognizes that current book value and earnings over the forecast horizon already reflect many of the cash flows expected to arrive after the forecast horizon. The approach builds directly on accrual accounting. For example, under accrual accounting book equity can be thought of as the minimum recoverable future benefits attributable to the firm's net assets. In addition, revenues are typically realized when earned, not when cash is received. The discounted cash flow approach, on the other hand, "unravels" all of the accruals, spreads the resulting cash flows over longer horizons, and then reconstructs its own "accruals" in the form of discounted expectations of future cash flows. The essential difference between the two approaches is that abnormal earnings valuation recognizes that the accrual process may already have performed a portion of the valuation task, whereas the discounted cash flow approach ultimately moves back to the primitive cash flows underlying the accruals.

The usefulness of the accounting-based perspective thus hinges on how well the accrual process reflects future cash flows. The approach is most convenient when the accrual process is "unbiased," so that earnings can be abnormal only as the result of economic rents and not as a product of accounting itself.[9] The forecast horizon then extends to the point where the firm is expected to approach a competitive equilibrium and earn only normal earnings on its projects. Subsequent abnormal earnings would be zero, and the terminal value at that point would be zero. In this case, *all* of the firm's value is reflected in the book value and earnings projected over the forecast horizon.

Of course, accounting rarely works so well. For example, in most countries research and development costs are expensed, and book values fail to reflect any research and development assets. As a result, firms that spend heavily on research and development—such as pharmaceutical companies—tend on average to generate abnormally high earnings even in the face of stiff competition. Purely as an artifact of research and development accounting, abnormal earnings would be expected to remain positive indefinitely for such firms, and the terminal value could represent a substantial fraction of total value.

If desired, the analyst can alter the accounting approach used by the firm in his or her own projections. "Better" accounting would be viewed as that which reflects a larger fraction of the firm's value in book values and earnings over the forecast horizon.[10] This same view underlies analysts' attempts to "normalize" earnings; the adjusted numbers are intended to provide better indications of value, even though they reflect performance only over a short horizon.

Recent research has focused on the performance of earnings-based valuation relative to discounted cash flow and discounted dividend methods. The findings indicate that over relatively short forecast horizons, ten years or less, valuation estimates using the abnormal earnings approach generate more precise estimates of value than either the discounted dividend or discounted cash flow models. This advantage for the earnings-based approach persists for firms with conservative or aggressive accounting, indicating that accrual accounting in the United States does a reasonably good job of reflecting future cash flows.[11]

Research also indicates that abnormal earnings estimates of value outperform traditional multiples, such as price-earnings ratios, price-to-book ratios, and dividend yields, for predicting future stock movements.[12] Firms with high abnormal earnings model estimates of value relative to current price show positive abnormal future stock returns, whereas firms with low estimated value-to-price ratios have negative abnormal stock performance.

Key Analysis Questions

The above discussion on the trade-offs between different methods of valuing a company raises several questions for analysts about how to compare methods and to consider which is likely to be most reliable for their analysis:

- What are the key performance parameters that the analyst forecasts? Is more attention given to forecasting accounting variables, such as earnings and book values, or to forecasting cash flow variables?
- Has the analyst linked forecasted income statements and balance sheets? If not, is there any inconsistency between the two statements, or in the implications of the assumptions for future performance? If so, what is the source of this inconsistency and does it affect discounted earnings-based and discounted cash flow methods similarly?
- How well does the firm's accounting capture its underlying assets and obligations? Does it do a good enough job that we can rely on book values as the basis for long-term forecasts? Alternatively, does the firm rely heavily on off-balance-sheet assets, such as R&D, which make book values a poor lower bound on long-term performance?
- Has the analyst made very different assumptions about long-term performance in the terminal value computations under the different valuation methods? If so, which set of assumptions is more plausible given the firm's industry and its competitive positioning?

SUMMARY

Valuation is the process by which forecasts of performance are converted into estimates of price. A variety of valuation techniques are employed in practice, and there is no single method that clearly dominates others. In fact, since each technique involves different advantages and disadvantages, there are gains to considering several approaches simultaneously.

For shareholders, a stock's value is the present value of future dividends. This chapter described three valuation techniques directly based on this dividend discount definition of value: discounted dividends, discounted abnormal earnings/ROEs, and discounted free cash flows. The discounted dividend method attempts to forecast dividends directly. The abnormal earnings approach expresses the value of a firm's equity as book value plus discounted expectations of future abnormal earnings. Finally, the discounted cash flow method represents a firm's stock value by expected future free cash flows discounted at the cost of capital.

Although these three methods were derived from the same dividend discount model, they frame the valuation task differently. In practice they focus the analyst's attention on different issues and require different levels of structure in developing forecasts of the underlying primitive, future dividends.

Price multiple valuation methods were also discussed. Under these approaches, analysts estimate ratios of current price to historical or forecasted measures of performance for comparable firms. The benchmarks are then used to value the performance of the firm being analyzed. Multiples have traditionally been popular, primarily because they do not require analysts to make multiyear forecasts of performance. However, it can be difficult to identify comparable firms to use as benchmarks. Even across highly related firms, there are differences in performance that are likely to affect their multiples.

The chapter discussed the relation between two popular multiples, value-to-book and value-earnings ratios, and the discounted abnormal earnings valuation. The resulting formulations indicate that value-to-book multiples are a function of future abnormal ROEs, book value growth, and the firm's cost of equity. The value-earnings multiple is a function of the same factors and also the current ROE.

DISCUSSION QUESTIONS

1. Joe Watts, an analyst at EMH Securities, states: "I don't know why anyone would ever try to value earnings. Obviously, the market knows that earnings can be manipulated and therefore it only values cash flows." Discuss.

2. Explain why terminal values in accounting-based valuation are significantly less than those for DCF valuation.

3. Manufactured Earnings is a "darling" of Wall Street analysts. Its current market price is $15 per share, and its book value is $5 per share. Analysts forecast that the firm's book value will grow by 10 percent per year indefinitely, and the cost of equity is 15 percent. Given these facts, what is the market's expectation of the firm's long-term average ROE?

4. Given the information in question 3, what will be Manufactured Earnings' stock price if the market revises its expectations of long-term average ROE to 20 percent?

5. Analysts reassess Manufactured Earnings' future performance as follows: growth in book value increases to 12 percent per year, but the ROE of the incremental book value is only 15 percent. What is the impact on the market-to-book ratio?

6. How can a company with a high ROE have a low PE ratio?

7. What types of companies have
   - a high PE and a low market-to-book ratio?
   - a high PE ratio and a high market-to-book ratio?
   - a low PE and a high market-to-book ratio?
   - a low PE and a low market-to-book ratio?

8. Free cash flows (FCF) used in DCF valuations discussed in the chapter are defined as follows:

   FCF to debt and equity = Earnings before interest and taxes $\times$ (1 $-$ tax rate)
   $+$ Depreciation and deferred taxes $-$ Capital
   expenditures $-/+$ Increase/decrease in working capital

   FCF to equity $=$ Net income $+$ Depreciation and deferred taxes
   $-$ Capital expenditures $-/+$ Increase/decrease in working
   capital $+/-$ Increase/decrease in debt

   Which of the following items affect free cash flows to debt and equity holders? Which affect free cash flows to equity alone? Explain why and how.
   - An increase in accounts receivable
   - A decrease in gross margins
   - An increase in property, plant, and equipment
   - An increase in inventory
   - Interest expense
   - An increase in prepaid expenses
   - An increase in notes payable to the bank

9. Starite Company is valued at $20 per share. Analysts expect that it will generate free cash flows to equity of $4 per share for the foreseeable future. What is the firm's implied cost of equity capital?

10. Janet Stringer argues that "the DCF valuation method has increased managers' focus on short-term rather than long-term performance, since the discounting process places much heavier weight on short-term cash flows than long-term ones." Comment.

NOTES

1. The incorporation of all non-capital equity transactions into income is called clean surplus accounting. It is analogous to comprehensive income, the concept defined in FAS 130.
2. Changes in book value also include new capital contributions. However, the dividend discount model assumes that new capital is issued at fair value. As a result, any incremental book value from capital issues is exactly offset by the discounted value of future dividends to new shareholders. Capital transactions, therefore, do not affect firm valuation.
3. Appendix C to this chapter provides a simple proof of the earnings-based valuation formula.
4. See P. M. Dechow, A. P. Hutton, and R. G. Sloan, "An empirical assessment of the residual income valuation model," *Journal of Accounting and Economics* 23, January 1999.
5. This formulation is a variant of a model proposed by J. Ohlson, "Earnings, book values, and dividends in security valuation," *Contemporary Accounting Research* 11, Spring 1995. Ohlson includes in his forecasts of future abnormal earnings a variable that reflects relevant information other than current abnormal earnings. This variable then also appears in the stock valuation formula. Empirical research by Dechow, Hutton, and Sloan, "An empirical assessment of the residual income valuation model," *Journal of Accounting and Economics* 23, January 1999, indicates that financial analysts' forecasts of abnormal earnings do reflect

considerable information other than current abnormal earnings, and that this information is useful for valuation.

6. This specification is similar to the model for dividends developed by J. Lintner, "Distribution of incomes of corporations among dividends, retained earnings, and taxes," *American Economic Review* 46 (May 1956): 97–113.

7. In practice, firms do not have to pay out all of their free cash flows as dividends; they can retain surplus cash in the business. The conditions under which a firm's dividend decision affects its value are discussed by M. H. Miller and F. Modigliani in "Dividend Policy, Growth and the Valuation of Shares," *Journal of Business* 34 (October 1961): 411–33.

8. Most finance texts implement the discounted cash flow model using cash flows attributable to all the firm's investors, both debt and equity. This generates the value of the firm's assets rather than the value of its equity. However, the value of the equity can easily be computed using this approach by deducting the value of the outstanding debt from the estimated value of the assets. Indeed, all of the valuation approaches discussed in this chapter can be structured to estimate the value of a firm's assets rather than its equity. Further discussion of these methods is shown in Appendix D.

9. Unbiased accounting is that which, in a competitive equilibrium, produces an expected ROE equal to the cost of capital. The actual ROE thus reveals the presence of economic rents. Market-value accounting is a special case of unbiased accounting that produces an expected ROE equal to the cost of capital, even when the firm is *not* in a competitive equilibrium. That is, market-value accounting reflects the present value of future economic rents in book value, driving the expected ROEs to a normal level. For a discussion of unbiased and biased accounting, see G. Feltham and J. Ohlson, "Valuation and Clean Surplus Accounting for Operating and Financial Activities," *Contemporary Accounting Research* 11, No. 2 (Spring 1995): 689–731.

10. In Bennett Stewart's book on EVA valuation, *The Quest for Value* (New York: Harper Business, 1999), he recommends a number of accounting adjustments, including the capitalization of research and development.

11. S. Penman and T. Sougiannis, "A Comparison of Dividend, Cash Flow, and Earnings Approaches to Equity Valuation," *Contemporary Accounting Research* (Fall 1998): 343–83, compares the valuation methods using actual realizations of earnings, cash flows, and dividends to estimate prices. J. Francis, P. Olsson, and D. Oswald, "Comparing Accuracy and Explainability of Dividend, Free Cash Flow and Abnormal Earnings Equity Valuation Models," *Journal of Accounting Research* 38 (Spring 2000): 45–70, estimates values using *Value Line* forecasts.

12. See C. Lee, J. Myers, and B. Swaminathan, "What is the Intrinsic Value of the Dow?" *Journal of Finance* (October 1999): 1693–1741.

APPENDIX A   Time Value of Money: Present and Future Values

The notion that $1 today is worth more than $1 received in one year is fundamental to finance. You may view this notion as obvious—after all, inflation reduces the value of nominal dollars over time and uncertainty about the receipt of future dollars increases the value of dollars already received today. But the finance concept does not rest upon these principles. Instead, it arises from the fact that the $1 received today can be invested at a positive interest rate to generate an amount greater than $1 in one year. This concept is known as the time value of money and is reflected in future and present value computations.

Future Values and Compounding

To understand future values, consider an opportunity to invest $1 in a bank (an investment that has no risk) that generates a 10 percent annual return. The amount you can expect to receive in one year is called the future value of $1 in one year at 10 percent FV($1, 10%, 1), and is computed as follows:

$$\begin{aligned} FV(\$1, 10\%, 1) &= \$1 + \$1 \times 10\% \\ &= \$1 \times (1 + 10\%) \\ &= \$1.10. \end{aligned}$$

Similarly, the future value of a dollar at 10% in two years is

$$\begin{aligned} FV(\$1, 10\%, 2) &= \$1 + \$1 \times 10\% + (\$1 + \$1 \times 10\%) \times 10\% \\ &= \$1 \times (1 + 10\%)^2 \\ &= \$1.121 \end{aligned}$$

More generally, we can write the future value of $1 at any interest rate R for any number of periods N as follows:

$$FV(\$1, R, N) = \$ \times (1 + R)^N$$

This process of converting dollars today into future dollars is called compounding. Among other things, it is useful for helping us to compute how much our savings will be worth upon retirement. For example, if I expect to retire in five years' time, my savings account that currently has a balance of $10,000 earning 5 percent per year will have grown to:

$$\begin{aligned} FV(\$10,000, 5\%, 5) &= \$10,000 \times (1 + 5\%)^5 \\ &= \$10,000 * 1.2763 = \$12,763 \end{aligned}$$

Notice that as interest rates increase, future values also increase. For example, if rates rise from 5 percent to 10 percent, the future value of my savings account will increase from $12,763 to $16,051, since I am now able to earn a much higher return on the savings.

Present Values and Discounting

The process of converting future dollars into today's dollars is called discounting. Using the examples above, $1.10 received in one year has a present value of $1 and $1.21 received in two years has a present value of $1. The present value of $1 received in one year, PV($1, 10%, 1), is therefore the amount that when invested today for one year at 10 percent would generate exactly $1, or PV($1, 10%, 1) × (1 + 10%) = $1. This implies that the present value itself is:

$$PV(1, 10\%, 1) = \$1/(1 + 10\%) = \$0.909$$

Similarly, the present value of $1 received in two years is PV($1, 10%, 2) × (1 + 10%)^2 = $1, so the present value itself is

$$PV(\$1, 10\%, 2) = \$1/(1 + 10\%)^2 = \$0.826$$

More generally, we can write the present value of $1 at any interest rate R for any number of periods N as follows:

$$PV(\$1, R, N) = \$1/(1 + R)^N$$

The present value concept can also help us to plan for our retirement. For example, if we decided that we wanted a nest egg of $1,000,000 for our planned retirement in twenty years, it can help us determine how much we would need to set aside in savings today to meet our goal. This is just the present value of $1,000,000 received in 20 years. If interest rates are 10 percent, this amount is

$$PV(\$1,000,000, 10\%, 20) = \$1,000,000/(1 + 10\%)^{20} = \$148.644$$

This means that if we invest $148,644 today, the interest that compounds on our investment will make it worth $1,000,000 in 20 years.

Notice that as interest rates decrease, the present value of dollars received in the future increase. For example, if interest rates fall from 10 percent to 5 percent, the present value of $1,000,000 in 20 years increases from $148,644 to $376,889. This arises because the lower interest rates require us to invest a greater amount today to generate $1,000,000 in the future.

As discussed in this chapter, the present value concept allows us to value stocks by discounting future dividends, cash flows, or earnings that the stock is expected to generate for shareholders. It also allows us to value bonds by discounting future receipts of bond interest and principal repayments.

Present Value of a Perpetuity

Some bonds, (such as British Consol bonds) pay off an identical amount each year. This is called a perpetuity. How do we value a perpetuity? It is actually remarkably simple. The perpetuity value (P) is simply the perpetuity amount (X) divided by the interest (or discount rate, as it is often called).

$$P = X/R$$

For example, if interest rates are 10 percent, a perpetual bond that pays interest of $10 per year is worth $100 ($10/0.10). Each year the investor receives $10 interest from the bond, generating a 10 percent return on the investment value of $100.

The perpetuity value is also very useful in valuing stocks, particularly for the terminal value computations. When a firm is in a stable steady state, its dividends, cash flows, or earnings may resemble a perpetuity. Stock perpetuities can also incorporate a constant growth rate over time. For example, a firm may generate cash flows of $10 for the first year, and these grow by 4 percent per year thereafter, perhaps reflecting the nominal rate of growth in the economy. A perpetuity with a constant growth rate is also relatively simple to value. If the first payment is X and the growth rate g, the perpetuity is valued as:

$$P = X/(R - g)$$

Hence, the perpetuity with a first payment of $10 and a constant growth rate of 4 percent is worth $10/(10% − 4%) or $166.67. This implies that the value of the growth component of the perpetuity is worth $66.67, since the non-growth perpetuity is worth $100.

Notice that the denominator for the growth perpetuity is R − g, the discount rate net of the growth rate. If the growth rate equals or exceeds the discount rate, the denominator is zero or negative and the perpetuity value is undefined or not meaningful. However, in practice once a firm has reached a steady state, this should not be expected to happen as firms that grow indefinitely at a rate that is much higher than the overall growth of the economy will soon dominate the economy.

APPENDIX B   Valuation Formulas

All of the valuation approaches discussed in this chapter can be expressed mathematically. The formulas for the various approaches are presented below:

Abnormal Earnings Valuation

Under the earnings-based approach, the value of the equity is

$$\text{Equity value} = BE_0 + \frac{NI_1 - R_e * BE_0}{(1 + R_e)} + \frac{NI_2 - R_e * BE_1}{(1 + R_e)^2} + \cdots$$

BE_0 is the firm's current book equity, BE_t is the expected beginning book equity in period t, NI_t is expected net income for period t, and R_e is the return required by the firm's equity investors.

Valuation Using Price Multiples

The abnormal earnings valuation can be restructured into the equity value-to-book value multiple by deflating the equity value by book equity by scaling. The valuation formula then becomes:

$$\frac{\text{Equity value}}{\text{Book equity}} = 1 + \frac{(ROE_1 - R_e) * GBE_0}{(1 + R_e)} + \frac{(ROE_2 - R_e) * GBE_1}{(1 + R_e)^2} + \frac{(ROE_3 - R_e) * GBE_2}{(1 + R_e)^3} + \cdots$$

ROE_t is net income in year t deflated by beginning book equity; GBE_t is expected book equity growth, defined as expected beginning book equity in year t (BE_t) deflated by the current book equity (BE_0); and R_e is the required return for equity investors.

Discounted Cash Flow Model

Under the free cash flow method, the value of equity is as follows:

$$\text{Equity value} = PV(\text{Expected free cash flows to equity})$$
$$= \frac{NI_1 - \Delta BVA_1 + \Delta BVND_1}{(1 + R_e)} + \frac{NI_2 - \Delta BVA_2 + \Delta BVND_2}{(1 + R_e)^2} + \cdots$$

NI is expected net income, ΔBVA is the change in expected book value of net operating assets (including changes in working capital plus capital expenditures less depreciation expense), $\Delta BVND$ is the change in expected book value of net debt (interest-bearing debt less excess cash), and R_e is the required return for equity investors.

APPENDIX C   Reconciling the Discounted Dividends and Discounted Abnormal Earnings Models

To derive the earnings-based valuation from the dividend discount model, consider the following two-period valuation:

$$\text{Equity value} = \frac{DIV_1}{(1 + r_e)} + \frac{DIV_2}{(1 + r_e)^2}$$

With clean surplus accounting, dividends (DIV) can be expressed as a function of net income (NI) and the book value of equity (BVE):

$$DIV_t = NI_t + BVE_{t-1} - BVE_t$$

Substituting this expression into the dividend discount model yields the following:

$$\text{Equity value} = \frac{\text{NI}_1 + \text{BVE}_0 - \text{BVE}_1}{(1 + r_e)} + \frac{\text{NI}_2 + \text{BVE}_1 - \text{BVE}_2}{(1 + r_e)^2}$$

This can be rewritten as follows:

$$\text{Equity value} = \frac{\text{NI}_1 - r_e\,\text{BVE}_0 + \text{BVE}_0(1 + r_e) - \text{BVE}_1}{(1 + r_e)}$$

$$+ \frac{\text{NI}_2 - r_e\,\text{BVE}_1 + \text{BVE}_1(1 + r_e) - \text{BVE}_2}{(1 + r_e)^2}$$

$$= \text{BVE}_0 + \frac{\text{NI}_1 - r_e\,\text{BVE}_0}{(1 + r_e)} + \frac{\text{NI}_2 - r_e\,\text{BVE}_1}{(1 + r_e)^2} - \frac{\text{BVE}_2}{(1 + r_e)^2}$$

As the forecast horizon expands, the final term (the present value of liquidating book value) becomes inconsequential. The value of equity is therefore the current book value plus the present value of future abnormal earnings.

APPENDIX D   Asset Valuation Methodologies

All of the valuation approaches discussed in this chapter can also be structured to estimate the value of a firm's assets (or the combined debt and equity) rather than its equity. Switching from equity valuation to asset valuation is often as simple as substituting financial measures related to equity for financial measures related to the entire firm. For example, in the earnings-based valuation model, Net Income (the earnings flow to equity) is replaced by NOPAT (the earnings available for debt and equity), and book values of net operating assets replace the book value of equity. Value multiples are based on ROEs for the equity formulation and on ROAs for valuing asset multiples. And the discount rate for equity models is the required return for equity owners compared to the weighted average cost of debt and equity owners, called the weighted average cost of capital (or WACC) for asset valuation models.

The formulas used for asset valuation under the various approaches are presented below:

Abnormal Earnings Valuation

Under the earnings-based approach, the value of the assets is

$$\text{Asset value} = \text{Book assets} + \text{PV(Expected abnormal NOPAT)}$$

$$= \text{BA}_0 + \frac{\text{NOPAT}_1 - \text{WACC} * \text{BA}_0}{(1 + \text{WACC})} + \frac{\text{NOPAT}_2 - \text{WACC} * \text{BA}_1}{(1 + \text{WACC})^2} + \cdots$$

BA is the book value of the firm's assets, NOPAT is net operating profit (before interest) after tax, and WACC is the firm's weighted-average cost of debt and equity. From this asset value, the analyst can deduct the market value of net debt to generate an estimate of the value of equity.

Valuation Using Price Multiples

The multiple valuation can be structured as the debt plus equity value-to-book assets ratio by scaling the abnormal NOPAT formula by book value of net operating assets. The valuation formula then becomes

$$\frac{\text{Asset value}}{\text{Book assets}} = 1 + \text{PV(Expected abnormal ROA} * \text{Expected beg. book asset growth)}$$

$$= 1 + \frac{(\text{ROA}_1 - \text{WACC}) * \text{GBA}_0}{(1 + \text{WACC})} + \frac{(\text{ROA}_2 - \text{WACC}) * \text{GBA}_1}{(1 + \text{WACC})^2} + \cdots$$

where ROA = Expected operating return on assets = NOPAT/(Operating working captial + Net long-term assets)

WACC = Weighted average cost of capital (debt and equity)

GBA = Book asset growth factor, defined as expected beginning book equity in year t (BE_t) deflated by the current book equity (BE_0).

The value of a firm's debt and equity to net operating assets multiple therefore depends on its ability to generate asset returns that exceed its WACC, and on its ability to grow its asset base. The value of equity under this approach is then the estimated multiple times the current book value of assets less the market value of debt.

Discounted Cash Flow Model

The free cash flow formulation can be structured by estimating the value of claims to net debt and equity and then deducting the market value of net debt. This approach is more widely used in practice because it does not require explicit forecasts of changes in debt balances. The value of debt plus equity is computed as follows:

$$\text{Asset value} = \text{PV(Expected free cash flows to net debt and equity owners)}$$

$$= \frac{\text{NOPAT}_1 - \Delta\text{BVA}_1}{(1 + \text{WACC})} + \frac{\text{NOPAT}_2 - \Delta\text{BVA}_2}{(1 + \text{WACC})^2} + \cdots$$

The firm's asset valuation therefore depends on the expected free cash flows to debt and equity holders during the forecast horizon, the forecasted terminal value of free cash flows, and the weighted average cost of capital.

Chapter 8

PROSPECTIVE ANALYSIS: VALUATION IMPLEMENTATION

To move from the valuation theory discussed in the previous chapter to the actual task of valuing a company, we have to deal with a number of issues. First, we have to make forecasts of financial performance stated in terms of abnormal earnings and book values, or free cash flows over the life of the firm. The forecasting task itself is divided into two subcomponents: (1) detailed forecasts over a finite number of years, and (2) a forecast of "terminal value," which represents a summary of performance beyond the detailed forecast horizon. And second, we have to estimate the cost of capital to discount our forecasts.

Continuing with our TJX example, this chapter builds on the forecasts developed in Chapter 6 and provides guidance on estimating the value of a firm's equity by computing a terminal value, calculating cost of equity, and synthesizing the different pieces of the analytical process to estimate the value of equity. We focus on valuing equity directly since this is typically the analyst's primary objective. However, as discussed in Appendix D of Chapter 7 and in the Appendix of this chapter, we recognize that a similar approach can be used to value a firm's assets (both debt and equity).

DETAILED FORECASTS OF PERFORMANCE

The horizon over which detailed forecasts are to be made is itself a choice variable. We will discuss later in this chapter how the analyst might make this choice. Once it is made, the next step is to consider the set of assumptions regarding a firm's performance that are needed to arrive at the forecasts. We described in Chapter 6 the general framework of financial forecasting and illustrated the approach using TJX.

The key to sound forecasts is that the underlying assumptions are grounded in a company's business reality. Strategy analysis provides a critical understanding of a company's value proposition and whether current performance is likely to be sustainable in the future. Accounting analysis and ratio analysis provide a deep understanding of a company's current performance and whether the ratios themselves are reliable indicators of performance. It is, therefore, important to see the valuation forecasts as a continuation of the earlier steps in business analysis rather than as a discrete and unconnected exercise from the rest of the analysis.

Since valuation involves forecasting over a long time horizon, it is not practical to forecast all the line items in a company's financial statements. Instead, the analyst has to focus on the key elements of a firm's performance. Specifically, we forecasted TJX's condensed income statement, beginning balance sheet, and free cash flows for a period

TABLE 8-1	Forecasting Assumptions for TJX									
Forecast Year	**2011**	**2012**	**2013**	**2014**	**2015**	**2016**	**2017**	**2018**	**2019**	**2020**
Sales growth rate	5.7%	6.6%	7.1%	6.9%	6.7%	6.5%	6.3%	6.1%	5.9%	5.7%
NOPAT margin	7.9%	7.5%	7.1%	6.7%	6.3%	5.9%	5.5%	5.0%	4.5%	4.0%
Beginning net operating working capital/sales	0.6%	1.0%	1.0%	1.0%	1.0%	1.0%	1.0%	1.0%	1.0%	1.0%
Beginning net operating long-term assets/sales	33.4%	34.0%	34.3%	34.5%	34.8%	35.0%	35.3%	35.5%	35.8%	36.0%
Beginning net debt to capital ratio	57.5%	57.5%	57.5%	57.5%	57.5%	57.5%	57.5%	57.5%	57.5%	57.5%
After-tax cost of debt	2.73	2.73	2.73	2.73	2.73	2.73	2.73	2.73	2.73	2.73

Source: © Cengage Learning 2013

of ten years starting in fiscal year 2011 (year beginning in February 2011), using as a base the adjusted financial statements detailed in Chapter 5. We will use these same forecasting assumptions and financial forecasts, which are repeated here in Tables 8-1 and 8-2, as a starting point to value TJX as of February 1, 2011.

Making Performance Forecasts for Valuing TJX

As discussed in Chapter 7, under the different approaches to valuation, the key forecasts required to convert the financial forecasts shown above into estimates of equity value are:

- Abnormal earnings: net income less shareholders' equity at the beginning of the year times shareholders' required return, termed the cost of equity,
- Abnormal ROE: abnormal ROE, or the difference between ROE and cost of equity, adjusted for growth in book equity, or
- Free cash flows to equity: net income less any increases in operating working capital and net long-term assets plus any increase in net debt.

In order to generate the forecasts of abnormal earnings and abnormal ROE, we need to establish an estimated cost of equity for the firm. For the purposes of this discussion we will take TJX's cost of equity as given at 8.8 percent; the detailed calculation of this estimate is discussed later in the chapter.

Table 8-3 shows TJX's performance forecasts for these three financial statement variables for the ten-year period 2011 to 2020.

As discussed earlier, to derive cash flows in 2020, we need to make assumptions about sales growth rate and balance sheet ratios in 2021. The cash flow forecasts shown in Table 8-3 are based on the assumption that the sales growth and beginning balance sheet ratios in 2021 remain the same as in 2020. We discuss the sensitivity of this assumption and the terminal value assumption later in the chapter.

TJX's projected abnormal ROE declines steadily over the forecast horizon, from 42.1 percent in 2011 to 13.0 percent in 2020, in keeping with the gradual attrition due to the forces of competition. A similar pattern is seen for abnormal earnings, which declines steadily over the course of the forecast period.

TERMINAL VALUES

Explicit forecasts of the various elements of a firm's performance generally extend for a period of five to ten years. The final year of this forecast period is labeled the "terminal year." Selection of an appropriate terminal year is discussed later in this section.

Prospective Analysis: Valuation Implementation **8-3**

TABLE 8-2 Forecasted Financial Statements for TJX

Forecast Year	2011	2012	2013	2014	2015	2016	2017	2018	2019	2020
Beginning Balance Sheet										
Beg. net working capital	144.1	247.2	264.8	283.1	302.0	321.7	341.9	362.8	384.2	406.1
+ Beg. net long-term assets	7,754.4	8,406.0	9,069.1	9,765.6	10,495.4	11,258.0	12,052.7	12,878.7	13,734.5	14,618.9
= net operating assets	7,898.5	8,653.3	9,333.9	10,048.7	10,797.4	11,579.7	12,394.7	13,241.4	14,118.7	15,025.0
Net Debt	4,541.4	4,975.3	5,366.6	5,777.6	6,208.1	6,657.9	7,126.5	7,613.4	8,117.8	8,638.9
+ Preferred stock	0.0	0.0	0.0	0.0	0.0	0.0	0.0	0.0	0.0	0.0
+ Shareholders' equity	3,357.1	3,677.6	3,967.2	4,271.0	4,589.3	4,921.8	5,268.2	5,628.1	6,001.0	6,386.2
= Net capital	7,898.5	8,653.3	9,333.9	10,048.7	10,797.4	11,579.7	12,394.7	13,241.4	14,118.7	15,025.0
Income Statement										
Sales	23,192.9	24,723.6	26,479.0	28,306.1	30,202.6	32,165.7	34,192.2	36,277.9	38,418.3	40,608.2
Net operating profits after tax	1,832.2	1,854.3	1,880.0	1,896.5	1,902.8	1,897.8	1,880.6	1,813.9	1,728.8	1,624.3
− Net interest expense after tax	123.9	135.7	146.4	157.6	169.4	181.6	194.4	207.7	221.5	235.7
= Net income	1,708.4	1,718.6	1,733.6	1,738.9	1,733.4	1,716.2	1,686.2	1,606.2	1,507.4	1,388.7
− Preferred dividends	0	0	0	0	0	0	0	0	0	0
= Net income to common	1,708.4	1,718.6	1,733.6	1,738.9	1,733.4	1,716.2	1,686.2	1,606.2	1,507.4	1,388.7
Operating return on assets	23.2%	21.4%	20.1%	18.9%	17.6%	16.4%	15.2%	13.7%	12.2%	10.8%
Return on common equity	50.9%	46.7%	43.7%	40.7%	37.8%	34.9%	32.0%	28.5%	25.1%	21.7%
Book value of assets growth rate	23.7%	9.6%	7.9%	7.7%	7.5%	7.2%	7.0%	6.8%	6.6%	6.4%
Book value of common equity growth rate	16.2%	9.6%	7.9%	7.7%	7.5%	7.2%	7.0%	6.8%	6.6%	6.4%
Net operating asset turnover	2.9	2.9	2.8	2.8	2.8	2.8	2.8	2.7	2.7	2.7
Cash Flow Data										
Net income	1,708.4	1,718.6	1,733.6	1,738.9	1,733.4	1,716.2	1,686.2	1,606.2	1,507.4	1,388.7
− Change in net working capital	103.1	17.6	18.3	19.0	19.6	20.3	20.9	21.4	21.9	23.2
− Change in net long-term assets	651.6	663.0	696.5	729.8	762.6	794.7	825.9	855.9	884.4	833.3
+ Change in net debt	434.0	391.3	411.0	430.5	449.8	468.6	486.9	504.4	521.1	492.4
= Free cash flow to equity	1,387.6	1,429.3	1,429.8	1,420.6	1,400.9	1,369.8	1,326.3	1,233.3	1,122.2	1,024.7
Net operating profit after tax	1,832.2	1,854.3	1,880.0	1,896.5	1,902.8	1,897.8	1,880.6	1,813.9	1,728.8	1,624.3
− Change in net working capital	103.1	17.6	18.3	19.0	19.6	20.3	20.9	21.4	21.9	23.2
− Change in net long-term assets	651.6	663.0	696.5	729.8	762.6	794.7	825.9	855.9	884.4	833.3
= Free cash flow to capital	1,077.5	1,173.7	1,165.2	1,147.7	1,120.5	1,082.8	1,033.8	936.6	822.5	767.9

Source: © Cengage Learning 2013

TABLE 8-3	Performance Forecast for TJX									
Forecast Year	2011	2012	2013	2014	2015	2016	2017	2018	2019	2020
Equity Valuation										
Abnormal earnings	1,413.9	1,396.0	1,385.7	1,364.3	1,330.9	1,284.5	1,224.1	1,112.6	981.1	828.6
Abnormal ROE	42.1%	38.0%	34.9%	31.9%	29.0%	26.1%	23.2%	19.8%	16.4%	13.0%
Free cash flow to equity	1,387.6	1,429.3	1,429.8	1,420.6	1,400.9	1,369.8	1,326.3	1,233.3	1,122.2	1,024.7
Equity discount factor	0.92	0.85	0.78	0.71	0.66	0.60	0.56	0.51	0.47	0.43
Equity growth factor	1.00	1.10	1.18	1.27	1.37	1.47	1.57	1.68	1.79	1.90

Source: © Cengage Learning 2013

Terminal value is then the present value of either abnormal earnings or free cash flows occurring beyond the terminal year. Since this involves forecasting performance over the remainder of the firm's life, the analyst must adopt some assumption that simplifies the process of forecasting. A key question is whether it is reasonable to assume a continuation of the terminal year performance or whether some other pattern is expected.

Clearly, the continuation of sales growth that is significantly greater than the average growth rate of the economy is unrealistic over a very long horizon. That rate would likely outstrip inflation in the dollar and the real growth rate of the world economy. Over many years, it would imply that the firm would grow to a size greater than that of all other firms in the world combined. But what would be a suitable alternative assumption? Should we expect the firm's sales growth rate to ultimately settle down to the rate of inflation? Or to a higher rate, such as the nominal GDP growth rate? And perhaps equally importantly, will a firm that earns abnormal profits continue to do so by maintaining its profit margins on a growing, or even existing, base of sales?

Ultimately, to answer these questions, we must consider how much longer the rate of growth in industry sales can outstrip overall economic growth and how long a firm's competitive advantages can be sustained. Clearly, looking eleven or more years into the future, any forecast is likely to be subject to considerable error.

Below we discuss a variety of alternative approaches to the task of calculating a terminal value.

Terminal Values with the Competitive Equilibrium Assumption

Fortunately, in many—if not most—situations, how we deal with the seemingly imponderable questions about long-range growth in sales simply *does not matter very much!* In fact, under plausible economic assumptions, there is no practical need to consider sales growth beyond the terminal year. Such growth may be *irrelevant*, so far as the firm's current equity value is concerned!

How can long-range growth in sales *not* matter? The reasoning revolves around the forces of competition. One impact of competition is that it tends to constrain a firm's ability to identify, on a consistent basis, growth opportunities that generate supernormal profits. The other dimension that competition tends to impact is a firm's margins. Ultimately, we would expect high profits to attract enough competition to drive down a firm's margins, and therefore its returns, to a normal level. At this point, the firm will earn its cost of capital, with no abnormal returns or terminal value. (Recall the evidence in Chapter 6 concerning the reversion of ROEs to normal levels over a horizon of five to ten years.)

Certainly, a firm may at a point in time maintain a competitive advantage that permits it to achieve returns in excess of the cost of capital. When that advantage is protected with patents or a strong brand name, the firm may even be able to maintain it for many years, perhaps indefinitely. With hindsight, we know that some such firms—Coca-Cola and Wal-Mart, for instance—were able not only to maintain their competitive edge but also to expand it across a dramatically increasing investment base. However, with a few exceptions, it is reasonable to assume that the terminal value of the firm will be zero under the competitive equilibrium assumption, obviating the need to make assumptions about long-term growth rates.

Competitive Equilibrium Assumption Only on Incremental Sales

An alternative version of the competitive equilibrium assumption is to assume that a firm will continue to earn abnormal earnings forever on the sales it had in the terminal year, but there will be no abnormal earnings on any incremental sales beyond that level. If we invoke the competitive equilibrium assumption on incremental sales beyond the terminal, then it does not matter what sales growth rate we use beyond that year, and we may as well simplify our arithmetic by treating sales *as if* they will be constant at the terminal year level. Then ROE, net income, and free cash flow to equity will all remain constant at the terminal year level.

For example, by treating TJX as if its competitive advantage can be maintained only on the *nominal* sales level achieved in the year 2020, we will be assuming that in *real* terms its competitive advantage will shrink. Under this scenario, it is simple to estimate the terminal value by dividing the 2020 level of abnormal earnings, abnormal ROEs, or free cash flow to equity by the appropriate discount rate. As one would expect, terminal values in this scenario will be higher than those with no abnormal returns on all sales in years 2021 and beyond. This is entirely due to the fact that we are now assuming that TJX can retain its superior performance on its existing base of sales indefinitely.

Terminal Value with Persistent Abnormal Performance and Growth

Each of the approaches described above appeals in some way to the competitive equilibrium assumption. However, there are circumstances where the analyst is willing to assume that the firm may defy competitive forces and earn abnormal rates of return on new projects for many years. If the analyst believes supernormal profitability can be extended to larger markets for many years, it can be accommodated within the context of a valuation analysis.

One possibility is to project earnings and cash flows over a longer horizon, i.e., until the competitive equilibrium assumption can reasonably be invoked. In the case of TJX, for example, we could assume that the supernormal profitability will continue for five years beyond 2020 (for a total forecasting horizon of 15 years from the beginning of the forecasting period), but after that period, the firm's ROE will equal its cost of equity.

Another possibility is to project growth in abnormal earnings or cash flows at some constant rate. For instance, one could expect TJX to maintain its advantage on a sales base that remains constant in *real* terms, implying that sales grow beyond the year 2020 at the long-run average U.S. inflation rate of 3.0 percent. Beyond our terminal year, 2020, as the sales growth rate remains constant at 3.0 percent, abnormal earnings, free cash flows, and book value of equity also grow at this same constant rate. This is simply because we held all other performance ratios constant in this period. As a result, abnormal ROE remains constant at the same level as in the terminal year.

This approach is more aggressive than the preceding assumptions about terminal value, but it may be more realistic. After all, there is no obvious reason why the *real* size of the investment base on which TJX earns abnormal returns should depend on inflation rates. The approach, however, still relies to some extent on the competitive equilibrium assumption. The assumption is now invoked to suggest that supernormal profitability can be extended only to an investment base that remains constant in real terms. In rare situations, if the company has established a market dominance that the analyst believes is immune to the threat of competition, the terminal value can be based on both positive real sales growth and abnormal profits. When we assume that the abnormal performance persists at the same level as in the terminal year, projecting abnormal earnings and free cash flows is a simple matter of growing them at the assumed sales growth rate. Since the rate of abnormal earnings and cash flows growth is constant starting in the year after the terminal year, it is also straightforward to discount those flows. The present value of the flow stream is the flow at the end of the first year divided by the difference between the discount rate and steady state growth rate, provided that the discount rate exceeds the growth rate. There is nothing about this valuation method that requires *any* reliance on the competitive equilibrium assumption; it could be used with *any* sales growth rate less than the discount rate. The question is not whether the arithmetic is available to handle such an approach, but rather how realistic it is.

Terminal Value Based on a Price Multiple

A popular approach to terminal value calculation is to apply a multiple to abnormal earnings, cash flows, or book values of the terminal period. The approach is not as *ad hoc* as it might first appear. Note that under the assumption of no sales growth, abnormal earnings or cash flows beyond the terminal year remain constant. Capitalizing these flows in perpetuity by dividing by the cost of capital is equivalent to multiplying them by the inverse of the cost of capital. For example, in the case of TJX, capitalizing free cash flows to equity at its cost of equity of 8.8 percent is equivalent to assuming a terminal cash flow multiple of 11.4. Thus, applying a multiple in this range to TJX is similar to discounting all free cash flows beyond 2020 while invoking the competitive equilibrium assumption on incremental sales.

The mistake to avoid here is to capitalize the future abnormal earnings or cash flows using a multiple that is too high. The earnings or cash flow multiples might be high currently because the market anticipates abnormally profitable growth. However, once that growth is realized, the PE multiple should fall to a normal level. It is that normal PE, applicable to a stable firm or one that can grow only through making investments that generate the cost of capital, that should be used in the terminal value calculation. Thus multiples in the range of 11.4—close to the reciprocal of cost of equity—should be used here. Higher multiples are justifiable only when there are still abnormally profitable growth opportunities beyond the terminal year. A similar logic applies to the estimation of terminal values using book value multiples.

Selecting the Terminal Year

A critical question posed by the above discussion is how long to make the detailed forecast horizon. When the competitive equilibrium assumption is used, the answer is whatever time is required for the firm's returns on incremental investment projects to reach that equilibrium—an issue that turns on the sustainability of the firm's competitive advantage. As indicated in Chapter 6, historical evidence indicates that most firms in the United States should expect ROEs to revert to normal levels within five to ten years. But for the typical firm, we can justify ending the forecast horizon even earlier—note that the return on *incremental* investment can be normal even while the return on *total* investment (and therefore ROE) remains abnormal. Thus a five- to ten-year forecast horizon should be more than sufficient for most firms. Exceptions would include firms so well insulated from competition (perhaps due to the power of a brand name) that they can extend their investment base to new markets for many years and still expect to generate supernormal returns.

Estimates of TJX's Terminal Value

Choosing a Terminal Year

Based on the foregoing strategic assessment of TJX, we have seen that the firm is facing challenges in both its established U.S. market and in the new markets where it sees its potential for long-term expansion. Despite those challenges, we have argued that TJX has created a competitive advantage that will resist a full reversion to the mean in the near term. With that in mind, we have chosen a ten-year forecast period beyond which we believe the firm's performance will have reached a steady state. Expanding the forecast horizon will therefore not provide further insights into how market dynamics will impact TJX's long-term performance. Table 8-2 shows that the ROE is forecasted to decline gradually over those ten years, from 50.9 percent in 2011 to 21.7 percent by 2020. At the 2020 level the company will earn an abnormal return on equity of approximately 13 percent, since its cost of equity is estimated to be 8.8 percent.

Terminal Value Under Varying Assumptions

Table 8-4 shows TJX's terminal value under the various theoretical approaches we discussed above. Scenario 1 of this table shows the terminal value if we assume that TJX will continue to grow its sales at 5.7 percent beyond fiscal year 2020, and that it will continue to earn the same level of abnormal returns as in 2020 (that is, we assume that all the other forecasting assumptions will be the same as in 2020). This scenario essentially summarizes TJX performance in perpetuity under the assumption that the firm will continue to make persistent abnormal returns and leads to a terminal value of $12.3 billion. Scenario 2 assumes that TJX is able to maintain its abnormal returns only

TABLE 8-4	Terminal Values Under Various Assumptions (Using Abnormal Earnings Methodology)			
Approach	Scenario	Terminal Sales Growth	Terminal NOPAT Margins	Value Beyond Forecast Horizon (Terminal Value $ in billions)
Persistent Abnormal Performance	Sales growth and margins based on detailed analysis and forecast	5.7%	4.0%	12.3
Abnormal Returns on Constant Sales (Real Terms)	Sales grow at the rate of inflation, margins maintained	3.0%	4.0%	6.4
Abnormal Returns on Constant Sales (Nominal Terms)	Essentially zero sales growth, margins maintained	0.0%	4.0%	4.1
Competitive Equilibrium	Margins reduced so no abnormal earnings	5.7%	2.0%	0.0

Source: © Cengage Learning 2013

on a base of sales that is constant in real terms. Scenario 2 calculates the terminal value assuming that TJX will maintain its margins only on sales that grow at the long-run expected rate of inflation, assumed to be 3.0 percent, reducing the terminal value to $6.4 billion. Scenario 3 shows the terminal value if we assume that the company's competitive advantage can be maintained only on the nominal sales level achieved in 2020. As a result, sales growth beyond the terminal year is assumed to be zero, which is equivalent to assuming that incremental sales do not produce any abnormal returns. The terminal value under this scenario drops to $4.1 billion. The final scenario invokes the competitive equilibrium assumption: margins will be eroded such that the firm will have no abnormal returns irrespective of the rate of sales growth, leading to no terminal value. For the sake of illustration, the expected sales growth of 5.7 percent is maintained. To represent the competitive equilibrium, margins are lowered to eliminate any of TJX's competitive advantage.

COMPUTING A DISCOUNT RATE

To value a company's equity, the analyst discounts abnormal earnings or cash flows available to equity holders using the cost of equity, which is the return required by equity investors. In our calculation of Abnormal Returns, Abnormal ROE, and Terminal Value above, we have assumed a cost of equity for TJX of 8.8 percent.

Estimating the cost of equity can be difficult, and a full discussion of the topic lies beyond the scope of this chapter. Even an extended discussion would not supply answers to all the questions that might be raised in this area because the field of finance is in a state of flux over what constitutes an appropriate measure of the cost of equity.

One common approach is to use the capital asset pricing model (CAPM), which expresses the cost of equity as the sum of a required return on riskless assets plus a premium for beta or systematic risk:

Cost of equity = Riskless rate of return + (Beta risk × Market risk premium)

To estimate the required return on riskless assets, analysts often use the rate on intermediate-term treasury bonds, based on the observation that it is cash flows beyond the short term that are being discounted.[1]

The systematic or beta risk of a stock reflects the sensitivity of its cash flows and earnings (and hence stock price) to economy-wide market movements.[2] A firm whose performance increases or decreases at the same rate as changes in the economy as a whole will have a beta of one. Firms whose performance is highly sensitive to economy-wide changes, such as luxury good producers, capital good manufacturers, and construction firms, will have betas that exceed one. And firms whose earnings and cash flows are less sensitive to economic changes, such as regulated utilities or supermarkets, will have betas that are lower than one. Financial services firms, such as Standard & Poor's and Value Line, provide estimates of beta for publicly listed companies that are based on the historical relation between their stock returns and the returns on the market index. These estimates, which are also reported on standard online financial sites such as Yahoo Finance and Google Finance, provide a useful way to assess publicly traded firms' beta risks.[3] For firms that are not publicly traded, analysts can use betas for publicly traded firms in the same industries as an indicator of their likely beta risks.

Finally, the market risk premium is the amount that investors demand as additional return for bearing beta risk. It is the excess of the expected return on the market index over the riskless rate. Over the 1926–2010 period, returns to the Standard and Poor's 500 index have exceeded the rate on intermediate-term treasury bonds by 6.7 percent.[4] As a result, many analysts assume that the market risk premium is around 7 percent. Others argue that a variety of changes in the U.S. economy make the historical risk premium an invalid basis for forecasting expected risk premium going forward. Evidence from some recent academic research suggests that the expected risk premium in the market in recent years has declined substantially to between 3 and 5 percent, leading some analysts to use these lower rates in their valuations.[5] However, questions have arisen about these approaches. In our calculation of TJX's cost of equity we therefore use the historic market risk premium of 6.7 percent.

Although the CAPM is often used to estimate the cost of equity, evidence indicates that the model is incomplete. Assuming stocks are priced competitively, stock returns should be expected just to compensate investors for the cost of their capital. Thus long-run average returns should be close to the cost of equity and should (according to the CAPM) vary across stocks according to their systematic risk. However, factors beyond just systematic risk seem to play some role in explaining variation in long-run average returns. The most important such factor is labeled the "size effect": smaller firms (as measured by market capitalization) tend to generate higher returns in subsequent periods. Why this is so is unclear. It could mean either that smaller firms are riskier than indicated by the CAPM or that they are underpriced at the point their market capitalization is measured, or some combination of both. Average stock returns for U.S. firms (including NYSE, AMEX, and NASDAQ firms) varied across size deciles from 1926 to 2010, as shown in Table 8-5. The table shows that, historically, investors in firms in the top two deciles of the size distribution have realized returns of 10.9 and 12.9 percent compared to significantly higher returns for firms in the smallest two size deciles, 17.2 to 21.0 percent respectively. Not surprisingly, large stocks have been significantly less risky than smaller stocks. Stocks in the largest decile have a beta of less than one compared to 1.41 for the smallest decile. After controlling for this difference in beta risk, we see that firms in the smallest decile have earned an average of 6.4 percent more than the theoretical CAPM return over time. Finance theorists have not developed a well-accepted explanation for why that should be the case.

TABLE 8-5	Stock Returns, Volatility, and Firm Size				
Size Decile	Market value of largest company in decile in 2010 ($ millions)	Fraction of total market value represented by decile in 2010 (%)	Average annual stock return 1926–2010 (%)	Beta, 1926–2010	Size premium (return in excess of CAPM - %)
1 – smallest	235.6	1.0	21.0	1.41	6.4
2	477.5	1.3	17.2	1.35	2.9
3	771.8	1.7	16.5	1.30	2.7
4	1,212.3	2.2	15.4	1.24	1.9
5	1,776.0	2.6	15.0	1.19	1.8
6	2,509.2	3.5	14.8	1.16	1.8
7	3,711.0	4.3	13.9	1.12	1.2
8	6,793.9	7.4	13.6	1.10	1.0
9	15,079.5	13.6	12.9	1.03	0.8
10 – largest	314,622.6	62.3	10.9	0.91	−0.4

Source: Ibbotson and Associates, *Market Results for Stocks, Bonds, Bills, and Inflation, 1926–2010 (2011)*

In recognition of their importance, we can use both the CAPM and the "size factors" to estimate a firm's cost of equity. The approach adjusts the CAPM-based cost of equity using the difference between the average return on the market index used in the CAPM (the Standard and Poor's 500) and the average return on firms of a size comparable to the firm being evaluated. The resulting cost of equity is the following:

$$\text{Cost of equity} = \text{Riskless rate of return} + (\text{Beta Risk} \times \text{Market risk Premium})$$
$$+ \text{Size premium}$$

In light of the continuing debate on how to measure the cost of equity, it is not surprising that managers and analysts often consider a range of estimates. Debates continue about whether or not the historical risk premium of approximately 7 percent is valid today, whether beta is a relevant measure of risk, and whether other metrics such as size should be reflected in cost of equity estimates. Since these debates are still unresolved, it is prudent for analysts to use a range of risk premium estimates in computing a firm's cost of equity.

Estimating TJX's Cost of Equity

To estimate the cost of equity for TJX, we note that the company's equity beta was reported by Value Line to be 0.8, and the ten-year Treasury bond in February/March 2011 was yielding roughly 3.4 percent. Using the historical risk premium for equities of 6.7 percent discussed above, we can calculate the cost of equity for TJX to be 8.8 percent as follows:

$$\text{Cost of equity} = \text{Riskless rate of return} + (\text{Beta Risk} \times \text{Market risk Premium})$$
$$8.8 \quad = \quad 3.4 \quad + (0.8 \quad \times \quad 6.7)$$

We do not include a size factor in computing TJX's cost of equity, since its market capitalization falls into the tenth decile, where the size premium is modest. However, it is important to remember that the 8.8 percent cost of equity used to discount forecasts of abnormal earnings and cash flows available to TJX's equity owners is only a starting point, and that the analyst can change the estimate by changing the assumed market risk premium or by making size effects adjustments.

Adjusting Cost of Equity for Changes in Leverage

The cost of equity changes as a function of a firm's leverage. As leverage increases, debt and equity become more risky and therefore more costly. If an analyst is contemplating making significant changes to the firm's capital structure during the forecasting time period relative to its historical capital structure, it is important to re-estimate the cost of debt and equity to take these changes into account.[6]

This is not a straightforward task. It requires estimating the changes in the costs of debt and equity that are likely to arise from changing the firm's capital structure. The change in the cost of debt can be estimated by examining the cost of debt for firms in the same or comparable industries that have the revised capital structure.

The change in the cost of equity can be estimated by computing the beta of the firm's assets, that is, the weighted average beta risk of its debt and equity, and then re-levering the firm using its new capital structure. The first step in this process is to infer the old and revised debt betas using the capital asset pricing model and given information on the former and revised costs of debt, the risk premium, and the risk-free rate. To compute the revised cost of debt, the analyst can estimate how the revised capital structure would change its debt rating (as discussed in Chapter 10). Higher or lower rated debt would increase or decrease the firm's cost of debt.

The second step is to estimate the firm's asset beta under the current (or old) capital structure, using the current betas for debt and equity, and the weightings of debt and equity in its market value:

$$\text{Asset beta risk} = \text{Equity beta risk}_{old} \times \% \text{ Equity}_{old} + \text{Debt beta risk}_{old} \\ \times \% \text{ Debt}_{old} \times (1 - \text{tax rate})$$

The asset beta risk represents the extent to which the cash flows generated by the firm's assets fluctuate with economic cycles. The %Equityold and %Debtold are the share of the firm's enterprise market or fair value currently financed by equity and debt, respectively, with an adjustment for the differential tax treatment of debt financing costs $(1 - \text{tax rate})$.

We are then in position to infer the revised equity beta under the new capital structure. To do so, we assume that the firm's asset beta is unchanged by the change in capital structure. Since we know the asset beta, the revised debt beta, and the new capital structure, we can solve for the new equity beta as follows:

$$\text{Equity beta risk}_{new} = (\text{Asset beta risk} - \text{Debt beta risk}_{new} \\ \times \% \text{ Debt}_{new} \times (1 - \text{tax rate}))/(\% \text{ Equity}_{new})$$

Finally, we can use the CAPM and the revised equity beta to compute the new cost of equity under the revised capital structure.

Given the complexity of this process, we recommend its use only when there are likely to be significant changes in a firm's capital structure.

COMPUTING EQUITY VALUE

Table 8-6 shows the estimated value of TJX's equity using the three different methods discussed in Chapter 7 (Abnormal earnings, Abnormal ROE, and Free cash flows to equity). To compute these values, TJX's cost of equity of 8.8 percent is first used to discount the performance forecasts in Table 8-3 and the terminal value forecast using the four scenarios presented above in Table 8-4. Those discounted forecasts are then added together with beginning book value (except in the free cash flows to equity calculation, which does not depend on beginning book value) to arrive at a total estimated value of TJX's equity under the various scenarios we have discussed. Depending on which assumption of TJX's earnings behavior over the long term we are examining, we can see that estimates of TJX's share price range from $29.78 to $61.36.

As discussed in Chapter 7, the Abnormal earnings, Abnormal ROE, and the Free cash flow methods generate the same equity values. Note also that TJX's terminal value represents a larger fraction of the total value of equity under the free cash flow method relative to the other methods. As discussed in Chapter 7, this is because the abnormal earnings and ROE methods rely on a company's book value of equity, so the terminal value forecasts are for incremental value over book value. In contrast, the free cash flow approach ignores the book value, implying that the terminal value forecasts represent total value during this period.

As a final note, the primary calculations in the above estimates treat all flows as if they arrive at the end of the year. In reality they will typically arrive throughout the year. If we choose to assume for the sake of simplicity that cash flows arrive at mid-year, then we should adjust our value estimates upward by $[1 + (R/2)]$, where R is the discount rate. This would increase the equity value estimates to a range of $31.09 to $64.06.

Value Estimates Versus Market Values

As the discussion above shows, valuation involves a substantial number of assumptions by analysts. Therefore, the estimates of value will vary from one analyst to the other. The only way to ensure that one's estimates are reliable is to make sure that the assumptions are grounded in the economics of the business being valued. It is also useful to check the assumptions against the time-series trends for performance ratios discussed in Chapter 6. While it is quite legitimate for an analyst to make assumptions that differ markedly from these trends in any given case, it is important for the analyst to be able to articulate the business and strategy reasons for making such assumptions.

When a company being valued is publicly traded, it is possible to compare one's own estimated value with the market value of a company. When an estimated value differs substantially from a company's market value, it is useful for the analyst to understand why such differences arise. A way to accomplish this is to reframe the valuation exercise to figure out what valuation assumptions are needed to arrive at the observed stock price. One can then examine whether the market's assumptions are more or less valid relative to one's own assumptions. As we discuss in the next chapter, such an analysis can be invaluable in using valuation to make buy or sell decisions in the security analysis context.

In the case of TJX, the observed value of the firm's equity on February 1, 2011 (the beginning of TJX's fiscal year 2011), was $47.94, placing it very close to our Scenario 2 value of $46.15 shown in Table 8-6.

TABLE 8-6	Equity Valuation Summary for TJX Under Varying Scenarios				
($000,000s)	Beginning Book Value	Value from Forecasts for 2011–2020	Value from Forecasts Beyond 2020 (Terminal Value)	Total Value	Value per Share ($)[1]
Scenario 1 – Persistent Abnormal Performance					
Abnormal Earnings	3,357.1	8,246.7	12,308.0	23,911.8	61.36
Abnormal ROE	3,357.1	8,246.7	12,308.0	23,911.8	61.36
Free Cash Flows to Equity	N/A	8,691.6	15,220.2	23,911.8	61.36
Scenario 2 – Abnormal Returns on Constant Sales (Real Terms)					
Abnormal Earnings	3,357.1	8,246.7	6,381.3	17,985.1	46.15
Abnormal ROE	3,357.1	8,246.7	6,381.3	17,985.1	46.15
Free Cash Flows to Equity	N/A	8,766.0	9,219.2	17,985.1	46.15
Scenario 3 – Abnormal Returns on Constant Sales (Nominal Terms)					
Abnormal Earnings	3,357.1	8,246.7	4,076.1	15,680.0	40.24
Abnormal ROE	3,357.1	8,246.7	4,076.1	15,680.0	40.24
Free Cash Flows to Equity	N/A	8,848.6	6,831.3	15,680.0	40.24
Scenario 4 – Competitive Equilibrium					
Abnormal Earnings	3,357.1	8,246.7	0.0	11,603.8	29.78
Abnormal ROE	3,357.1	8,246.7	0.0	11,603.8	29.78
Free Cash Flows to Equity	N/A	8,691.6	2,912.2	11,603.8	29.78

[1]Shares of TJX outstanding used in the calculation of equity per share 389.7 million per Thomson ONE database, accessed July, 2011.
Source: © Cengage Learning 2013

Sensitivity Analysis

The broad range of estimated equity values shown in Table 8-6 above demonstrates that changes in assumptions can significantly affect an analyst's equity valuation for a company. As noted above, the market's valuation of TJX in early 2011 falls close to our Scenario 2 valuation, indicating that the market expected TJX to be able to continue to generate abnormal returns beyond the forecast horizon. However, in Chapter 6, we recognized that the company's future could play out in multiple ways. If, for instance, TJX is able to resist the long run pressure for its ROEs to revert to the mean in its U.S. and Canadian markets, address its problems in Europe, and replicate its U.S. success in other new markets, its abnormal real returns or even overall abnormal returns could persist beyond the terminal year, leading to a much higher valuation (see Table 8-6). Alternatively, if the U.S. and Canadian markets revert toward the mean, the European business fails to recover, and its model fails to translate successfully to new markets, TJX's terminal year performance may be better reflected by reversion to competitive equilibrium. The differences in values of these scenario values were driven primarily by long-term differences in sales growth and margins, performance measures that are strongly affected by the forces of competition.

SOME PRACTICAL ISSUES IN VALUATION

The above discussion provides a blueprint for doing valuation. In practice, the analyst has to deal with a number of other issues that have an important effect on the valuation task. We discuss below three frequently encountered complications—accounting distortions, negative book values, and excess cash.

Dealing with Accounting Distortions

We know from the discussion in Chapter 7 that accounting methods per se should have no influence on firm value, despite the fact that abnormal returns and earnings valuation approaches used here are based on numbers that vary with accounting method choices.

Since accounting choices must affect both earnings *and* book value, and because of the self-correcting nature of double-entry bookkeeping (all "distortions" of accounting must ultimately reverse), estimated values will not be affected by accounting choices, *as long as the analyst recognizes the accounting distortions.*[7] When a company uses "biased" accounting—conservative or aggressive—the analyst needs to recognize the bias to ensure that value estimates are not biased. If a thorough analysis is not performed, a firm's accounting choices can influence analysts' perceptions of the real performance of the firm and hence the forecasts of future performance. Accounting choice would affect expectations of future earnings and cash flows, and distort the valuation, regardless of whether the valuation is based on DCF or discounted abnormal earnings.[8] For example, if a firm overstates current revenue growth through aggressive revenue recognition, failure to appreciate the effect is likely to lead the analyst to overstate future revenues, affecting both earnings and cash flow forecasts. An analyst who encounters biased accounting has two choices—either to adjust current earnings and book values to eliminate managers' accounting biases, or to recognize these biases and adjust future forecasts accordingly. Whereas both approaches lead to the same estimated firm value, the choice will have an important impact on what fraction of the firm's value is captured within the forecast horizon and what remains in the terminal value.

Holding forecasting horizon and future growth opportunities constant, higher accounting quality generally allows a higher fraction of a firm's value to be captured by the current book value and the abnormal earnings within the forecasting horizon. Accounting can be of low quality either because it is unreliable or because it is extremely conservative. If accounting reliability is a concern, the analyst has to expend resources on "accounting adjustments." If accounting is conservative, the analyst is forced to increase the forecasting horizon to capture a given fraction of a firm's value or to rely on relatively more uncertain terminal values estimates for a large fraction of the estimated value.

In the case of TJX, in Chapter 5 we reported the impact on financial ratios and other measures of firm performance of adjusting for the firm's use of off–balance sheet lease accounting. We saw that the major effects of adjusting for that accounting choice were to increase earnings in the current period (due to the lower depreciation of the newly "acquired" assets versus the previously expensed leases), and to significantly increase both long-term assets and debt (with resultant impact on the related ratios). In valuing TJX, we have recognized these effects in estimating forecasts for TJX by using adjusted financials that reflect the full impact of the operating leases. Another way the analyst could choose to address the issue would be by acknowledging that TJX, with its low asset base, would be expected to maintain a return on operating assets that resists a full reversion to the mean. In that case, this strong near-term performance would also result in less of TJX's value being reflected in its terminal value.

Dealing with Negative Book Values

A number of firms have negative earnings and/or negative values of book equity. Firms in the start-up phase have negative equity, as do those in high technology industries. These firms incur large investments whose payoff is uncertain. Accountants write off these investments as a matter of conservatism, leading to negative book equity. Examples of firms in this situation include biotechnology firms, Internet firms, telecommunication firms, and other high technology firms. A second category of firms with negative book equity are those that are performing poorly, resulting in cumulative losses exceeding the original investment by the shareholders.

Negative book equity makes it difficult to use the accounting-based approach to value a firm's equity. There are several ways to get around this problem. The first is to value the firm's assets (using, for example, abnormal operating ROA or abnormal NOPAT) rather than equity. Then, based on an estimate of the value of the firm's debt, one can estimate the equity value. Another alternative is to "undo" accountants' conservatism by capitalizing the investment expenditures written off. This is possible if the analyst is able to establish that these expenditures are value creating. A third alternative, feasible for publicly traded firms, is to start from the observed stock price and work backward. Using reasonable estimates of cost of equity and steady-state growth rate, the analyst can calculate the average long-term level of abnormal earnings needed to justify the observed stock price. Then the analytical task can be framed in terms of examining the feasibility of achieving this abnormal earnings "target."

It is important to note that the value of firms with negative book equity often consists of a significant option value. For example, the value of high-tech firms is not only driven by the expected earnings from their current technologies but also by the payoff from technology options embedded in their research and development efforts. Similarly, the value of troubled companies is driven to some extent by the "abandonment option"— shareholders with limited liability can turn over the firm to debt holders and creditors. One can use the options theory framework to estimate the value of these "real options."

Dealing with Excess Cash and Excess Cash Flow

Firms with excess cash balances, or large free cash flows, also pose a valuation challenge. In our projections for TJX, we implicitly assumed that cash beyond the level required to finance the company's operations will be paid out to the firm's shareholders either in the form of dividends or stock repurchases. Notice that these cash flows are already incorporated into the valuation process when they are earned, so there is no need to take them into account when they are paid out.

It is important to recognize that both the accounting-based valuation and the discounted cash flow valuation assume a dividend payout that can potentially vary from period to period. This dividend policy assumption is required as long as one wishes to assume a constant level of financial leverage and stable equity risk used to compute the cost of equity in the valuation calculations. Firms rarely have such a variable dividend policy in practice. However, this in itself does not make the valuation approaches invalid, as long as a firm's dividend policy does not affect its value. That is, the valuation approaches assume that the well-known Modigliani-Miller theorem regarding the irrelevance of dividends holds.

A firm's dividend policy can affect its value if managers do not invest free cash flows optimally. For example, if a firm's managers use excess cash to undertake value-destroying acquisitions, then our approach overestimates the firm's value. Firms that suffer from such "agency" costs are likely to have ineffective corporate governance (discussed in chapter 12). One approach that the analyst can use to reflect these types of concerns into a valuation is to first estimate the firm value according to the approach described earlier and then adjust the estimated value for whatever agency costs the firm's managers may impose on its investors.

SUMMARY

We illustrate in this chapter how to apply the valuation theory discussed in Chapter 7. The chapter explains the set of business and financial assumptions one needs to make to conduct the valuation exercise. It also illustrates the mechanics of making detailed valuation forecasts and terminal values of earnings, free cash flows, and accounting rates of return. We discuss how to compute the cost of equity. Using a detailed example, we show how a firm's equity value can be computed using earnings, cash flows, and rates of return. Finally, we offer ways to deal with some commonly encountered practical issues, including accounting distortions, negative book values, and excess cash balances.

DISCUSSION QUESTIONS

1. How will the forecasts in Table 8-2 change if TJX maintains a sales growth rate of 10 percent per year from 2011 to 2020 (and all the other assumptions are kept unchanged)?
2. Recalculate the forecasts in Table 8-2, assuming that the NOPAT profit margin is held steady for the first five years of the forecast and then declines by 0.1 percentage points per year thereafter (keeping all the other assumptions unchanged).
3. Recalculate the forecasts in Table 8-3, assuming that the ratio of net operating working capital to sales is 3 percent and the ratio of net long-term assets to sales is 33.4 percent for all the years from fiscal 2011 to fiscal 2020. Keep all the other assumptions unchanged.
4. Calculate TJX's cash payouts to its shareholders in the years 2011–2020 that are implicitly assumed in the projections in Table 8-2.
5. How will the abnormal earnings calculations in Table 8-3 change if the cost of equity assumption is changed to 12 percent?

6. What would be the total equity value (as calculated for scenarios in Table 8-6 using abnormal earnings) if the sales growth in years 2021 and beyond is 8.5 percent and the company is able to generate abnormal returns at the same level as in fiscal 2020 forever (keeping all the other assumptions in the table unchanged)?

7. Calculate the proportion of terminal value to total estimated value of equity under the abnormal earnings method and the discounted cash flow method for the Scenario 2 results shown in Table 8-6. Why are these proportions different?

8. What will TJX's cost of equity be if the equity market risk premium is 5 percent?

9. Assume that TJX changes its capital structure so that its market value weight of debt to capital increases to 30 percent, and its after-tax interest rate on debt at this new leverage level is 3.5 percent. Assume that the equity market risk premium is 6.7 percent. What will be the cost of equity at the new debt level? What will be the new weighted average cost of capital?

10. Nancy Smith says she is uncomfortable making the assumption that TJX's dividend payout will vary from year to year. If she makes a constant dividend payout assumption, what changes does she have to make in her other valuation assumptions to make them internally consistent with each other?

NOTES

1. See T. Copeland, T. Koller, and J. Murrin, *Valuation: Measuring and Managing the Value of Companies*, 2nd edition (New York: John Wiley & Sons, 1994). Theory calls for the use of a short-term rate, but if that rate is used here, a difficult practical question rises: how does one reflect the premium required for expected inflation over long horizons? While the premium could, in principle, be treated as a portion of the term $[E(rm) - rf]$, it is probably easier to use an intermediate- or long-term riskless rate that presumably reflects expected inflation.

2. One way to estimate systematic risk is to regress the firm's stock returns over some recent time period against the returns on the market index. The slope coefficient represents an estimate of β. More fundamentally, systematic risk depends on how sensitive the firm's operating profits are to shifts in economy-wide activity, and the firm's degree of leverage. Financial analysis that assesses these operating and financial risks should be useful in arriving at reasonable estimates of β

3. These betas are typically estimated by regressing five years of daily firm stock returns on the return on a market index, such as the Standard & Poor's 500. These estimates can be heavily influenced by extremely positive or negative firm-specific news (and stock returns) during the five-year estimation period, generating betas that are implausibly high or low. Since it uses a more complex estimation approach, Value Line betas are less likely to be subject to these biases and are used throughout this book.

4. The average return reported here is the arithmetic mean as opposed to the geometric mean. Ibbotson and Associates explain why this estimate is appropriate in this context (see *Stocks, Bonds, Bills, and Inflation, 2010 Yearbook*, Chicago).

5. See W. Gebhardt, C. Lee, and B. Swaminathan, "Toward an Implied Cost of Capital," *Journal of Accounting Research* 39, no. 1 (2001): 135–176; and J. Claus and J. Thomas, "The Equity Premium Is Much Lower Than You Think It Is: Empirical Estimates from a New Approach," *Journal of Finance* 56 (2001): 1,629–1,666.

6. For TJX, adjustments to bring the operating leases onto the balance sheet change the company's leverage and other capital structure ratios from those reported. However, we do not consider it necessary to re-estimate TJX's cost of debt and equity for these

changes since the adjustments are made to provide a better economic picture of the firm's current capital structure, not to change TJX's capital structure. The implicit assumption underlying this approach is that estimates of the firm's equity and debt beta risks reflect its current economic capital structure, rather than that reported. Given that rating agencies typically make adjustments to increase leverage for the effect of debt from operating leases, this seems a reasonable assumption.

7. Valuation based on discounted abnormal earnings does require one property of the forecasts: that they be consistent with "clean surplus accounting." Such accounting requires the following relation:

$$\text{End-of-period book value} = \text{Beginning book value} \times \text{earnings} - \text{dividends} \\ \pm \text{capital contributions/withdrawals}$$

Clean surplus accounting rules out situations where some gain or loss is excluded from earnings but is still used to adjust the book value of equity. For example, under U.S. GAAP, gains and losses on foreign currency translations are handled this way. In applying the valuation technique described here, the analyst would need to deviate from GAAP in producing forecasts and treat such gains/losses as a part of earnings. However, the technique does not require that clean surplus accounting has been applied in the past—so the existing book value, based on U.S. GAAP or any other set of principles, can still serve as the starting point. All the analyst has to do is apply clean surplus accounting in his/her forecasts, which is not only easy but also is usually the natural thing to do anyway.

8. It is important to recognize that when the analyst uses the "indirect" cash flow forecasting method, undetected accounting biases can influence not only future earnings forecasts but also future free cash flow forecasts. In the current example, since accounts receivables are overstated, the analyst will assume that they will be collected as cash in some future period, leading to a higher future cash flow estimate.

APPENDIX   Estimating TJX's Overall Asset Value

Our primary focus in this chapter has been on valuing TJX's equity. But it can also be useful for the analyst to value the firm's assets. As we discussed in Chapter 7, under the different approaches to valuation, the key forecasts required to convert the financial forecasts shown in Tables 8-1 and 8-2 into estimates of asset value are the following:

- Abnormal NOPAT: NOPAT less total net capital at the beginning of the year times the weighted average cost of capital;
- Abnormal operating ROA: the difference between operating ROA and the weighted average cost of capital; or
- Free cash flows to capital: NOPAT less the increase in operating working capital less the increase in new long-term assets.

In the same way that we used the cost of equity to discount TJX's forecasted equity performance and value its equity, we need to come up with a cost of all capital provided, termed the weighted average cost of capital (WACC), to discount the forecasts of asset performance and value its assets. As discussed in Appendix D of Chapter 7, the weighted average cost of capital (WACC) is used to discount the abnormal earnings or free cash flows to all investors in the company. WACC is the average cost to a firm of obtaining capital from both debt and equity sources. It is, literally, the weighted after-tax cost of debt financing (i.e., the return required by providers of debt to the firm on an after-tax basis) and the weighted return required by equity providers, where the weights are the percentages of debt and equity (at their fair or market values) to the enterprise market value.

To estimate the WACC for TJX, we start with the assumption that its pre-tax cost of debt is 4.4 percent, based on the average yield of similarly rated company debt during 2010 (we discuss this in more detail in Chapter 10). Given TJX's marginal tax rate of 38 percent, the after-tax cost of debt is 2.7 percent [4.4% × (1−38%)]. As discussed in the chapter, TJX's cost of equity is estimated at 8.8 percent, reflecting the company's equity beta of 0.8, the ten-year Treasury bond yield of 3.4 percent, and the historical risk premium for equities of 6.7 percent.

TJX's estimated equity value seen in our Scenario 2 estimate detailed above (which most closely tracks actual equity market value during the same time period) was $18.0 billion; its net book debt (using our adjusted numbers) was $4.5 billion. Using these numbers we can calculate the "market value" weights of debt and equity in the company's capital structure as 20 percent and 80 percent respectively. Given these weightings and the costs of equity and debt, TJX's WACC in February 2011 is estimated at 7.6 percent.

TJX's Weighted Average Cost of Capital

	Cost of funds	× Market Weighting	= Weighted cost
Debt	2.7%	20.0%	0.6%
Equity	8.8%	80.0%	7.0%
Capital			7.6%

Now that we have estimated TJX's WACC, we can forecast the variables needed to compute an overall asset value for TJX. Table A-1 shows forecasts for the three financial statement variables—abnormal NOPAT, abnormal operating ROA, and free cash flow to capital—for the ten-year period 2011 to 2020.

To derive cash flows in 2020, we need to make assumptions about the sales growth rate and balance sheet ratios in 2021. The cash flow forecasts shown in Table A-1 are based on the assumption that the sales growth and beginning balance sheet ratios will track those shown in Scenario 2 above, which assumes a sales growth rate of 3.0 percent with other beginning balance sheet ratios remaining the same as in 2020.

To complete our analysis, Table A-2 shows the estimated value of TJX's assets using the three methods discussed in Chapter 7 for Scenario 2 (abnormal returns on constant sales) shown in the body of the chapter. To compute this value, TJX's performance forecasts in Table A-1 and its terminal value forecast for Scenario 2 are discounted at the weighted

TABLE A-1	Asset Valuation Performance Forecasts for TJX									
Forecast year	2011	2012	2013	2014	2015	2016	2017	2018	2019	2020
Abnormal NOPAT	1,235.0	1,200.0	1,174.2	1,136.7	1,086.3	1,022.2	943.3	812.6	661.2	488.2
Abnormal operating ROA	15.6%	13.9%	12.6%	11.3%	10.1%	8.8%	7.6%	6.1%	4.7%	3.3%
Free cash flow to capital	1,077.5	1,173.7	1,165.2	1,147.7	1,120.5	1,082.8	1,033.8	936.6	822.5	1,173.6
Asset discount factor	0.93	0.86	0.80	0.75	0.69	0.65	0.60	0.56	0.52	0.48
Asset growth factor	1.00	1.10	1.18	1.27	1.37	1.47	1.57	1.68	1.79	1.90

Source: © Cengage Learning 2013

TABLE A-2	Asset Valuation Summary for TJX Under Scenario 2			
($000,000s)	Beginning Book Value	Value from Forecasts for 2011–2020	Value from Forecasts Beyond 2020 (Terminal Value)	Total Value
Scenario 2 – Abnormal Returns on Constant Sales (Real Terms)				
Abnormal NOPAT	7,898.5	6,991.2	5,317.9	20,207.6
Abnormal Operating ROA	7,898.5	6,991.2	5,317.9	20,207.6
Free Cash Flows to Capital	N/A	7,423.8	12,783.8	20,207.6

Source: © Cengage Learning 2013

average cost of capital of 7.6 percent. These discounted forecasts are then summed and combined with beginning book value of net operating assets (except in the free cash flows to equity calculation, which does not depend on beginning book value) to arrive at a total estimated value of TJX's assets under Scenario 2 of $20.2 billion.

Finally, by deducting the book value of debt ($4.5 billion), the analyst can generate the implied value of the equity under Scenario 2. This equity valuation is different from that reported in Table 8-6 in this chapter, when we valued equity directly. Several factors underlie the difference. First, the asset valuation uses the value of equity, an output of the analysis, as an input to compute the WACC. If the computed equity value differs from that used to estimate WACC, there is an internal inconsistency in the analysis. This can be resolved by re-running the valuation, discounting the forecasts of asset profits / cash flows using the value of equity from the first estimation in generating a new WACC. This process can be repeated until the equity weight used in the WACC computation and the final asset/equity valuation converge.

A second explanation for the valuation difference is that the book value of assets, used to compute TJX's WACC, is only an approximation of the market or fair value of debt. The average coupon rate TJX pays on its outstanding debt is 5.5 percent, which exceeds the current pre-tax cost of debt of 4.4 percent, implying that the market value of its debt exceeds its book value and that TJX's actual WACC is lower than the estimate used in the above analysis.

Given these challenges in determining economic leverage, we recommend valuing equity directly as we did in the body of the chapter.

PART

3

BUSINESS ANALYSIS AND VALUATION APPLICATIONS

CHAPTER 9
Equity Security Analysis

CHAPTER 10
Credit Analysis and Distress Prediction

CHAPTER 11
Mergers and Acquisitions

CHAPTER 12
Communication and Governance

Chapter 9

EQUITY SECURITY ANALYSIS

Equity security analysis is the evaluation of a firm and its prospects from the perspective of a current or potential investor in the firm's stock. Security analysis is, however, just one step in a larger investment process that involves (1) establishing the objectives of the investor, (2) forming expectations about the future returns and risks of individual securities, and then (3) combining individual securities into portfolios to maximize progress toward the investment objectives.

Security analysis is the foundation for the second step of projecting future returns and assessing risk. Security analysis is typically conducted with an eye toward identifying mispriced securities in the hopes of generating returns that more than compensate the investor for risk. However, that need not be the case. For analysts who do not have a comparative advantage in identifying mispriced securities, the focus should be on gaining an appreciation for how a security would affect the risk of a given portfolio and whether it fits the profile that the portfolio is designed to maintain.

Security analysis is undertaken by individual investors, by analysts at brokerage houses and investment banks (sell-side analysts), and by analysts that work at the direction of fund managers for various institutions (buy-side analysts). The institutions employing buy-side analysts include mutual funds, hedge funds, insurance companies, universities, and others.

A variety of questions are dealt with in security analysis:

- A sell-side analyst asks: Is the industry I am covering attractive, and if so why? How do different firms within the industry position themselves? What are the implications for my earnings forecasts? Given my expectations for a firm, does its stock appear to be mispriced? Should I recommend this stock as a buy, a sell, or a hold?

- A buy-side analyst for a "value stock fund" asks: Does this stock possess the characteristics we seek in our fund; that is, does it have a relatively low ratio of price–earnings, low price-to-book value, and other fundamental indicators? Do its prospects for earnings improvement suggest good potential for high future returns on the stock?

- An individual investor asks: Does this stock present the risk profile that suits my investment objectives? Does it enhance my ability to diversify the risk of my portfolio? Is the firm's dividend payout rate low enough to minimize my tax liability while I continue to hold the stock?

As the above questions underscore, there is more to security analysis than estimating the value of stocks. Nevertheless, for most sell-side and buy-side analysts, the key goal remains the identification of mispriced stocks.

INVESTOR OBJECTIVES AND INVESTMENT VEHICLES

The investment objectives of individual savers in the economy are highly idiosyncratic. For any given saver they depend on factors such as income, age, wealth, tolerance for risk, and tax status. For example, savers with many years until retirement are likely to prefer to have a relatively large share of their portfolio invested in equities, which offer a higher expected return than fixed income (or debt) securities and higher short-term variability. Investors in high tax brackets are likely to prefer to have a large share of their portfolio in stocks that generate tax-deferred capital gains rather than stocks that pay dividends or interest-bearing securities.

Mutual funds (or unit trusts as they are termed in some countries) have become popular investment vehicles for savers to achieve their investment objectives. Mutual funds sell shares in professionally managed portfolios that invest in specific types of stocks and/or fixed income securities. They therefore provide a low-cost way for savers to invest in a portfolio of securities that reflects their particular appetite for risk.

The major classes of mutual fund include (1) money market funds that invest in CDs and treasury bills, (2) bond funds that invest in debt instruments, (3) equity funds that invest in equity securities, (4) balanced funds that hold money market, bond, and equity securities, and (5) real estate funds that invest in commercial real estate. Within the bond and equities classes of funds, however, there are wide ranges of fund types. For example, bond funds include

- *Corporate bond funds* that invest in investment-grade rated corporate debt instruments,
- *High yield funds* that invest in non-investment-grade rated corporate debt,
- *Mortgage funds* that invest in mortgage-backed securities, and
- *Municipal funds* that invest in municipal debt instruments, which generate income that can be exempt from federal and often state and local taxes.

Equity funds include

- *Income funds* that invest in stocks that are expected to generate dividend income,
- *Growth funds* that invest in stocks expected to generate long-term capital gains,
- *Income and growth funds* that invest in stocks that provide a balance of dividend income and capital gains,
- *Value funds* that invest in equities that are considered to be undervalued,
- *Short funds* that sell short equity securities that are considered to be overvalued,
- *Index funds* that invest in stocks that track a particular market index, such as the S&P 500,
- *Size-based funds* that invest based on the market capitalization of the company, such as large-cap and small-cap funds,
- *Sector funds* that invest in stocks in a particular industry segment, such as the technology or health sciences sectors, and
- *Regional funds* that invest in equities from a particular country or geographic region, such as Japan, Europe, or the Asia-Pacific region.

Since the 1990s, hedge funds have gained increased prominence, and the assets controlled by these funds have grown significantly. While generally open only to institutional investors and certain qualified wealthy individuals, hedge funds are becoming an increasingly important force in the market. Hedge funds employ a variety of investment strategies including

- *Market neutral funds* that typically invest equal amounts of money in purchasing undervalued securities and shorting overvalued ones to neutralize market risk,
- *Short-selling funds,* which short sell the securities of companies that they believe are overvalued, and
- *Special situations funds* that invest in undervalued securities in anticipation of an increase in value resulting from a favorable turn of events.

These fund types employ very different strategies. But for many, fundamental analysis of companies is the critical task. This chapter focuses on applying the tools we have developed in Part 2 of the book to analyze equity securities.

EQUITY SECURITY ANALYSIS AND MARKET EFFICIENCY

How a security analyst should invest his or her time depends on how quickly and efficiently information flows through markets and becomes reflected in security prices. In the extreme, information would be reflected in security prices fully and immediately upon its release. This is essentially the condition posited by the *efficient markets hypothesis.* This hypothesis states that security prices reflect all available information, as if such information could be costlessly digested and translated immediately into demands for buys or sells without regard to frictions imposed by transaction costs. Under such conditions, it would be impossible to identify mispriced securities on the basis of public information.

In a world of efficient markets, the expected return on any equity security is just enough to compensate investors for the unavoidable risk the security involves. Unavoidable risk is that which cannot be "diversified away" simply by holding a portfolio of many securities. Given efficient markets, the investor's strategy shifts away from the search for mispriced securities and focuses instead on maintaining a well-diversified portfolio. Aside from this, the investor must arrive at the desired balance between risky securities and risk-free short-term government bonds. The desired balance depends on how much risk the investor is willing to bear for a given increase in expected returns.

The above discussion implies that investors who accept that stock prices already reflect available information have no need for analysis involving a search for mispriced securities. If all investors adopted this attitude, of course no such analysis would be conducted, mispricing would go uncorrected, and markets would no longer be efficient![1] This is why the efficient markets hypothesis cannot represent an equilibrium in a strict sense. In equilibrium there must be just enough mispricing to provide incentives for the investment of resources in security analysis.

The existence of some mispricing, even in equilibrium, does not imply that it is sensible for just anyone to engage in security analysis. Instead, it suggests that securities analysis is subject to the same laws of supply and demand faced in all other competitive industries: it will be rewarding only for those with the strongest comparative advantage. How many analysts are in that category depends on a number of factors, including the liquidity of a firm's stock and investor interest in the company.[2] For the smallest publicly traded firms in the United States, there is typically no formal following by analysts, and would-be investors and their advisors are left to form their own opinions on a stock. Recent research shows a trend of reduced sell-side analyst coverage following new regulations for investment banks following the scandals of the late 1990s.[3] Coverage of IBM, for example, has declined from about 40 sell-side professional analysts in March 2003 to 32 analysts in October 2011. This decline has been at least partially offset by an increase in the number of analysts employed on the buy-side.

Market Efficiency and the Role of Financial Statement Analysis

The degree of market efficiency that arises from competition among analysts and other market agents is an empirical issue addressed by a large body of research spanning the last three decades. Such research has important implications for the role of financial statements in security analysis. Consider, for example, the implications of an extremely efficient market, where information is fully impounded in prices within minutes of its revelation. In such a market, agents could profit from digesting financial statement information in two ways. First, the information would be useful to the select few who receive newly announced financial data, interpret it quickly, and trade on it within minutes. Second, and probably more important, the information would be useful for gaining an understanding of the firm, so as to place the analyst in a better position to interpret future news (from financial statements as well as other sources) as it arrives.

On the other hand, if securities prices fail to reflect financial statement data fully, even days or months after its public revelation, market agents could profit from such data by creating trading strategies designed to exploit any systematic ways in which the publicly available data are ignored or discounted in the price-setting process.

Market Efficiency and Managers' Financial Reporting Strategies

The degree to which markets are efficient also has implications for managers' approaches to communicating with their investment communities. The issue becomes most important when the firm pursues an unusual strategy, or when the usual interpretation of financial statements would be misleading in the firm's context. In such a case, the communication avenues that managers can successfully pursue depend not only on management's credibility but also on the degree of understanding present in the investment community. We will return to the issue of management communications in more detail in Chapter 12.

Evidence of Market Efficiency

There is an abundance of evidence consistent with a high degree of efficiency in the primary U.S. securities markets.[4] In fact, during the 1960s and 1970s, the evidence was so one-sided that the efficient markets hypothesis gained widespread acceptance within the academic community and had a major impact on the practicing community as well.

Evidence pointing to very efficient securities markets comes in several forms:

- When information is announced publicly, the markets react *very* quickly.
- It is difficult to identify specific funds or analysts who have consistently generated abnormally high returns.
- A number of studies suggest that stock prices reflect a rather sophisticated level of fundamental analysis.

While a large body of evidence consistent with efficiency exists, recent years have witnessed a re-examination of the once widely accepted thinking. A sampling of the research includes the following:

- On the issue of the speed of stock price response to news, a number of studies suggest that even though prices react quickly, the initial reaction tends to be incomplete.[5]
- A number of studies point to trading strategies that could have been used to outperform market averages.[6]

- Related evidence—still subject to ongoing debate about its proper interpretation—suggests that even though market prices reflect some relatively sophisticated analysis, prices still do not fully reflect all the information that could be garnered from publicly available financial statements.[7]

The controversy over the efficiency of securities markets is unlikely to be resolved soon. However, there are some lessons that are accepted by most researchers. First, securities markets not only reflect publicly available information, but they also anticipate much of it before it is released. The open question is what fraction of the response remains to be impounded in price once the day of the public release comes to a close. Second, even in most studies that suggest inefficiency, the degree of mispricing is relatively small for large stocks.

Finally, even if some of the evidence is currently difficult to align with the efficient markets hypothesis, it remains a useful benchmark (at a minimum) for thinking about the behavior of security prices. The hypothesis will continue to play that role unless it can be replaced by a more complete theory. Some researchers are developing theories that encompass the existence of market agents who are forced to trade for unpredictable "liquidity" reasons, and prices that differ from so-called "fundamental values," even in equilibrium.[8] Also, behavioral finance models recognize that cognitive biases can affect investor behavior.[9]

APPROACHES TO FUND MANAGEMENT AND SECURITIES ANALYSIS

Approaches used in practice to analyze securities and manage funds are quite varied. One dimension of variation is the extent to which the investments are actively or passively managed. Another is whether a quantitative or a traditional fundamental approach is used. Security analysts also vary considerably in terms of whether they produce formal or informal valuations of the firm.

Active Versus Passive Management

Active portfolio management relies heavily on security analysis to identify mispriced securities. The passive portfolio manager serves as a price taker, avoiding the costs of security analysis and turnover while typically seeking to hold a portfolio designed to match some overall market index or sector performance. Combined approaches are also possible. For example, one may actively manage 20 percent of a fund balance while passively managing the remainder. The widespread growth of passively managed funds in the United States over the past 20 years serves as testimony to the growing belief that it is difficult to consistently earn returns that are superior to broad market indices such as the S&P 500 Index.

Quantitative Versus Traditional Fundamental Analysis

Actively managed funds must depend on some form of security analysis. Some funds employ *technical analysis,* which attempts to predict stock price movements on the basis of market indicators (prior stock price movements, volume of shares traded, etc.). In contrast, *fundamental analysis,* the primary approach for security analysis, attempts to evaluate the current market price relative to projections of the firm's future earnings and cash-flow generating potential. Fundamental analysis involves all the steps described in the previous chapters of this book: business strategy analysis, accounting analysis, financial analysis, and prospective analysis (forecasting and valuation). In recent years, some analysts have supplemented traditional fundamental analysis, which involves a substantial amount of subjective judgment, with more quantitative approaches.

The quantitative approaches themselves are quite varied. Some involve simply "screening" stocks on the basis of some set of factors, such as trends in analysts' earnings revisions, price-earnings ratios, price-to-book ratios, and so on. Whether such approaches are useful depends on the degree of market efficiency relative to the screens. Quantitative approaches can also involve implementation of some formal model to predict future stock returns. Longstanding statistical techniques such as regression analysis and probit analysis can be used, as can more recently developed, computer-intensive techniques such as neural network analysis. Again, the success of these approaches depends on the degree of market efficiency and whether the analysis can exploit information in ways not otherwise available to market agents as a group.

Quantitative approaches play a more important role in security analysis today than they did a decade or two ago. However, by and large, analysts still rely primarily on fundamental analysis involving complex human judgments.

Formal Versus Informal Valuation

Full-scale, formal valuations based on the methods described in Chapter 7 have become more common in recent years. However, less formal approaches are also popular. For example, an analyst can compare his or her long-term earnings projection with the consensus forecast to generate a buy or sell recommendation. Another possible approach, that might be labeled "marginalist," involves no attempt to value the firm. The analyst simply assumes that if he or she has unearthed favorable (or unfavorable) information believed not to be recognized by others, the stock should be bought (or sold).

Unlike many security analysts, investment bankers produce formal valuations as a matter of course. Investment bankers, who estimate values for the purpose of bringing a private firm to the public market, for evaluating a merger or buyout proposal, for issuing a fairness opinion or for making a periodic managerial review, must document their valuation in a way that can readily be communicated to management and, if necessary, to the courts.

THE PROCESS OF COMPREHENSIVE SECURITY ANALYSIS

Given the variety of approaches practiced in security analysis, it is impossible to summarize all of them here. Instead, we briefly outline steps to be included in a comprehensive security analysis. The amount of attention focused on any given step varies among analysts.

Selection of Candidates for Analysis

No analyst can effectively investigate more than a small fraction of the securities on a major exchange, and thus some approach to narrowing the focus must be employed. Sell-side analysts are often organized within an investment house by industry or sector. Thus they tend to be constrained in their choices of firms to follow. However, from the perspective of a fund manager or an investment firm as a whole, there is usually the freedom to focus on any firm or sector.

As noted earlier, funds typically specialize in investing in stocks with certain risk profiles or characteristics (e.g., growth stocks, "value" stocks, technology stocks, and cyclical stocks). Managers of these types of funds seek to focus the energies of their analysts on identifying stocks that fit their fund objective. In addition, individual investors who seek to maintain a well-diversified portfolio without holding many stocks also need information about the nature of a firm's risks and how they fit with the risk profile of their overall portfolio.

An alternative approach to stock selection is to screen firms on the basis of some potential mispricing followed by a detailed analysis of only those stocks that meet the specified criteria. For example, one fund managed by a large U.S. insurance company screens stocks on the basis of recent "earnings momentum" as reflected in revisions in the earnings projections of sell-side and buy-side analysts. Upward revisions trigger investigations for possible purchase. The fund operates on the belief that earnings momentum is a positive signal of future price movements. Another fund complements the earnings momentum screen with one based on recent short-term stock price movements, in the hopes of identifying earnings revisions not yet reflected in stock prices.

Key Analysis Questions

Depending on whether fund managers follow a strategy of targeting stocks with specific types of characteristics, or of screening stocks that appear to be mispriced, the following types of questions are likely to be useful:

- What is the risk profile of a firm? How volatile is its earnings stream and stock price? What are the most likely bad outcomes in the future? What is the upside potential? How closely linked are the firm's risks to the health of the overall economy? Are the risks largely diversifiable, or are they systematic?
- Does the firm possess the characteristics of a growth stock? What is the expected pattern of sales and earnings growth for the coming years? Is the firm reinvesting most or all of its earnings?
- Does the firm match the characteristics desired by "income funds"? Is it a mature or maturing company, prepared to "harvest" profits and distribute them in the form of high dividends?
- Is the firm a candidate for a "value fund"? Does it offer measures of earnings, cash flow, and book value that are high relative to the price? What specific screening rules can be implemented to identify misvalued stocks?

Inferring Market Expectations

If the security analysis is conducted with an eye toward the identification of mispricing, it must ultimately involve a comparison of the analyst's expectations with those of "the market." One possibility is to view the observed stock price as the reflection of market expectations and to compare the analyst's own estimate of value with that price. However, a stock price is only a "summary statistic." It is useful to have a more detailed idea of the market's expectations about a firm's future performance, expressed in terms of sales, earnings, and other measures. For example, assume that an analyst has developed new insights about a firm's near-term sales. Whether those insights represent new information for the stock market, and whether they indicate that a "buy" recommendation is appropriate, can be easily determined if the analyst knows the market consensus sales forecast.

Around the world a number of agencies summarize analysts' forecasts of sales and earnings. Forecasts for the next year or two are commonly available, and for many firms, a "long-run" earnings growth projection is also available—typically for three to five years. Some financial information providers in the United States provide continuous online updates to such data, so if an analyst revises a forecast, that revision can be made known to fund managers and other analysts within seconds.

As useful as analysts' forecasts of sales and earnings are, they do not represent a complete description of expectations about future performance, and there is no guarantee that consensus analyst forecasts are the same as those reflected in market prices. Further, financial analysts typically forecast performance for only a few years, so it is helpful to understand what types of long-term forecasts are reflected in stock prices. Armed with the model in Chapters 7 and 8 that expresses price as a function of future cash flows or earnings, an analyst can draw some educated inferences about the expectations embedded in stock prices.

For example, consider the valuation of General Electric Company (GE), the global diversified technology, services, and finance company. On June 30, 2011, GE's stock price closed at $18.86, giving it a market capitalization of $199.9 billion. Earnings per share (EPS) had declined from $2.20 in fiscal year 2007 to $1.06 in fiscal year 2010. The stock price had fallen more than 50 percent since early 2007, significantly underperforming other global industrial conglomerates such as Honeywell (32 percent increase), 3M (25 percent increase), United Technologies (44 percent increase), and Danaher Corporation (54 percent increase).[10] An article in *Fortune* Magazine in February 2011 titled, "Grading Jeff Immelt," noted the difficult first ten years of his tenure as CEO and compared current GE metrics against those of the company when Immelt took over from previous CEO Jack Welch.[11] However, analysts were encouraged as 2011 progressed, as GE reduced its financial services operations and increased investment in the technology and industrial sectors, and they headed their reports with titles such as, "'Shareholder Value Supercollider' Now Being Lit…"[12] and "2Q Shows Industrial Spring is Loading."[13] Performance in the quarter ended June 30, 2011, showed early evidence of this rebound as second quarter profits rose 21 percent from the previous year.

The market expected GE to generate EPS of $1.35 in 2011, a 27 percent increase from the prior year, followed by increases of 23 percent in 2012 and 19 percent in 2013, bringing GE's EPS to $1.97 in 2013. Most analysts projected earnings only over a three-year period.[14]

How do these forecasts by analysts reconcile with the actual market valuation of GE? What were the market's implicit assumptions about the short-term and long-term earnings growth for the company? By altering key value drivers and arriving at a combination that generates an estimated value equal to the observed market price, the analyst can infer what the market might have been expecting for GE in July 2011.

A reasonable estimate of GE's cost of equity can be calculated using a measure of risk free return, GE's beta, and the historic market risk premium discussed in Chapter 8. On June 30, 2011, the ten year Treasury bill was yielding 3.17 percent. Value Line reported GE's beta as 1.2 and the historic market risk premium we discussed in Chapter 8 is 6.7 percent. Given these figures, we can estimate GE's cost of equity using the method discussed in Chapter 8 as 11.2 percent. Focusing on earnings as the value driver, critical questions for judging the market valuation of GE are (1) how quickly the company's earnings are expected to rebound to approach and exceed the levels of 2007, and how that compares to the analyst's view of the firm's near-term earnings growth prospects, and (2) what the current valuation assumes in terms of long-term earnings growth rate as compared to the earnings growth rate of the average firms in the economy (which historically has been about 4 percent), and again how comfortable the analyst feels with this assumption.[15]

The analysis in Table 9-1 shows a scenario for GE's future performance that would justify its current stock price, assuming a cost of equity capital of 11.2 percent, and

TABLE 9-1	Assumptions About Value Drivers for GE Consistent with Observed Market Price of $18.86 (Assuming 11.2 Percent Cost of Equity Capital)					
Analysts' Mean Earnings Forecast Through 2013	**2011**	**2012**	**2013**	**2014**	**2015**	**Post 2015**
Earnings Growth	27.4%	23.0%	18.7%	12.0%	12.0%	3.2%
Earnings Per Share	1.35	1.66	1.97	2.21	2.47	
Return on Equity	12.1%	14.5%	16.5%	16.5%	16.5%	

Source: © Cengage Learning 2013

using the three-year estimates of the various sell-side analysts covering the stock. Using the market's estimates for the first three years, GE would need to maintain a strong rate of earnings growth through 2015, with the company returning to 2007 level EPS by 2014. Furthermore, this scenario requires continued earnings growth beyond the forecast horizon—GE would need to maintain an earnings growth rate of slightly over 3 percent in perpetuity, with an ROE which stabilizes at 16.5 percent—a bit above the ROE time series reversions we examined in Chapter 6. In general, then, the market is assuming that not only will GE be successful in recovering from its stagnant performance of the past several years, but that it will be able to show continued strong performance over the long term.

This type of scenario analysis provides the analyst with insights about investors' expectations for GE and is useful for judging whether the stock is correctly valued. Security analysis need not involve such a detailed attempt to infer market expectations. However, whether or not an explicit analysis is made, a good analyst understands what economic scenarios could plausibly be reflected in the observed price.

Key Analysis Questions

By using the discounted abnormal earnings/ROE valuation model, analysts can infer the market's expectations for a firm's future performance. This permits analysts to ask whether the market is over- or undervaluing a company. Typical questions that analysts might ask from this analysis include the following:

- What are the market's assumptions about long-term ROE and growth? For example, is the market forecasting that the company can grow its earnings without a corresponding level of expansion in its asset base (and hence equity)? If so, how long can this persist?
- How do changes in the cost of capital affect the market's assessment of the firm's future performance? If the market's expectations seem to be unexpectedly high or low, has the market reassessed the company's risk? If so, is this change plausible?

Developing the Analyst's Expectations

Ultimately, a security analyst must compare his or her own view of a stock with the view embedded in the market price. The analyst's view is generated using the same analytical tools discussed in Chapters 2 through 8. The final product of this work is, of course, a forecast of the firm's future earnings and cash flows and an estimate of the firm's value.

However, that final product is less important than the understanding of the business and its industry that the analysis provides. It is such understanding that enables the analyst to interpret new information as it arrives and to infer its implications.

Key Analysis Questions

In developing expectations about a firm's future performance using the financial analysis tools discussed throughout this book, the analyst is likely to ask the following types of questions:

- How profitable is the firm? In light of industry conditions, the firm's corporate strategy, and its barriers to competition, how sustainable is that rate of profitability?
- What are the opportunities for growth for this firm?
- How risky is this firm? How vulnerable are operations to general economic downturns? How highly leveraged is the firm? What does the riskiness of the firm imply about its cost of capital?
- How do answers to the above questions compare to the expectations embedded in the observed stock price?

The Final Product of Security Analysis

For financial analysts, the final product of security analysis is a recommendation to buy, sell, or hold the stock (or some more refined ranking). The recommendation is supported by a set of forecasts and a report summarizing the foundation for the recommendation. Analysts' reports often delve into significant detail and include an assessment of a firm's business as well as a line-by-line income statement, balance sheet, and cash flow forecasts for one or more years.

In making a recommendation to buy or sell a stock, the analyst has to consider the investment time horizon required to capitalize on the recommendation. Are anticipated improvements in performance likely to be confirmed in the near term, allowing investors to capitalize quickly on the recommendation? Or do expected performance improvements reflect long-term fundamentals that will take several years to play out? Longer investment horizons impose greater risk to investors that the company's performance will be affected by changes in economic conditions that cannot be anticipated by the analyst, reducing the value of the recommendation. Consequently, thorough analysis requires the ability not only to recognize whether a stock is misvalued, but also to anticipate when a price correction is likely to take place.

Because there are additional investment risks from following recommendations that require long-term commitments, security analysts tend to focus on making recommendations that are likely to pay off in the short term. This might explain why so few analysts recommended selling dot-com and technology stocks during the late 1990s when their prices would be difficult to justify on the basis of long-term fundamentals. It also explains why analysts recommended Enron's stock at its peak, even though the kind of analysis performed in this chapter would have shown that the future growth and ROE performance implied by this price would be extremely difficult to achieve. It implies as well that to take advantage of long-term fundamental analysis can often require access to patient, long-term capital.

PERFORMANCE OF SECURITY ANALYSTS AND FUND MANAGERS

There has been extensive research on the performance of sell-side security analysts and fund managers during the last three decades. A few of the key findings are summarized below.

Performance of Sell-Side Analysts

Despite the failure of sell-side analysts to foresee the dramatic price declines for dot-com and telecommunications stocks, and to detect the financial shenanigans and overvaluation of companies such as Enron and WorldCom, research shows that analysts generally add value in the capital market. Analysts' earnings forecasts are more accurate than those produced by time series models that use past earnings to predict future earnings.[16] Of course, this should not be too surprising since analysts can update their earnings forecasts between quarters to incorporate new firm and economy information, whereas time-series models cannot. In addition, stock prices tend to respond positively to upward revisions in analysts' earnings forecasts and recommendations, and negatively to downward revisions.[17] Further, recent research indicates that sell-side analysts' buy recommendations outperform the market index and risk benchmarks by 6.5 percent and 7.5 percent per year, respectively.[18] Roughly 50 percent of this superior performance can be traced to sell-side analysts' recommending purchase of small less liquid stocks. Finally, recent research finds that analysts play a valuable role in improving market efficiency. For example, stock prices for firms with higher analyst following incorporate information on accruals and cash flows more rapidly than prices of less followed firms.[19]

Several factors seem to be important in explaining analysts' earnings forecast accuracy. Not surprisingly, forecasts of near-term earnings are much more accurate than those of long-term performance.[20] This probably explains why analysts typically make detailed forecasts for only one or two years ahead. Studies of differences in earnings forecast accuracy among analysts find that the more accurate ones tend to specialize by industry and work for large, well-funded firms that employ other analysts who follow the same industry.[21]

Although analysts perform a valuable function in the capital market, research shows that their forecasts and recommendations tend to be biased. Early evidence on bias indicated that analysts' earnings forecasts tended to be optimistic and that their recommendations were almost exclusively for buys.[22] Several factors potentially explain this finding. First, security analysts at brokerage houses are typically compensated on the basis of the trading volume that their reports generate. Given the costs of short selling and the restrictions on short selling by many institutions, brokerage analysts have incentives to issue optimistic reports that encourage investors to buy stocks rather than to issue negative reports that create selling pressure.[23] Second, until 2003 analysts that worked for investment banks were rewarded for promoting public issues by current clients and for attracting new banking clients, creating incentives for optimistic forecasts and recommendations. Studies show that analysts who work for lead underwriters make more optimistic long-term earnings forecasts and recommendations for firms raising equity capital than unaffiliated analysts.[24]

Evidence indicates that during the late 1990s there was a marked decline in analyst optimism in forecasts of near-term earnings.[25] One explanation offered for this change is that during this time analysts relied heavily on private discussions with top management to make their earnings forecasts. Management allegedly used these personal connections to manage analysts' short-term expectations downward so that the firm could subsequently report earnings that beat analysts' expectations. In response to concerns about this practice, in October 2000 the SEC approved Regulation Fair Disclosure, which prohibits management from making selective disclosures of nonpublic information. Studies show that this regulatory intervention has led to greater independence from management by analysts and an increased effort in independent information discovery.[26]

There has also been a general decline in sell-side analysts' optimistic recommendations during the past few years. Many large investment banks now require analysts to use a forced curve to rate stocks, leading to a greater number of the lowest ratings. Factors that underlie this change include a sharp rise in trading by hedge funds, which actively seek stocks to short sell. In contrast, traditional money management firms are typically restricted from short selling, and are more interested in analysts' buy recommendations than their sells. Second, regulatory changes in the United States under the Global Settlement require tight separation between investment banking and equity research at investment banks.

Performance of Fund Managers

Measuring whether mutual and pension fund managers earn superior returns is a difficult task for several reasons. First, there is no agreement about how to estimate benchmark performance for a fund. Studies have used a number of approaches; some have used the Capital Asset Pricing Model (CAPM) as a benchmark, while others have used multifactor pricing models. For studies using the CAPM, there are questions about what type of market index to use. For example, should it be an equal- or value-weighted index, a NYSE index, or a broader market index? Second, many of the traditional measures of fund performance abstract from market-wide performance, which understates fund abnormal performance if fund managers can time the market by reducing portfolio risk prior to market declines and increasing risks before a market run-up. Third, the overall volatility of stock returns stretches the limits of statistical power needed to measure fund performance. Finally, tests of fund performance are likely to be highly sensitive to the time period examined. Value or momentum investing could therefore appear to be profitable depending on when the tests are conducted.

Perhaps because of these challenges, there is no consistent evidence that actively managed mutual funds generate superior returns for investors. While some studies find evidence of positive abnormal returns for the industry, others conclude that returns are generally negative.[27] Of course even if mutual fund managers on average can only generate "normal" returns for investors, it is still possible for the best managers to show consistently strong performance. Some studies do in fact document that funds earning positive abnormal returns in one period continue to outperform in subsequent periods. However, more recent evidence suggests that these findings are caused by general momentum in stock returns or are offset by high fund expenses from management fees and/or trading costs.[28] Researchers have also examined which, if any, investment strategies are most successful. However, no clear consensus appears; several studies have found that momentum and high turnover strategies generate superior returns, whereas others conclude that value strategies are better.[29]

Finally, recent research has examined whether fund managers tend to buy and sell many of the same stocks at the same time. There is evidence of "herding" behavior, particularly by momentum fund managers.[30] This could arise because managers have access to common information, because they are affected by similar cognitive biases, or because they have incentives to follow the crowd.[31] For example, consider the rationale of a fund manager who holds a stock but who, through long-term fundamental analysis, estimates that it is misvalued. If the manager changes the fund's holdings accordingly and the stock price returns to its intrinsic value in the next quarter, the fund will show superior relative portfolio performance and will attract new capital. However, if the stock continues to be misvalued for several quarters, the informed fund manager will underperform the benchmark and capital will flow to other funds. In contrast, a risk-averse manager who simply follows the crowd will not be rewarded for detecting the misvaluation, but neither will this manager be blamed for a poor investment decision when the stock price ultimately corrects, since other funds made the same mistake.

There has been considerably less research on the performance of pension fund managers. Overall, the findings show little consistent evidence that pension fund managers either over- or under-perform traditional benchmarks.[32]

SUMMARY

Equity security analysis is the evaluation of a firm and its prospects from the perspective of a current or potential investor in the firm's stock. Security analysis is one component of a larger investment process that involves (1) establishing the objectives of the investor or fund, (2) forming expectations about the future returns and risks of individual securities, and then (3) combining individual securities into portfolios to maximize progress toward the investment objectives.

Some security analysis is devoted primarily to assuring that a stock possesses the proper risk profile and other desired characteristics prior to inclusion in an investor's portfolio. However, especially for many professional buy-side and sell-side security analysts, the analysis is also directed toward the identification of mispriced securities. In equilibrium, such activity will be rewarding for those with the strongest comparative advantage. They will be the ones able to identify any mispricing at the lowest cost and exert pressure on the price to correct the mispricing. What kinds of efforts are productive in this domain depends on the degree of market efficiency. A large body of evidence exists that is supportive of a high degree of efficiency in the U.S. market, but recent studies have reopened the debate on this issue.

In practice, a wide variety of approaches to fund management and security analysis are employed. However, at the core of the analyses are the same steps outlined in Chapters 2 through 8 of this book: business strategy analysis, accounting analysis, financial analysis, and prospective analysis (forecasting and valuation). For the professional analyst, the final product of the work is, of course, a forecast of the firm's future earnings and cash flows, and an estimate of the firm's value. But that final product is less important than the understanding of the business and its industry, which the analysis provides. It is such understanding that positions the analyst to interpret new information as it arrives and infer its implications.

Finally, the chapter summarizes some key findings of the research on the performance of both sell-side and buy-side security analysts.

DISCUSSION QUESTIONS

1. Despite many years of research, the evidence on market efficiency described in this chapter appears to be inconclusive. Some argue that this is because researchers have been unable to link company fundamentals to stock prices precisely. Comment.

2. Geoffrey Henley, a professor of finance, states, "The capital market is efficient. I don't know why anyone would bother devoting time to following individual stocks

and doing fundamental analysis. The best approach is to buy and hold a well-diversified portfolio of stocks." Do you agree? Why or why not?

3. What is the difference between fundamental and technical analysis? Can you think of any trading strategies that use technical analysis? What are the underlying assumptions made by these strategies?

4. Investment funds follow many different types of investment strategies. Income funds focus on stocks with high dividend yields, growth funds invest in stocks that are expected to have high capital appreciation, value funds follow stocks that are considered to be undervalued, and short funds bet against stocks they consider to be overvalued. What types of investors are likely to be attracted to each of these types of funds? Why?

5. Intergalactic Software Company went public three months ago. You are a sophisticated investor who devotes time to fundamental analysis as a way of identifying mispriced stocks. Which of the following characteristics would you focus on in deciding whether to follow this stock?
   - The market capitalization
   - The average number of shares traded per day
   - The bid–ask spread for the stock
   - Whether the underwriter that brought the firm public is a top tier investment banking firm
   - Whether the firm's audit company is a Big Four firm
   - Whether there are analysts from major brokerage firms following the company
   - Whether the stock is held mostly by retail or by institutional investors

6. Intergalactic Software Company's stock has a market price of $20 per share and a book value of $12 per share. If its cost of equity capital is 15 percent and its book value is expected to grow at 5 percent per year indefinitely, what is the market's assessment of its steady state return on equity? If the stock price increases to $35 and the market does not expect the firm's growth rate to change, what is the revised steady state ROE? If instead the price increase was due to an increase in the market's assessments about long-term book value growth rather than long-term ROE, what would the price revision imply for the steady state growth rate?

7. There are two major types of financial analysts: buy-side and sell-side. Buy-side analysts work for investment firms and make stock recommendations that are available only to the management of funds within that firm. Sell-side analysts work for brokerage firms and make recommendations that are used to sell stock to the brokerage firms' clients, which include individual investors and managers of investment funds. What would be the differences in tasks and motivations of these two types of analysts?

8. Many market participants believe that sell-side analysts are too optimistic in their recommendations to buy stocks and too slow to recommend sells. What factors might explain this bias?

9. Joe Klein is an analyst for an investment banking firm that offers both underwriting and brokerage services. Joe sends you a highly favorable report on a stock that his firm recently helped go public and for which it currently makes the market. What are the potential advantages and disadvantages in relying on Joe's report in deciding whether to buy the stock?

10. Joe states, "I can see how ratio analysis and valuation help me do fundamental analysis, but I don't see the value of doing strategy analysis." Can you explain to him how strategy analysis could be potentially useful?

NOTES

1. P. Healy and K. Palepu, "The Fall of Enron," *Journal of Economic Perspectives* 17, no. 2 (Spring 2003): 3–26, discuss how weak money manager incentives and a lack of proper long-term analysis contributed to the stock price run-up and subsequent collapse of Enron. A similar discussion on factors affecting the rise and fall of dot-com stocks is provided in "The Role of Capital Market Intermediaries in the Dot-Com Crash of 2000," Harvard Business School Case 9-101–110, 2001.

2. See R. Bhushan, "Firm Characteristics and Analyst Following," *Journal of Accounting and Economics* 11 (2/5), July 1989: 255–75, and P. O'Brien and R. Bhushan, "Analyst Following and Institutional Ownership," *Journal of Accounting Research* 28, Supplement (1990): 55–76.

3. P. Mohanram and S. Sunder, "How Has Regulation FD Affected the Operations of Financial Analysts?" *Contemporary Accounting Research* 23, no. 2 (2006): 491–525.

4. Reviews of evidence on market efficiency are provided by E. Fama, "Efficient Capital Markets: II," *Journal of Finance* 46 (December 1991): 1,575–1,617; S. Kothari, "Capital Markets Research in Accounting," *Journal of Accounting and Economics* 31 (September 2001): 105–231; and C. Lee, "Market Efficiency in Accounting Research," *Journal of Accounting and Economics* 31 (September 2001): 233–53.

5. For example, see V. Bernard and J. Thomas, "Evidence That Stock Prices Do Not Fully Reflect the Implications of Current Earnings for Future Earnings," *Journal of Accounting and Economics* 13 (December 1990): 305–41.

6. For example, the superior returns earned by pursuing a "value stock" strategy were examined by J. Lakonishok, A. Shleifer, and R. Vishny, "Contrarian Investment, Extrapolation, and Risk," *Journal of Finance* 49 (December 1994): 1,541–78, and R. Frankel and C. Lee, "Accounting Valuation, Market Expectation, and Cross-Sectional Stock Returns," *Journal of Accounting and Economics* 25 (June 1998): 283–319.

7. For example, see J. Ou and S. Penman, "Financial Statement Analysis and the Prediction of Stock Returns," *Journal of Accounting and Economics* 11 (November 1989): 295–330; R. Holthausen and D. Larcker, "The Prediction of Stock Returns Using Financial Statement Information," *Journal of Accounting and Economics* 15 (June/September 1992): 373–412; and R. Sloan, "Do Stock Prices Fully Reflect Information in Accruals and Cash Flows about Future Earnings?" *Accounting Review* 71 (July 1996): 298–325.

8. A. Shleifer, "Do Demand Curves for Stocks Slope Down," *Journal of Finance and Quantitative Analysis* 34 (March 1986): 579–90, argues that stocks show positive abnormal returns immediately after entering the S&P 500 Index as a result of increased demand from index funds. While extensive research exists on the idea that trading as a result of investor preference creates short-term price pressure in spin-off transactions, J. Abarbanell, B. Bushee, and J. Raedy, "Institutional Investor Preferences and Price Pressure: The Case of Corporate Spin-Offs," *Journal of Business* 76 (2003): 233–61, find that this trading is not associated with abnormal price movements for parents or subsidiaries around the spin-off.

9. For an overview of research in behavioral finance, see R. Thaler, *Advances in Behavioral Finance* (New York: Russell Sage Foundation, 1993), and A. Shleifer, *Inefficient Markets: An Introduction to Behavioral Finance* (Oxford: Oxford University Press, 2000). Numerous studies have documented the bias introduced by various elements of irrational behavior such as overconfidence, herding, regret, and loss aversion.

10. Company data taken from Thomson ONE, accessed October 2011.

11. G. Colvin, "Grading Jeff Immelt," *Fortune*, February 10, 2011, http://management. fortune.cnn.com/2011/02/10/grading-jeff-immelt/, accessed October 2011.

12. N. Heymann and J. Calabrese, "General Electric Company: 'Shareholder Value Supercollider' Now Being Lit as Industrial Order Outlook Improves for Infrastructure," William Blair & Company, July 26, 2011, via Thomson ONE, accessed October 2011.

13. J.P. Morgan Securities LLC, "General Electric Co. 2Q Shows Industrial Spring is Loading," July 25, 2011, via Thomson ONE, accessed October 2011.

14. These forecasts were taken from Thomson One Analytics, accessed October 2011.

15. For historic earnings growth rate analysis, see for instance data from Robert Shiller showing earnings from 1871 in data file labeled, "Stock Market Data Used in 'Irrational Exuberance' Princeton University Press, 2000, 2005, updated," www.irrational exuberance.com, accessed January 2012. Since 1980 the average growth is more in the range of 6 percent.

16. See L. Brown and M. Rozeff, "The Superiority of Analyst Forecasts as Measures of Expectations: Evidence from Earnings," *Journal of Finance* 33 (1978): 1–16; L. Brown, P. Griffin, R. Hagerman, and M. Zmijewski, "Security Analyst Superiority Relative to Univariate Time-Series Models in Forecasting Quarterly Earnings," *Journal of Accounting and Economics* 9 (1987): 61–87; and D. Givoly, "Financial Analysts' Forecasts of Earnings: A Better Surrogate for Market Expectations," *Journal of Accounting and Economics* 4, no. 2 (1982): 85–108.

17. See D. Givoly and J. Lakonishok, "The Information Content of Financial Analysts' Forecasts of Earnings: Some Evidence on Semi-Strong Efficiency," *Journal of Accounting and Economics* 2 (1979): 165–86; T. Lys and S. Sohn, "The Association Between Revisions of Financial Analysts' Earnings Forecasts and Security Price Changes," *Journal of Accounting and Economics* 13 (1990): 341–64; and J. Francis and L. Soffer, "The Relative Informativeness of Analysts' Stock Recommendations and Earnings Forecast Revisions," *Journal of Accounting Research* 35, no. 2 (1997): 193–212.

18. See B. Groysberg, P. Healy, C. Chapman, and Y. Gui, "Do Buy-Side Analysts Out-Perform the Sell-Side?" (working paper, Harvard Business School, June 2006). The study also finds that buy-side analysts at a large money management firm make more optimistic earnings forecasts and less profitable buy recommendations than sell-side analysts.

19. See M. Brennan, N. Jegadeesh, and B. Swaminathan, "Investment Analysis and the Adjustment of Stock Prices to Common Information," *Review of Financial Studies* 6, no. 4 (1993): 799–824, and B. Ayers and R. Freeman, "Evidence That Analyst Following and Institutional Ownership Accelerate the Pricing of Future Earnings," *Review of Accounting Studies* 8, no. 1 (2003): 47–67.

20. See P. O'Brien, "Forecasts Accuracy of Individual Analysts in Nine Industries," *Journal of Accounting Research* 28 (1990): 286–304.

21. See M. Clement, "Analyst Forecast Accuracy: Do Ability, Resources, and Portfolio Complexity Matter?" *Journal of Accounting and Economics* 27 (1999): 285–304; J. Jacob, T. Lys, and M. Neale, "Experience in Forecasting Performance of Security Analysts." *Journal of Accounting and Economics* 28 (1999): 51–82; and S. Gilson, P. Healy, C. Noe, and K. Palepu, "Analyst Specialization and Conglomerate Stock Breakups," *Journal of Accounting Research* 39 (December 2001): 565–73.

22. See L. Brown, G. Foster, and E. Noreen, "Security Analyst Multi-Year Earnings Forecasts and the Capital Market," *Studies in Accounting Research*, no. 23, American Accounting Association (Sarasota, FL), 1985. In addition, M. McNichols and P. O'Brien, in "Self-Selection and Analyst Coverage," *Journal of Accounting Research*,

Supplement (1997): 167–208, find that analyst bias arises primarily because analysts issue recommendations on firms for which they have favorable information and withhold recommending firms with unfavorable information.

23. See A. Cowen, B. Groysberg, and P. Healy, "Which Types of Analyst Firms Are More Optimistic?" *Journal of Accounting and Economics* 41 (2006): 119–146.

24. See H. Lin and M. McNichols, "Underwriting Relationships, Analysts' Earnings Forecasts and Investment Recommendations," *Journal of Accounting and Economics* 25, no. 1 (1998): 101–28; R. Michaely and K. Womack, "Conflict of Interest and the Credibility of Underwriter Analyst Recommendations," *Review of Financial Studies* 12, no. 4 (1999): 653–86; and P. Dechow, A. Hutton, and R. Sloan, "The Relation Between Analysts' Forecasts of Long-Term Earnings Growth and Stock Price Performance Following Equity Offerings," *Contemporary Accounting Research* 17, no. 1 (2000): 1–32.

25. See L. Brown, "Analyst Forecasting Errors: Additional Evidence," *Financial Analysts' Journal* (November/December 1997): 81–88, and D. Matsumoto, "Management's Incentives to Avoid Negative Earnings Surprises," *Accounting Review* 77 (July 2002): 483–515.

26. See P. Mohanram and S. Sunder, "How Has Regulation FD Affected the Functioning of Financial Analysts?" *Contemporary Accounting Research* 23, no. 2 (2006): 491–525.

27. For example, evidence of superior fund performance is reported by M. Grinblatt and S. Titman, "Mutual Fund Performance: An Analysis of Quarterly Holdings, *Journal of Business* 62 (1994), and by D. Hendricks, J. Patel, and R. Zeckhauser, "Hot Hands in Mutual Funds: Short-Run Persistence of Relative Performance," *Journal of Finance* 48 (1993): 93–130. In contrast, negative fund performance is shown by M. Jensen, "The Performance of Mutual Funds in the Period 1945–64," *Journal of Finance* 23 (May 1968): 389–416, and B. Malkiel, "Returns from Investing in Equity Mutual Funds from 1971 to 1991," *Journal of Finance* 50 (June 1995): 549–73.

28. M. Grinblatt and S. Titman, "The Persistence of Mutual Fund Performance," *Journal of Finance* 47 (December 1992): 1,977–86, and D. Hendricks, J. Patel, and R. Zeckhauser, "Hot Hands in Mutual Funds: Short-Run Persistence of Relative Performance," *Journal of Finance* 48 (March 1993): 93–130, find evidence of persistence in mutual fund returns. However, M. Carhart, "On Persistence in Mutual Fund Performance," *Journal of Finance* 52 (March 1997): 57–83, shows that much of this is attributable to momentum in stock returns and to fund expenses; B. Malkiel, "Returns from Investing in Equity Mutual Funds from 1971 to 1991," *Journal of Finance* 50 (June 1995): 549–73, shows that survivorship bias is also an important consideration.

29. See M. Grinblatt, S. Titman, and R. Wermers, "Momentum Investment Strategies, Portfolio Performance, and Herding: A Study of Mutual Fund Behavior," *American Economic Review* 85 (December 1995): 1,088–1,105.

30. For example, J. Lakonishok, A. Shleifer, and R. Vishny, "Contrarian Investment, Extrapolation, and Risk," *Journal of Finance* 49 (December 1994): 1541–79, find that value funds show superior performance, whereas M. Grinblatt, S. Titman, and R. Wermers, "Momentum Investment Strategies, Portfolio Performance, and Herding: A Study of Mutual Fund Behavior," *American Economic Review* 85 (December 1995): 1,088–1,105, find that momentum investing is profitable.

31. See D. Scharfstein and J. Stein, "Herd Behavior and Investment," *American Economic Review* 80 (June 1990): 465–80, and P. Healy and K. Palepu, "The Fall of Enron," *Journal of Economic Perspectives* 17, no. 2 (Spring 2003): 3–26.

32. For evidence on performance by pension fund managers, see J. Lakonishok, A. Shleifer, and R. Vishny, "The Structure and Performance of the Money Management Industry," *Brookings Papers on Economic Activity*, Washington, DC (1992): 339–92; T. Coggin, F. Fabozzi, and S. Rahman, "The Investment Performance of U.S. Equity Pension Fund Managers: An Empirical Investigation," *Journal of Finance* 48 (July 1993): 1,039–56; and W. Ferson and K. Khang, "Conditional Performance Measurement Using Portfolio Weights: Evidence for Pension Funds," *Journal of Financial Economics* 65 (August 2002): 249–282.

Chapter 10

CREDIT ANALYSIS AND DISTRESS PREDICTION

C redit analysis is the evaluation of a firm from the perspective of a holder or potential holder of its debt, which includes trade payables, loans, and public debt securities. A key element of credit analysis is the prediction of the likelihood a firm will face financial distress. Credit analysis is involved in a wide variety of decision contexts:

- A commercial banker asks: Should we extend a loan to this firm? If so, how should it be structured? How should it be priced?
- If the loan is granted, the banker must later ask: Are we still providing the services, including credit, that this firm needs? Is the firm still in compliance with the loan terms? If not, is there a need to restructure the loan, and if so, how? Is the situation serious enough to call for accelerating the repayment of the loan?
- A potential investor asks: Are these debt securities a sound investment? What is the probability that the firm will face distress and default on the debt? Does the yield provide adequate compensation for the default risk involved?
- An investor contemplating purchase of debt securities in default asks: How likely is it that this firm can be turned around? In light of the high yield on this debt relative to its current price, can I accept the risk that the debt will not be repaid in full?
- A potential supplier asks: Should I sell products or services to this firm? The associated credit will be extended only for a short period, but the amount is large and I should have some assurance that collection risks are manageable.

Finally, there are third parties—those other than borrowers and lenders—who are interested in the general issue of how likely it is that a firm will avoid financial distress:

- An auditor asks: How likely is it that this firm will survive beyond the short run? In evaluating the firm's financials, should I consider it a going concern?
- A credit rating analyst asks: What is the likelihood that the firm will default on its debt obligations?
- An actual or potential employee asks: How confident can I be that this firm will be able to offer employment over the long term?
- A potential customer asks: What assurance is there that this firm will survive to provide warranty services, replacement parts, product updates, and other services?

- A competitor asks: Will this firm survive the current industry shakeout? What are the implications of potential financial distress at this firm for my pricing and market share?

This chapter develops a framework to evaluate a firm's creditworthiness and assess the likelihood of financial distress.

WHY DO FIRMS USE DEBT FINANCING?

Before discussing the credit market and credit analysis, it is worth understanding why firms use debt financing. Debt financing is attractive to firms for two key reasons:

- *Corporate interest tax shields.* In many countries, including the United States, tax laws provide for the corporate tax deductibility of interest paid on debt. No such corporate tax shield is available for dividend payments or retained earnings. Therefore, corporate tax benefits should encourage firms with high effective tax rates and few forms of tax shields other than interest to favor debt financing.
- *Management incentives for value creation.* Firms with relatively high leverage face pressures to generate cash flows to meet payments of interest and principal, reducing resources available to fund unjustifiable expenses and investments that do not maximize shareholder value. Debt financing, therefore, focuses management on value creation, reducing conflicts of interest between managers and shareholders.

However, there are also costs of debt financing. As a firm increases its use of debt financing, it increases the likelihood of financial distress, where it is unable to meet interest or principal repayment obligations to creditors. This forces the firm to restructure its financial claims, either under formal bankruptcy proceedings or out of bankruptcy. Financial distress has multiple negative consequences for the firm:

- *Legal costs of financial distress.* Restructurings are likely to be costly, since the parties involved have to hire lawyers, bankers, and accountants to represent their interests and must pay court costs if there are formal legal proceedings. These are often called the direct costs of financial distress.
- *Costs of foregone investment opportunities.* Distressed firms face significant challenges in raising capital as potential new investors and creditors will be wary of becoming embroiled in the firm's legal disputes. Thus, firms in distress are often unable to finance new investments even though they may be profitable for its owners.
- *Costs of conflicts between creditors and stockholders.* When faced with financial distress, creditors focus on the firm's ability to service its debt while shareholders worry that their equity will revert to the creditors if the firm defaults. Thus, managers face increased pressure to make decisions that typically serve the interests of the stockholders, and creditors react by increasing the costs of borrowing for the firm's stockholders.

Firms are more likely to fall into financial distress if they have high business risks, and their assets are easily destroyed in financial distress. For example, firms with human capital and brand intangibles are particularly sensitive to financial distress since dissatisfied employees and customers can leave or seek alternative suppliers. In contrast, firms with tangible assets can sell their assets if they get into financial distress, providing additional security for lenders and lowering the costs of financial distress. Firms with intangible assets are therefore less likely to be highly leveraged than firms whose assets are mostly tangible.

TABLE 10-1	Median Leverage in Selected Industries – Year-end 2010	
	Net Interest-Bearing Debt-to-Book Equity	
Industry	All Listed Firms	NYSE Firms
Prepackaged Computer Software	−41.9%	−49.4%
Pharmaceuticals	−60.2%	−7.5%
Crude Petroleum and Natural Gas	10.8%	22.2%
Industrial Inorganic Chemicals	3.1%	26.3%
Electric Services	74.2%	79.5%
Water Supply	81.7%	90.5%

Source: Standard and Poor's Compustat 2011.

The above discussion implies that a firm's long-term decisions on the use of debt financing reflect a trade-off between the corporate interest tax shield and incentive benefits of debt against the costs of financial distress. As the firm becomes more highly leveraged, the costs of leverage presumably begin to outweigh the tax and monitoring benefits of debt.

Table 10-1 shows median leverage ratios for all publicly-traded stocks in selected industries for the year ended December 31, 2010. Median debt-to-book equity ratios are highest for the water supply and electric services industries, which are typically not highly sensitive to economy risk and whose core assets are primarily physical equipment and property that are readily transferable to debt holders in the event of financial distress. In contrast, the software and pharmaceutical industries' core assets are their research staffs. Ownership of these types of assets cannot be easily transferred to debt holders if the firm is in financial distress, and researchers are sensitive to budget cuts. As a result, firms in these industries have relatively conservative capital structures. Firms in the crude petroleum and natural gas and industrial inorganic chemicals industries have leverage in between these extremes, reflecting the need to balance the impact of having extensive physical assets and being subject to more volatile revenue streams.

It is also interesting to note that NYSE firms in the majority of industries shown here tend to have higher debt financing than non-NYSE firms in the same industries, with the difference most pronounced in pharmaceuticals. This probably reflects the fact that larger NYSE firms tend to have more product offerings and to be more diversified geographically, reducing their vulnerability to negative events for a single product or market, and enabling them to take on more debt.

THE MARKET FOR CREDIT

An understanding of credit analysis requires an appreciation for the various players in the market for credit. We briefly describe below the major suppliers of debt financing.

Commercial Banks

Commercial banks are important players in the market for credit. Since banks tend to provide a range of services to a client, and have intimate knowledge of the client and its operations, they have a comparative advantage in extending credit in settings where

(1) knowledge gained through close contact with management reduces the perceived riskiness of the credit and (2) credit risk can be contained through careful monitoring of the firm.

Bank lending operations are constrained by a low tolerance for risk to ensure that the overall loan portfolio will be of acceptably high quality to bank regulators. Because of the importance of maintaining public confidence in the banking sector and the desire to shield government deposit insurance from risk, governments have incentives to constrain banks' exposure to credit risk. Banks also tend to shield themselves from the risk of shifts in interest rates by avoiding fixed-rate loans with long maturities. Since banks' capital comes mostly from short-term deposits, such long-term loans leave them exposed to increases in interest rates, unless the risk can be hedged with derivatives. Thus banks are less likely to play a role when a firm requires a very long-term commitment to financing. However, in some cases banks place the debt with investors looking for longer-term credit exposure.

Non-Bank Financial Institutions

Banks face competition in the commercial lending market from a variety of sources. In the United States, there is competition from savings and loans institutions, though these firms tend to focus on financing mortgages. Finance companies compete with banks in the market for asset-based lending (i.e., the secured financing of specific assets such as receivables, inventory, or equipment). Insurance companies are also involved in a variety of lending activities. Since life insurance companies face obligations of a long-term nature, they often seek investments of long duration (e.g., long-term bonds or loans to support large, long-term commercial real estate and development projects). Investment bankers are prepared to place debt securities with private investors or in the public markets (discussed later). Various government agencies are also a source of credit.

Public Debt Markets

Some firms have the size, strength, and credibility necessary to bypass the banking sector and seek financing directly from investors, either through sales of commercial paper or through the issuance of bonds. Such debt issues are facilitated by the assignment of a debt rating, which measures the underlying credit strength of the firm and determines the yield that must be offered to investors.

Banks often provide financing in tandem with a public debt issue or other source of financing. In highly levered transactions, such as leveraged buyouts, banks commonly provide financing along with public debt that has a lower priority in case of bankruptcy. The bank's "senior financing" would typically be scheduled for earlier retirement than the public debt, and it would carry a lower yield. For smaller or start-up firms, banks often provide credit in conjunction with equity financing from venture capitalists. Note that in the case of both the leveraged buyout and the start-up company, the bank helps provide the cash needed to make the deal happen, but it does so in a way that shields it from risks that would be unacceptably high for the banking sector.

Sellers Who Provide Financing

Another sector of the market for credit is manufacturers and other suppliers of goods and services. As a matter of course, such firms tend to finance their customers' purchases on an unsecured basis for periods of 30 to 60 days. Suppliers will, on occasion, also agree to provide more extended financing, usually with the support of a secured note. A supplier may be willing to grant such a loan in the expectation that the creditor will survive a cash shortage and remain an important customer in the future. However, the customer would typically seek such an arrangement only if bank financing is unavailable because it could constrain flexibility in selecting among and/or negotiating with suppliers.

THE CREDIT ANALYSIS PROCESS IN PRIVATE DEBT MARKETS

Credit analysis is more than just establishing the creditworthiness of a firm, that is, its ability to pay its debts at the scheduled times. The decision to extend credit is not a binary one—the firm's exact value, its upside potential, and its distance from the threshold of creditworthiness are all equally important. There are ranges of credit-worthiness, and it is important for purposes of pricing and structuring a loan to understand where a firm lies within that range. While downside risk must be the primary consideration in credit analysis, a firm with growth potential offers opportunities for future income-generating financial services from a continued relationship.

This broader view of credit analysis involves most of the issues already discussed in the prior chapters on business strategy analysis, accounting analysis, financial analysis, and prospective analysis. Perhaps the greatest difference is that credit analysis rarely involves any explicit attempt to estimate the value of the firm's equity. However, the determinants of that value are relevant in credit analysis because a larger equity cushion translates into lower risk for the creditor.

Below we describe a representative but comprehensive series of steps that is used by commercial lenders in credit analysis. However, not all credit providers follow these guidelines. For example, when compared to a banker, manufacturers conduct a less extensive analysis on their customers since the credit is very short-term and the manufacturer is willing to bear some credit risk in the interest of generating a profit on the sale.

We present the steps in a particular order, but they are in fact all interdependent. Thus analysis at one step may need to be rethought, depending on the analysis at some later step.

Step 1: Consider the Nature and Purpose of the Loan

Understanding the purpose of a loan is important not only for deciding whether it should be granted but also for structuring the loan based on duration, purpose, and size. Loans might be required for only a few months, for several years, or even as a permanent part of a firm's capital structure. Loans might be used for replacement of other financing, to support working capital needs, or to finance the acquisition of long-term assets or another firm.

The required amount of the loan must also be established. In the case of small- and medium-sized companies, bankers typically prefer to be the sole financier of the business. This preference is not only to gain an advantage in providing a menu of financial services to the firm but also to maintain a superior interest in case of bankruptcy. If other creditors are willing to subordinate their positions to the bank, that would of course be acceptable as far as the bank is concerned.

Often the commercial lender deals with firms that may have parent-subsidiary relations, posing the question of the appropriate counterparty. In general, the entity that owns the assets that will serve as collateral (or that could serve as such if needed in the future) acts as the borrower. If this entity is the subsidiary and the parent presents some financial strength independent of the subsidiary, a guarantee of the parent could be considered.

Step 2: Consider the Type of Loan and Available Security

The type of loan is a function not only of its purpose but also of the financial strength of the borrower. Thus, to some extent, the loan type will be dictated by the financial analysis described in Step 3. Some of the possible loan types are as follows:

- *Open line of credit.* An open line of credit permits the borrower to receive cash up to some specified maximum on an as-needed basis for a specified term, such as one year. To maintain this option, the borrower pays a fee (e.g., 3/8 of 1 percent) on the unused balance in addition to a market rate of interest on any used amount. An open line of credit is useful in cases where the borrower's cash needs are difficult to anticipate.

- *Revolving line of credit.* When it is clear that a firm will need credit beyond the short run, financing may be provided in the form of a "revolver." The terms of a revolver, which is sometimes used to support working capital needs, requires the borrower to make payments as the operating cycle proceeds and inventory and receivables are converted to cash. However, it is also expected that cash will continue to be advanced as long as the borrower remains in good standing. In addition to interest on amounts outstanding, a fee is charged on the unused line.

- *Working capital loan.* Such a loan is used to finance inventory and receivables, and it is usually secured. The maximum loan balance may be tied to the balance of the working capital accounts. For example, the loan may be allowed to rise to no more than 80 percent of receivables less than 60 days old.

- *Term loan.* Term loans are used for long-term needs and are often secured with long-term assets such as plants or equipment. Typically, the loan will be amortized, requiring periodic payments to reduce the loan balance.

- *Trade credit.* Trade credit generally takes two forms—an interim loan to an exporter to be repaid when the exports are paid for by the foreign importer or credit extended by an exporter to an importer, allowing them to pay at some time after they take delivery.

- *Mortgage loan.* Mortgages support the financing of real estate, have long terms, and generally require periodic amortization of the loan balance.

- *Lease financing.* Lease financing can be used to facilitate the acquisition of any asset but is most commonly used for equipment, including vehicles and buildings. Leases may be structured over periods of 1 to 15 years, depending on the life of the underlying asset.

Much bank lending is done on a secured basis, especially with smaller and more highly levered companies. Security will be required unless the loan is short-term and the borrower exposes the bank to only minimal default risk. When security is required, an important consideration is whether the amount of available security is sufficient to support the loan. The amount that a bank will lend based on a given security involves business judgment and depends on a variety of factors that affect the liquidity of the security should the firm face financial distress. The following are some rules of thumb often applied in commercial lending to various categories of security:

- *Receivables.* Accounts receivable are usually considered the most desirable form of security because they are the most liquid. One large regional bank allows loans of 50 to 80 percent of the balance of non-delinquent accounts. The percentage applied is lower when (1) there are many small accounts that would be costly to collect in case the firm is distressed; (2) there are a few very large accounts, such that problems with a single customer could be serious; and/or (3) the customer's financial health is closely related to that of the borrower, so that collectability is endangered just when the borrower is in default. On the latter score, banks often refuse to accept receivables from affiliates as effective security.

- *Inventory.* The desirability of inventory as security varies widely. The best-case scenario is inventory consisting of a common commodity that can easily be sold to other parties if the borrower defaults. More specialized inventory, with appeal to only a limited set of buyers or that is costly to store or transport, is less desirable. The large regional bank mentioned above lends up to 60 percent on raw materials, 50 percent on finished goods, and 20 percent on work in process.
- *Machinery and equipment.* Machinery and equipment are less desirable as collateral. They are likely to be used and must be stored, insured, and marketed. Keeping the costs of these activities in mind, banks typically will lend only up to 50 percent of the estimated value of such assets in a forced sale such as an auction.
- *Real estate.* The value of real estate as collateral varies considerably. Banks will often lend up to 80 percent of the appraised value of readily salable real estate. On the other hand, a factory designed for a unique purpose and thus not easy to sell would be much less desirable.

Even when a loan is not secured initially, a bank can require a "negative pledge" on the firm's assets—a pledge that the firm will not use the assets as security for any other creditor. In that case, if the borrower begins to experience difficulty and defaults on the loan, and if there are no other creditors in the picture, the bank can demand that the loan become secured if it is to remain outstanding.

Step 3: Conduct a Financial Analysis of the Potential Borrower

This portion of the analysis involves all the steps discussed in our chapters on business strategy analysis, accounting analysis, and financial analysis. The emphasis, however, is on the firm's ability to service the debt at the scheduled rate. All the factors that could impact that ability, such as the presence of off-balance-sheet lease obligations and the sustainability of the firm's operating profit stream, need to be carefully examined. The focus of the analysis depends on the type of financing under consideration. For example, if a short-term loan is needed to support seasonal fluctuations in inventory, the emphasis would be on the ability of the firm to convert the inventory into cash on a timely basis. In contrast, a term loan to support plant and equipment must be made with confidence in the long-run earnings prospects of the firm. This step incorporates both an assessment of the potential borrower's financial status, using ratio analysis, and a forecast to determine future payment prospects.

Ratio Analysis

Ultimately, since the key issue in the financial analysis is the likelihood that cash flows will be sufficient to repay the loan, lenders focus much attention on solvency ratios: the magnitude of various measures of profits and cash flows relative to debt service and other requirements. Therefore, ratio analysis from the perspective of a creditor differs somewhat from that of an owner. There is greater emphasis on cash flows and earnings available to *all* claimants (not just owners) *before* taxes (since interest is tax-deductible and paid out of pretax dollars). The *funds flow coverage ratio* illustrates the creditor's perspective:

$$\text{Funds flow coverage} = \frac{\text{EBIT} + \text{Depreciation}}{\text{Interest} + \frac{\text{Debt repayment}}{(1 - \text{tax rate})} + \frac{\text{Preferred dividends}}{(1 - \text{tax rate})}}$$

Earnings before both interest and taxes in the numerator is compared directly to the interest expense in the denominator, because interest expense is paid out of pre-tax dollars. In contrast, any payment of principal scheduled for a given year is non-deductible and must be made out of after-tax profits. In essence, with a 50 percent tax rate, one dollar of principal payment is "twice as expensive" as a one-dollar interest payment. Scaling the payment of principal by (1 − tax rate) accounts for this. The same idea applies to preferred dividends, which are not tax deductible.

The funds flow coverage ratio provides an indication of how comfortably the funds flow can cover unavoidable expenditures. The ratio excludes payments such as common dividends and capital expenditures on the premise that they could be reduced to zero to make debt payments if necessary.[1] Clearly, however, if the firm is to survive in the long run, funds flow must be sufficient to service debt while also maintaining plant assets. Thus long-run survival requires a funds flow coverage ratio well in excess of 1.[2]

To the extent the ratio exceeds 1, it indicates the "margin of safety" the lender faces. When such a ratio is combined with an assessment of the variance in its numerator, it provides an indication of the probability of nonpayment. However, it would be overly simplistic to establish any particular threshold above which a ratio indicates a loan is justified. A creditor clearly wants to be in a position to be repaid on schedule, even when the borrower faces a reasonably foreseeable difficulty. That argues for lending only when the funds flow coverage is expected to exceed 1, even in a recession scenario—and higher if some allowance for capital expenditures is prudent.

The financial analysis should produce more than an assessment of the risk of nonpayment. It should also identify the nature of the significant risks. At many commercial banks it is standard operating procedure to summarize the analysis of the firm by listing the key risks that could lead to default and factors that could be used to control those risks if the loan were made. That information can be used in structuring the detailed terms of the loan so as to trigger default when problems arise, at a stage early enough to permit corrective action.

Forecasting

Implicit in the discussion of the ratio analysis is a forward-looking view of the firm's ability to service the loan. Good credit analysis should also be supported by explicit forecasts. The basis for such forecasts is usually management, though lenders perform their own tests as well. An essential element of this step is a sensitivity analysis to examine the ability of the borrower to service the debt under a variety of scenarios such as changes in the economy or in the firm's competitive position. Ideally, the firm should be strong enough to withstand downside risks such as a drop in sales or a decrease in profit margins.

At times it is possible to reconsider the structure of a loan so as to permit it to "cash flow." That is, the term of the loan might be extended or the amortization pattern changed. Often a bank will grant a loan with the expectation that it will be continually renewed, thus becoming a permanent part of the firm's financial structure (labeled an "evergreen" loan). In that case the loan will still be written as if it is due within the short term, and the bank must assure itself of a viable "exit strategy." However, the firm would be expected to service the loan by simply covering interest payments.

Step 4: Assemble the Detailed Loan Structure, Including Loan Covenants

If the analysis thus far indicates that a loan is in order, the final step is to assemble the detailed structure. Having previously determined the type of loan and repayment schedule, the focus shifts to the loan covenants and pricing.

Writing Loan Covenants

Loan covenants specify mutual expectations of the borrower and lender by specifying actions the borrower will and will not take. Covenants generally fall into three categories: (1) those that require certain actions such as regular provision of financial statements; (2) those that preclude certain actions such as undertaking an acquisition without the permission of the lender; and (3) those that require maintenance of certain financial ratios. Loan covenants must strike a balance between protecting the interests of the lender and providing the flexibility management needs to run the business. The covenants represent a mechanism for ensuring that the business will remain as strong as the two parties anticipated at the time the loan was granted.

The principal covenants that govern the management of the firm include restrictions on other borrowing, pledging assets to other lenders, selling substantial assets, engaging in mergers or acquisitions, and paying dividends. The financial covenants should seek to address the significant risks identified in the financial analysis or to at least provide early warning that such risks are surfacing. Some commonly used financial covenants follow:

- *Maintenance of minimum net worth.* This covenant assures that the firm will maintain an "equity cushion" to protect the lender. Covenants typically require a level of net worth rather than a particular level of income. In the final analysis, the lender may not care whether that net worth is maintained by generating income, cutting dividends, or issuing new equity. Tying the covenant to net worth offers the firm the flexibility to use any of these avenues to avoid default.
- *Minimum coverage ratio.* Especially in the case of a long-term loan, such as a term loan, the lender may want to supplement a net worth covenant with one based on coverage of interest or total debt service. The funds flow coverage ratio presented above would be an example. Maintenance of some minimum coverage helps ensure that the ability of the firm to generate funds internally is strong enough to justify the long-term nature of the loan.
- *Maximum ratio of total liabilities to net worth.* This ratio constrains the risk of high leverage and prevents growth without either retaining earnings or infusing equity.
- *Minimum net working capital balance or current ratio.* Constraints on this ratio force a firm to maintain its liquidity by using cash generated from operations to retire current liabilities (as opposed to acquiring long-lived assets).
- *Maximum ratio of capital expenditures to earnings before depreciation.* Constraints on this ratio help prevent the firm from investing in growth (including the illiquid assets necessary to support growth) unless such growth can be financed internally, with some margin remaining for debt service.

Required financial ratios are typically based on the levels that existed at the time that the agreement was executed, perhaps with some allowance for deterioration but often with some expected improvement over time. Violation of a covenant represents an event of default that could cause immediate acceleration of the debt payment, but in most cases the lender uses the default as an opportunity to re-examine the situation and either waive the violation or renegotiate the loan.

Covenants are included not only in private lending agreements but also in public debt agreements. However, public debt agreements tend to have less restrictive covenants for two reasons. First, since negotiations resulting from a violation of public debt covenants are costly (possibly involving not just the trustee but bondholders as well), the covenants are written to be triggered only in serious circumstances. Second, public debt is usually issued by stronger, more credit-worthy firms, though there is a large market for high-yield debt. For the most financially healthy firms with strong debt ratings, very few covenants will be used, generally only those necessary to limit dramatic changes in the firm's operations, such as a major merger or acquisition.

Loan Pricing

A detailed discussion of loan pricing falls outside the scope of this text. The essence of pricing is to assure that the yield on the loan is sufficient to cover (1) the lender's cost of borrowed funds; (2) the lender's costs of administering and servicing the loan; (3) a premium for exposure to default risk; and (4) at least a normal return on the equity capital necessary to support the lending operation. The price is often stated in terms of a deviation from the bank's prime rate (the rate charged to stronger borrowers). For example, a loan might be granted at prime plus 1.5 percent. An alternative base is LIBOR, or the London Interbank Offer Rate, the rate at which large banks from various nations lend blocks of funds to each other.

Banks compete actively for commercial lending business, and it is rare that a yield includes more than 2 percentage points to cover the cost of default risk. If the spread to cover default risk is, say, 1 percent, and the bank recovers only 50 percent of amounts due on loans that turn out bad, then the bank can afford only 2 percent of their loans to fall into that category. This underscores how important it is for banks to conduct a thorough analysis and to contain the riskiness of their loan portfolio.

FINANCIAL STATEMENT ANALYSIS AND PUBLIC DEBT

Fundamentally, the issues involved in analysis of public debt are no different from those of bank loans and other private debt issues. Institutionally, however, the contexts are different. Bankers can maintain very close relations with clients so as to form an initial assessment of their credit risk and monitor their activities during the loan period. In the case of public debt, the investors are distanced from the issuer. To a large extent, they must depend on professional debt analysts, including debt raters, to assess the riskiness of the debt and monitor the firm's ongoing activities. Such analysts and debt raters thus serve an important function in closing the information gap between issuers and investors.

The Meaning of Debt Ratings

A firm's debt rating influences the yield that must be offered to sell the debt instruments. After the debt issue, the rating agencies continue to monitor the firm's financial condition. Changes in the rating are associated with fluctuation in the price of the securities. The two major debt rating agencies in the United States are Moody's and Standard and Poor's. Other rating agencies include Fitch Ratings, A.M. Best, and Dun & Bradstreet.

Using the Standard and Poor's labeling system, the highest possible rating is AAA. Proceeding downward from AAA, the ratings are AA, A, BBB, BB, B, CCC, CC, C, and D, where D indicates debt in default. Table 10-2 presents examples of firms in rating categories AAA through D, as well as average yields across all firms in each category. Less than 1 percent of the public non-financial companies rated by Standard & Poor's have the financial strength to merit a AAA rating. Among the few are Exxon Mobil, Johnson & Johnson, and Microsoft—all among the largest, most profitable firms in the world. AA firms are also very strong and include General Electric, Wal-Mart, and Canon. Firms rated AAA and AA have the lowest costs of debt financing; at year-end 2010, their average yields averaged 3.2 to 3.4 percent over the 12-month LIBOR rate.

To be considered investment grade, a firm must achieve a rating of BBB or higher, which is an important threshold as many funds are precluded by their charters from investing in any bonds below that grade. Even to achieve a grade of BBB is difficult. Daimler, the automobile manufacturer and owner of Mercedes Benz, one of the world's most recognizable brands, was rated BBB, or barely investment grade, in 2010. Its large U.S. rivals, General Motors and Ford, were rated BB and B, respectively, at the same time. Some of the world's largest airlines, including British Airways and American Airlines, were also rated below investment grade.

Table 10-2 shows that the cost of debt financing rises markedly once firms' debt falls below investment grade. For example, in 2010, yields for BBB rated debt issues were a

TABLE 10-2	Debt Ratings: Example Firms and Average Yields by Category			
S&P debt rating	Example firms in 2010	Percentage of public industrials given same rating by S&P	Average yield, 2010	Average spread over 12-month LIBOR rate
AAA	Exxon Mobil Johnson & Johnson Microsoft	0.4%	4.0%	3.2%
AA	General Electric Wal-Mart Canon	2.1%	4.2%	3.4%
A	Coca-Cola McDonald's TJX	11.7%	4.4%	3.6%
BBB	Daimler Nordstrom Best Buy	29.7%	4.9%	4.1%
BB	General Motors Fiat Netflix	27.3%	6.4%	5.6%
B	Ford Motor Company Eastman Kodak American Airlines (AMR)	27.7%	8.0%	7.2%
CCC	E-Trade Sbarro's Clearwire	1.1%	9.9%	9.1%
CC	Realogy	<0.1%	13.6%[a]	12.8%
D	Blockbuster A&P	<0.1%	30%+[a]	30%+

[a]Representative yields as most securities not actively traded.
Source: Standard and Poor's Compustat 2011.

TABLE 10-3	Debt Ratings: Median Financial Ratios by Category			
	Median ratios for overall category in January 2011 (excludes financial firms)			
S&P debt rating	Earnings before interest and taxes to net capital	Pretax interest coverage	Cash flow from operations to total debt	Net debt to net capital
AAA	41.6%	105.4	317%	−33%
AA	25.9%	14.6	47%	31%
A	23.5%	11.5	57%	22%
BBB	16.1%	5.9	35%	32%
BB	15.4%	3.7	28%	37%
B	9.6%	1.5	14%	58%
CCC	−2.6%	−0.3	>0.1%	87%

Source: Standard and Poor's Compustat 2011.

little over 4 percent over the 12-month LIBOR rate, whereas yields for B rated issues were more than 7 percent above LIBOR rates. Yields for firms with CCC rated debt, which were close to bankruptcy, were more than 9 percent over LIBOR, and the debt securities of a few firms in default that were still traded were yielding over 30 percent above the benchmark.

Table 10-3 shows median financial ratios for firms by debt rating category. Firms with AAA and AA ratings have very strong earnings and cash flow performance as well as minimal leverage. AAA rated firms often have large surpluses of cash such that net debt is negative. Firms in the BBB class are only moderately leveraged, with about 32 percent of net capitalization coming from net debt. Earnings tend to be relatively strong, as indicated by a pretax interest coverage (EBIT/interest) of 5.9 and a cash flow debt coverage (cash flow from operations / total debt) of 35 percent. Firms toward the bottom of the ratings spectrum, however, face significant risks: they typically report losses, have high leverage, and have interest coverage ratios less than 1.

Factors That Drive Debt Ratings

Research using quantitative models of debt ratings demonstrates that some of the variation in ratings can be explained by selected financial statement ratios. Some debt rating agencies rely heavily on these types of quantitative models, and they are also commonly used by insurance companies, banks, and others to assist in the evaluation of the riskiness of debt issues for which a public rating is not available.

Table 10-4 lists the factors used by three different firms in their quantitative debt-rating models. The firms include one insurance company and one bank, which use the models in their private placement activities, and an investment research firm, which employs the model in evaluating its own debt purchases and holdings. In each case, profitability and leverage play an important role in the rating. One firm also uses size as an indicator, with larger size associated with higher ratings.

TABLE 10-4	Factors Used in Quantitative Models of Debt Ratings		
	Firm 1	**Firm 2**	**Firm 3**
Profitability measures	Return on long-term capital	Return on long-term capital	Return on long-term capital
Leverage measures	Long-term debt to capitalization	Long-term debt to capitalization Total debt to total capital	Long-term debt to capitalization
Profitability and leverage	Interest coverage Cash flow to long-term debt	Interest coverage Cash flow to long-term debt	Fixed charge coverage Coverage of short-term debt and fixed charges
Firm size	Sales	Total assets	
Other		Standard deviation of return Subordination status	

Source: © Cengage Learning

Several researchers have developed quantitative models of debt ratings. Two of these models, both by Kaplan and Urwitz and shown in Table 10-5, highlight the relative importance of the different factors.[3] Model 1 has a greater ability to explain variation in bond ratings. However, it includes some factors based on stock market data, which are not available for all firms. Model 2 is based solely on financial statement data.

The factors in Table 10-5 are listed in the order of their statistical significance in Model 1. An interesting feature is that the most important factor explaining debt ratings is not a financial ratio at all—it is simply firm size! Large firms tend to get better ratings than small firms. Whether the debt is subordinated or unsubordinated is next most important, followed by a leverage indicator. Profitability appears less important, but in part that reflects the presence in the model of multiple factors (ROA and interest coverage) that capture profitability. The explanatory power of profitability is then divided between these two variables.

When applied to a sample of bonds that were not used in the estimation process, the Kaplan-Urwitz Model 1 predicted the rating category correctly in 44 of 64 cases, or 63 percent of the time. Where it erred, the model was never off by more than one category, and in about half of those cases its prediction was more consistent with the market yield on the debt than was the actual debt rating. The discrepancies between actual ratings and those estimated using the Kaplan-Urwitz model indicate that rating agencies incorporate factors other than financial ratios in their analysis. These are likely to include the types of strategic, accounting, and prospective analyses discussed throughout this book.

Although debt ratings can be explained reasonably well in terms of a handful of financial ratios based on publicly available data, ratings changes have an important signaling effect. Debt rating downgrades are greeted with drops in both bond and stock prices,[4] even though the capital markets anticipate much of the information reflected in rating changes. This is due to the fact that changes often represent reactions to recent known events, and the rating agencies typically indicate in advance that a change is being considered.

		Coefficients	
TABLE 10-5 Kaplan-Urwitz Models of Debt Ratings			
Firm or debt characteristic	**Variable reflecting characteristic**	**Model 1**	**Model 2**
	Model intercept	5.67	4.41
Firm size	Total assets[a]	.0009	.0011
Subordination status of debt	1 = subordinated; 0 = unsubordinated	−2.36	−2.56
Leverage	Long-term debt to total assets	−2.85	−2.72
Systematic risk	Market model beta, indicating sensitivity of stock price to market-wide movements (1 = average)[b]	−.87	—
Profitability	Net income to total assets	5.13	6.40
Unsystematic risk	Standard deviation of residual from market model (average = .10)[b]	−2.90	—
Riskiness of profit stream	Coefficient of variation in net income over five years (standard deviation/ mean)	—	−.53
Interest coverage	Pretax funds flow before interest to interest expense	.007	.006

The score from the model is converted to a bond rating as follows:

If score > 6.76, predict AAA

    score > 5.19, predict AA

    score > 3.28, predict A

    score > 1.57, predict BBB

    score < 0.00, predict BB

[a]The coefficient in the Kaplan-Urwitz model was estimated at .005 (Model 1) and .006 (Model 2). Its scale has been adjusted to reflect that the estimates were based on assets measured in dollars from the early 1970s. Given that $1 from 1972 is approximately equivalent to $5.33 in 2011, the original coefficient estimate has been divided by 5.33.

[b]Market model is estimated by regressing stock returns on the market index, using monthly data for the prior 5 years.

Source: © Cengage Learning

PREDICTION OF DISTRESS AND TURNAROUND

The key task in credit analysis is assessing the probability that a firm will face financial distress and fail to repay a loan. A related analysis, relevant once a firm begins to face distress, involves considering whether it can be turned around. In this section, we consider evidence on the predictability of these states.

The prediction of either distress or turnaround is a complex, difficult, and subjective task that involves all of the steps of analysis discussed throughout this book: business strategy analysis, accounting analysis, financial analysis, and prospective analysis. Purely quantitative models of the process can rarely serve as substitutes for the hard work the analysis involves. However, research on such models does offer some insight into which financial indicators are most useful in the task. Moreover, there are some settings where extensive credit checks are too costly to justify and where quantitative distress prediction models are useful.

Models for Distress Prediction

Several distress prediction models have been developed over the years.[5] They are similar to the debt rating models, but instead of predicting ratings, they predict whether a firm will face some state of distress, typically defined as bankruptcy, within a specified period such as one year. One study suggests that the factors most useful (on a stand-alone basis) in predicting bankruptcy one year in advance are the firm's level of profitability, the volatility of that profitability (as measured by the standard deviation of ROE), and its leverage.[6] Interestingly, liquidity measures turn out to be much less important. Current liquidity will not save an unhealthy firm if it is losing money at a fast pace.

A number of more robust, multifactor models have also been designed to predict financial distress. One such model, the Altman Z-score model, weights five variables to compute a bankruptcy score.[7] For public companies the model is as follows[8]:

$$Z = 1.2(X_1) + 1.4(X_2) + 3.3(X_3) + 0.6(X_4) + 1.0(X_5)$$

where

X_1 = net working capital/total assets (measure of liquidity)

X_2 = retained earnings/total assets (measure of cumulative profitability)

X_3 = EBIT/total assets (measure of return on assets)

X_4 = market value of equity/book value of total liabilities (measure of market leverage)

X_5 = sales/total assets (measure of sales generating potential of assets)

The model predicts bankruptcy when $Z < 1.81$. The range between 1.81 and 2.67 is labeled the "gray area."

The following table presents calculations for two companies, Canon, Inc. and Eastman Kodak Company, at the end of 2010:

	Model Coefficient	Canon, Inc. Dec. 31, 2010		Eastman Kodak Company Dec. 31, 2010	
		Ratios	Score	Ratios	Score
Net working capital/Total assets	1.2	0.079	0.09	−0.112	−0.13
Retained earnings/ Total assets	1.4	0.771	1.08	0.896	1.25
EBIT/Total assets	3.3	0.096	0.32	−0.074	−0.24
Market value of equity/ Book value of total liabilities	0.6	4.934	2.96	0.218	0.13
Sales/Total assets	1.0	0.900	0.90	1.296	1.30
Altman Z-score:			5.35		2.31

Source: Thomson ONE, accessed October 2011.

The table shows the wide performance gap between two of the largest and best-known competitors in imaging technology products and services. Canon's Z score demonstrates its financial strength and reflects its AA rating. Canon has delivered generally steady sales and earnings growth over the past ten years, and its liabilities are only 20 percent of its market capitalization, indicating relatively low financial leverage. Kodak's Z score, on the other hand, highlights its difficulty in recovering from its late and poorly executed shift to digital imaging technology. Kodak has posted an annual loss since 2005, as the company has adopted a series of unsuccessful strategies aimed at replacing lost revenues and profitability from its declining film business. At the end of 2010, Kodak's liabilities were almost five times larger than its market capitalization, an indication of its declining financial state. As a result, Kodak's debt was downgraded to CCC in early 2011, with a negative outlook, and by mid 2011 with losses mounting, reports circulating of the company accessing lines of credit at a higher than normal rate, and the stock hovering around $1.50 per share, rumors abounded about a possible bankruptcy filing.

Such models have some ability to predict failing and surviving firms. Altman reports that when the model was applied to a holdout sample containing 33 failed and 33 non-failed firms (the same proportion used to estimate the model), it correctly predicted the outcome in 63 of 66 cases. However, the performance of the model would degrade substantially if applied to a holdout sample where the proportion of failed and non-failed firms was not forced to be the same as that used to estimate the model.

The commercially available ZETA model, also developed by Altman, improves on the predictive power and accuracy of the Z-score model. The ZETA model incorporates seven variables and includes measures of the stability of earnings, debt service coverage, and firm size.[9] While distress prediction models cannot serve as a replacement for in-depth analysis of the kind discussed throughout this book, they do provide a useful reminder of the power of financial statement data to summarize important dimensions of a firm's performance. In addition, they can be useful for screening large numbers of firms prior to more in-depth analysis of corporate strategy, management expertise, market position, and financial ratio performance. The ZETA model, for instance, is used by some manufacturers and other firms to assess the creditworthiness of their customers.

Investment Opportunities in Distressed Companies

The debt securities of firms in financial distress trade at steep discounts to par value. Some hedge fund managers and investment advisors specialize in investing in these securities—even purchasing the debt of firms operating under bankruptcy protection. Investors in these securities can earn attractive returns if the firm recovers from its cash flow difficulties.[10]

Distressed debt investors assess whether the firm is likely to overcome its immediate cash flow problems and whether it has a viable long-run future. Two elements of the framework laid out in Part 2 of this book are particularly relevant to analyzing distressed opportunities. The first is a thorough analysis of the firm's industry and competitive positioning and an assessment of its business risks. This is followed by the construction of well-reasoned forecasts of its future cash flow and earnings performance in light of the business analysis.

CREDIT RATINGS AND THE SUBPRIME CRISIS

While the focus of this chapter is on the credit analysis and distress prediction of corporate debt, there are also important lessons to be learned from examining the role that credit analysis and ratings of securitized financial instruments (primarily asset-backed securities) played in the 2008 financial crisis. We touch on these briefly here.

Much of the research into the causes of the financial crisis has focused on the application of securitization to the U.S. subprime mortgage market.[11] The securitization of mortgage debt, which involved the pooling of individual mortgages and the slicing of that pool into layers ("tranches") with progressive levels of seniority, enabled the development of securities which could be widely sold in the financial markets—something not possible at the individual mortgage level. In addition, the securitization process was expected to mitigate the individual risk of default of the underlying securities by filling the pool with securities whose default risk was not highly correlated, allowing the creation of securities with different levels of default risk—some (or many, depending on the specifics) with a lower risk of default than the average of the underlying mortgages in the pool.

As banks refined and expanded these offerings to capitalize on the burgeoning subprime mortgage market, they pushed the ratings agencies, which up until that time had focused on the rating of corporate debt, to rate the securities so as to make them more widely acceptable both to institutional investors who were restricted in their ability to invest in non-rated securities and to the broader market, which looked more favorably on securities given the stamp of approval of an investment-grade rating. The agencies complied and saw their revenues jump dramatically until this part of their revenue stream in many cases constituted the majority of their revenues.

When the housing market experienced a significant downturn beginning in late 2005, it became clear that the credit agencies and the market had underestimated the riskiness of these securities and their potential exposure to the broad market downturn that occurred. Also, the crisis raised questions about the quality of the ratings in general, especially as it related to the agency/banking relationship dynamic.

While much of the discussion into the role of the credit rating agencies in the crisis has been around the conflict of interest inherent in the agencies' relationship to their banking clients and its potential compromising impact on the quality of its rating of the client's products, researchers have also examined factors inherent in the agencies' own rating methodologies that contributed to a systemic underestimation of the risk of the securitized subprime mortgage product.[12] In general, the ratings agencies were more familiar with corporate debt ratings—they had only recently moved into rating financial instruments—and their models did not seem adequate to handle the complexity of the structured products they were being asked to rate. Also, the embedded nature of many of these products meant that small errors in estimates had big impacts on default risk calculations. For instance, one product known as a CDO^2 (collateralized debt obligation squared) was made up of the most junior tranches of other CDOs, pooled and tranched again, which magnified this type of instrument's exposure to estimate error risk. Also, structured products in general replace the of individual default with the risk of systematic default (i.e., failure of the whole system), which made the mortgage-based product highly exposed to losses in broad downturns such as occurred beginning in 2005. Despite this critical risk, ratings agency models did not even account for the potential of a significant housing downturn since there had not been one in recent memory. Finally, in general the ratings agencies did not have good historical data on subprime defaults since subprime lending was a relatively new phenomenon. In total, it is clear that while conflict of interest issues were an important factor in the crisis, another perhaps equally important factor was that the analysis performed by the agencies in assigning ratings to these securities was not adequate to assess their true creditworthiness.

The Dodd-Frank Wall Street Reform and Consumer Protection Act, which was passed in the wake of the financial crisis, was an attempt to address through regulation some of the key causes of the financial crisis, and included increased oversight of the ratings agencies. Among its key provisions related to credit agencies:[13]

- *Creation of an Office of Credit Ratings at the SEC*—with its own compliance staff and the authority to fine agencies, and the mandate to examine the ratings agencies at least once a year.
- *Increased disclosure requirements for the ratings agencies*—of their methodologies, their use of third parties for due diligence efforts, and their ratings track record.
- *Required use of independent information by the ratings agencies*—from sources other than organizations being rated, if credible.
- *Increased limitations on activities involving potential conflict of interest*—prohibits compliance officers from working on ratings, and other reporting requirements.
- *Increased potential liability*—removes liability exemptions for ratings agencies, allowing investors to bring private rights of action against agencies.
- *Gives SEC right to deregister a ratings agency*—for providing bad ratings over time.
- *Increased education requirements*—requires ratings analysts to pass qualifying exams and to participate in continuing education.
- *Elimination of statutory and regulatory requirements for use of ratings*—in an attempt to reduce over-reliance on ratings.
- *Increased independence of agency boards*—requires at least 50 percent of agency boards to hold no financial stake in credit ratings.
- *New SEC mechanism to prevent "shopping for ratings"*—to prevent issuers of securities from picking the agency most likely to give their product a favorable rating.

SUMMARY

Debt financing is attractive to firms with high marginal tax rates and few non-interest tax shields, making interest tax shields from debt valuable. Debt can also help create value by deterring management of firms with high, stable income/cash flows and few new investment opportunities from over-investing in unprofitable new ventures.

However, debt financing also creates the risk of financial distress, which is likely to be particularly severe for firms with volatile earnings and cash flows, and intangible assets that are easily destroyed by financial distress.

Prospective providers of debt use credit analysis to evaluate the risks of financial distress for a firm. Credit analysis is important to a wide variety of economic agents—not only bankers and other financial intermediaries but also public debt analysts, industrial companies, service companies, and others.

At the heart of credit analysis lie the same techniques described in Chapters 2 through 8: business strategy analysis, accounting analysis, financial analysis, and portions of prospective analysis. The purpose of credit analysis in private debt markets goes beyond the assessment of the likelihood that a potential borrower will fail to repay the loan. It also serves to identify the nature of the main risks involved and to guide how the loan might be structured to mitigate or control those risks. A well-structured loan provides the lender with a viable "exit strategy," even in the case of default. Properly designed accounting-based covenants are essential to this structure.

Fundamentally, the issues involved in analysis of public debt are no different from those involved in evaluating bank loans or other private debt. Institutionally, however, the contexts are different. Investors in public debt are usually not close to the borrower and must rely on other agents, including debt raters and other analysts, to assess creditworthiness. Debt ratings, which depend heavily on firm size and financial measures of performance, have an important influence on the market yields that must be offered to issue debt.

The primary task in credit analysis is assessment of the probability of default. The task is complex, difficult, and to some extent, subjective. A few financial ratios can help predict financial distress with some accuracy. The most important indicators for this purpose are profitability, volatility of profits, and leverage. While there are a number of models that predict distress based on financial indicators, they cannot replace the in-depth forms of analysis discussed in this book.

The financial crisis of 2008 is an example of a major miscalculation of the probability of default for asset-backed securities due to the complex, not well understood nature of the financial instruments. Government legislation put in place after the financial crisis attempts to impose additional controls on ratings agencies who had significant conflict of interest and whose models did not fully understand the complex securities that they were being asked to rate given their historic background in rating corporate debt.

DISCUSSION QUESTIONS

1. Financial analysts typically measure financial leverage as the ratio of debt to equity. However, there is less agreement on how to measure debt, or even equity. How would you treat the following items in computing this ratio? Justify your answers.
   - Revolving credit agreement with bank
   - Cash and marketable securities
   - Operating leases
   - Unrecorded pension commitments
   - Deferred tax liabilities
   - Preferred stock
   - Convertible debt

2. U.S. public companies with "low" leverage have an interest-bearing net debt-to-equity ratio of 0 percent or less, firms with "medium" leverage have a ratio between 1 and 62 percent, and "high" leverage firms have a ratio of 63 percent or more. Given these data, how would you classify the following firms in terms of their optimal debt-to-equity ratio (high, medium, or low)?
   - a successful pharmaceutical company
   - an electric utility
   - a manufacturer of consumer durables
   - a commercial bank
   - a start-up software company

3. What are the critical performance dimensions for (a) a retailer and (b) a financial services company that should be considered in credit analysis? What ratios would you suggest looking at for each of these dimensions?

4. Why would a company pay to have its public debt rated by a major rating agency (such as Moody's or Standard and Poor's)? Why might a firm decide not to have its debt rated?

5. Some have argued that the market for original-issue junk bonds developed in the late 1970s as a result of a failure in the rating process. Proponents of this argument suggest that rating agencies rated companies too harshly at the low end of the rating scale, denying investment grade status to some deserving companies. What are proponents of this argument effectively assuming were the incentives of rating agencies? What economic forces could give rise to this incentive?

6. Many debt agreements require borrowers to obtain the permission of the lender before undertaking a major acquisition or asset sale. Why would the lender want to include this type of restriction?

7. Betty Li, the CFO of a company applying for a new loan, states, "I will never agree to a debt covenant that restricts my ability to pay dividends to my shareholders because it reduces shareholder wealth." Do you agree with this argument?

8. Cambridge Construction Company follows the percentage-of-completion method for reporting long-term contract revenues. The percentage-of-completion is based on the cost of materials shipped to the project site as a percentage of total expected material costs. Cambridge's major debt agreement includes restrictions on net worth, interest coverage, and minimum working capital requirements. A leading analyst claims that "the company is buying its way out of these covenants by spending cash and buying materials, even when they are not needed." Explain how this might be possible.

9. Can Cambridge improve its Z score by behaving as the analyst claims in Question 8? Is this change consistent with economic reality?

10. A banker asserts, "I avoid lending to companies with negative cash from operations because they are too risky." Is this a sensible lending policy?

11. A leading retailer finds itself in a financial bind. It does not have sufficient cash flow from operations to finance its growth, and it is close to violating the maximum debt-to-assets ratio allowed by its covenants. The Vice-President for Marketing suggests, "We can raise cash for our growth by selling the existing stores and leasing them back. This source of financing is cheap since it avoids violating either the debt-to-assets or interest-coverage ratios in our covenants." Do you agree with his analysis? Why or why not? As the firm's banker, how would you view this arrangement?

NOTES

1. The same is true of preferred dividends. However, when preferred stock is cumulative, any dividends missed must be paid later, when and if the firm returns to profitability.

2. Other relevant coverage ratios are discussed in Chapter 5.

3. R. Kaplan and G. Urwitz, "Statistical Models of Bond Ratings: A Methodological Inquiry," *Journal of Business* (April 1979): 231–61.

4. See R. Holthausen and R. Leftwich, "The Effect of Bond Rating Changes on Common Stock Prices," *Journal of Financial Economics* (September 1986): 57–90 and J. Hand, R. Holthausen, and R. Leftwich, "The Effect of Bond Rating Announcements on Bond and Stock Prices," *Journal of Finance* (June 1992): 733–52.

5. See E. Altman, "Financial Ratios, Discriminant Analysis, and the Prediction of Corporate Bankruptcy," *Journal of Finance* (September 1968): 589–609; E. Altman, *Corporate Financial Distress* (New York: John Wiley, 1993); W. Beaver, "Financial Ratios as Predictors of Distress," *Journal of Accounting Research*, Supplement (1966): 71–111; J. Ohlson, "Financial Ratios and the Probabilistic Prediction of Bankruptcy," *Journal of Accounting Research* (Spring 1980): 109–131; and M. Zmijewski, "Predicting Corporate Bankruptcy: An Empirical Comparison of the Extant Financial Distress Models" (working paper, SUNY at Buffalo, 1983).

6. Zmijewski, op. cit.

7. Altman, *Corporate Financial Distress*, op. cit.

8. For private firms, Altman, ibid., adjusts the public model by changing the numerator for the variable X_4 from the market value of equity to the book value. The revised model follows:

$$Z = .717(X_1) + .847(X_2) + 3.11(X_3) + 0.420(X_4) + .998(X_5)$$

Where
   X_1 = net working capital/total assets
   X_2 = retained earnings/total assets
   X_3 = EBIT/total assets
   X_4 = book value of equity/book value of total liabilities
   X_5 = sales/total assets

The model predicts bankruptcy when $Z < 1.23$. The range between 1.23 and 2.90 is labeled the "gray area."

9. See Altman, *Corporate Financial Distress*, op. cit.
10. In the period from January 1994 through July 2011, distressed investing outperformed 10 out of 11 other strategies that were tracked by the Dow Jones Credit Suisse Hedge Fund Index. The average annual return over that period was 10.6 percent versus a return of 8.0 percent for the S&P 500 index (assuming dividends were reinvested in the index).
11. For a background on the development of the subprime mortgage market, see, for instance, S. Chomsisengphet and A. Pennington-Cross, "The Evolution of the Subprime Mortgage Market," *Federal Reserve Bank of St. Louis Review*, January/February 2006, 88(1): pp. 31–56, http://research.stlouisfed.org/publications/review/06/01/ChomPennCross.pdf, accessed February 2012.
12. For instance, the following conclusions are drawn by J. D. Coval, J. Jurek, and E. Stafford, "The Economics of Structured Finance," HBS working paper 09-060, 2008.
13. Detail on the Act from "Brief Summary of the Dodd-Frank Wall Street Reform and Consumer Protection Act," www.banking.senate.gov, accessed February 2012. The entire Act can be seen at Dodd-Frank Wall Street Reform and Consumer Protection Act, 111th Congress, 2nd session, www.sec.gov/about/laws/wallstreetreform-cpa.pdf, accessed February 2012.

Chapter 11

MERGERS AND ACQUISITIONS

Mergers and acquisitions have long been a popular form of corporate investment, particularly in countries with Anglo-American forms of capital markets. There is no question that these transactions provide a healthy return to target stockholders. However, their value to acquiring shareholders is less understood. Many skeptics point out that given the hefty premiums paid to target stockholders, acquisitions tend to be negative-valued investments for acquiring stockholders.[1]

A number of questions can be examined using financial analysis for mergers and acquisitions:

- Securities analysts can ask: Does a proposed acquisition create value for the acquiring firm's stockholders?
- Risk arbitrageurs can ask: What is the likelihood that a hostile takeover offer will ultimately succeed, and are there other potential acquirers likely to enter the bidding?
- Acquiring management can ask: Does this target fit our business strategy? If so, what is it worth to us, and how can we make an offer that can be successful?
- Target management can ask: Is the acquirer's offer a reasonable one for our stockholders? Are there other potential acquirers that would value our company more than the current bidder?
- Investment bankers can ask: How can we identify potential targets that are likely to be a good match for our clients? And how should we value target firms when we are asked to issue fairness opinions?

In this chapter we focus primarily on the use of financial statement data and analysis directed at evaluating whether a merger creates value for the acquiring firm's stockholders. However, our discussion can also be applied to these other merger analysis contexts. The topic of whether acquisitions create value for acquirers focuses on evaluating the (1) motivations for acquisitions, (2) pricing of offers, (3) forms of payment, and (4) likelihood that an offer will be successful. Throughout the chapter we use Pfizer Inc.'s acquisition of Wyeth in 2009 to illustrate how financial analysis can be used in a merger context.

MOTIVATION FOR MERGER OR ACQUISITION

There are a variety of reasons that firms merge or acquire other firms. Some acquiring managers may want to increase their own power and prestige. Others, however, realize that business combinations provide an opportunity to create new economic value for their stockholders. New value can be created in the following ways:

1. *Taking advantage of economies of scale.* Mergers are often justified as a means of providing the two participating firms with increased economies of scale. Economies of scale arise when one large firm can perform a function more efficiently than two smaller firms. While Pfizer did not consider this the primary reason for the acquisition of Wyeth, management did forecast potential operational savings of $4 billion that would result from combining the operations of the two firms.[2]

2. *Improving target management.* Another common motivation for acquisition is to improve target management. A firm is likely to be a target if it has systematically underperformed its industry. Historically poor performance could be due to bad luck, but it could also be due to the firm's managers making poor investment and operating decisions or deliberately pursuing goals that increase their personal power but cost stockholders.

3. *Combining complementary resources.* Firms may decide that a merger will create value by combining complementary resources of the two partners. For example, Pfizer viewed Wyeth's strong presence in biotech drugs, vaccines, and consumer health products as complementary to its own primarily prescription medicine focus, with the combination resulting in a broadly diversified health care company.

4. *Capturing tax benefits.* In the United States, the 1986 Tax Reform Act eliminated many of the tax benefits from mergers and acquisitions. However, several merger tax benefits remain. The major benefit is the acquisition of operating tax losses. If a firm does not expect to earn sufficient profits to fully utilize operating tax loss carryforward benefits, it may decide to buy another firm that is earning profits. The operating losses and loss carryforwards of the acquirer can then be offset against the target's taxable income.[3] A second tax benefit often attributed to mergers is the tax shield that comes from increasing leverage for the target firm. This was particularly relevant for leveraged buyouts in the 1980s.[4]

5. *Providing low-cost financing to a financially constrained target.* If capital markets are imperfect, perhaps because of information asymmetries between management and outside investors, firms can face capital constraints. Information problems are likely to be especially severe for newly formed, high-growth firms. These firms can be difficult for outside investors to value since they have short track records, and their financial statements provide little insight into the value of their growth opportunities. Further, since they typically have to rely on external funds to finance their growth, capital market constraints for high-growth firms are likely to affect their ability to undertake profitable new projects. Public capital markets are therefore likely to be costly sources of funds for these types of firms. An acquirer that understands the business and is willing to provide a steady source of finance may therefore be able to add value.[5]

6. *Creating value through restructuring and break-ups.* Acquisitions are often pursued by financial investors such as leveraged buy-out firms that expect to create value by significantly restructuring or even breaking up the firm. The break-up value is expected to be larger than the aggregate worth of the entire firm. Often, a financial investor will acquire a firm with a view of unlocking value from various

components of the firm's asset base. For example, in 2011 investor Carl Icahn made a series of unsolicited bids for Clorox Co., the U.S.-based consumer products maker. Analysts and news media at the time speculated that his goal was to break up the company and sell off the company's many popular brands such as Clorox bleach products, Kingsford charcoal, Brita water filters, Glad trash bags, and Hidden Valley Ranch salad dressings.[6]

7. *Penetrating new geographies.* Cross-border acquisitions are pursued by firms to expand product markets, to capitalize on new technologies, and to capture labor cost advantages that presumably could not have been achieved through joint ventures or supplier contracts. In the 25-year period between 1986 and 2010, over 12 percent of all acquisitions in the United States were led by foreign buyers, with nearly 1,500 such deals announced in 2010 alone.[7]

8. *Increasing product-market rents.* Firms can also have incentives to merge in order to increase product-market rents. By merging and becoming a dominant firm in the industry, two smaller firms can collude to restrict their output and raise prices, thereby increasing their profits. This circumvents problems that arise in cartels of independent firms, where firms have incentives to cheat on the cartel and increase their output.

   While product-market rents make sense for firms as a motive for merging, the two partners are unlikely to announce their intentions when they explain the merger to their investors, since most countries have antitrust laws that regulate mergers between two firms in the same industry. For example, in the United States there are three major antitrust statutes—The Sherman Act of 1890, The Clayton Act of 1914, and The Hart Scott Rodino Act of 1976.

   Anti-competitive concerns were potentially significant for Pfizer's acquisition of Wyeth, since at the time of the merger announcement, Pfizer and Wyeth were the largest and twelfth-largest pharmaceutical companies in the world, respectively.[8] Merger approval was required by the U.S. Federal Trade Commission (FTC), the European Commission, and regulatory bodies in China, Australia, and Canada. All did eventually approve the merger but required the combined firm to sell assets in certain businesses and regions to preserve competition.

While many of the motivations for acquisitions are likely to create new economic value for shareholders, some are not. Firms that are flush with cash but have few new profitable investment opportunities are particularly prone to using their surplus cash to make acquisitions. Stockholders of these firms would probably prefer that managers pay out any surplus cash flows as dividends or use the funds to repurchase the firm's stock. However, these options reduce the size of the firm and the assets under management's control. Management may therefore prefer to invest the free cash flows to buy new companies, even if they do not create value for stockholders. Of course, managers will never announce that they are buying a firm because they are reluctant to pay out funds to stockholders. They may explain the merger using one of the motivations discussed above, or they may argue that they are buying the target at a bargain price.

Another motivation for mergers that is valued by managers but not stockholders is diversification, which was a popular motivation for acquisitions in the 1960s and early 1970s. Acquirers sought to dampen their earnings volatility by buying firms in unrelated businesses. Diversification as a motive for acquisitions has since been widely discredited. Modern finance theorists point out that in a well-functioning capital market, investors can diversify for themselves and do not need managers to do so for them. In addition, diversification has been criticized when leading firms lose sight of their major competitive strengths and expand into businesses where they do not have expertise.[9] These firms eventually recognize that diversification-motivated acquisitions do not create value, leading to divestitures of business units. Divestitures have been the source of almost a third of all acquisitions over the past 25 years, and in 2010 alone, close to 3,100 deals were a result of corporate divestitures.[10]

Key Analysis Questions

In evaluating a proposed merger, analysts are interested in determining whether the merger creates new wealth for acquiring and target stockholders, or whether it is motivated by managers' desires to increase their own power and prestige. Key questions for financial analysis are likely to include:

- *What is the motivation(s) for an acquisition and the anticipated benefits disclosed by acquirers or targets?*
- *What are the industries of the target and acquirer?* Are the firms related horizontally or vertically? How close are the business relations between them? If the businesses are unrelated, is the acquirer cash-rich and reluctant to return free cash flows to stockholders?
- *What are the key operational strengths of the target and the acquirer?* Are these strengths complementary? For example, does one firm have a renowned research group and the other a strong distribution network?
- *Is the acquisition a friendly one, supported by target management, or hostile?* In the case of a hostile takeover, which is more likely to occur for targets with poor-performing management, will the transaction go through despite the opposition of management who will want to preserve its jobs? Will the hostile acquirer have sufficient access to information to mitigate the risk of overpayment?
- *What is the premerger performance of the two firms?* Performance metrics are likely to include ROE, gross margins, general and administrative expenses to sales, and working capital management ratios. On the basis of these measures, is the target a poor performer in its industry, implying that there are opportunities for improved management? Is the acquirer in a declining industry and searching for new directions?
- *What is the tax position of both firms?* What are the average and marginal current tax rates for the target and the acquirer? Does the acquirer have operating loss carryforwards and the target taxable profits?

This analysis should help the analyst understand what specific benefits, if any, the merger is likely to generate.

Motivation for Pfizer's Acquisition of Wyeth

There were important industry-wide and company-specific factors in 2009 that motivated Pfizer to acquire Wyeth.[11] Across the pharmaceutical industry in the late 2000s, competition from generic drugs was increasingly making the traditional strategy of reliance on a few blockbuster drugs obsolete, as difficult economic conditions and the increased pervasiveness of managed care increased demand for the lower-priced generics. Also, the profitability of blockbusters was being further reduced as specialty manufacturers found increasing success in gaining approval for drugs that closely replicated the blockbuster drug without infringing on its patent. In addition, a tougher regulatory approval climate made the in-house development of new ground-breaking drugs more expensive, time-consuming, and risky, leading large firms such as Pfizer to acquire proven products rather than to develop them in-house. Also, global demand was increasing—with much of the higher growth opportunities in developing countries such as Latin America, the Middle East, and China necessitating an increasingly global footprint in order to take advantage of the growth in those markets.[12] Finally, the rapidly growing biotech segment represented an attractive diversification option for the large pharmaceutical companies, who again viewed acquisition or partnering as a more attractive option than developing capabilities in-house. As a result of these market dynamics, large pharmaceutical firms increasingly moved to broaden their product offerings, keep their pipelines full, and to expand their geographic coverage—often by acquisition.

For Pfizer, the most pressing motivation in early 2009 was the impending loss of patent protection for the blockbuster drug Lipitor (the world's top selling drug, which accounted for 29 percent of Pfizer's pharmaceutical revenues in 2008)[13] which, combined with the inability of Pfizer to create a successful follow-up drug, threatened to create a huge revenue hole for the company in the next few years (torcetrapib, a promising potential replacement, had recently failed in late-stage testing). This looming issue, combined with a lack of other high-quality prospects in its development pipeline, a languishing company stock (which in early 2009 was trading at about a third of its July 2000 peak), and $23 billion in cash holdings, had analysts and shareholders pressuring management to make a big move. Historically, as well, Pfizer had grown by acquisition rather than by developing its own blockbuster drugs, with major acquisitions of Warner-Lambert in 2000 for $89 billion and Pharmacia in 2003 for $60 billion keeping its product line full and giving it status as the world's largest pharmaceutical company.

Operationally, Pfizer's acquisition of Wyeth would provide significant diversification for the combined company, complementing Pfizer's strength in human health pharmaceuticals with Wyeth's strong presence in vaccines, injectable biologic drugs, veterinary medicine, Alzheimer's disease drugs, and consumer products such as Chapstick, Centrum, Anacin, and Preparation H. In fact, in the combined company no drug would represent more than 10 percent of total revenue,[14] buffering it from sudden future revenue loss of a blockbuster such as Lipitor. In addition, management stressed the enhanced global coverage of the combined company in both developed and emerging markets.[15]

Potential cost savings due to streamlining were also a potential positive in a time of reduced profit margins and increased competition. At the time of the merger, Pfizer projected potential savings at $4 billion from increased economies of scale and consolidation of redundant operations, and announced plans to cut the combined work force by 15 percent (which represented 20,000 jobs).[16]

Analysts and the financial media were mixed on the economic benefits that potentially would be derived from the acquisition. While the pressing need for Pfizer to replace the impending loss of revenue from the Lipitor patent expiration was recognized, some nevertheless expressed concern as to whether Wyeth, with the patent expiration of its two top drugs coming in the next two years, was the best target.[17]

ACQUISITION PRICING

A well considered economic motivation for a merger or acquisition is a necessary but not sufficient condition for it to create value for acquiring stockholders. The acquirer must be careful to avoid overpaying for the target. Overpayment makes the transaction highly desirable and profitable for target stockholders, but it diminishes the value of the deal to acquiring stockholders. A financial analyst can use the following methods to assess whether the acquiring firm is overpaying for the target.

Analyzing Premium Offered to Target Stockholders

One popular way to assess whether the acquirer is overpaying for a target is to compare the premium offered to target stockholders to premiums offered in similar transactions. If the acquirer offers a relatively high premium, the analyst is typically led to conclude that the transaction is less likely to create value for acquiring stockholders.

Premiums differ significantly for friendly and hostile acquisitions. Premiums tend to be about 30 percent higher for hostile deals than for friendly offers, implying that hostile acquirers are more likely to overpay for a target.[18] There are several reasons for this. First, a friendly acquirer has access to the internal records of the target, improving the accuracy in valuing the target and making it less likely that it will be surprised by hidden liabilities or problems once it has completed the deal. In contrast, a hostile acquirer does not have this advantage in valuing the target during negotiations and is more likely to overpay. Second, the delays that typically accompany a hostile acquisition often provide opportunities for competing bidders to make an offer for the target, leading to a bidding war.

Comparing a target's premium to values for similar types of transactions is straightforward but has several practical problems. First, it is not obvious how to define a comparable transaction. Figure 11-1 shows the mean and median premiums paid for U.S. targets over a 25-year period between 1986 and 2010. Average premiums rose from around 40 percent through the mid-1990s to between 50 and 60 percent in 1999–2001. Median premiums also increased during this period, from around 30 percent to 40 percent. Despite the increase in M&A activity in 2004 and 2005, both average and median premiums dropped significantly from the highs of 1999–2001 to only 31 to 35 and 23 to 24 percent, respectively. Recently, premiums have rebounded—in 2008–2010 average premiums ranged again between 50 and 60 percent, with median premiums in the 35 to 40 percent range.[19] However, mean and median premiums have to be interpreted

| FIGURE 11-1 | Merger Activity and Premium Paid: 1981–2010 |

Source: Mergerstat Review 2011 (FactSet Mergerstat, LLC).

with caution since there is considerable variation across transactions, making it difficult to use these estimates as a benchmark.

A second problem in using premiums offered to target stockholders to assess whether an acquirer overpaid is that measured premiums can be misleading if an offer is anticipated by investors. The stock price run-up for the target will then tend to make estimates of the premium appear relatively low. This limitation can be partially offset by using target stock prices one month prior to the acquisition offer as the basis for calculating premiums. However, in some cases offers may have been anticipated for even longer than one month.

Finally, using target premiums to assess whether an acquirer overpaid ignores the value of the target to the acquirer after the acquisition. The acquirer expects to benefit from the merger by improving the target firm's operating performance through a combination of economies of scale, improved management, tax benefits, and spillover effects derived from the acquisition. Clearly, acquirers will be willing to pay higher premiums for targets that are expected to generate higher merger benefits. Thus, examining the premium alone cannot determine whether the acquisition creates value for acquiring stockholders.

Analyzing Value of the Target to the Acquirer

A second and more reliable way of assessing whether the acquirer has overpaid for the target is to compare the offer price to the estimated value of the target to the acquirer. This latter value can be computed using the valuation techniques discussed in Chapters 7 and 8. The most popular methods of valuation used for mergers and acquisitions are earnings multiples and discounted cash flows. Since a comprehensive discussion of these techniques is provided earlier in the book, we focus here on implementation issues that arise for valuing targets in mergers and acquisitions.

We recommend first computing the value of the target as an independent firm. This provides a way of checking whether the valuation assumptions are reasonable, since for publicly listed targets we can compare our estimate with premerger market prices. It also provides a useful benchmark for thinking about how the target's performance, and hence its value, is likely to change once it is acquired.

Earnings Multiples

To estimate the value of a target to an acquirer using earnings multiples, we have to forecast earnings for the target and decide on an appropriate earnings multiple, as follows:

Step 1: Forecasting earnings Earnings forecasts are usually made by first forecasting next year's net income for the target, assuming no acquisition. Historical sales growth rates, gross margins, and average tax rates are useful in building a pro forma income model. Once we have forecasted the income for the target as an independent firm, we can incorporate into the pro forma model any improvements in earnings performance that we expect to result from the acquisition. Performance improvements can be modeled on numerous dimensions including:

- Higher operating margins through economies of scale in purchasing, or increased market power;
- Reductions in expenses as a result of consolidating research and development staffs, sales forces, and/or administration; or
- Lower average tax rates from taking advantage of operating tax loss carryforwards.

Step 2: Determining the price-earnings multiple How do we determine the earnings multiple to be applied to our earnings forecasts? If the target firm is listed, it may be tempting to use the preacquisition price-earnings multiple to value postmerger earnings. However, there are several limitations to this approach. First, for many targets, earnings growth expectations are likely to change after a merger, implying that there will be a difference between the pre- and postmerger price-earnings multiples. Postmerger earnings should then be valued using a multiple for firms with comparable growth and risk characteristics. A second problem is that premerger price-earnings multiples are unavailable for unlisted targets. Once again it becomes necessary to decide which types of listed firms are likely to be good comparables. In addition, since the earnings being valued are the projected earnings for the next 12 months or the next full fiscal year, the appropriate benchmark ratio should be a *forward* price-earnings ratio. Finally, if a premerger price-earnings multiple is appropriate for valuing postmerger earnings, care is required to ensure that the multiple is calculated prior to any acquisition announcement, since the price will increase in anticipation of the premium to be paid to target stockholders.

The following table summarizes how price-earnings multiples are used to value a target firm before an acquisition (assuming it will remain an independent entity) and to estimate the value of a target to a potential acquirer:

Summary of Price-Earnings Valuation for Targets

Value of target as an independent firm	Target earnings forecast for the next year, assuming no change in ownership, multiplied by its *premerger* forward PE multiple.
Value of target to potential acquirer	Target *revised* earnings forecast for the next year, incorporating the effect of any operational changes made by the acquirer, multiplied by its *postmerger* forward PE multiple.

Limitations of Price-Earnings Valuation As explained in Chapter 7, there are serious limitations to using earnings multiples for valuation. In addition to these limitations, the method has two more that are specific to merger valuations:

1. PE multiples assume that merger performance improvements come either from an immediate increase in earnings or from an increase in earnings growth (and hence an increase in the postmerger PE ratio). In reality, improvements and savings can come in many forms—gradual increases in earnings from implementing new operating policies, eliminating overinvestment, managing working capital better, or paying out excess cash to stockholders. These types of improvements are not naturally reflected in PE multiples.
2. PE models do not easily incorporate any spillover benefits from an acquisition for the acquirer since they focus on valuing the earnings of the target.

Discounted Abnormal Earnings or Cash Flows

As discussed in Chapters 7 and 8, we can also value a company using the discounted abnormal earnings and discounted free cash flow methods. These require us to first forecast the abnormal earnings or free cash flows for the firm and then discount them at the cost of capital, as follows.

Step 1: Forecasting abnormal earnings / free cash flows A pro forma model of expected future income and cash flows for the firm provides the basis for forecasting abnormal earnings / free cash flows. As a starting point, the model should be constructed under the assumption that the target remains an independent firm. The model should reflect the best estimates of future sales growth, cost structures, working capital needs, investment and research and development needs, and cash requirements for known debt retirements, developed from a financial analysis of the target. The abnormal earnings method requires that we forecast abnormal earnings or net operating profit after tax (NOPAT) for as long as the firm expects new investment projects to earn more than their cost of capital. Under the free cash flow approach, the pro forma model will forecast free cash flows to either the firm or to equity, typically for a period of five to ten years. Once we have a model of the abnormal earnings or free cash flows, we can incorporate any improvements in earnings / free cash flows that we expect to result from the acquisition. These will include the cost savings, cash received from asset sales, benefits from eliminating overinvestment, improved working capital management, and excess cash paid out to stockholders.

Step 2: Compute the discount rate If we are valuing the target's postacquisition abnormal NOPAT or cash flows to the firm, the appropriate discount rate is the weighted average cost of capital (WACC) for the target, using its expected *postacquisition* capital structure. Alternatively, if the target's equity cash flows are being valued directly or if we are valuing abnormal earnings, the appropriate discount rate is the target's *postacquisition cost of equity* rather than its WACC. Two common mistakes are to use the acquirer's cost of capital or the target's *preacquisition* cost of capital to value the postmerger abnormal earnings / cash flows from the target.

The computation of the target's postacquisition cost of capital can be complicated if the acquirer plans to make a change to the target's capital structure after the acquisition, since the target's costs of debt and equity will change. As discussed in Chapter 8, this involves estimating the asset beta for the target, calculating the new equity and debt betas under the modified capital structure, and finally computing the revised cost of equity capital or WACC. As a practical matter, the effect of these changes on the WACC is likely to be quite small unless the revision in leverage has a significant effect on the target's interest tax shields or its likelihood of financial distress.

The following table summarizes how the discounted abnormal earnings / cash flow methods can be used to value a target before an acquisition (assuming it will remain an independent entity) and to estimate the value of a target firm to a potential acquirer.

Summary of Discounted Abnormal Earnings / Cash Flow Valuation for Targets

Value of target as an independent firm	(a) Present value of abnormal earnings / free cash flows to target equity assuming no acquisition, discounted at *premerger* cost of equity, or (b) Present value of abnormal NOPAT / free cash flows to target debt and equity assuming no acquisition, discounted at *premerger* WACC, less value of debt.
Value of target to potential acquirer	(a) Present value of abnormal earnings / free cash flows to target equity, *including benefits from merger*, discounted at *postmerger* cost of equity, or (b) Present value of abnormal NOPAT / free cash flows to target debt and equity, *including benefits from merger*, discounted at *postmerger* WACC, less value of debt.

Step 3: Analyze sensitivity Once we have estimated the expected value of a target, we will want to examine the sensitivity of our estimate to changes in the model assumptions.

For example, answering the following questions can help the analyst assess the risks associated with an acquisition:

- What happens to the value of the target if it takes longer than expected for the benefits of the acquisition to materialize?
- What happens to the value of the target if the acquisition prompts its primary competitors to respond by also making an acquisition? Will potential changes in industry dynamics affect the firm's plans and estimates?

Key Analysis Questions

To analyze the pricing of an acquisition, the analyst is interested in assessing the value of the acquisition benefits to be generated by the acquirer relative to the price paid to target stockholders. Analysts are therefore likely to be interested in answers to the following questions:

- *What is the premium that the acquirer paid for the target's stock?* What does this premium imply for the acquirer in terms of future performance improvements to justify the premium?
- *What are the likely performance improvements that management expects to generate from the acquisition?* For example, are there likely to be increases in the revenues for the merged firm from new products, increased prices, or better distribution of existing products? Alternatively, are there cost savings as a result of taking advantage of economies of scale, improved efficiency, or a lower cost of capital for the target?
- *What is the value of any performance improvements?* Values can be estimated using multiples or discounted abnormal earnings / cash flow methods.

Pfizer's Pricing of Wyeth

Pfizer's $68 billion price for Wyeth represented a 29 percent premium to target stockholders over the market value on January 22, 2009, the day before the *Wall Street Journal* reported on the possible deal. This was below the mean and median premiums reported for all acquisitions during that year (shown in Figure 11-1 as 58.7 percent and 39.8 percent, respectively), perhaps in some part reflecting its timing as the first major deal announcement since the beginning of the global financial crisis.

In terms of traditional multiples-based forms of valuation, Pfizer's pricing of Wyeth appears to be reasonable. For example, at the time of the announcement of Pfizer's offer, the PE multiple for other firms in the pharmaceutical and biotech industries that were comparable to Wyeth ranged from 13.7 to 18.6. Pfizer's offer valued Wyeth at 15.4 times current earnings.[20]

The market reaction to the acquisition announcement suggests that analysts believed that the deal was not necessarily a positive one for Pfizer's stockholders—Pfizer's stock price dropped by a little over 10 percent on January 26, 2009, the day the deal was announced (the S&P 500 registered a .6 percent gain on that day), and throughout 2009, Pfizer stock continued to underperform the market index. By October 15, the date the deal closed, Pfizer stock had regained ground, increasing 13 percent since the deal announcement, but it still lagged the 31 percent rebound of the S&P 500 index during the same period. Pfizer stock ended 2009 with a loss of .5 percent for the year, compared to a gain for the S&P 500 market index of 20 percent.[21] All else being equal, it seems that investors were not convinced that the deal made sense for Pfizer.

Subsequent short-term results for Pfizer suggested that at least on the cost-cutting front the merger was resulting in expected synergies. In late 2010, Pfizer reported that it had achieved approximately one half of the forecast $4–5 billion in cost savings announced at the time of the merger.[22] However, the longer term issue of revenue loss due to expiring patents (with Lipitor and eight other high revenue drugs coming off patent protection by 2015) continued to weigh on the company stock; as of the end of third quarter 2011, Pfizer stock had increased a total of 13 percent since the merger announcement, well underperforming the S&P 500, which increased 35 percent over the same period.[23]

ACQUISITION FINANCING AND FORM OF PAYMENT

Even if an acquisition is undertaken to create new economic value and is priced judiciously, it may still destroy shareholder value if it is inappropriately financed. Several financing options are available to acquirers, including issuing stock or warrants to target stockholders, or acquiring target stock using surplus cash or proceeds from new debt. The trade-offs between these alternatives from the standpoint of target stockholders usually hinge on their tax and transaction cost implications. For acquirers, they can affect the firm's capital structure and provide new information to investors.

As we will discuss, the financing preferences of acquiring and target stockholders can diverge. Financing arrangements can therefore increase or reduce the attractiveness of an acquisition from the standpoint of acquiring stockholders. As a result, a complete analysis of an acquisition will include an examination of the implications of the financing arrangements for the acquirer.

Effect of Form of Payment on Acquiring Stockholders

From the perspective of the acquirer, the form of payment is essentially a financing decision. As discussed in Chapter 10, in the long term firms choose whether to use debt or equity financing to balance the tax and incentive benefits of debt against the risks of financial distress. For acquiring stockholders, the costs and benefits of different financing alternatives therefore usually depend on three factors described below: how the offer affects their firm's capital structure, any information effects associated with different forms of financing, and control issues arising from the form of payment.

Capital Structure Effects of Form of Financing

In acquisitions where debt financing or surplus cash are the primary form of consideration for target shares, the acquisition increases the net financial leverage of the acquirer. This increase in leverage may be part of the acquisition strategy, since one way an acquirer can add value to an inefficient firm is to lower its taxes by increasing interest tax shields. However, in many acquisitions an increase in postacquisition leverage is a side effect of the method of financing and not part of a deliberate tax-minimizing strategy. Demands by target shareholders for consideration in cash could lead the acquirer to have a postacquisition capital structure that can potentially reduce shareholder value for the acquirer by increasing the risk of financial distress.

To assess whether an acquisition leads an acquirer to have too much leverage, financial analysts can assess the acquirer's financial risk following the proposed acquisition by these methods:

- Analyze the business risks and the volatility of the combined, postacquisition cash flows against the level of debt in the new capital structure, and the implications for possible financial distress.

- Assess the pro forma financial risks for the acquirer under the proposed financing plan. Popular measures of financial risk include debt-to-equity and interest-coverage ratios, as well as projections of cash flows available to meet debt repayments. The ratios can be compared to similar performance metrics for the acquiring and target firms' industries to determine whether postmerger ratios indicate that the firm's probability of financial distress has increased significantly.
- Examine whether there are important off-balance-sheet liabilities for the target and/or acquirer that are not included in the pro forma ratio and cash flow analysis of postacquisition financial risk.
- Determine whether the pro forma assets for the acquirer are largely intangible and therefore sensitive to financial distress. Measures of intangible assets include such ratios as market to book equity and tangible assets to the market value of equity.

Information Problems and the Form of Financing

In the short term, information asymmetries between managers and external investors can make managers reluctant to raise equity to finance new projects. Managers' reluctance arises from their fear that investors will interpret the decision as an indication that the firm's stock is overvalued. In the short term, this effect can lead managers to deviate from the firm's long-term optimal mix of debt and equity. As a result, acquirers are likely to prefer to use internal funds or debt to finance an acquisition since these forms of consideration are less likely to be interpreted negatively by investors.[24]

The information effects imply that firms forced to use stock financing are likely to face a stock price decline when investors learn of the method of financing.[25] From the viewpoint of financial analysts, the financing announcement may, therefore, provide valuable news about the acquiring managers' views of their own company's value prior to the acquisition. On the other hand, it should have no implications for analysis of whether the acquisition creates value for acquiring shareholders since the news reflected in the financing announcement is about the *preacquisition* value of the acquirer and not about the *postacquisition* value of the target to the acquirer.

A second information problem arises if the acquiring management does not have good information about the target. Stock financing then provides a way for acquiring stockholders to share the information risks with target shareholders. If the acquirer finds out after the acquisition that the value of the target is less than previously anticipated, the accompanying decline in the acquirer's equity price will be partially borne by target stockholders who continue to hold the acquirer's stock. In contrast, if the target's shares were acquired in a cash offer, any postacquisition loss would be fully borne by the acquirer's original stockholders. The risk-sharing benefits from using stock financing appear to be widely recognized for acquisitions of private companies, where public information on the target is largely unavailable.[26] In practice it appears to be considered less important for acquisitions of large public corporations.

Control and the Form of Payment

There is a significant difference between the use of cash and stock in terms of its impact on the voting control of the combined firm postacquisition. Financing an acquisition with cash allows the acquirer to retain the structure and composition of its equity ownership. On the other hand, depending on the size of the target firm relative to the acquirer, an acquisition financed with stock could have a significant impact on the ownership and control of the firm postacquisition. This could be particularly relevant to a family-controlled acquirer. Therefore, the effects of control need to be balanced against the other costs and benefits when determining the form of payment.

Over the last 25 years, offers that are 100 percent cash have comprised 49 percent of all acquisitions, exceeding all-stock offers (26 percent) and mixed stock and cash offers (25 percent). The popularity of all-cash offers has increased since 2000, rising to 60 percent of all deals in 2010 whereas the use of all-stock offers has declined to only 21 percent.[27]

Effect of Form of Payment on Target Stockholders

The key payment considerations for target stockholders are the tax and transaction cost implications of the acquirer's offer.

Tax Effects of Different Forms of Consideration

Target stockholders care about the after-tax value of any offer they receive for their shares. In the United States, whenever target stockholders receive cash for their shares, they are required to pay capital gains tax on the difference between the takeover offer price and their original purchase price. Alternatively, if they receive shares in the acquirer as consideration and the acquisition is undertaken as a tax-free reorganization, they can defer any taxes on the capital gain until they sell the new shares.

As a result, U.S. tax laws appear to cause target stockholders to prefer a stock offer to a cash one. This is certainly likely to be the case for a target founder who still has a significant stake in the company. If the company's stock price has appreciated over its life, the founder will face a substantial capital gains tax on a cash offer and will therefore probably prefer to receive stock in the acquiring firm. However, cash and stock offers can be tax-neutral for some groups of stockholders. For example, consider the tax implications for risk arbitrageurs, who take a short-term position in a company that is a takeover candidate in the hope that other bidders will emerge and increase the takeover price. They have no intention of holding stock in the acquirer once the takeover is completed and will pay ordinary income tax on any short-term trading gain. Cash and stock offers therefore have identical after-tax values for risk arbitrageurs. Similarly, tax-exempt institutions are likely to be indifferent to whether an offer is in cash or stock.

Transaction Costs and the Form of Payment

Transaction costs are another factor related to the form of payment that can be relevant to target stockholders. Transaction costs are incurred when target stockholders sell any stock received as consideration for their shares in the target. These costs will not be faced by target stockholders if the bidder offers them cash. Transaction costs are unlikely to be significant for investors who intend to hold the acquirer's stock following a stock acquisition. However, they may be relevant for investors who intend to sell, such as risk arbitrageurs.

Key Analysis Questions

For an analyst focused on the acquiring firm, it is important to assess how the method of financing affects the acquirer's capital structure and its risks of financial distress by asking the following questions:

- *What is the leverage for the newly created firm?* How does this compare to leverage for comparable firms in the industry?

> • *What are the projected future cash flows for the merged firm?* Are these sufficient to meet the firm's debt commitments? How much of a cushion does the firm have if future cash flows are lower than expected? Is the firm's debt level likely to impair its ability to finance profitable future investments if future cash flows are below expectations?

Pfizer's Financing of Wyeth

Pfizer offered Wyeth shareholders $33 in cash and 0.985 shares of Pfizer stock for each Wyeth share. With the stock component valued at $17.19 per share, the combined cash and equity implied a total offer of roughly $68 billion. While the premerger equity value of Wyeth represented 31 percent of the combined market value, the large cash component of the deal caused the postmerger proportion of ownership to drop to about 16 percent for Wyeth shareholders and to rise to 84 percent for Pfizer shareholders.

The merger was structured as a taxable transaction for federal income tax purposes. This implied that Wyeth shareholders would recognize capital gain or loss for federal income tax purposes as a result of the transaction. By using debt in addition to stock and cash to finance the acquisition, Pfizer increased its financial leverage significantly—increasing total debt as a percentage of equity from 30 percent prior to the acquisition to 54 percent at the end of 2009. Also, in order to help finance the large cash outlay required for the acquisition, Pfizer cut its dividend by 50 percent upon announcing the deal (which likely also contributed to the significant drop in share price when the deal was announced). Reacting to this material change in Pfizer's financial structure, Standard and Poor's downgraded Pfizer's credit rating from AAA to AA on October 16, 2009—the day after the Wyeth acquisition closed, with the other agencies following suit.[28]

ACQUISITION OUTCOME

The final question of interest to the analyst evaluating a potential acquisition is whether it will indeed be completed. If an acquisition has a clear value-based motive, the target is priced appropriately, and its proposed financing does not create unnecessary financial risks for the acquirer, it may still fail because the target receives a higher competing bid, there is opposition from entrenched target management, or the transaction fails to receive necessary regulatory approval. Therefore, to evaluate the likelihood that an offer will be accepted, the financial analyst has to understand whether there are potential competing bidders who could pay an even higher premium to target stockholders than is currently offered. They also have to consider whether target managers are entrenched and likely to oppose an offer to protect their jobs, as well as the political and regulatory environment in which the target and the acquirer operate.

Other Potential Acquirers

If there are other potential bidders for a target, especially ones who place a higher value on the target, there is a strong possibility that the bidder in question will be unsuccessful. Target management and stockholders have an incentive to delay accepting the initial offer to give potential competitors time to also submit a bid. From the perspective of the initial bidder, this means that the offer could potentially reduce stockholder value by the cost of making the offer (including substantial investment banking and legal fees). In practice, a losing bidder can usually recoup these losses and sometimes even make healthy profits from selling to the successful acquirer any shares it has accumulated in the target.

On some occasions, the original bidder includes a break-up fee in the acquisition contract that is payable should the target company choose to be acquired by a different partner. For example, in late 2005 Johnson & Johnson signed an agreement to acquire Guidant Corporation for about $21 billion. A takeover battle for Guidant resulted when Boston Scientific made a higher offer. Over the ensuing seven weeks (from December 2005 to January 2006), both Johnson & Johnson and Boston Scientific increased their bids on multiple occasions. Eventually, Boston Scientific won with a $27 billion offer. However, in addition to the purchase price, Boston Scientific had to reimburse Guidant the termination fee of $705 million payable to Johnson & Johnson.

Key Analysis Questions

The financial analyst can determine whether there are other potential acquirers for a target and how they value the target by asking the following questions:

- *Who are the acquirer's major competitors?* Could any of these firms provide an even better fit for the target?
- *Are there other firms that could also implement the initial bidder's acquisition strategy?* For example, if this strategy relies on developing benefits from complementary assets, look for potential bidders who also have assets complementary to the target. If the goal of the acquisition is to replace inefficient management, what other firms in the target's industry could provide management expertise?

Target Management Entrenchment

If target managers are entrenched and fearful for their jobs, it is likely that they will oppose a bidder's offer. Some firms have implemented "golden parachutes" for top managers to allay their concerns about job security at the time of an offer. Golden parachutes provide top managers of a target firm with attractive compensation rewards should the firm get taken over.[29] However, many firms do not have such schemes, and opposition to an offer from entrenched management is a very real possibility.

More generally, there are a variety of structural impediments known as takeover defense mechanisms that provide a disincentive to acquiring firms. Many such defenses were used during the turbulent 1980s, when hostile acquisitions were at their peak. Some of the most widely adopted include poison pills, staggered boards, super-majority rules, dual-class recapitalizations, fair-price provisions, ESOP plans, and changes in states of incorporation to states with more restrictive anti-takeover laws. While the existence of takeover defenses for a target indicates that its management is likely to fight a bidding firm's offer, defenses have typically not prevented an acquisition from taking place. Instead, they tend to cause delays, which increase the likelihood that there will be competing offers made for the target, including offers by friendly parties solicited by target management, called "white knights." Takeover defenses, therefore, increase the likelihood that the bidder in question will be outbid for the target, or that it will have to increase its offer significantly to win a bidding contest. Given these risks, some have argued that acquirers are now less likely to embark on a potentially hostile acquisition.

Key Analysis Questions

To assess whether the target firm's management is entrenched and therefore likely to oppose an acquisition, analysts can ask the following questions:

- *Does the target firm have takeover defenses designed to protect management?*
- *Has the target been a poor performer relative to other firms in its industry?* If so, management's job security is likely to be threatened by a takeover, leading it to oppose any offers.
- *Is there a golden parachute plan in place for target management?* Golden parachutes provide attractive compensation for management in order to deter opposition to a takeover for job security reasons.

Antitrust and Security Issues

Regulators such as the Federal Trade Commission in the U.S. and the European Competition Commission assess the effects of an acquisition on the competitive dynamics of the industry in which the firms operate. The objective is to ensure that no one firm, through mergers and acquisitions, creates a dominant position that can impede effective competition in specific geographies or product markets. For instance, in August 2011 the U.S. Justice Department sued to block AT&T's proposed $39 billion purchase of rival T-Mobile USA on the grounds that the merger would substantially reduce competition for mobile phone services in the United States.[30]

In addition, political concerns around firms that have an impact on the national and economic security of a country come under the scrutiny of local lawmakers, whose opposition can often derail cross-border acquisition efforts. The United States, for instance, has a specific inter-agency committee that vets foreign takeovers of U.S. assets on national security grounds. Two recent high profile cases—China's CNOOC oil company's proposed acquisition of California-based Unocal in mid-2005 and Dubai Ports World's acquisition of U.S. port terminals in March 2006—underscore the importance of assessing this risk. Chevron, another interested bidder for Unocal, used CNOOC's links to the Chinese government to generate political opposition to the CNOOC bid, which eventually led CNOOC to drop its offer. Similarly, political opposition based on the United Arab Emirates government's control of Dubai Ports World and the national security concerns over port infrastructure forced the company to sell the U.S. operations as part of its acquisition of British port operator P&O.

Key Analysis Questions

To assess whether the regulators and/or government is likely to oppose an acquisition, analysts can ask the following questions:

- *What proportion of industry sales do the two firms control?* Is this likely to be of concern to regulators in countries in which the firms operate? Are the combined firms likely to be able to reduce regulatory opposition by selling certain business units?
- *Is the target firm or the industry in which it operates of strategic importance or in the national interest of the country in which it is located?* Is the ownership structure of the acquirer likely to create political opposition to the deal?

Analysis of Outcome of Pfizer's Offer for Wyeth

Analysts covering Wyeth had little reason to question whether Wyeth would be sold to Pfizer. The offer was a friendly one that had received the approval of Wyeth's management and board of directors. There was some risk of another major pharmaceutical company entering the bidding for Wyeth—in fact, in the S-4 filed by Pfizer in March of 2009, there is mention of a "Company X" that approached Wyeth in December of 2008 to explore making a competitive bid (rumored at the time to be Abbott Labs).[31, 32] After discussions with both companies, Wyeth management accepted Pfizer's bid, determining that difficult current market conditions and potential anti-competitive issues would likely make a more attractive bid unlikely, and in the end no competing bid was made.

The complementary nature of the two companies' product lines on the human health side meant that the deal raised few antitrust concerns on that front. However, Pfizer and Wyeth's similar strength in animal health products was seen as a potential antitrust issue. Consequently, regulators in the United States and in the European Union, Canada, China, and Australia required the combined company to divest certain animal health assets in those countries as a condition of approval. Pfizer agreed to the conditions, and the acquisition was completed on October 15, 2009, nine months after announcement of the initial agreement.

SUMMARY

This chapter summarizes how financial statement data and analysis can be used by financial analysts interested in evaluating whether an acquisition creates value for an acquiring firm's stockholders. Obviously, much of this discussion is also likely to be relevant to other merger participants, including target and acquiring management and their investment banks.

For the external analyst, the first task is to identify the acquirer's acquisition strategy. We discuss a number of strategies. Some of these are consistent with maximizing acquirer value, including acquisitions to take advantage of economies of scale, improve target management, combine complementary resources, capture tax benefits, provide low-cost financing to financially constrained targets, and increase product-market rents.

Other strategies appear to benefit managers more than stockholders. For example, some unprofitable acquisitions are made because managers are reluctant to return free cash flows to shareholders, or because managers want to lower the firm's earnings volatility by diversifying into unrelated businesses.

The financial analyst's second task is to assess whether the acquirer is offering a reasonable price for the target. Even if the acquirer's strategy is based on increasing shareholder value, it can overpay for the target. Target stockholders will then be well rewarded but at the expense of acquiring stockholders. We show how the ratio analysis, forecasting, and valuation techniques discussed earlier in the book can all be used to assess the worth of the target to the acquirer.

The method of financing an offer is also relevant to a financial analyst's review of an acquisition proposal. If a proposed acquisition is financed with surplus cash or new debt, it increases the acquirer's financial risk. Financial analysts can use ratio analysis of the acquirer's postacquisition balance sheet and pro forma estimates of cash flow volatility and interest coverage to assess whether demands by target stockholders for consideration in cash lead the acquirer to increase its risk of financial distress.

Finally, the financial analyst is interested in assessing whether a merger is likely to be completed once the initial offer is made, and at what price. This requires the analyst to determine whether there are other potential bidders, whether target management is entrenched and likely to oppose a bidder's offer, or whether the deal could fail due to antitrust or security concerns.

DISCUSSION QUESTIONS

1. Since the year 2000, there has been a noticeable increase in mergers and acquisitions among firms in different countries (termed cross-border acquisitions). What factors could explain this increase? What special issues can arise in executing a cross-border acquisition and in ultimately meeting one's objectives for a successful combination?

2. Private equity firms have become an important player in the acquisition market. These private investment groups offer to buy a target firm, often with the cooperation of management, and then take the firm private. Private equity buyouts rose from just 2 percent of U.S. merger and acquisition activity in 2000 to 15 percent as of December 2005. Private equity buyers tend to finance a significant portion of the acquisition with debt.

   a. What types of firms would make ideal candidates for a private equity buyout? Why?

   b. How might the buyout firm add sufficient value to the target to justify a high buyout premium?

3. Kim Silverman, CFO of the First Public Bank Company, notes, "We are fortunate to have a cost of capital of only 7 percent. We want to leverage this advantage by acquiring other banks that have a higher cost of funds. I believe that we can add significant value to these banks by using our lower cost financing." Do you agree with Silverman's analysis? Why or why not?

4. The Boston Tea Company plans to acquire Hi Flavor Soda Co. for $60 per share, a 50 percent premium over current market price. John E. Grey, the CFO of Boston Tea, argues that this valuation can easily be justified using a price-earnings analysis: "Boston Tea has a price-earnings ratio of 15, and we expect that we will be able to generate long-term earnings for Hi Flavor Soda of $5 per share. This implies that Hi Flavor is worth $75 to us, well below our $60 offer price." Do you agree with this analysis? What are Grey's key assumptions?

5. You have been hired by GT Investment Bank to work in the merger department. The analysis required for all potential acquisitions includes an examination of the target for any off-balance-sheet assets or liabilities that have to be factored into the valuation. Prepare a checklist for your examination.

6. A target company is currently valued at $50 in the market. A potential acquirer believes that it can add value in two ways: $15 of value can be added through better working capital management, and an additional $10 of value can be generated by making available a unique technology to expand the target's new product offerings. In a competitive bidding contest, how much of this additional value will the acquirer have to pay out to the target's shareholders to emerge as the winner?

7. In 2011 Comcast acquired a majority stake in NBC Universal in a deal that valued the company at more than $30 billion. Analysts at the time tended to define the rationale for the acquisition as being one of "conduit" acquiring "content". Evaluate the potential strategic merits of this rationale.

8. A leading oil exploration company decides to acquire an Internet company at a 50 percent premium. The acquirer argues that this move creates value for its own stockholders because it can use its excess cash flows from the oil business to help

finance growth in the new Internet segment. Evaluate the economic merits of this claim.

9. Under current U.S. accounting standards, acquirers are required to capitalize good-will and report any subsequent declines in value as an impairment charge. What performance metrics would you use to judge whether goodwill is impaired?

10. As an external adviser to the U.S. Government's interagency committee that vets foreign takeovers, you have been asked to provide expert testimony on the proposed takeover of a major U.S. airport by a Dutch airport management services company. Would you recommend that the acquisition be granted regulatory approval? What are the different issues you will examine and present to the committee?

NOTES

1. In a review of studies of merger returns, Michael Jensen and Richard Ruback conclude that target shareholders earn positive returns from takeovers, but that acquiring shareholders only break even. See M. Jensen and R. Ruback, "The Market for Corporate Control: The Scientific Evidence," *Journal of Financial Economics* 11 (April 1983): 5–50.

2. "Pfizer to Acquire Wyeth, Creating the World's Premier Biopharmaceutical Company," Pfizer press release, January 26, 2009, http://www.pfizer.com/news/press_releases/pfizer_press_release_archive.jsp#guid=20090126005624en&source=RSS_2009&page=13, accessed October 2011.

3. Of course, another possibility is for the profitable firm to acquire the unprofitable one. However, in the United States the IRS will disallow the use of tax loss carry-forwards by an acquirer if it appears that an acquisition was tax-motivated.

4. See S. Kaplan, "Management Buyouts: Evidence on Taxes as a Source of Value," *Journal of Finance* 44 (1989): 611–632.

5. K. Palepu, "Predicting Takeover Targets: A Methodological and Empirical Analysis," *Journal of Accounting and Economics* 8 (March 1986): 3–36.

6. See, for instance, "Carl Icahn's Latest Quest: Cleaning up with Clorox," July 26, 2011, post on blog "Schumpeter," *The Economist*, http://www.economist.com/blogs/schumpeter/2011/07/carl-icahns-latest-quest, accessed October 2011, also "Pending a Takeover, Clorox's multiple Brands come into Question," Jennifer Collins, Marketplace Morning Report for Wednesday, August 2, 2011, http://marketplace.publicradio.org/display/web/2011/08/03/am-pending-a-takeover-cloroxs-multiple-brands-come-into-question/, accessed October 2011.

7. FactSet Mergerstat, LLC, *Mergerstat Review 2011* (Newark, NJ, 2011): 194–195.

8. *Statement of the Federal Trade Commission Concerning Pfizer/Wyeth*, FTC File No. 091-0053, http://www.ftc.gov/os/caselist/0910053/091014pwyethstmt.pdf, accessed October 2011.

9. Chapter 2 discusses the pros and cons of corporate diversification and evidence on its implications for firm performance.

10. FactSet Mergerstat, LLC, *Mergerstat Review 2011* (Newark, NJ, 2011), pp. 194–195.

11. General pharmaceutical industry context from David Collis and Troy Smith, "Strategy in the Twenty-First Century Pharmaceutical Industry: Merck & Co. and Pfizer Inc.," HBS No. 707-509 (Boston: Harvard Business School Publishing, 2007), http://www.hbsp.com, accessed October 2011.

12. This was cited as a reason for the Wyeth acquisition in "Pfizer to Acquire Wyeth, Creating the World's Premier Biopharmaceutical Company," Pfizer press release, January

26, 2009, http://www.pfizer.com/news/press_releases/pfizer_press_release_archive.jsp#guid=20090126005624en&source=RSS_2009&page=13, accessed October 2011.

13. Pfizer Inc., December 31, 2008 Form 10-K (filed February 27, 2009), http://www.pfizer.com/investors/sec_filings/sec_filings.jsp?month=2&day=27&year=2009&month1=2&day1=28&year1=2009&filing=10-K&x=43&y=4, accessed October 2011.

14. "Pfizer And Wyeth Become One: Working Together for a Healthier World," Pfizer press release, October 16, 2009, http://www.pfizer.com/news/press_releases/pfizer_press_release_archive.jsp#guid=20091016005880en&source=RSS_2009&page=4, accessed October 2011.

15. "Pfizer to Acquire Wyeth, Creating the World's Premier Biopharmaceutical Company," Pfizer press release, January 26, 2009, http://www.pfizer.com/news/press_releases/pfizer_press_release_archive.jsp#guid=20090126005624en&source=RSS_2009&page=13, accessed October 2011.

16. Ibid.

17. See, for instance, William Patalon III, "Pfizer-Wyeth Merger Underscores That Bigger Isn't Better," February 2, 2009, blog post on DailyMarkets.com, http://www.dailymarkets.com/stock/2009/02/02/pfizer-wyeth-merger-underscores-that-bigger-isn%E2%80%99t-better/, accessed October 2011, also Catherine Arnst, "A Pfizer-Wyeth Merger Isn't the Cure all," January 24, 2009, *Bloomberg Businessweek*, http://www.businessweek.com/technology/content/jan2009/tc20090123_516076.htm, accessed October 2011, also "Pfizer Eyes Wyeth. We Ask 'Why?'" January 29, 2009, blog post on Zacks.com, http://www.zacks.com/stock/news/16958/Pfizer+Eyes+Wyeth.+We+Ask+%26quot%3BWhy%3F%26quot%3B, accessed October 2011.

18. See P. Healy, K. Palepu, and R. Ruback, "Which Mergers Are Profitable—Strategic or Financial?" *Sloan Management Review* 38, no. 4 (Summer 1997): 45–58.

19. FactSet Mergerstat, LLC, *Mergerstat Review 2011* (Newark, NJ, 2011): 25, 194–195.

20. Thomson ONE accessed October 2011.

21. Ibid.

22. "Its Acquisition of Wyeth Appears to be Paying off for Pfizer," Associated Press, August 3, 2010, http://www.nytimes.com/2010/08/04/business/04pfizer.html, accessed October 2011.

23. Thomson ONE, accessed October 2011.

24. See S. Myers and N. Majluf, "Corporate Financing and Investment Decisions When Firms Have Information That Investors Do Not," *Journal of Financial Economics* (June 1984): 187–221.

25. For evidence see N. Travlos, "Corporate Takeover Bids, Methods of Payments, and Bidding Firms' Stock Returns," *Journal of Finance* 42 (1987): 943–963.

26. See S. Datar, R. Frankel, and M. Wolfson, "Earnouts: The Effects of Adverse Selection and Agency Costs on Acquisition Techniques," *Journal of Law, Economics, and Organization* 17 (2001): 201–238.

27. FactSet Mergerstat, LLC, *Mergerstat Review 2011* (Newark, NJ, 2011): 16.

28. At the same time, Fitch downgraded Pfizer from AA to AA-, Moody's Aa2 to A1.

29. H. Singh and F. Harianto, "Management–Board Relationships, Takeover Risk, and the Adoption of Golden Parachutes," *Academy of Management Journal* 32 (1989): 7–24, find that entrenched managers create golden parachute contracts to avoid the disciplinary effect of corporate takeovers. J. Machlin, H. Choe, and J. Miles, "The Effects of Golden Parachutes on Takeover Activity," *Journal of Law and Economics* 36 (1993): 861–876, find that golden parachutes increase the likelihood of an acquisition.

30. T. Catan and S. E. Ante, "U.S. Sues to Stop AT&T Deal," *Wall Street Journal*, September 1, 2011, http://online.wsj.com/article/SB10001424053111904716604576542373831069388.html, accessed October 2011.

31. Pfizer Inc., March 27, 2009, Form S4, http://www.pfizer.com/investors/sec_filings/sec_filings.jsp?month=3&day=26&year=2009&month1=3&day1=27&year1=2009&x=44&y=3, accessed October 2011.

32. A. Johnson, "'Company X': Who was Wyeth's Other Suitor?" post on "Health Blog," *Wall Street Journal*, http://blogs.wsj.com/health/2009/03/27/company-x-who-was-wyeths-other-suitor/, accessed October 2011.

Chapter 12

COMMUNICATION AND GOVERNANCE

Corporate governance has become an increasingly important issue in capital markets throughout the world during the turbulent first decade of the new century, with the financial market meltdowns in Asia and the United States in the early 2000s, the global financial crisis that began in 2008, and the European Debt crisis of 2010–11. These market collapses exposed problems of accounting misstatements and lack of corporate transparency, as well as governance problems and conflicts of interest among the intermediaries charged with monitoring management and corporate disclosures.

The breakdowns have increased the challenge for managers in communicating credibly with skeptical outside investors, making it more difficult for new (and in some cases even established) firms to raise capital. Financial reports, the traditional platform for management to communicate with investors, have increasingly come to be viewed with skepticism following a number of widely publicized audit failures; the demise of Enron, Worldcom, and Arthur Andersen in the United States; and lack of transparency of financial firms in their exposures to subprime mortgage instruments in the 2008 financial crisis.

The market crashes have also raised questions about improving the quality of governance by information and financial intermediaries, and have resulted in the passage of legislation attempting to address such deficits. The Sarbanes-Oxley Act in the United States (discussed in Chapter 1) attempts to increase accountability and financial competence for audit committees and external auditors, who are charged with reviewing the financial reporting and disclosure process, and accountability for the CEO and CFO, who are required to certify the validity of both financial statements and internal controls. The Dodd-Frank Act (also discussed in Chapter 1) attempts to protect investors by increasing the transparency and accountability of credit rating agencies and to improve the financial security of large financial institutions.

Throughout this book we have focused primarily on showing how financial statement data can be helpful for analysts and outside investors in making a variety of decisions. In this chapter we change our emphasis and focus primarily on management communication and the role of governance agents. Of course an understanding of the management communication process and corporate governance is also important for security analysts and investors. The approach taken here, however, is more germane to insiders since most of the types of analyses we discuss are not available to outsiders.

In the sections that follow we discuss how many of the financial analysis tools developed in Chapters 2 through 8 can be used by managers to develop a coherent disclosure strategy, and by corporate board members and external auditors to improve the quality of their work. The following types of questions are dealt with:

- Managers ask: Is our current communication policy effective in helping investors understand the firm's business strategy and expected future performance, thereby ensuring that our stock price is not seriously over- or undervalued?
- Audit committee members ask: What are the firm's key business risks? Are they reflected appropriately in the financial statements? How is management communicating on important risks that cannot be reflected in the financial statements? Is information on the firm's performance as presented to the board consistent with that provided to investors in the financial report and firm disclosures?
- External auditors ask: What are the firm's key business risks, and how are they reflected in the financial statements? Where should we focus our audit tests? Is our assessment of the firm's performance consistent with that of external investors and analysts? If not, are we overlooking something, or is management misrepresenting the firm's true performance in disclosures?

GOVERNANCE OVERVIEW

As we discuss throughout this book, outside investors require access to reliable information on firm performance, both to value their debt and equity claims and to monitor the performance of management. When investors agree to provide capital to the firm, they require that managers provide information on their company's performance and future plans.

However, left to their own devices, managers are likely to paint a rosy picture of the firm's performance in their disclosures. There are three reasons for manager optimism in reporting. First, most managers are genuinely positive about their firms' prospects, leading them to unwittingly emphasize the positive and downplay the negative.

Second, management optimism in reporting arises because firm disclosures play an important role in mitigating "agency" problems between managers and investors.[1] Investors use firm disclosures to judge whether managers have either run the firm in the investors' best interests or abused their authority and control over firm resources. Reporting consistently poor earnings increases the likelihood that top management will be replaced, either by the board of directors or by an acquirer who takes over the firm to improve its management.[2] Of course, managers are aware of this and have incentives to show positive performance.

Third, managers are also likely to make optimistic disclosures prior to issuing new equity. Recent evidence indicates that entrepreneurs tend to take their firms public after disclosure of strong reported, but frequently unsustainable, earnings performance. Also, seasoned equity offers (additional offers of equity made by an already public firm) typically follow strong, but again unsustainable, stock and earnings performance. The strong earnings performance prior to IPOs and seasoned offers appears to be at least partially due to earnings management.[3] Rational outside investors recognize management's incentives to manage earnings and inflate expectations prior to a new issue. They respond by discounting the stock, demanding a hefty new issue discount, and (in extreme cases) refusing to purchase the new stock. This raises the cost of capital and potentially leaves some of the best new ventures and projects unfunded.[4]

As discussed in Chapter 1, financial and information intermediaries help reduce agency and information problems faced by outside investors. These intermediaries

Communication and Governance

FIGURE 12-1   The Intermediation Chain Between Managers and Investors

Information Demand Side

Information Supply Side

Source: © Cengage Learning

evaluate the quality of management representation in the firm's disclosures, provide their own analysis of firms' (and managers') performance, and make investment recommendations and decisions on behalf of investors. As presented in Figure 12-1, these intermediaries include internal governance agents, assurance professionals, information analyzers, and professional investors. The importance of these intermediaries is underscored by the magnitude of the fees that they collectively receive from investors and entrepreneurs.

Internal governance agents, such as corporate boards, audit committees and internal auditors, are responsible for monitoring a firm's management. Their functions include reviewing business strategy, evaluating and rewarding top management, and assuring the flow of credible information to external parties. Assurance professionals, such as external auditors, enhance the credibility of financial information prepared by managers. Information analyzers, such as financial analysts and ratings agencies, are responsible for gathering and analyzing information to provide performance forecasts and investment recommendations to both professional and retail individual investors. Finally, professional investors (such as banks, investment advisors, private equity firms, hedge funds, mutual funds, insurance companies, and venture capital firms) make investment decisions on behalf of dispersed investors. They are therefore responsible for valuing and selecting investment opportunities in the economy.

In this framework, management, internal governance agents, and assurance professionals are charged with supplying information. The demand for information comes from individual and professional investors and information analyzers. Both the supply and demand sides are governed by a variety of regulatory institutions. In the United States, these include public regulators such as the Securities and Exchange Commission (SEC), the Public Company Accounting Oversight Board (PCAOB), and bank regulators, as well as private sector bodies such as the Financial Accounting Standards Board (FASB), the American Institute of Certified Public Accountants (AICPA), and stock exchanges. Other countries have similar types of institutions.

The level and quality of information and residual information and agency problems in capital markets are determined by the organizational design of these intermediaries and regulatory institutions. Key organizational design questions include: What are the optimal incentive schemes for rewarding top managers? What should be the composition and charter of corporate boards? Should auditors assure that financial reports comply with accounting standards or represent a firm's underlying economics? Should there be detailed accounting standards or a few broad accounting principles? What should be the organizational form and business scope of auditors and analysts? What incentive schemes should be used for professional investors to align their interests with individual investors?

A variety of economic and institutional factors are likely to influence the answers to these design questions. Examples include the ability to write and enforce optimal contracts, proprietary costs that might make disclosure costly for investors, and regulatory imperfections. The spectacular collapses of companies like Enron and Lehman Brothers, and their impact on equity and credit markets, suggest that these limitations can have a first-order effect on the functioning of capital markets.

While it is interesting to speculate on how to improve the functioning of capital markets through changes in organizational design, that issue goes beyond the scope of this chapter. Instead, we discuss how the financial analysis tools developed in Chapters 2 through 8 can be used to improve the performance of some of the information intermediaries who were widely criticized following revelations of financial reporting improprieties at companies such as Enron, WorldCom, Tyco, and Lehman Brothers.[5]

We have already discussed the application of financial analysis tools to equity and credit analysts and to professional investors in Chapters 9 through 11. In the remainder of this chapter, we discuss how these tools can be used by managers to develop a strategy for effective communication with investors, by members of boards of directors and audit committees in overseeing management and the audit process, and by audit professionals.

MANAGEMENT COMMUNICATION WITH INVESTORS

Some managers argue that communication problems are not worth worrying about. They maintain that as long as managers make investment and operating decisions that enhance shareholder value, investors will value their performance and the firm's stock accordingly. While this is true in the long run, since all information is eventually public, it may not hold in the short or even medium term. If investors do not have access to the same information as management, they will probably find it difficult to value new and innovative investments, or to assess intelligently the degree of risk inherent in a company's operations or positions. In an efficient capital market, they will not consistently over- or undervalue these new investments or risks, but their valuations can be noisy. This can make stock prices and a company's overall cost of capital relatively noisy, leading management at various times to consider their firms to be either seriously over- or undervalued.

Does it matter if a firm is over- or undervalued for a period? Most managers would prefer to not have their stock undervalued or lenders over-estimate their firms' risk, since it makes it more costly to raise new financing. They may also worry that undervaluation is likely to increase the chance of a takeover by a hostile acquirer, with an accompanying reduction in their job security. Also, the financial crisis of 2008 demonstrated the importance of investor confidence for the effective operation of financial markets and the risk of financial distress for firms that lose that confidence. Managers of firms that are overvalued may also be concerned about the market's assessment, since they are legally liable for failing to disclose information relevant to investors.[6] Therefore, they may not wish to see their stock seriously overvalued, even though overvaluation provides opportunities to issue new equity at favorable rates.

A Word of Caution

As noted above, it is natural that many managers believe that firms are undervalued by the capital market. This frequently occurs because it is difficult for managers to be objective about their company's future performance. After all, it is part of their job to sell the company to new employees, customers, suppliers, and investors. In addition, forecasting the firm's future performance objectively requires them to judge their own capabilities as managers. Thus, it is not surprising that many managers argue that investors are uninformed and that their firm is undervalued. Only some managers can back that up with solid evidence.

If management decides that the firm does face a genuine information problem, it can begin to consider whether and how this could be redressed. Is the problem potentially serious enough that it is worth doing something to alter investors' perceptions? Or is the problem likely to resolve itself within a short period? Does the firm have plans to raise new equity or to use equity to acquire another company? Is management's job security or the company's viability threatened? As we discuss below, management has a wide range of options in this situation.

Key Analysis Questions

We recommend that before jumping to the conclusion that their firms are undervalued, managers should analyze their firms' performance and compare their own forecasts of future performance with those of analysts, using the following approach:

- *Is there a significant difference between internal management forecasts of future earnings and cash flows and those of outside analysts?*
- *Do any differences between managers' and analysts' forecasts arise because of different expectations about economy-wide performance?* Managers may understand their own businesses better than analysts, but they may not be any better at forecasting macroeconomic conditions.
- *Can managers identify any factors that might explain a difference between analysts' and managers' forecasts of future performance?* For example, are analysts unaware of positive new R&D results, do they have different information about customer responses to new products and marketing campaigns, etc.? These types of differences could indicate that the firm faces an information problem.

Example: Communication Issues for Jefferies Group, Inc.

In 2011, Jefferies Group, Inc. was a mid-sized global securities and investment banking firm that had been in business for almost 50 years. The firm's strong balance sheet had enabled it to successfully weather the 2008 financial crisis without government support, and provided it with the financial flexibility to expand its global operations aggressively following the crisis. At its fiscal 2010 year end on November 30, 2010, Jefferies had a book value per share of $16.37, a price-to-book value of 1.7, a price to earnings multiple of 20.3, and an equity beta of 1.7.

However, during 2011, the Jefferies stock price declined precipitously from $26.63 to a low of $11.60 in early October, recovering somewhat to $14.72 as of October 28. This drop was attributed to concerns about the firm's exposure to the growing European debt crisis, a concern that was magnified by the firm's aggressive expansion in Europe since 2008. On October 31, the stock's recovery was abruptly halted when MF Global, a commodities broker-dealer that dealt with Jefferies, filed for bankruptcy protection, citing losses resulting from European sovereign debt exposure. Over the next few days Jefferies stock fell almost 20 percent as investors tried to assess potential indirect and direct exposure to MF Global and the sovereign debt crisis.

The firm's management issued a press release on October 31 explaining that it had only minimal exposure to MF Global and to European sovereign debt. But this failed to stem the market's concerns. As one blogger at the *Wall Street Journal* explained, "Yes, Jefferies says it has no 'meaningful exposure' to the government debt of the PIIGS. Trouble is, since the financial crisis, investors shoot first and ask questions later."

On November 3, ratings agency Egan-Jones downgraded Jefferies debt, citing concern over the company's potential exposure to European sovereign debt. Jefferies was quick to respond, issuing two increasingly detailed press releases on the same day disclosing its limited exposure. The stock remained stable for the next few days, but then continued its downward trajectory, trading as low as $9.50 on November 17.

The sharp decline in its price raises questions about the valuation of Jefferies stock. At the November 17, 2011, close, the price-to-book ratio was well below 1, and the price-to-earnings multiple was 6.9. The market, therefore, expected that the company would generate a return on equity somewhat lower than its cost of capital—a dramatic turnaround from the market's perception at the beginning of 2011. Jefferies management expressed surprise and frustration at the sharp drop in price and argued that the market was unjustly punishing the firm for exposure that it did not have. However, before reaching this conclusion, a number of questions need to be answered:

- Was the firm previously overvalued? If so, what forces were behind the market's high valuation of the company? Had management been painting too rosy a picture for the company's future in its meetings with analysts?
- What were the financial implications of the events that precipitated the company's drop in stock value? As noted above, the primary question for analysts was the extent of the firm's exposure—either directly or indirectly, to the European debt crisis. Management needed to make sure it had a deep understanding of both the macro- and micro-economic aspects of the issue to assess the implications for the company's future performance.
- If management believed that the firm was actually being undervalued, what options were available to correct the market's view of the company?

COMMUNICATION THROUGH FINANCIAL REPORTING

Financial reports are the most popular format for management communication. Below we discuss the role of financial reporting as a means of investor communication, the institutions that make accounting information credible, and the situations in which the reporting is likely to be ineffective.

Accounting as a Means of Management Communication

As we discussed in Chapters 3 and 4, financial reports are an important medium for management communication with external investors. Reports provide investors with an explanation of how their money has been invested, a summary of the performance of those investments, and a discussion of how current performance fits within the firm's overall philosophy and strategy.

Accounting reports not only provide a record of past transactions but also reflect management estimates and forecasts of the future. For example, they include estimates of bad debts, forecasts of the lives of tangible assets, and implicit forecasts that outlays will generate future cash flow benefits that exceed their cost. Since management is likely to be in a position to make forecasts of these future events that are more accurate than those of external investors, financial reports are a potentially useful way of communicating with investors. However, as discussed, investors are also likely to be skeptical of reports prepared by management. The Sarbanes-Oxley Act requires the CEO and CFO to certify that the financials fairly represent the financial performance of the company and that internal controls are adequate to support those financial statements. This requirement increases the accountability of senior management and mitigates some of the investors' skepticism.

Factors That Increase the Credibility of Accounting Communication

A number of mechanisms mitigate conflicts of interest in financial reporting and increase the credibility of accounting information that is communicated to investors. These include accounting standards, auditing, monitoring of management by financial analysts and ratings agencies, and management reputation.

Accounting Standards and Auditing

Accounting standards, such as those promulgated by the FASB and the SEC in the United States and the IASB and country-specific standard setters and regulators globally, provide guidelines for managers on how to make accounting decisions and furnish outside investors with a way of interpreting these decisions. Uniform accounting standards attempt to reduce managers' ability to record similar economic transactions in different ways, either over time or across firms. Compliance with these standards is enforced by external auditors who attempt to ensure that managers' estimates are reasonable. Auditors, therefore, reduce the likelihood of earnings management.

Monitoring by Financial Analysts and Ratings Agencies

Information intermediaries such as financial analysts and ratings agencies also limit management's ability to manage earnings and understate risk. Financial analysts and ratings agencies specialize in developing firm- and industry-specific knowledge, enabling them to assess the quality of a firm's reported numbers and to make any necessary adjustments. These information analyzers evaluate the appropriateness of management's forecasts implicit in accounting method choices and reported accruals. This requires a thorough understanding of the firm's business and the relevant accounting rules used in the preparation of its financial reports. Superior analysts adjust reported accrual numbers, if necessary, to reflect economic reality, perhaps by using the cash flow statement and the footnote disclosures.

Analysts' business and technical expertise as well as their legal liability and incentives differ from those of auditors. Consequently, analyst reports can provide information to investors on whether the firm's accounting decisions are appropriate or whether managers are overstating the firm's economic performance (or understating its risk) to protect their jobs.[7]

Management Reputation

A third factor that can counteract external investors' natural skepticism about financial reporting is management reputation. Managers that expect to have an ongoing relation with external investors and financial intermediaries may be able to build a track record for unbiased financial reporting. By making accounting estimates and judgments that are supported by subsequent performance, managers can demonstrate their competence and reliability to investors and analysts. As a result, managers' future judgments and accounting estimates are more likely to be viewed as credible.

Limitations of Financial Reporting for Investor Communication

While accounting standards, auditing, monitoring of management by financial analysts, and management concerns about its reputation increase the credibility and informativeness of financial reports, these mechanisms are far from perfect. Consequently, there are times when financial reporting breaks down as a means for management to communicate with external investors. These breakdowns can arise when (1) there are no accounting rules to guide practice or the existing rules do not distinguish between poor and successful performers, (2) auditors and analysts do not have the expertise to judge new products or business opportunities, or (3) management faces credibility problems.

Accounting Rule Limitations

Despite the rapid increase in new accounting standards, accounting rules frequently do not distinguish between good and poor performers. For example, current accounting rules do not permit managers to show on their balance sheets in a timely fashion the benefits of investments in quality improvements, human resource development programs, research and development (with the exception of software development costs), and customer service.

Some of the problems with accounting standards arise because it takes time for standard setters to develop appropriate standards for many new types of economic transactions. Other difficulties arise because standards are the result of compromises between different interest groups (e.g., auditors, investors, corporate managers, and regulators).

Auditor, Analyst, and other Intermediary Limitations

While auditors and analysts may have a good understanding of a firm's business, they do not have the same depth of information as managers. The discrepancy between managers' and auditors'or analysts' business assessments is likely to be most severe for firms with distinctive business strategies, or firms that operate in emerging industries or in industries with constantly evolving, very complex products (such as financial services). In addition, auditors' decisions in these circumstances are likely to be dominated by concerns about legal liability, hampering management's ability to use financial reports to communicate effectively with investors.

Finally, conflicts of interest faced by auditors, analysts, and other intermediaries make their analysis imperfect. Conflicts can potentially induce auditors to side with management to retain the firm as an audit client. They can also arise for analysts who provide favorable ratings and research on companies to increase their firm's investment banking business and trading volume among less-informed investors, and for credit ratings agencies who earn their revenue from the firms they are rating. Regulations that increase oversight of audit firms by the Public Company Accounting Oversight Board and limit the impact of investment banking on financial analysts' incentives, were put in place as part of Sarbanes-Oxley and the Global Settlement to reduce auditor and analyst conflicts of interest, while the Dodd-Frank Act sought, among other things, to increase the transparency and accountability of ratings agencies.

Management Credibility Problems

There is limited evidence on when management is likely to face credibility problems with investors. However, managers of new firms, firms with volatile earnings, firms in financial distress, and firms with poor track records in communicating with investors should expect to find it difficult to be seen as credible reporters.

If management has a credibility problem, financial reports are likely to be viewed with considerable skepticism. Investors will view financial reporting estimates that increase income as evidence that management is padding earnings. This makes it very difficult for management to use financial reports to communicate positive news about current or future performance.

Example: Accounting Communication for Jefferies

Jefferies exposure to European sovereign debt is reported in the company's August 31, 2011, balance sheet. The asset, "Government, Federal Agency, and Other Sovereign Obligations," which amounts to $5.5 billion, aggregates European sovereign debt with U.S. and other debt. Footnote disclosure reveals that "Sovereign obligations" were $2.7 billion and were offset by a $2.5 billion liability "Financial instruments sold, not yet purchased," suggesting that the firm was effectively hedged in the event of European sovereign debt defaults. In addition, management explained that increases in sovereign debt inventory during 2010 and 2011 arose from the firm being designated as a Primary Dealer in several European jurisdictions. These exposures "are substantially comprised of the most liquid securities in the asset class with a significant portion in holdings of securities of G-7 countries. Our market risk exposure to Portugal, Italy, Ireland, Greece, and Spain was modest at August 31, 2011." However, management may have raised questions about the firm's exposure when in another part of the same report it warned that: "Europe's debt crisis could have a material adverse effect on our business, financial condition, and liquidity."

Although the third quarter financial statements were unaudited, there is reason to expect that Jefferies management would have some credibility with analysts. The company's CEO, Richard Handler, who had led the company since 2000, had successfully helped navigate the firm through the 2008 financial crisis, and had a reputation among analysts for a deep understanding of the firm's businesses, and for eschewing the opulent banking lifestyle common among leading investment banks.

Yet the ratings agency, Egan-Jones, raised questions about the credibility of the firm's hedge and financial reporting. In explaining the debt downgrade, Egan-Jones principal Shaun Egan commented: "They claim it's beautifully hedged. Our view is that we're skeptical until we see complete proof of that. In the past, the hedges haven't been as perfect as originally presented. We don't know how those shorts are set up and whether they completely offset their $2.7 billion [exposure]."

Key Analysis Questions

For management interested in understanding how effectively the firm's financial reports help it communicate with outside investors, the following questions are likely to provide a useful starting point:

- *What are the primary business risks that have to be managed effectively? What processes and controls are in place to manage the business risks? How are these risks reflected in the financial statements?* For example, credit risks are reflected in the bad debt allowance, and product quality risks are reflected in allowances for product returns and the method of revenue recognition. For these types of risks, what message is the firm sending on the management of these risks through its estimates or choices of accounting methods? Has the firm been unable to deliver on the forecasts underlying these choices? Alternatively, does the market seem to be ignoring the message underlying the firm's financial reporting choices, indicating a lack of credibility?

- *How does the firm communicate about important risks that cannot be reflected in accounting estimates or methods?* For example, a company such as Jefferies has direct and indirect exposure to major external market shocks such as the European debt crisis which is difficult to fully reflect in its financial statements; hence, investors and information intermediaries may still have questions about this business issue.

COMMUNICATION THROUGH FINANCIAL POLICIES

Managers can also use financing policies to communicate effectively with external investors. One important difference between this type of communication and additional disclosure is that the firm does not provide potentially proprietary information to competitors. Financial policies that are useful in this respect include dividend payouts, stock repurchases, financing choices, and hedging strategies.

Dividend Payout Policies

A firm's dividend payout decisions can provide information to investors on managers' assessments of the firm's future prospects. Dividend payout, defined as cash dividends as a percentage of income available to common shareholders, reflects the extent to which a company pays out profits or retains them for reinvestment. Because paying dividends reduces financial slack and is thus costly, a firm's dividend policy can help management communicate effectively with external investors. Investors recognize that managers will only increase their firm's dividend rate if they anticipate that the payout will not have a serious effect on the firm's future financing options. Thus, the decision to increase dividends can help investors appreciate management's optimism about the firm's future performance and ability to finance growth. This arises because dividend payouts tend to be sticky, as managers are reluctant to cut dividend payouts. Managers will only increase dividends when they are confident that they will be able to sustain the increased payout rate in future years. Consequently, investors interpret dividend increases as signals of managers' confidence in the quality of current and future earnings.[8]

As a result, managers in high-growth firms tend to set low dividend payout policies and retain their internally generated funds for reinvestment to minimize any costs from capital market constraints on financing growth options. On the other hand, firms with high and stable operating cash flows and few investment opportunities have high dividend payouts to reduce managers' incentives to reinvest free cash flows in unprofitable ventures.

Stock Repurchases

In some countries, such as the United States and the United Kingdom, managers can use stock repurchases to communicate with external investors. Under a stock repurchase, the firm buys back its own stock, either through a purchase on the open market, through a tender offer, or through a negotiated purchase with a large stockholder. Of course a stock repurchase, particularly a tender offer repurchase, is an expensive way for management to communicate with outside investors that they believe the firm is undervalued. Firms typically pay a hefty premium to acquire their shares in tender offer repurchases, potentially diluting the value of the shares that are not tendered or not accepted for tender. In addition, the fees to investment banks and lawyers, and for share solicitation, are not trivial. Given these costs, it is not surprising that research findings indicate that stock repurchases are effective signals to investors about the level and risk of future earnings performance.[9] Research findings also suggest that firms that use stock repurchases to communicate with investors have accounting assets that are less reflective of firm value and have high general information asymmetry.[10]

Financing Choices

Firms that have problems communicating with external investors may be able to use financing choices to reduce them. For example, a firm that is unwilling to provide proprietary information to help dispersed public investors value it appropriately may be willing to provide such information to a knowledgeable private investor, which can become a large stockholder/creditor, or to a bank that agrees to provide the company with a significant new loan. A firm with credibility problems in financial reporting can also sell stock or issue debt to an informed private investor such as a large customer who has superior information about the quality of its product or service. For example, Warren Buffett's investment of $5 billion in Bank of America in August of 2011 was widely viewed as enhancing the bank's credibility. Investors responded accordingly, increasing the stock by 20 percent in the three trading days following the announcement.

Such changes in financing and ownership can mitigate communication problems in two ways. First, the terms of the new financing arrangement and the credibility of the new lender or stockholder can provide investors with information to reassess the value of the firm. Second, the accompanying increased concentration of ownership and the role of large block holders in corporate governance can have a positive effect on valuation. If investors are concerned about management's incentives to increase shareholder value, the presence of a new block shareholder or significant creditor on the board can be reassuring. This type of monitoring arises in leveraged buyouts, startups backed by venture capital firms, and firms with equity partnership investments. In Japanese and German corporations, it may also arise because large banks own both debt and equity and have close working relationships with firms' managers.

Of course, in the extreme, management can decide that the best option for a firm is to no longer operate as a public company. This can be accomplished by a management buyout, where a buyout group (including management) leverages its own investment (using bank or public debt finance), buys the firm, and takes it private. The buyout group hopes to run the firm for several years and then take the company public again, hopefully with a track record of improved performance that enables investors to value the firm more effectively.

Hedging

An important source of mispricing arises if investors are unable to distinguish between unexpected changes in reported earnings due to management performance and transitory shocks that are beyond managers' control (e.g., foreign currency translation gains and losses). Managers can counteract these effects by hedging such "accounting" risks. Even though hedging may be costly, it is valuable if it reduces information problems that potentially lead to misvaluation.

Example: Financial Policies at Jefferies

Jefferies took several financial policy actions in 2011 in efforts to communicate its financial strength to the market. On September 20, 2011, the firm announced that its Board of Directors had approved a share repurchase program authorizing the repurchase of up to 20 million shares—or a little over 10 percent—of its common stock, and followed through with purchases of about 5 million shares of stock under the program in the following two months. In November the firm reported that it had also repurchased $50 million of its 2012 bonds on the open market. On November 3–4—coinciding with the company's debt downgrade by Egan-Jones—the company's largest shareholder, Leucadia National (which held more than 25 percent of the company stock at the time), bought an additional 1.5 million shares of common stock. Finally, company insiders purchased significant shares in 2011, signaling to investors their faith in the company. Board members Ian Cumming and Joseph Steinberg, co-founders of Leucadia National, purchased a total of 1.5 million shares on November 3 and 4. On November 15, the Chairman and CEO Richard Handler (who owned more than 6 percent of company shares), purchased more than 80,000 of the bank's shares. Overall in 2011, insider buys outweighed sales by a ratio of 57 to 3.

These combined actions, however, did not arrest the stock's slide, as worries about the firm's exposure to the European debt crisis continued to build. On the day before the share buyback announcement (which was announced in conjunction with the company reporting a 53 percent increase in third quarter profits over the previous year), the shares closed at $14.12. By November 1, the day after the MF Global bankruptcy was announced, the shares had fallen to $12.01. The slide continued through the month of November, reaching a low of $10.20 on November 21, a drop of over 60 percent year to date.

Key Analysis Questions

For management considering whether to use financing policies to communicate more effectively with investors, the following questions are likely to provide a useful starting point for analysis:

- *Have other, potentially less costly actions, such as expanded disclosure or accounting communication, been considered? If not, would these alternatives provide a lower-cost means of communication?* Alternatively, if management is concerned about providing proprietary information to competitors, or has low credibility, these options may not be effective.
- *Does the firm have sufficient free cash flow to be able to implement a share repurchase program or to increase dividends?* If the firm has excess cash available today but expects to be constrained in the future, a stock repurchase may be more effective. Alternatively, if management expects to have some excess cash available each year, a dividend increase may be in order.
- *Is the firm cash constrained and unable to increase disclosure for proprietary reasons?* If so, management may want to consider changing the mix of owners as a way of indicating to investors that another informed outsider is bullish on the company. Of course, another possibility is for management itself to increase its stake in the company.

ALTERNATE FORMS OF INVESTOR COMMUNICATION

Given the limitations of accounting standards, auditing, and monitoring by financial analysts, as well as the reporting credibility problems faced by management, firms that wish to communicate effectively with external investors are often forced to use alternative methods. We discuss two additional ways that managers can communicate with external investors and analysts below.

Analyst Meetings

One popular way for managers to help mitigate communication problems is to meet regularly with financial analysts that follow the firm. At these meetings, management will field questions about the firm's current financial performance and discuss its future business plans. In addition to holding analyst meetings, many firms appoint a director of public relations, who provides further regular contact with analysts seeking more information on the firm.

In the last twenty years, conference calls have become a popular forum for management to communicate with financial analysts. Research finds that firms are more likely to host calls if they are in industries where financial statement data fail to capture key business fundamentals on a timely basis.[11] In addition, conference calls themselves appear to provide new information to analysts about a firm's performance and future prospects.[12] Smaller and less heavily traded firms in particular benefit from initiating investor conference calls.[13]

In the 1990s, firms typically had closed conference calls with key analysts and institutional investors. However, under Regulation Fair Disclosure (or Reg FD), implemented in October 2000, the SEC encouraged firms to open these meetings to the public. Reg FD required firms that provided material nonpublic information to security analysts or professional investors to simultaneously (or promptly thereafter) disclose the information to the public. While Reg FD has reduced the information that managers disclose in private meetings, research also shows that the regulation has enhanced the conference call's ability to improve analyst forecast accuracy and consensus by eliminating selective disclosure.[14]

Voluntary Disclosure

Another way for managers to improve the credibility of their financial reporting is through voluntary disclosure. Accounting rules usually prescribe minimum disclosure requirements, but they do not restrict managers from voluntarily providing additional information. These could include an articulation of the company's long-term strategy, specification of nonfinancial leading indicators that are useful in judging the effectiveness of the strategy implementation, explanation of the relation between the leading indicators and future profits, forecasts of future performance, additional financial or nonfinancial information to rebut an incorrect view in the market, or information on corporate sustainability initiatives designed to create long-term, sustainable value, but which is not necessarily reflected in the current stock price. Voluntary disclosures can be reported in the firm's annual report, in brochures created to describe the firm to investors, in management meetings with analysts, or in investor relations' responses to information requests.[15]

One constraint on expanded disclosure is the competitive dynamics in product markets. Disclosure of proprietary information on strategies and their expected economic consequences may hurt the firm's competitive position. Managers then face a trade-off between providing information that is useful to investors in assessing the firm's economic performance and withholding information to maximize the firm's product market advantage.

A second constraint in providing voluntary disclosure is management's legal liability. Forecasts and voluntary disclosures can potentially be used by dissatisfied shareholders to bring civil action against management for providing misleading information. This seems ironic, since voluntary disclosures should provide investors with additional information. Unfortunately, it can be difficult for courts to decide whether managers' disclosures were good faith estimates of uncertain future events that later did not materialize, or whether management manipulated the market. Consequently many corporate legal departments recommend against management providing much voluntary disclosure. One aspect of voluntary disclosure, earnings guidance, has been particularly controversial. There is growing evidence that the guidance provided by management plays an important role in leading analysts' expectations toward achievable earnings targets, and that management guidance is more likely when analysts' initial forecasts are overly optimistic.[16]

Finally, management credibility can limit a firm's incentives to provide voluntary disclosures. If management faces a credibility problem in financial reporting, any voluntary disclosure it provides is also likely to be viewed skeptically. In particular, investors may be concerned about what management is not telling them, particularly since such disclosures are not audited.

Example: Other Forms of Communication at Jefferies

Beginning on the day of the MF Global bankruptcy, and continuing with its debt rating downgrade, the decline in its share price, and ongoing questions about the firm's viability, the board and management of Jefferies provided extensive voluntary disclosures in an effort to regain investor confidence.

On October 31, 2011, within hours of the MF Global bankruptcy news breaking, Jefferies sought to quell rumors that it had significant exposure to MF Global, issuing a press release that "its exposure to MF Global Holdings Ltd. Debt securities … is less than $9 million in marked-to-market positions." The next day, the firm issued another press release, this time to dispel rumors about its exposure to European debt. The release reaffirmed statements in its SEC filings that it "currently has no meaningful exposure to the sovereign debt of the nations of Portugal, Italy, Ireland, Greece, and Spain" and sought to reassure investors that it had no "repo-to-maturity or related off-balance-sheet derivative activity" that could generate losses, such as those incurred by several leading financial institutions during the 2008 financial crisis.

In response to the November 3 ratings downgrade, which cited concerns over its potential exposure to European sovereign debt, Jefferies management issued a series of additional press releases providing material new information intended to disprove the assumptions behind the downgrade. The first such report disclosed the firm's net exposure to European sovereign debt by country. It was followed by a second release later the same day, informing investors that it held, "no credit-default swaps hedging its sovereign debt positions." These actions appeared to slow the stock price drop—the shares closed down only about 2 percent for the trading day after being down as much as 20 percent earlier in the session. One day later, in response to further inquiries, the company disclosed details of all short and long positions by country. In explaining the firm's actions, Chairman and CEO Richard Handler noted that "these are fragile times in the financial market and we decided the only way to conclusively dispel rumors, misinformation and misplaced concerns is with unprecedented transparency about internal information that is rarely, if ever, publicly disclosed."

The firm's efforts to reassure the markets continued on November 7 with a press release announcing that it had reduced its gross holding of European sovereign debt by 50 percent, with "no meaningful profit or loss on today's trading activity or our remaining positions." This news prompted the head of one research firm to observe that the company "has certainly sent a message to the market that they are aggressively attending to this criticism, whether it's founded or not."

These efforts were of limited help in restoring confidence in the company. The stock continued to fall, closing at $10.20 on November 21, 2011. On that day, Handler took the offensive, posting a six-page letter on the Jefferies website to rebut what he saw as continued false impressions about the company. Handler argued that:

> Throughout the month of November, Jefferies has been barraged by a group of people maliciously spreading rumors, half-truths and outright lies through every means possible, including calling analysts and security holders, as well as using the mass media in an effort to amplify and legitimize their efforts. Last week, a representative of a hedge fund, who we understand has been spreading false rumors about Jefferies, sent us a letter with a series of questions that for the most part show what we must presume is an intentional misreading of our public filings to try to support these rumors. All these folks seem to be trying to take advantage of the MF Global bankruptcy and the volatile market environment with a view to harming Jefferies and all of us, presumably for personal gain. With the facts and truth on our side, we have responded to all this directly and completely. Fortunately, those who take the time to understand and truly analyze the facts are reaching the right conclusion. While it may be necessary for us to continue to respond to these ill-conceived attacks, we fortunately can do so on a firm foundation and with confidence in our funding and business model.

Handler pointed out that the firm's net exposure was an insignificant $134 million, or 3.8 percent of equity.

Handler's strong response and the coverage it received proved to be a turning point for the stock, which rose from $10.20 on the date of the letter to more than $13.00 in early December. In late December, Jefferies announced strong fourth quarter earnings, providing further support for management's position, and the stock jumped 23 percent to close at $14.50 on December 20.

The Role of the Auditor

In the United States the auditor is responsible for providing investors with assurance that the financial statements are prepared in accordance with U.S. Generally Accepted Accounting Principles, or U.S. GAAP, and that the company maintains effective internal control over its financial reporting. This requires the auditor to evaluate whether transactions are recorded in a way that is consistent with the rules produced by regulators (including the FASB, PCAOB, and SEC), whether management estimates reflected in the financial statements are reasonable, and whether the company maintained effective internal financial control systems. The results of the audit are disclosed in the audit report, which is part of the financial statements. The auditor issues an unqualified report if (a) the firm's financial statements conform to U.S. GAAP, (b) the accounting methods are applied consistently throughout the prior three years, (c) the internal financial reporting controls are adequate as of the end of the audit period, and (d) there is no substantial doubt about the firm's ability to survive. If the financials do not conform to U.S. GAAP, the auditor is required to issue a qualified or an adverse report that provides information to investors on the discrepancies. If the auditor is uncertain about whether the firm can survive during the coming year, a going concern report that discusses the firm's survival risks is issued.

In contrast, in the United Kingdom and countries that have adopted the U.K. system, such as Australia, New Zealand, Singapore, Hong Kong, and India, auditors undertake a broader review than their U.S. counterparts. Their audits are required to not only assess whether the financial statements are prepared in accordance with accounting standards, but also to judge whether they present a "true and fair view" of the client's underlying economic performance. This additional assurance requires more judgment on the part of the auditor and increases the value of the audit to outside investors.

The essential procedures involved in a typical audit include (1) understanding the client's business and industry to identify key risks for the audit, (2) evaluating the firm's internal control system to assess whether it is likely to produce reliable information, (3) performing preliminary analytic procedures to identify unusual events and possible errors, and (4) collecting specific evidence on controls, transactions, and account balance details to form the basis for the auditor's opinion. In most cases client management is willing to respond to issues raised by the audit to ensure that the company receives an unqualified audit opinion. Once the audit is completed, the auditor presents a summary of audit scope and findings to the Audit Committee of the firm's board of directors.

It is worth noting that in both the U.S. and U.K. systems (and for that matter elsewhere), the audit is not intended to detect fraud. Of course in some cases it may do so, but that is not its purpose. The detection of fraud is the domain of the internal audit department of the firm itself.

Role of Financial Analysis Tools in Auditing

How can the financial analysis tools discussed in this book be used by audit professionals? The relevance to the audit of the four steps in financial analysis—strategy analysis, accounting analysis, financial analysis, and prospective analysis—is discussed briefly next.

Strategy Analysis Strategy analysis is critical to the first stage of the audit, understanding the client's business and industry. It is important that the auditor develop the expertise to be able to identify the chief risks facing its client. Given the sheer volume of activity, it is impossible to review all the transactions of the firm during the audit. Time and attention should be focused on the areas that investors need in order to evaluate the firm's value proposition and how well it is managing key success factors. These are also likely to be the areas worth further testing and analysis by the auditor, to assess their impact on the financial statements.

Accounting Analysis For the auditor, accounting analysis involves two steps. First, the auditor must understand how the key success factors and risks are reflected in the financial statements. The second step in accounting analysis is for the auditor to evaluate management judgment reflected in the critical financial statements items.

Financial Analysis Financial ratios help auditors judge whether there are any unusual performance changes for their client, either relative to past performance or relative to their competitors. Any such changes merit further investigation to ensure that the reasons for the change can be fully explained and to determine what additional tests are required to satisfy the auditor that the reported changes in performance are justified. Careful ratio analysis can also reveal whether clients are facing business problems that might induce management to conceal losses or keep significant obligations off the balance sheet. Such information should alert auditors that extra care and additional detailed tests are likely to be required to reach a conclusion on the client's financial statements.

Prospective Analysis Auditors use prospective analysis to assess whether estimates and forecasts made by management are consistent with the firm's economic position. In addition, the market's perception of a client's future performance provides a useful benchmark for affirming or questioning the auditor's assessment of the client's prospects. If the auditor concludes that the market is either overly optimistic or pessimistic about a client, he or she can determine whether additional disclosure will help investors develop a more realistic view of the company's prospects.

Key Analysis Questions

The following questions are likely to provide a useful starting point for auditors in their analysis of a client's financial statements:

- *What are the chief business risks facing the firm?* How well are these risks managed?
- *What are the accounting policies and estimates that reflect the firm's principal risks?* What tests and evidence are required to evaluate management judgment that is reflected in these accounting decisions?
- *Do the critical ratios indicate any unusual changes in client performance?* What tests and evidence are required to understand the causes of such changes?
- *Has firm performance deteriorated, creating pressure on management to manage earnings or record off-balance-sheet transactions?* If so, what additional tests and evidence are required to provide assurance that the financial statements are consistent with GAAP?
- *How is the market assessing the client's prospects?* If different from the auditor, what is the reason for the difference? If the market is overly optimistic or pessimistic, are there implications for client disclosure or accounting estimates?

Example: Auditing Jefferies

The European crisis raises several questions for the firm's auditors. The company's management of its net market exposure to increasingly risky debt instruments and its continued ability to access funds are critical success factors. The stock price volatility appears to be largely driven by changing perceptions of this risk, potentially affecting the fair values of assets and liabilities reported on the balance sheet, and write-downs in the income statement. These should be a principal focus of the audit.

Questions for the auditor include the following:

- Has the company properly recorded and provided sufficient explanation of positions held?
- Has the company appropriately disclosed the use of off-balance sheet instruments, including disclosure of recourse provisions and other critical details?
- Why has the market reacted so negatively to Jefferies over the past year? Is there something that the market recognizes that Jefferies management does not? What information is available about the specific hedging strategies that Jefferies claims is minimizing its market exposure?
- Is the firm's classification of assets into Level 1, Level 2, and Level 3 appropriate? What information is there about the models used to value Level 3 assets?

- If the firm's positions appear to be reasonable and well established, what additional information can the firm provide to investors to address their concerns? Will this information need to be audited?

THE ROLE OF THE AUDIT COMMITTEE IN THE UNITED STATES

Audit committees are responsible for overseeing the work of the auditor, for ensuring that the financial statements are properly prepared, and for reviewing the internal controls at the company. Audit committees, which are mandated by many stock exchanges and by the SEC, typically comprise three to four outside directors who meet regularly before or after the full board meetings.

In the last 15 years, requirements for audit committees have been expanded and formalized. In December 1999, the SEC, the national stock exchange(s), and the Auditing Standards Board issued new audit committee rules based largely on recommendations of the Blue Ribbon Committee (BRC) on Improving the Effectiveness of Corporate Audit Committees. The new rules defined best practices for judging audit committee members' independence and qualifications.

Following the collapse of Enron, additional audit committee requirements were created under the Sarbanes-Oxley Act. The Act requires that audit committees take formal responsibility for appointing, overseeing, and negotiating fees with external auditors. Audit committee members are required to be independent directors with no consulting or other potentially compromising relation to management. It is recommended that at least one member of the committee have financial expertise, such as being a CFO, CEO, or retired audit partner.

The audit committee is expected to be independent of management and to take an active role in reviewing the propriety of the firm's financial statements. Committee members are expected to question management and the auditors about the quality of the firm's financial reporting, the scope and findings of the external audit, and the quality of internal controls.

In reality, however, the audit committee has to rely extensively on information from management as well as internal and external auditors. Given the ground that it has to cover, its limited available time, and the technical nature of accounting standards, audit committees are not in a position to catch management fraud or auditors' failures on a timely basis.

How then can the audit committee add value?[17] We believe that many of the financial analysis tools discussed in this book can provide a useful way for audit committees to approach their tasks. Many of the applications of the financial analysis steps discussed for auditors also apply for audit committees.

In its scrutiny of financial statements, the committee should use the 80–20 rule, devoting most of its time to assessing the effectiveness of those *few* policies and decisions that have the *most* impact on investors' perceptions of the company's critical performance indicators. This should not require any additional work for committee members, since they should already have a good understanding of the firm's key success factors and risks from discussions of the full board.

Audit committee members should also have sufficient financial background to identify where in the financial statements the important risks are reflected. Their discussions with management and external auditors should focus on these risks. How well are they being managed? How are the auditors planning their work to focus on these areas? What evidence have they gathered to judge the adequacy of the financial statement estimates?

The audit committee also receives regular reviews of company performance from management as part of their board duties. Committee members should be especially proactive in requesting information that helps them evaluate how the firm is managing its key risks, since this information can also help them judge the quality of the financial statements.

Audit committee members need to ask: Is information on company performance we are receiving in our regular board meetings consistent with the picture portrayed in the financial statements? If not, what is missing? Are additional disclosures required to ensure that investors are well informed about the firm's operations and performance?

Finally, audit committees need to focus on capital market expectations, not just statutory financial reports. In today's capital markets, the game begins when companies set expectations via analyst meetings, press releases, and other forms of investor communications. Indeed, the pressure to manage earnings is often a direct consequence of Wall Street's unrealistic expectations, either deliberately created by management or sustained by their inaction. Thus, it is also important for audit committees to oversee the firm's investor relations strategy and ensure that management sets realistic expectations for both the short and long term.

Key Analysis Questions

The following questions are likely to provide a useful starting point for audit committees in their discussions with management and auditors about the firm's financial statements:

- *How are the critical business risks facing the firm being managed?*
- *How are these risks reflected by accounting policies and estimates in the financial statements?* What was the basis for the external auditor's assessment of these items?
- *Is information on the critical value drivers and firm performance presented to the full board consistent with the picture of the firm reflected in the financial statements and MD&A?*
- *What expectations is management creating in the capital market?* Are these likely to cause undue pressure to manage earnings?

SUMMARY

This chapter discussed how many of the financial analysis tools developed in Chapters 2 through 8 can be used by managers to develop a coherent disclosure strategy, and by corporate board members and external auditors to improve the quality of their work.

By communicating effectively with investors, management can potentially reduce information problems for outside investors, lowering the likelihood that the stock will be mispriced or unnecessarily volatile, or that the market will lose confidence in the company and limit its access to capital entirely. This can be important for firms that wish to raise new capital or avoid takeovers, or whose management is concerned that its true job performance is not reflected in the firm's stock price. Finally, as we saw in the 2008 financial crisis and in the Jefferies example more recently, financial markets are fragile and can easily lose confidence in a company and its management. As a result, the quality and effectiveness of management communication can sometimes have a significant impact on a company's financial viability.

The typical way for firms to communicate with investors is through financial reporting. Accounting standards and auditing make the reporting process a way for managers to not only provide information about the firm's current performance but also indicate, through accounting estimates, where they believe the firm is headed in the future.

However, financial reports are not always able to convey the type of forward-looking information that investors need. Accounting standards often do not permit firms to capitalize outlays, such as R&D, that provide significant future benefits to the firm.

A second way that management can communicate with investors is through nonaccounting means. We discussed several such mechanisms, including using financial policies (such as stock repurchases, dividend increases, and hedging) to help signal management's optimism about the firm's future performance; meeting with financial analysts to explain the firm's strategy, current performance, and outlook; and disclosing additional information, both quantitative and qualitative, to provide investors with information similar to that of management.

In this chapter we have stressed the importance of communicating effectively with investors. But firms also have to communicate with other stakeholders, including employees, customers, suppliers, and regulatory bodies. Many of the same principles discussed here can also be applied to management communication with these other stakeholders.

Finally, we examined the capital market role of governance agents, such as external auditors and audit committees. Both have faced considerable public scrutiny following a series of financial reporting meltdowns in the United States. Much has been done to improve the governance and independence of these intermediaries. We focus on how the financial analysis tools developed in the book can be used to improve the quality of audit and audit committee work. The tools of strategy analysis, accounting analysis, financial analysis, and prospective analysis can help auditors and audit committee members to identify the key issues in the financial statements to focus on and provide common sense ways of assessing whether there are potential reporting problems that merit additional testing and analysis.

DISCUSSION QUESTIONS

1. Amazon's inventory increased from $3.2 billion on December 31, 2010, to $5.0 billion one year later. In addition, sales for the fourth quarter of those years increased from $12.9 billion in 2010 to $17.4 billion in 2011. What is the implied annualized inventory turnover for Amazon for these years? What different interpretations about future performance could a financial analyst infer from this change? What information could Amazon's management provide to investors to clarify the change in inventory turnover? What are the costs and benefits to Amazon from disclosing this information? What issues does this change raise for the auditor? What additional tests would you want to conduct as Amazon's auditor?

2. a. What are likely to be the long-term critical success factors for the following types of firms?
   - a high technology company such as Microsoft
   - a large low-cost retailer such as Wal-Mart

   b. How useful is financial accounting data for evaluating how well these two companies are managing their critical success factors? What other types of information would be useful in your evaluation? What are the costs and benefits to these companies from disclosing this type of information to investors?

3. Management frequently objects to disclosing additional information on the grounds that it is proprietary. For instance, when the FASB proposed to expand disclosures on (a) accounting for stock-based employee compensation (issued in December 2002) and (b) business segment performance (issued in June 1997), many corporate managers expressed strong opposition to both proposals. What are the potential proprietary costs from expanded disclosures in each of these areas? If you conclude

that proprietary costs are relatively low for either, what alternative explanations do you have for management's opposition?

4. In contrast to U.S. GAAP, IFRS permits management to reverse impairment on fixed assets that have increased in value since the time of their impairment. Revaluations are typically based on estimates of realizable value made by management or independent valuers. Do you expect that these accounting standards will make earnings and book values more or less useful to investors? Explain why or why not. How can management make these types of disclosures more credible?

5. Under a management buyout, the top management of a firm offers to buy the company from its stockholders, usually at a premium over its current stock price. The management team puts up its own capital to finance the acquisition, with additional financing typically coming from a private buyout firm and private debt. If management is interested in making such an offer for its firm in the near future, what are its financial reporting incentives? How do these differ from the incentives of management that are not interested in a buyout? How would you respond to a proposed management buyout if you were the firm's auditor? What about if you were a member of the audit committee?

6. You are approached by the management of a small start-up company that is planning to go public. The founders are unsure about how aggressive they should be in their accounting decisions as they come to the market. John Smith, the CEO, asserts, "We might as well take full advantage of any discretion offered by accounting rules, since the market will be expecting us to do so." What are the pros and cons of this strategy? As the partner of a major audit firm, what type of analysis would you perform before deciding to take on a startup that is planning to go public?

7. Two years after a successful public offering, the CEO of a biotechnology company is concerned about stock market uncertainty surrounding the potential of new drugs in the development pipeline. In his discussion with you, the CEO notes that even though they have recently made significant progress in their internal R&D efforts, the stock has performed poorly. What options does he have to help convince investors of the value of the new products? Which of these alternatives are likely to be feasible?

8. Why might the CEO of the biotechnology firm discussed in Question 7 be concerned about the firm being undervalued? Would the CEO be equally concerned if the stock were overvalued? Do you believe that the CEO would attempt to correct the market's perception in this overvaluation case? How would you react to company concern about market under- or overvaluation if you were the firm's auditor? Or if you were a member of the audit committee?

9. When companies decide to shift from private to public financing by making an initial public offering for their stock, they are likely to face increased costs of investor communications. Given this additional cost, why would firms opt to go public?

10. German firms are traditionally financed by banks, which have representatives on the companies' boards. How would communication challenges differ for these firms relative to U.S. firms, which rely more on public financing?

NOTES

1. M. Jensen and W. Meckling, "Theory of the Firm: Managerial Behavior, Agency Costs, and Capital Structure," *Journal of Financial Economics* 3 (October 1976): 305–360, analyzes agency problems between managers and outside investors. Subsequent work by Bengt Holmstrom and others examines how contracts between managers and outside investors could mitigate the agency problem.

2. K. Murphy and J. Zimmerman, "Financial Performance Surrounding CEO Turnover," *Journal of Accounting and Economics* 16 (January/April/July 1993): 273–315, find a strong relation between CEO turnover and earnings-based performance.

3. See S. Teoh, I. Welch, and T. Wong, "Earnings Management and the Long-Run Market Performance of Initial Public Offerings," *The Journal of Finance* 63 (December 1998): 1,935–1,974, and S. Teoh, I. Welch, and T. Wong, "Earnings Management and the Underperformance of Seasoned Equity Offerings," *Journal of Financial Economics* 50 (October 1998): 63–99.

4. This market imperfection, often referred to as a "lemons" or "information" problem, is also discussed in Chapter 1. It was first studied by George Akerlof in relation to the used car market in "The Market for 'Lemons': Quality Uncertainty and the Market Mechanism," *Quarterly Journal of Economics* 90 (1970): 629–650.

5. Of course, improved analysis alone is unlikely to be sufficient to improve market intermediation if the structural reforms implemented by Regulation Fair Disclosure, the Sarbanes-Oxley Act, the Global Settlement, and the Dodd-Frank Act fail to correct the conflicts of interest for intermediaries that we have witnessed in the last few years.

6. D. Skinner, "Earnings Disclosures and Stockholder Lawsuits," *Journal of Accounting and Economics* (November 1997): 249–283, finds that firms with bad earnings news tend to predisclose this information, perhaps to reduce the cost of litigation that inevitably follows bad news quarters.

7. For example, G. Foster, "Briloff and the Capital Market," *Journal of Accounting Research* 17, no. 1 (Spring 1979): 262–274, finds firms that are criticized for their accounting by Abraham J. Briloff in *Barron's* on average suffer an 8 percent decline in their stock price around the article publication date. H. Desai and P. Jain, "Long-Run Stock Returns Following Briloff's Analyses," *Financial Analysts Journal* 60, no. 2 (March/April 2004): 47–56, find significant declines in one- and two-year performance of the firms that Briloff criticized.

8. Findings by P. Healy and K. Palepu in "Earnings Information Conveyed by Dividend Initiations and Omissions," *Journal of Financial Economics* 21 (September 1988): 149–175, indicate that investors interpret announcements of dividends initiations and omissions as managers' forecasts of future earnings performance.

9. See L. Dann, R. Masulis, and D. Mayers, "Repurchase Tender Offers and Earnings Information," *Journal of Accounting and Economics* (September 1991): 217–252, and M. Hertzel and P. Jain, "Earnings and Risk Changes Around Stock Repurchases," *Journal of Accounting and Economics* (September 1991): 253–276.

10. See M. Barth and R. Kasznik, "Share Repurchases and Intangible Assets," *Journal of Accounting and Economics* 28 (December 1999): 211–241.

11. See S. Tasker, "Bridging the Information Gap: Quarterly Conference Calls as a Medium for Voluntary Disclosure." *Review of Accounting Studies* 3, nos. 1–2 (1998): 137–167.

12. See R. Frankel, M. Johnson, and D. Skinner, "An Empirical Examination of Conference Calls as a Voluntary Disclosure Medium," *Journal of Accounting Research* 37, no. 1 (Spring 1999): 133–150.

13. See M. Kimbrough, "The Effect of Conference Calls on Analyst and Market Underreaction to Earnings Announcements," *The Accounting Review* 80, no. 1 (January 2005): 189–219.

14. See A. Irani, "The Effect of Regulation Fair Disclosure on the Relevance of Conference Calls to Financial Analysts," *Review of Quantitative Finance and Accounting* 22, no. 1 (January 2004): 15–28.

15. Research on voluntary disclosure includes M. Lang and R. Lundholm, "Cross-Sectional Determinants of Analysts' Ratings of Corporate Disclosures," *Journal of Accounting Research* 31 (Autumn 1993): 246–271; M. Lang and R. Lundholm, "Corporate Disclosure Policy and Analysts," *The Accounting Review* 71 (October 1996): 467–492; M. Welker, "Disclosure Policy, Information Asymmetry and Liquidity in Equity Markets," *Contemporary Accounting Research* (Spring 1995): 801–827; C. Botosan, "The Impact of Annual Report Disclosure Level on Investor Base and the Cost of Capital," *The Accounting Review* (July 1997): 323–350; and P. Healy, A. Hutton, and K. Palepu, "Stock Performance and Intermediation Changes Surrounding Sustained Increases in Disclosure," *Contemporary Accounting Research* 16, no. 3 (Fall 1999): 485–521. This research finds that firms are more likely to provide high levels of disclosure if they have strong earnings performance, issue securities, have more analyst following, and have less dispersion in analyst forecasts. In addition, firms with high levels of disclosure policies tend to have a lower cost of capital and bid–ask spread. Finally, firms that increase disclosure have accompanying increases in stock returns, institutional ownership, analyst following, and stock liquidity. In addition, in "The Role of Supplementary Statements with Management Earnings Forecasts," *Journal of Accounting Research* 41 (December 2003): 867–890, A. Hutton, G. Miller, and D. Skinner examine the market response to management earnings forecasts and find that bad news forecasts are always informative but that good news forecasts are informative only when they are supported by verifiable forward-looking statements.
16. See J. Cotter, I. Tuna, and P. Wysocki, "Expectations Management and Beatable Targets: How do Analysts React to Explicit Earnings Guidance?" *Contemporary Accounting Research* 23, no. 3 (Autumn 2006): 593–628.
17. See P. Healy and K. Palepu, "Audit the Audit Committees: After Enron Boards Must Change the Focus and Provide Greater Financial Transparency," *Financial Times*, June 10, 2002, p. 14.

Note: In each entry, the first number is the chapter number; the number(s) following the hyphen (-) is(are) the page or range of pages on which the entry appears. Italic type indicates the page numbers of charts and tables. An "n" after a page number indicates that the entry is an author's note.